Reconsiderations in
Southern African History

Richard Elphick, Editor

A World of Their Own
A History of South African Women's Education

Meghan Healy-Clancy

University of Virginia Press *Charlottesville and London*

University of Virginia Press
Originally published in 2013 by the University of KwaZulu-Natal Press
© 2013 by Meghan Healy-Clancy

Printed in the United States of America on acid-free paper

First University of Virginia Press edition published 2014

ISBN 978-0-8139-3608-6

9 8 7 6 5 4 3 2 1

Library of Congress Cataloging-in-Publication Data is available from the Library of Congress.

Contents

Tables and Figures

On Terminology and Orthography

Racial terminology presents manifold problems when writing after – and when attempting to write ourselves *out of* – apartheid. While some scholars have tried to minimise their use of such terminology as a protest against its persistent racialising logic, I use the terms 'African', 'black' and 'white' in order to analyse most fully a nation whose past was shaped by these social categories and which (like the United States) has plainly not become 'post-racial' after the dismantling of legal regimes of racial inequality. I employ the term 'African' to refer to those South Africans classified as 'Native' or 'Bantu' by colonial and apartheid officials. When I use the term 'black', I refer to all South Africans historically classified as 'Non-European' or 'Non-White' – including those classified as 'African', 'Coloured', 'Asiatic' or 'Indian'. When applied to South Africans, the term 'white' refers to those historically classified as 'European' or 'White'. I refer to 'black Americans' and 'African Americans' interchangeably. I also refer to 'white Americans' on occasion, but because the vast majority of the missionaries herein were white, this is less often specified.

Orthography presents problems that are less political than logistical. IsiZulu orthography changed over the period that this study covers, meaning that the names of certain individuals have been variously spelt over the course of their lives in published and archival materials. I have used the spelling that individuals used themselves in personal correspondence or publications as adults.

Abbreviations

AME	African Methodist Episcopal
ANC	African National Congress
HSRP	Historic Schools Restoration Project
ICU	Industrial and Commercial Workers Union
ISOGA	Inanda Seminary Old Girls Association
LMS	London Missionary Society
MEDUNSA	Medical University of Southern Africa
SANNC	South African Native National Congress
SASO	South African Students' Organisation
UCBWM	United Church Board for World Ministries
UCCSA	United Congregational Church of Southern Africa
UCT	University of Cape Town
UDF	United Democratic Front

Acknowledgements

As a close reader of acknowledgement pages, I have learned that writing good history hinges on having good friendships. I can only hope that this study is as rich as the intellectual comradeship that went into it.

First, the women and men affiliated with Inanda Seminary, past and present, gave life to this project. Their contributions – interviews and archival materials, gathered from Connecticut to Cape Town – are evident throughout its pages. Thanks to my interviewees Roger Aylard, Thuthula Balfour-Kaipa, Lindiwe Baloyi, Nomangcobo Bhengu, Mwelela Cele, Mabel Christofersen, Carohn Cornell, Bongi Dlomo, Thandeka Dloti, B.K. Dludla, Pam Dube, Melodious Gumede, Andile Hawes, Carroll Jacobs, Nonhlanhla Khumalo, Cecilia Khuzwayo, Siphokazi Koyana, Constance Koza, Khanyisile Kweyama, Lungi Kwitshana, Nomsa Makhoba, Gloria Malindi, Nozizwe Maneli, Dorcas Meyiwa, Ntombi Mngomezulu, Khosi Mpanza, Rudo Mphasane, Thembi Msane, Vuyo Ncwaiba, Lauretta Ngcobo, Mamsie Ntshangase, Ndo Nyembezi, Faith Nyongo, Karen Roy-Guglielmi, Esther Sangweni, Caroline Sililo, Darlene Woodburn, Kho Zimu, Dumi Zondi, Thembekile Zondi and Mandisa Zungu. Special thanks to Inanda's former principal Dumi Zondi, who first provided me with access to Inanda's wide-ranging collection of archival materials and who contextualised these materials with his knowledge of the school's past. Thanks as well to Inanda's principal Judy Tate, chaplain Susan Valiquette and development manager Scott Couper. They have been unwaveringly supportive of my research without attempting to direct my research agenda – a rare and wonderful combination for a historian. Scott has also been a stimulating and dedicated colleague, despite his hectic schedule.

This book came out of my 2011 Harvard University doctoral dissertation in African Studies. Thanks to my advisor, Emmanuel Akyeampong, who patiently worked to rein in my verbosity, to curtail my descents into narrative history and to tease out my embedded arguments – and who first observed that the core tensions I was describing were tensions over social reproduction. My other Harvard committee members, Caroline Elkins and Evelyn Higginbotham, helped me see the bigger picture – beyond Inanda Seminary, South Africa, and the African continent – that my musings on the politics of social reproduction illuminate. Through Carrie and Evelyn's mentorship, I had the privilege to become a part of the other pillars of African Studies at Harvard, the Committee on African Studies and the Du Bois Institute for African and African American Research. Thanks to the support of the Institute's Director, Henry Louis Gates, Jr, and Executive Director Vera Grant, I benefited from the collegial support of my fellow Du Bois Fellows, as well as from the intrepid research assistance of Emily Jendzejec and Yvette Ramirez. As a postgraduate and now as a lecturer at Harvard, I have benefited from conversations with many other wonderful colleagues and students, particularly Sibusisiwe Khuluse, Matthew Kustenbauder, Margot Leger, Daniel Liss, Carla Martin, Erin Mosely, Amber Moulton and Zolisa Shokane. Jeanne Follansbee and Anya Bernstein Bassett have made the Committees on Degrees in History and Literature and in Social Studies ideal places for me to research and teach.

I conducted research for this project between 2007 and 2010 – at a most fascinating time in South Africa, and in the company of scholars who have become some of my favourite people in the world. Thanks to Nonhlanhla Mbeje and colleagues in the Fulbright-Hays Zulu Group Program Abroad in Pietermaritzburg, who laboured to teach isiZulu to this wooden-tongued American and who introduced me to KwaZulu-Natal in the cold southern winter of 2007. When I returned to Durban on a Harvard grant between September 2008 and June 2009, I was fortunate to undertake much of my research at the Campbell Collections of the University of KwaZulu-Natal, where I met my dear friend Mwelela Cele – the consummate librarian, with incredible knowledge of and passion for South African history. It is fitting that we first bonded over our enthusiasm for the work of

Mark Gevisser and Shula Marks, as Mwelela has taught me much about the power of biography as history. I was also privileged to be affiliated with the Department of Historical Studies at the University of KwaZulu-Natal in Durban, during the brilliant Catherine Burns' tenure at the helm of its History and African Studies Seminar. Through this seminar, I met Jason Hickel and Jeff Guy. Many of the best ideas in this thesis – particularly around domesticity and state power – came out of conversations with Jason over cappuccino or pinotage. With great patience for my historian's obsession with detail, he asked hard questions of my project as it unfolded, which tricked me into theorising; he has been a wonderful friend to me and to this project. During my academic year in Durban and since, Jeff has been an ideal mentor and friend: he understood the value of my project before I did, and he continuously reminded me of the value of institutional history for unearthing continuities underlying seismic socio-political changes. His model of unmitigated intellectual curiosity and committed scholarship is one that I will always work to emulate. Jeff invited me to join his Tradition, Authority and Power (TAP) research group, where I had the privilege to work with other extraordinary colleagues. Eva Jackson is a bona fide rock star, activist and very smart historian. We have had many fabulous conversations about the relationships between women's power and marginality, which have shaped this project and my future research trajectory significantly. Percy Ngonyama, Mark Hunter and visiting researchers involved with TAP deeply stimulated my thinking about these concepts in KwaZulu-Natal, and beyond. Rochelle Burgess, Adriaan Diederichs, Xolani Dube, Paul and Maggie McIlroy, Scott Naysmith and Clara Rubincam also made living in Durban fun.

In addition to sharing my research in fora at Harvard and the University of KwaZulu-Natal, I presented at conferences and workshops at the University of Sheffield, Boston University, the Massachusetts Institute of Technology, the North Eastern Workshop on Southern Africa, the African Studies Association and the University of the Witwatersrand. Thanks to all participants in these fora, particularly Frederick Cooper, Deborah Gaitskell, Tim Gibbs, Janet Giele, Robert Houle, Rachel Johnson, Daniel Magaziner and Amy Stambach. I have also benefited from conversations and exchanges of archival and scholarly work with many people, especially Roger Aylard, Zabeth Botha, Jean and John Comaroff, Carohn Cornell, Heidi Gengenbach, Leslie Hadfield, Lauren Jarvis, Peter Kallaway, Cherif Keita, Jill Kelly, Ntongela Masilela, Seán Morrow, Lauretta Ngcobo, Karen Roy-Guglielmi and Liz Thornberry. The financial support of Harvard and the US Department of Education made my work possible.

At University of KwaZulu-Natal Press, Debra Primo, Louis Gaigher, Lisa Compton and Adele Branch have made an excellent editorial team. Alternative versions of Chapters 1 and 2 have also appeared as articles: Meghan Elisabeth Healy, ' "Like a Family": Global Models, Familial Bonds, and the Making of an American School for Zulu Girls', *Safundi: The Journal of South African and American Studies* 11, no. 3 (July 2010): 279–300; and Healy, ' "To Control Their Destiny": The Politics of Home and the Feminisation of Schooling in Colonial Natal', *Journal of Southern African Studies* 37, no. 2 (June 2011): 247–264. Thanks as well to my anonymous reviewers.

So much love goes to my family and family-like friends. My parents, Dan and Judy Healy, have been remarkably tolerant of their peripatetic only child. I suppose a historian is what you get when you indulge your daughter's interests in reading, writing and travel, and unceasingly take her to folk art and social history museums. I especially thank my mother for her incredible endurance at the scanning machine. Daniel Higgins, Katie Foss, the Clancys and the Bourrets have been very supportive. Special thanks to Meghan Clancy for her heroic digitisation efforts, which enabled me to carry hundreds of books around the world. Finally, my husband, Seamus Clancy, kept me happy and comfortable throughout my graduate school career, which was not always an easy feat. I thank him for making me laugh and making me dinner in Cambridge, for following me to South Africa and keeping me in Spain. Wherever we are, I am home. I thank him for evincing continual faith not just in my project, but in me.

Introduction

Inanda Seminary stands some fifteen miles north of Durban, Kwa-Zulu-Natal, its verdant campus separated from the township around it by a long driveway and an electric fence. Amidst whitewashed buildings and jacarandas, neatly attired schoolgirls file between classrooms, the doors to which almost invariably remain unlocked. On the 140th anniversary of the high school's 1869 founding under the auspices of the American Zulu Mission of the American Board of Commissioners for Foreign Missions, these students greeted alumnae who call themselves 'Old Girls' and who include some of South Africa's most prominent women. Among these alumnae was the then deputy president Baleka Mbete, class of 1968, who highlighted her alma mater's role in the struggle that had culminated in the 1994 victory of her party, the African National Congress. 'Thinking back to the 140 years of this seminary's existence is like walking through the heritage route of the liberation struggle that brought us our freedom in 1994,' Mbete declared, as it was out of Inanda that so many activist women had come.[1]

These linkages between mission schooling, nationalist struggle and post-colonial leadership may seem familiar to scholars of anti-colonialism elsewhere. Like educated elites throughout much of Africa in the late nineteenth through mid-twentieth centuries, mission-educated Africans in South Africa found that the skills and expectations they had forged in the classroom clashed radically with the constraints facing them outside, and many articulated their grievances in nationalist movements. Yet while their counterparts in west and east Africa would achieve national sovereignty in the 1950s and 1960s, educated elite South Africans encountered the elaboration of apartheid. And as the apartheid state introduced the Bantu

Education Act of 1953, it closed or took over almost all mission schools. As elites elsewhere attempted to deploy schooling for nation building, black South Africans found their political organisations banned and their children mostly consigned to inferior state schools, where youth forged the visions that culminated in the Soweto schools boycotts of 1976 and the protests and reforms that followed. Thus what Mbete called the 'heritage route of the liberation struggle' was in fact a more winding road.

This book follows the winding road through Inanda's past to reveal a tradition of educated black women's social leadership that predated and has survived apartheid. This tradition has been almost wholly neglected in the historiography, despite a profusion of studies that have elaborated an intersecting tradition of educated black men's political leadership in the nineteenth and twentieth centuries.[2] Understanding this enduring women's tradition enables reconsiderations of not only 'the liberation struggle' of which Mbete spoke but also a longer history of gendered struggles. In these latter struggles— with black and white men, with white women, and amongst themselves—black women have claimed schools as sites at which to develop, through idioms of 'social service', a moral authority that could transcend the limitations of a racialised patriarchy.

Through the first social history of Inanda Seminary,[3] this book offers the first exploration of the expansion of black women's education in South Africa—across the longue durée of colonialism, segregation, and apartheid. This study shows how schools have been women's spaces since the nineteenth-century expansion of mission education, which provided nearly all schooling available to Africans before apartheid. By the early twentieth century, over half of all African students in South Africa were female. Yet strikingly, it was only during apartheid that women began to meet or exceed the educational achievements of men at all levels. This study examines why black women's educational opportunities expanded in this period of racial oppression, and to what ends. It explains the expansion of African women's schooling as an outcome of what I term a 'politics of social reproduction', building upon a nuanced conception of social reproduction as 'the gendered processes by which workers and children survive and are reproduced'.[4]

Figures 1 and 2
Inanda Township and Inanda Seminary, September 2008. (Photographs by
the author)

With the rise of Christianity and colonial capitalism, African women's historical roles at the heart of production and reproduction in rural homesteads shifted. As missionary and *kholwa* (African Christian) ideals emphasised women's nurturance above all else, educated women claimed new roles as intermediaries between their families and the state—mediating and ameliorating crises of colonial change. Through discourses of 'social service', women like 1910 Inanda alumna, teacher and pioneering social worker Sibusisiwe Makhanya effectively cultivated new political communities. But colonial and segregationist officials tended to see women's social leadership as far more innocuous than male-led African political movements. Rather than threatening state power, women's engagement in social service seemed that it might enable the reproduction of a black workforce on a shoestring.

The gendered implications of this politics of social reproduction for apartheid education were profound. When apartheid officials came to power in 1948, they needed the skills of an African middle class to govern. But they needed to undermine this class politically to rule. These tensions came to a head in the Bantu Education Act of 1953, which sought to resolve them through a gendered strategy: officials encouraged African women's training as teachers and health workers, even as they attempted to limit African male-led political agitation by nationalising most mission schools and generally limiting curricula to preparation for semi-skilled labour.

Yet officials' attempts to harness women's education to their narrow goals ultimately failed. Instead of fulfilling official expectations that they would reproduce a divided society, women could build upon a gendered tradition of social leadership and moral authority to nurture alternative political visions. Inanda Seminary was a critical site at which women cultivated these alternative possibilities through the apartheid years.

* * *

Scholarly acknowledgements of southern Africa's long history of women's schooling are remarkably diffuse. In the Cape, site of the earliest evangelising, scholars have documented that more African girls than boys attended mission schools from at least the mid-nineteenth century. Anthropologist Monica Wilson, the first observer of this trend, attributed it to regional social and economic patterns.[5] Wilson suggested that, in a pastoral society, girls could more readily combine their domestic responsibilities with schooling. Gendered conversion patterns may also have played a role, as black women tended to be more rapid and fervent converts than black men, prompting mothers' espousal of mission schooling for their daughters but fathers' disavowal of schooling for their sons. In the view of this daughter of missionaries, the Cape's feminisation of schooling was a trend with 'profound' cultural implications: African Christian women assumed significant social influence as they 'laboured to build a civilized society'.[6] Sociologist Jacklyn Cock, however, has more darkly described how young women were clustered in the lower grades and channelled into a narrow range of professions: domestic service, teaching, housewifery and later nursing. Cock saw their schooling as education for 'ultra-exploitability', as 'it operated in the main coercively, as an agency of socialization, tying women to subordinate roles in colonial society'.[7] As missionary schooling expanded across southern Africa with the mineral revolution of the late nineteenth century, new migrant labour regimes extended these gendered patterns. While mission schooling catered overwhelmingly to male students across the rest of colonial Africa, historian Claire Robertson noted in 1980 that an unusual 'Southern African complex' of girls' numerical dominance in all but the highest grades of school emerged out of an economic context 'where boys usually herd and then work in South Africa's extractive industries, neither of which requires formal education. Bridewealth, which is still important, is increased by girls' education.'[8]

In apartheid South Africa, a handful of scholars have pointed out that African women's access to schooling expanded, even as they faced deepening gendered and racialised constraints (see Table 1). Elaine Unterhalter, who has done more than anyone else to place this issue on the scholarly agenda, has emphasised the contradictions that accompanied the feminisation of schooling in a profoundly anti-feminist historical context, demonstrating that young women's high rates of access to apartheid schooling did not give rise to gender equality, as they faced school environments shaped by racism, sexism and casual violence.[9] Yet scholars have insufficiently addressed the relationship between gender, schooling and ideologies of separate development. They have dismissed the feminisation of schooling as 'an ironic effect of Bantu Education', which 'unintentionally addressed gender inequalities by producing high participation rates by African girls'.[10] Moreover, they have not explained why, in such dismal contexts, young women in fact *pursued* schooling at higher rates than young

Table 1 The apartheid-era expansion of women's schooling

Year	Percentage and number of female African students			
	Lower primary	**Higher primary**	**Lower secondary**	**Higher secondary**
1960	48.9% (535 700)	53% (191 300)	51.4% (23 400)	27% (700)
1965	48.6% (647 100)	52.6% (244 600)	51% (29 700)	27% (1 000)
1970	48.6% (917 000)	52.5% (383 100)	54.5% (61 800)	32% (2 900)
1975	48.7% (1 151 100)	52.5% (532 000)	55.3% (161 000)	39.2% (10 700)
1980	48.9% (1 386 600)	52.2% (640 200)	55.7% (359 800)	50.1% (64 100)
1985	48.8% (1 597 100)	52.2% (807 200)	55.4% (513 700)	54.5% (145 200)

Source: Elaine Unterhalter, 'The Impact of Apartheid on Women's Education in South Africa', *Review of African Political Economy* 48 (Autumn 1990): 66–75, pp. 70–71. Based on census figures.

men.[11] In their studies of nursing and teaching, however, historians Shula Marks and Deborah Gaitskell have suggested that the expansion of the feminised professions was a political choice that apartheid officials made in their efforts at social engineering.[12] As this study will show, this choice made new educational space for young women, within which they could envision and sometimes enact new possibilities for their lives.

The reasons for this underdeveloped scholarship on the meanings of the feminisation of schooling are clear: as Bantu Education developed, critical research focused on overarching issues of race and class. So few Africans had historically enjoyed schooling beyond a basic level that the gender composition of an African educated elite seemed irrelevant to early scholars of black education.[13] After the Soweto uprising of 1976, a growing share of scholarship focused on the politics of schooling. This work was wide-ranging in its theoretical scaffolding, innovative in its methods and bold in its claims.[14] But when radical critiques incorporated women's experiences, they often did so with ancillary notes.[15] Post-apartheid scholars have explored apartheid policies as racialised variations on a modern global theme of mass schooling, and they have examined student resistance with nuance. But most continue to neglect the gendered relations structuring missionary and state schooling.[16]

By rethinking the development of black education from Inanda Seminary's vantage, it becomes clear not only that we cannot understand the historical politics of education without a gendered analysis; we also cannot understand the politics of the cultural class that mission institutions like Inanda cultivated without attention to that class's gendered traditions of leadership. In discussing my research with South Africans—black and white—I have encountered the sentiment that Inanda reflects a 'hidden history of the black middle class': a history of how essentially *kholwa* values of 'respectability' and a commitment to 'racial progress' through elite achievement survived apartheid. Indeed, this study shows the enduring resonance of a 'middle-class' belief in schooling as integral in coming of age and achieving social mobility, even as schools became sites of unrest and violence. During the apartheid years and into the present, this has particularly been the case for young women with family histories of 'middle-class' aspiration. To understand the nuanced cultural politics of class over time, I examine its intersections with race, gender and generation.[17]

Through the history of the educated black women at the seams of what feminist scholar Belinda Bozzoli has termed South Africa's '"patchwork quilt" of patriarchies',[18] this study provides a new take on the consequences of an extractive economy premised on outsourcing core burdens of social reproduction onto black women.[19] While scholars have often examined how women's productive and reproductive labours had enabled the resilience of traditionalist homesteads in the nineteenth century,[20] this study reveals how women's labours also enabled the resilience of a tenuous black 'middle class' in the twentieth century. But educated black women's social centrality came with an 'emerging irony', to borrow Bozzoli's term.[21] Although both educated black men and officials invoked women's social roles to justify their marginalization from formal politics, women found in education opportunities to politicize their social leadership.

This study thus provides fresh insights into how gender relations have been constitutive of pre-colonial, colonial and apartheid politics, building on a rich regional literature[22] that explores how 'women's power and women's marginality were structurally linked'.[23] It also speaks to a global literature on social reproduction,[24] which has emphasised how states look to women to maintain political and economic stability.[25] Ultimately, as education and social service professions feminise on a global level, this study provides an historical perspective on the ironies and political possibilities of that process.

* * *

This study reflects my engagement with an eclectic range of institutional, personal and official archives from South Africa and the United States, placed into conversation with oral historical research with Inanda affiliates. 'Intertextual' connections within this corpus of sources emerge often in this book, revealing how a tradition of women's social leadership endured and transformed across generations.

For instance, I encountered an early alumna named Talitha Hawes in several places, which presented different dimensions of this historiographically obscure but influential woman. In missionary correspondence and reports in the archives of the American Board of Commissioners for Foreign Missions at Harvard University and in the National Archives of South Africa in Pietermaritzburg, KwaZulu-Natal, she appears as a dedicated companion of Inanda's founder Mary Edwards, with whom she had moved in as a 'little lame girl'.

In the records of the Secretary for Native Affairs in Pietermaritzburg, she appears as an independent young teacher successfully applying for exemption from native law, enabling her to inherit and maintain her father's farm as an unmarried woman. In an Inanda Seminary campus archive file on a 1940 essay contest to commemorate alumnae who had 'brought help, inspiration, and uplift into unnumbered homes and communities', she appears as the subject of the prize-winning essay, penned by a student who had come to Inanda from the elementary school that Hawes founded. In the memory and family archive of a descendent of one of her siblings whom I interviewed, that school emerges at the heart of the Hawes family's independent *kholwa* mission. This was a place called Ebusisweni, where Talitha Hawes broke away from the control of her benefactor Mary Edwards to educate African youth on her own terms. (I discuss Hawes at length in Chapter One.)

The subject of the runner-up in that 1940 essay contest was another early alumna named Agnes Mdladla Cele, the essay written by her granddaughter, 1949 Inanda alumna Lauretta Ngcobo. In that essay, the youthful Ngcobo remembered her grandmother as a force inspiring education amongst her neighbors, with whom she owned a farm in the Inanda valley. In her interview with me, Ngcobo emphasised the influence of her grandmother and her mother, a teacher, on her own embrace of education, which she deployed to become a feminist novelist and anti-apartheid activist. (I discuss Ngcobo's family and personal history in Chapters Two, Three and Four.)

My research methodologies thus combined sources conventional to political history—official sources in KwaZulu-Natal as well as Pretoria and Cape Town—and to institutional history—prolific missionary collections—with alternative archives, emanating from Inanda affiliates. I combed through boxes of family archives and historical newspapers in isiZulu and English—the 'women's pages' of which often included reportage by and about women at Inanda Seminary and peer institutions, from as far back as the late nineteenth century.

Feminist historians of South Africa and elsewhere have stressed the challenges of unearthing women's 'voices' from under layers of representation, leading many simply to privilege oral sources. This has had benefits: feminist scholars have been at the forefront of methodological innovations in oral history. But it also reflects certain problematic theoretical assumptions of gender history in South Africa, and of the social history tradition out of which it developed in the late 1970s and 1980s. While it did allow for some attention to (male) political leaders, the social history tradition prioritized the stories of 'ordinary' people—leaving the history of the elite women that I explore strangely neglected. My work with a range of conventional and alternative archives reveals how, by triangulating such evidence, historians might construct a more complete portrait of the making of black politics and society in modern South Africa.

My presence on Inanda's campus also enabled me to observe regular contemporary evocations of the history of the school and its alumnae. Stories of founder Mary Edwards' tenacity in the face of patriarchal and colonial opposition to African girls' education loomed large in the school's 'At Home' reunion, which takes place each year in October, and at its 140th anniversary celebrations in March 2009, where Mbete and other luminaries underscored the school's subversiveness during apartheid. In the campus archive, through which student volunteers now guide campus visitors, and in their classes and daily chapel services, students learn of Inanda's distinguished history—and they hear repeatedly that as Inanda girls they bear a special responsibility to improve their society. While the careers for which Inanda students prepare have changed—ranging widely through the arts and sciences, far transcending the limited choices of teaching and nursing with which students were long presented—the idioms of 'social service' as *kholwa* women remain strong. And although black girls now have the option to attend more elite, historically white schools, many choose Inanda because of this tradition.

At the October 2008 reunion and the March 2009 anniversary, hundreds of alumnae—who had attended Inanda from the 1930s through recent years—convened on campus. Many of these women were regular visitors to their alma mater. Some had become more personally involved since the school faced financial crises and academic decline in the late 1990s. Alumnae came together to mobilise support from the state and industry to restore Inanda's physical premises and to hire new staff members, espousing a renewed commitment to making Inanda an exceptional academic institution for African girls. My presence on campus enabled me to connect with several of these highly active alumnae, but I also sought to speak with former students, staff and other affiliates outside of this core network who might convey a broader (and possibly more critical) sense of the Inanda community. Beginning with affiliates I had met at the October and March events and moving outward to reach a broader network through referrals from these affiliates, current Inanda staff, colleagues and friends, I arranged interviews with forty-one affiliates, whose personal or familial connections at Inanda stretched from the school's founding through the present.

Thirty of my interviewees were alumnae, the oldest of whom attended Inanda from 1934 to 1936. Fourteen of these alumnae had attended Inanda prior to 1976, and sixteen had attended after 1976. Five of these alumnae returned to Inanda as teachers or principals. Additionally, I interviewed nine former staff members: four American mission appointees who worked at Inanda between 1946 and 1985, including the first white male principal (1970–1973); Dumi Zondi, the first African male principal (1974–1976); the Governing Council chair from 1965 to 1981; and three South African teachers, serving between 1954 and 1984. I also interviewed Mwelela Cele and Andile Hawes about the role of Inanda Seminary in their families' pasts.[26] These interviews took place in English, in which all of my interviewees were fluent first- or second-language speakers, although some moved into isiZulu at moments.

In addition to spending between one and three hours speaking with me, several interviewees shared photographs, correspondence, course materials and genealogies. Most of my older interviewees also offered me tea. Alumnae from the 1930s through the 1950s remarked on Inanda graduates' domestic prowess, while former staff referred to the racial politics of staff tea rooms at Inanda and other schools during apartheid. Alumnae from the 1960s through the 1980s were less likely to stress the domestic aspects of their education; several proudly emphasised that Inanda alumnae tended to be weak in the domestic arts. But all were exceedingly warm. While conducting her research on South African women's clubs in 1993 and 1994, Deborah

Mindry also reflected upon her interviewees' teatime rituals, emphasising the common gendered values that such exchanges embodied.[27] Although she was a white South African woman based at an American university, she found that her black interviewees often assumed that she was American, as they imagined that white South African women would never travel as she did and relate to them on a basis of equality. The context has changed since Mindry's research, but in my case too my unusual social position seemed to ease my interactions with my black and white South African and white American interviewees. I was clearly both an outsider in South Africa—a young, white American woman, but not a missionary—and an insider, as I shared my knowledge and questions about the school's survival and significance. With their pots of tea and recollections of Inanda's role in their lives, my interviewees welcomed me into the school's transnational extended community.

With alumnae, I conducted 'directed life history interviews', asking about their experiences at Inanda and in their broader lives.[28] Sixteen of these interviews were one-on-one, and the others took place in a pair, one group of three, one group of four and one group of five. The group interviews took place at the request of participants, and they were conducive towards my goal of cultivating conversations rather than inquisitions, as the interviewees shared and contested their memories together. Staff interviews were one-on-one, and my questions tended to centre more on their work at Inanda than on their life histories. But they pushed me to see that staff's time at Inanda may have been as formative for them as for students, as the school offered such a distinct community.

Across generations, interviewees described a core tradition in which young women claimed Inanda as a space of protection and preparation from which they might improve the world beyond their campus. Yet this was a difficult and compromised space, in which young women's preparation for lives of 'service' was charged with gender, sexual, racial and class politics. First, all emphasised the distinct intimacy of Inanda's community within the broader landscape of South Africa. Students who attended after 1953 underscored this point particularly. Staff and students frequently introduced this point through stories of travel between school and home, and the inequities and indignities of which it reminded them. Second, most emphasised the sense of order underlying this community—students were made acutely self-conscious of their role as social models and the need for 'respectability' and, particularly, sexual restraint that such a role demanded. Students who attended prior to 1953 and under the 1980–1986 principalship of Constance Koza—the first black woman in the post and a proud alumna of the class of 1945, whom I also interviewed—emphasised Inanda's strictness particularly, and reflected upon it in both positive and critical terms through discussion of routines, labour and sexual crises. Third, despite their teachers' emphasis on discipline, restraint and routines, most alumnae highlighted the liveliness of debate and discussion that took place—connecting their protective campus to a changing world beyond, and empowering them with a sense of self-efficacy to face that world, and to change it. Students who attended in the 1960s and 1970s emphasised this most searingly.

I have also tried to integrate my interviewees' words into this narrative as fully as possible. Although these interviews contributed most significantly to my reconstruction of the years that affiliates were personally involved with the school, several interviewees added to my knowledge of earlier periods, as their mothers, aunts and grandmothers had attended Inanda. Researchers may access interview transcripts at Inanda and Campbell Collections, or on my website.

*   *   *

This book combines a historical ethnography of Inanda's formal and informal (or 'hidden') educational culture with a broader analysis of the changing gendered politics of black education in order to chart the disjunctions within Inanda's community, and between Inanda and the world beyond its campus.[29] To deconstruct the making of gendered categories and the politics of social reproduction in apartheid South Africa, the first three chapters treat the years before 1948. Chapters 1 and 2 examine how Africans, missionaries and political authorities came to a working consensus around African women's centrality in social reproduction in the nineteenth century, and how this consensus engendered the regional expansion of young women's schooling amidst the transformations of industrialising southern Africa. Chapter 3 turns to the roles of educated African women in segregationist South Africa, charting the politicisation of social reproduction in a context of deepening African nationalism.

Chapter 1, 'Social Reproduction in the Making of a "Benevolent Empire": 1835–1885', demonstrates how, in the global Protestant mission movement as in southern Africa, evangelisation hinged upon self-replicating domestic transformations in which women—foreign and local—played central roles. Through a study of the exertions of Inanda's founding missionaries, the women and men of the Boston-based American Board of Commissioners for Foreign Missions, this chapter shows that missionaries looked to young women's education to enact evangelical transformations because they believed that women possessed a deeper familial and social influence than men. This belief was rooted not only in missionaries' experiences in the industrialised societies whence they came, but also in women's apparent abilities to inhibit or encourage conversion in southern Africa and in other evangelical 'fields'. Upon Inanda's 1869 founding as a southern African version of the Mount Holyoke Female Seminary in Massachusetts, African Christian families from across Natal sent their daughters to school to enable their familial social mobility: educated daughters could earn salaries as teachers, marry professional men and enhance their family's security. So, too, did a small number of traditionalist families and a few chiefly royals, who sought to empower their children with literacy to navigate a changing society.

Chapter 2, 'Domestic Revolutions and the Feminisation of Schooling in Natal: 1885–1910', examines the period in which colonial encroachment, agricultural crisis and male labour migration wrought domestic crises that impelled rising numbers of young women to seek schooling at Inanda and other mission schools. While some traditionalist families and chiefs supported them, others opposed girls' schooling vehemently. Angry patriarchs presented a profound challenge to a colonial system predicated on an interlocking web of patriarchal authority. Thus officials deferred to fathers' authority in deciding which young women could attend school, resulting in spectacular cases of 'kraal girls' forced to leave school against their will. At the same time that the legal exigencies of patriarchal colonial governance circumscribed the educational options of girls whose fathers opposed their educations, however, the head of a nascent educational bureaucracy argued that African girls' education in Western domesticity would be essential in creating different sorts of families with different sorts of needs. In monogamous families, the Native Education Inspector imagined, husbands and sons would be taught to 'want' enough to impel them to labour for wages—but they would also be sufficiently satisfied by their domestic comforts to avoid political unrest. Even as officials clamped down on African boys' curricula—attempting to restrict it to the barest preparation for unskilled wage labour—they allowed missionaries more autonomy in the education of young women, whose role in the social reproduction of new sorts of families made their education appear to be a benefit to governance. As young men pursued work in Natal, the Cape and the booming goldfields of the Witwatersrand, young African women began to outnumber their male peers in mission school classrooms, except at the highest levels. They pursued a narrow range of professions—domestic service for those who did not progress very far in school, and teaching for those who went farther.

Chapter 3, 'New African Women's Work in Segregationist South Africa: 1910–1948', demonstrates how educated African women drew upon their schooling to establish gendered social authority within a racialised patriarchy, and it illuminates the stakes of this authority in the development of the segregationist state. Between the Union of South Africa's 1910 formation and the 1940s, African women asserted their leadership in a growing range of social service professions. As the state sought to ensure the reproduction of a black labour force on a shoestring, it depended significantly on the labours of women at all economic levels. And as the degradation of rural African 'reserves' made total segregation an impossibility and African urbanisation an inexorable fact, the state relied particularly on the labours of educated women working in social service professions: teaching, nursing and social work. While the state had long outsourced core responsibilities of African education and medical care to missionaries, missionaries and state officials relied increasingly in this period upon the professional work of African women. As black men grew more deeply disenfranchised in the 1930s, they too looked to women's social leadership to keep their communities resilient and resistant. White missionaries and educated African men regarded African women's role in social 'uplift' with both appreciation and some trepidation, as African women asserted their autonomy from maternalistic female missionaries and paternalistic African men. But agents of the segregationist state did not see African women as a serious political threat. Rather, as African male students and young adults grew more politically assertive during the Second World War and in its aftermath, state officials continued to see African female students and teachers as stabilising forces.

By the eve of apartheid, Inanda Seminary had become the largest and most prestigious all-female high school for African students in the country. Chapter 4, 'Education Policy and the Gendered Making of Separate Development: 1948–1976', demonstrates why, as apartheid bureaucrats elaborated a system of mass African education that excluded most of the missionaries to whom the state had long delegated responsibilities for black social welfare, they would retain a space for Inanda and its socially useful graduates. This chapter underscores that Bantu Education sought to cultivate complacent masses of semi-skilled black workers—male and female. But for Bantu Education to work—indeed, for apartheid to work—schools also needed to train a smaller professional stratum of teachers and health professionals to sustain segregated social institutions. Like missionaries before them, the architects of Bantu Education looked to African women to serve as nurses and teachers—seeing women as intrinsically nurturing, and black women as uniquely equipped to tend to black bodies and minds. Black women also made appealing helping professionals because they were systematically paid less, and officials deemed them more politically tractable—particularly when isolated from the malevolent influence of activist men in all-female institutions. In other words, educated black women seemed both less politically threatening than educated black men and more socially necessary. By this gendered logic, the state nationalised most teacher training colleges and then restricted their male enrolment. By this same gendered logic, officials tolerated Inanda's continuation as an elite, all-female school, which grew more prestigious and cosmopolitan as Bantu Education foreclosed African students' options for a quality education elsewhere.

After the Soweto students' uprising of 1976 rendered apartheid schooling a central site of political struggle, educated African women seized the limited openings that a reformist apartheid state made in its efforts to co-opt a black bourgeoisie. Chapter 5, 'Educated African Women in a Time of Political Revolution: 1976–1994', examines how African women availed themselves of new opportunities to attend historically white universities and to work in an expanding range of professions—particularly medical and corporate work—and used these new opportunities to push for transformations in their lives, and in their country. But at the same time that the African educated elite feminised, schooling became a site of political crisis and gender-linked violence became epidemic. This chapter explores the tensions and possibilities that accompanied the expansion of young black women's schooling in the late-apartheid state, from Inanda's vantage point.

The Epilogue examines Inanda's position since South Africa's democratic transition, situating its resilience within the context of the broader appeal of historic mission schools and single-sex women's institutions. The appeal of single-sex boarding schooling to students, their families, state officials and benefactors reveals the contradictions accompanying the coeval feminisation of schooling and poverty in South Africa. In a time of expanding female access to education, but also deepening unemployment and gender-linked violence, Inanda's model of schooling seems to suggest solutions to ongoing crises of social reproduction.

CHAPTER ONE

Social Reproduction in the Making of a 'Benevolent Empire'
1835–1885

'The whole system of schools in this mission needs reforming,' Henry Bridgman wrote to the American Board of Commissioners for Foreign Missions on behalf of his American Zulu Mission in 1864. 'We absolutely need <u>now</u>, a girls Seminary, modelled after Mt. Holyoke Sem. as much as the case will admit. We absolutely need a boys Seminary for training up teachers & evangelists.'[1]

Bridgman's call for a school in the African countryside modelled on the Mount Holyoke Female Seminary in Massachusetts may seem strange. But the American Zulu Mission and Mount Holyoke were coeval parts of American Protestants' 'benevolent empire'.[2] In 1835, as the first Americans arrived in Natal, Mary Lyon was raising funds to train women as teachers and missionary wives at Holyoke, which opened two years later. Four alumnae were American Zulu Mission appointees in the 1840s; others, including Bridgman's wife, Laura, soon followed.[3] By the late 1880s, over a fifth of all American Board women came from Mount Holyoke.[4] Holyoke women in the United States and abroad ran schools modelled on their alma mater, and they served not only white Americans like the bulk of Board appointees, but also Christian girls in Persia (1843), Cherokee girls in Arkansas (1851) and Hindu girls in India (1853).[5] In 1874, two Holyoke alumnae would organise the Huguenot Seminary in Cape Colony as a 'daughter school' for white girls, upon the invitation of a Dutch Reformed Church pastor there.[6] Holyoke pedagogies translated unevenly across these institutions, where women's ambitions often ran up against cultural incompetence, as well as political and financial constraints.[7]

But like Holyoke, which was so regimented that contemporaries called it a 'Protestant nunnery', these schools encouraged self-discipline and self-sacrifice within practically self-sufficient institutions.[8] American missionaries hoped that each young woman trained at these institutions would work to forge a new Christian society 'by the power of her uniform and consistent example', like a Mount Holyoke graduate.[9]

Holyoke values broadly complemented the ideals of the man to whom Bridgman appealed, Board Secretary Rufus Anderson. Anderson's 'three-self' theory of evangelism espoused the eventual formation of self-governing, self-supporting and self-propagating local churches. But until missionaries were sure that converts would not 'backslide' in their faith, the three-self theory demanded a programme of education for 'native agency' under the paternalistic authority of American ministers.[10] American ministers retained authority over stations that relied upon the labours of many local male and female 'native assistants', of smaller numbers of local male preachers – and of missionary wives. Marriage was a prerequisite for the first American Zulu Mission appointees, and Anderson often suggested that unmarried aspirant missionaries marry Holyoke alumnae.[11] Ministers throughout the Board's missions brought their wives to work with women and children, while ministers trained local men as evangelists.[12]

Inanda Seminary was thus founded to replicate missionary divisions of labour within *kholwa* (African Christian) families, drawing upon women's socially reproductive labours to effect a self-sustaining chain of Christian transformations. While men would train as preachers and teachers at the American Board's all-male Amanzimtoti Seminary, women would prepare to be wives and teachers at a school modelled on that which Henry Bridgman's own wife had attended. A gendered pair of seminaries seemed 'indispensable' to salvaging the Board's fledgling mission in Natal, as they would ultimately make 'native agency' possible.[13] Indeed, during Inanda's first two decades, graduates of Inanda, Amanzimtoti and similar seminaries around the globe sustained the broader American missionary enterprise. In the process, new global and local templates for women's authority emerged. But even as women assumed roles other than those of wife and mother in an expanding benevolent empire, the associations between women and social reproduction grew deeply entrenched. Women's professional labours as teachers and 'native assistants' were structured by a set of familial idioms, through which women were empowered as well as confined.

Engendering education for 'native agency'

The Board had been chartered in 1812 as the first American mission society; early supporters were mostly Congregationalist, and they imagined that citizens of a Christian republic must prepare the world for divine judgement.[14] It remained the largest American mission society through its first half-century, and it 'was also, in its combination of breadth with provincialism, an epitome of the enterprise at large'.[15] In India (from 1813), Ceylon (1817), the Hawaiian Islands (1819), the Ottoman Empire (1820) and Persia (1820), and with Native Americans (1817), the Board had laboured to reproduce idealised New England socio-religious mores.[16] Acculturating youth to these mores through schooling had been an early imperative. In 1817, the Board began a school in Connecticut, for 'the education in our own country of Heathen Youths, in such manner, as, with subsequent professional instruction will qualify them to become useful Missionaries, Physicians, Surgeons, School Masters, or Interpreters; and to communicate to the Heathen Nations such knowledge in agriculture and the arts, as may prove the means of promoting Christianity and civilization'.[17] But this model of education within the United States came to its end in 1827, after two Native American graduates apparently went too far in their acculturation by marrying white women.[18]

The Board contended that '[t]he best education of youth born heathen, having reference to their success as teachers of their brethren, must be given through the instrumentality of missionary institutions in their respective countries', although 'under the paternal care' of American missionaries there.[19] A model of in-country education was developing in Ceylon, where Americans ran 'Common schools' with Tamil instruction for boys and girls and a smaller number of 'English schools' for advanced male pupils.[20] In 1823, a men's seminary opened for 'English school graduates', and later that year the Oodooville Female Boarding School opened to train 'more suitable and acceptable companions' for this elite.[21] Girls left home between the ages of six and eight, remaining in school until they were married to seminary men; some took on new names, as missionaries named them after family members or supporters. Under an American minister, assisted by American and Tamil women, girls learned to read and write Tamil and English and studied the Bible, needlework, arts and sciences.[22]

By the time the Board launched its African missions, then, links between schooling, control over social reproduction and the cultivation of 'native agency' were established. The Board selected Liberia and the port of Natal as its initial entry points into the continent because its leaders believed that people there could be rapidly educated to evangelise the interior. 'Having made a successful beginning among the tribes of the coast, around the colonies, we shall, as our laborers increase, and the roads are opened, advance into the interior with our permanent establishments,' the Board advised John Leighton Wilson, the Liberian mission leader, in 1833. 'Wherever we go, seminaries must be founded for educating schoolmasters, catechists, and naive preachers. The language must be learned and reduced to writing. Printing-presses must be erected, and the natives taught to work them. Constellations of Christian schools must be called into being, and shine around these.'[23] John Philip, of the London Missionary Society (LMS) mission in the Cape, assured the Board that the 'Zoolahs' – subjects of the Zulu king Dingane and the breakaway leader Mzilikazi – lived in complex societies that were as yet unserved by evangelists; with a little education, they, too, would make ideal evangelists.[24] With this espousal, 'light gleamed unexpectedly from the southeastern shore, and laid open to our view a promising and accessible field'.[25]

These grand expectations of continental conversion almost immediately gave way to grander disappointments. Early in 1834, the Maryland Colonization Society sent an exploratory mission to Monrovia and Cape Palmas; Wilson returned to Cape Palmas with his wife and an unmarried African American female teacher at the year's end to launch the mission. Within the next several years, three other white American ministers and their wives joined them, as well as an African American printer and his wife and a single black male minister. Of this group of twelve, four had died by 1843. This unhealthy port was also politically contentious, as missionaries were often at odds with Liberian colonists. The Board opened a new mission on the Gabon River, in a territory that had not yet been claimed by any other missionaries; but soon thereafter, the French military claimed the area. By the late 1850s, there were only twelve members of the mission church, and movement into the interior remained a distant dream.[26] Dramatic challenges also met the American Zulu Mission. In December 1834, as the other Americans settled at Cape Palmas, six ministers and their wives departed for Cape Town. From there three couples were to travel inland to establish a mission amongst Mzilikazi's subjects, while the other three pairs were to sail to Port Natal, whence they would convert Dingane's subjects up to Delagoa Bay. Following Philip's suggestion, the Americans came looking for nations to transform into self-governing bodies of Christians that would in turn effect a chain of conversions.[27] They came into a region marked by incomplete Zulu hegemony and incipient white settlement, and in which the mass of their potential converts did not define themselves in ethnic terms, but rather by their political affiliations.[28] They arrived amidst the immigration of Afrikaner 'trekkers' from the Cape, culminating in the trekkers' 1839 declaration of Natal as an Afrikaner republic, Dingane's 1840 murder and his brother Mpande's authority over a smaller Zulu kingdom.

The first agents of the mission 'to the Zoolahs' were all quite green. They were also all white, unlike their counterparts in western Africa, where some black American involvement had emerged through the colonisationist movement.[29] The inland contingent comprised Southern Presbyterians, and the coastal group New England Congregationalists. Thirty-three-year-old Daniel Lindley, who would found the mission at Inanda, was the eldest, and the only agent with any ministerial experience; he had preached in North Carolina. He was accepted by the Board in late 1833, met Lucy Allen in April 1834 and proposed within three weeks; they married in November and sailed for Cape Town two weeks later. Before meeting her husband, Lucy Lindley had worked as a governess on a Virginia plantation, where she reportedly evangelised to slaves and dreamed of mission work. Her friend Jane Smithey married another of the six missionaries, Dr Alexander Wilson, a North Carolina physician who had trained with Daniel Lindley at Union Theological Seminary in Virginia; Jane

Wilson died in Natal in 1836. The Lindleys and the Wilsons travelled inland with Union graduate Henry Venable of Kentucky and his wife. Aldin Grout was in his final year at Andover Theological Seminary upon his appointment. After his wife died in the field in 1836, he returned to his Massachusetts home, then in late 1838 came back to Natal with a new wife, recent Holyoke graduate Charlotte Bailey Grout.[30] Andover alumnus George Champion of Connecticut joined with his wife, as did Dr Newton Adams of New York, who had no theological training. The wives were all 'Assistant Missionaries'.[31] The upheaval they encountered pushed the Venables, the Champions and Wilson out of the mission. The Lindleys relocated to the trekkers' capital of Pietermaritzburg to minister to them in 1840, and Mpande pushed the Grouts out of his domain in 1842.[32] When the British annexed Natal in 1843, only Adams' station near the Umlazi River seemed remotely promising. The Board considered abandoning the mission upon the fear that the British would constrain their efforts to cultivate autonomous Christian communities.

But after another intervention by Philip of the LMS, the Board decided to stay. While the decade before Philip had encouraged the Americans to build a 'civilized community' from the people of sovereign, 'powerful chiefs', in 1843 he encouraged them to make the best of the stability that British rule might provide.[33] The Cape governor appointed Grout and Adams official missionaries to Natal Africans, while he appointed Lindley to Natal's Afrikaners.[34] In 1846, Lindley and Adams served on the Locations Commission with 'Diplomatic Agent to the Native Tribes' Theophilus Shepstone, delimiting land for African occupation.[35] The next year, the Lindleys assumed residence on the Inanda location, land then occupied predominantly by the amaQadi. The Qadi, a chiefdom within the Ngcobo paramountcy of the Thukela Valley, had been one of the first groups that Shaka kaSenzangakhona had incorporated into the Zulu state in the late 1810s. Then in 1837, Shaka's successor, Dingane, murdered Qadi Chief Dube, pushing his subjects south to Port Natal; Dube's son and successor, Dabeka, died the next year in an expedition against the Zulus. When the Lindleys arrived at Inanda, the Qadi were living under Dabeka's son Mqhawe, who regarded them with suspicion in light of these struggles with usurping authority.[36] Daniel

Lindley, who had been unable to examine the Inanda location until its boundaries had been set on account of floods, complained that 'a more broken, worthless region could hardly be found', claiming to have 'wasted a small vocabulary in grumbling at Government, for allowing the natives to have a settlement in such a wretched region'.[37] But he stayed on, and the colony soon granted the Americans an 11 500-acre 'mission reserve' – land to be administered by resident missionaries.[38] Such would become the American Zulu Mission's pattern in colonial Natal – rueing colonial policies but seeing colonial order as conducive to their work.[39]

The mission had hoped to convert Dingane's and Mzilikazi's followers in one generation, leading to their rapid conversion of the rest of the 'Zoolah race' as the missionaries construed it, thence to the glorious conversion of the interior.[40] But the Americans were unable to accomplish much amidst the political chaos of the 1830s and 1840s. Where stations were established, they were unable to sustain interest beyond initial curiosity in most African communities, as conversion and its cultural trappings demanded ontological transformations few were willing to make. Polygynous homesteads comprised the fundamental social, spiritual and economic bases of African societies in the region. Missionaries demanded that their converts transform, or break with, kin and ancestors that sustained these homesteads to enter into new and uncertain communities, predicated on a new and uncertain god. Christianity thus appeared inviting only to those with few other options.

Fortunately for the Lindleys, one of these desperate people around Inanda was a Qadi royal widow. Early in 1849, Chief Dube's widow Mayembe took refuge at the Lindleys' station to escape an *ukungena* marriage – marriage to her late husband's brother, a custom that would cause much hand-wringing amongst missionaries in years to come, and enable many more conversions. Baptised Dalida Dube, the royal widow engendered such hope in the Lindleys that they formed a church around her. She was their second convert, after Shaka's former soldier John Mavuma; the third was Dube's nineteen-year-old son, Ukakonina, baptised James. Uncle of Chief Mqhawe, James Dube would grow close to Daniel Lindley, who charged him with teaching in Inanda's school and ordained him in 1871.[41] Upon the Lindleys'

1873 retirement, James Dube would replace Daniel Lindley as Inanda's pastor. Dube's wife, Elizabeth Nomanzi Dube, did 'more than any other person' in the community to educate youth, with help from her nine children.[42]

This model of 'native agency' remained exceptional, however. James Dube was only the third African to be ordained in the mission. After Grout's expulsion in 1842, Americans would not return to work in the Zulu kingdom until British control extended north following the Anglo-Zulu War of 1879. By 1880 there were fewer than 10 000 *amakholwa* in Natal, less than 10 per cent of the colony's African population; in Zululand, *amakholwa* numbered in the hundreds.[43] The Americans plainly had not been able to convert a nation in one generation. And half a century into their mission, they were not alone in their exertions. They were instead sharing one of the densest evangelical fields in the world with a range of British and European Protestants and Catholics – a far cry from the open landscape that Philip had conjured.[44] By this time, others had also come to Natal: Indian indentured workers first arrived to work on sugar plantations in 1860, followed by free Indian immigrants. Yet the Americans did not evangelise or educate Indians, seeing these tasks as the domain of British missionaries.[45]

In the mid-nineteenth century, then, the Americans were struggling in a colony characterised by political and social changes that they could neither control nor fully comprehend. As they had before in Ceylon, missionaries in southern Africa saw boarding schools as appealing sites at which to gather young and impressionable prospective Christians, whose evangelical labours in their homes, communities and further afield might sustain the fledgling mission. By 1849, the mission was planning for a male seminary 'to give increased efficiency to our system of native agency' by training local preachers in a course of history, ancient languages and science modelled on American missionaries' own training; their plans resulted in 1853 in the Amanzimtoti Seminary, which pre-dated similar schools for white men in Natal by some twenty years.[46] But Amanzimtoti operated unevenly after its founding missionary fell ill in 1856.[47] A decade later, as *amakholwa* of sufficient means were beginning to send their sons to more established – and racially integrated – Cape Colony schools like the Free Church of Scotland's Lovedale, the Americans urged the Board to revitalise their own 'infant and short-lived Seminary', to provide teachers for a struggling mission.[48] In 1864, Daniel Lindley warned, 'We shall yet reap the fruit of our not doing in former years.' He fretted that 'we ought to have been prepared for the present call for teachers' emanating both from his station's small community of *amakholwa* and, auspiciously, from Mqhawe, who had asked Lindley to send an African male teacher to teach reading on his homestead.[49]

To undergird the work of African male teachers and preachers, Lindley and his colleagues suggested that the Board establish a female counterpart to Amanzimtoti: 'The usefulness of our native teachers & other assistants of various kinds will be helped or hindered by the standing & character of their wives. For the training of girls who may become the trainers of others & examples to them, we need a school of a different character from any we now have.'[50] Critically, the men of the mission envisioned a female seminary that, like Mount Holyoke, would train teachers and evangelists. More importantly, the school would systematically train wives, who would sustain their own Christian homes and effect a self-perpetuating series of transformations through their public example of piety and service. At the time of Inanda's founding, missionaries were convinced that

[t]he Female Boarding School is vitally connected with the success of the missionary enterprise. Its object is to educate suitable companions for the native preachers and teachers, and for other educated Christian young men; that in every native community there may be at least one household illustrative of the fruits of Christian culture. The example of such families will act as leaven to promote the social and moral regeneration of the people, and will especially tend to the elevation of the female sex. The basis of a true Christian civilization must be laid in the homes as well as in the hearts of the people.[51]

Prior to the 1860s, however, the Board had elaborated few seminaries to train men or women. It had mostly held makeshift classes, often in missionary homes.

The Lindleys' household was an exemplar of this model. Lucy deployed her eleven children to go through 'the alphabet of civilization' with African girls. Daniel's biographer recounts that she always had four, five, or six of them in the house to be watched over and taught various things, from the use of soap and water, of forks and dishcloths and tablecloths, to the fashioning and putting on of clothes. Everyone in the family had to help in some way. The daughter whose week it was to look after the girls had to transplant herself with her lesson-books into the kitchen and mix history, philosophy, mathematics, and poetry, with pots and pans and dishwater.

Homeschooling was integral to the social reproduction of *kholwa* society: 'As soon as the girls were tolerably trained, some young men would be found hovering about quite frequently, and soon there would be weddings and new homes for the missionary to inspect on Saturday.'[52] Newton Adams hailed such 'family schools'; he and his wife had even paid parents at Amanzimtoti to keep their children in his home, where they worked and studied.[53]

Despite missionaries' tendencies to represent these 'family schools' as organic solutions to pleas for schooling, they were by gendered design integral to their work. Model marriages were mandatory for missionaries. In 1870, the Board explained:

> The Christian family, the Christian home, the social and moral elevation of women, illustrated in the family and home of our missionaries, have been, and still constitute a prime agency in the great change now in progress, and preeminently justify the policy of the American Board in its decided preference for married missionaries. Indeed, some of the late calls for missionaries have been not only for married men, but for men with a family of children.[54]

But by that time, family schools no longer seemed sufficient to produce and reproduce an African Christian class, given the Americans' manifest failures three decades into their work. Within a couple days of Lindley's missive warning the Board of their need for African teachers in mid-1864, Henry Bridgman issued another, more plaintive call for an African Holyoke: 'We have here some six young misses, that should go to a good Female Seminary at once. But, Female Seminary's <u>we</u>

have none; I say it with sorrow.' This presented a crisis for the Board's visions of 'native agency', as 'now is the time, to secure the "First-fruits" from amongst the children of Believing Parents on our different stations, and prepare them (as far as human agency can) as an offering to the Lord's service in this land'. And 'native agency' must be facilitated by American Christian women:

> In what one way could the 'King's Daughters' in the American churches, make themselves, and their, to be pitied, Zulu Sisters, still more glorious, than by imparting from their Abundance, (and poverty too, it may be) Funds and Teachers, to found a Seminary among the degraded Zulus, after the Pattern of that showed us in the Mount. I mean of course, the one at the Mount Holyoke. Let us have at least 'a reflection' of that goodly Pattern, that the lower half (for in Heathen lands I believe women are the worse half) of these sin-ridden, sin degraded Zulus, passing and expanding under its influence, may be enabled.[55]

Many 'King's Daughters' were keen to take Bridgman up on his challenge. Family schools were also straining to contain the ambitions of increasingly well-educated American women to work more systematically for their 'Zulu Sisters'.[56] Lucy Lindley and other wives in the mission's Maternal Association reportedly discussed the need for a women's school, prayed about the subject and pushed their husbands to act.[57] By 1866, Daniel Lindley had launched construction of a ten-room school for women with neither the funds to complete it nor a teacher to serve there; it was his daughter Mary, working as a governess in New York, who raised funds from affluent American friends to absolve the debt he incurred.[58] In building new schools, missionary families pushed for systemisation of the divisions of labour that had long undergirded their households.

Schooling, homemaking and social transformation at Inanda and Amanzimtoti

The Amanzimtoti Institute opened in 1866 under William Ireland, who had been working with his wife in Natal since 1848. Although inexperienced as a teacher, Ireland was conversant in isiZulu and rooted in the area.[59] From about sixteen pupils in 1866, Ireland would claim over forty in 1870.[60] Ireland boasted that 'in reading, writing, spelling, Geography, Arithmetic, vocal music and in committing to memory, they cannot be outdone by English boys who have enjoyed like advantages'.[61] By 1869, two of these students had joined Ireland as assistant teachers at the school.[62] The next year, Ireland reported that five married men had come for more advanced theological training; one of them had attended the first iteration of Amanzimtoti fifteen years before and had been working as a 'native assistant' since.[63] As the first cohort of African pastors was ordained and as the Native Home Missionary Society of non-ordained African evangelists developed, Amanzimtoti was a crucial institution for the development of 'native agency' in Natal, but Ireland worried that its results were limited. Of an estimated 150 pupils enrolled between the school's founding and 1877, fewer than a third had become teachers or preachers.[64] While the mission left no record of the others' occupations, they likely engaged in trade, farming or transport-riding (carrying trade goods on ox-drawn wagons) – professions that offered men more independence and pay than the mission.[65] This seemed 'a sad waste of what might become, an efficient native agency, that so many of our graduates are now engaging in secular pursuits'.[66]

Ireland's successor, Herbert Goodenough, put the school's role in a broader light in an appeal for funds from the Board to construct a new hostel on campus in 1882:

These boys have never had a home as we understand the word. The influences that have surrounded them all their lives have been more or less heathenish. Not that many of them come from heathen parents, though that is the case with perhaps half a dozen of the boys, but they are from a heathen uncivilized people, and the customs and thoughts of heathenism cling to the best of them. They are surrounded by and breathe an atmosphere of corrupt and degrading influences. Of how great importance is it then, that for the few years we can have these boys, they should be brought under the best possible influences in every respect, but most emphatically, those of a Christian home ... To hold and mold them to a higher idea of Christian living, to train up young men who shall be leaders of a truer type of Christianity, and from whose members may be chosen faithful preachers and Christian teachers – this we understand to be our work. It is not necessary to state how much we should be helped in this.

This appeal apparently resonated with the Board, as it gave $10 000 for this 'home'.[67]

Between its revitalisation and the turn of the century, the Amanzimtoti Institute became known more often as Adams, in honour of Newton Adams, the first missionary at Amanzimtoti and an exponent of 'family schools' that combined work, study and domestic routines. The name was apt, as the school operated upon a series of familial idioms that naturalised a staggering amount of student labour under the authority of Goodenough and his colleague, Annie Dixon, whom pupils called 'our dear mother'. In 1886, students unable to pay their fees – half the student body – were compelled to work five and a half hours a day, in the homes of Dixon or Goodenough, in the school or in fields which produced much of their food.[68]

The mission would go to greater pains to make Inanda Seminary into a model 'home' – Amanzimtoti's ideal complement. Upon her appointment as the school's first principal, Mary Edwards was a widowed, middle-aged schoolteacher who had hitherto encountered the 'Zooloos' only in the periodicals she followed as secretary of the Ladies Missionary Society of the First Presbyterian Church in Troy, Ohio, giving her vague knowledge of the mission's field.[69] Undeterred, in August 1868 she boarded a ship with her worldly possessions packed into forty boxes – including all of the furnishings necessary to make an American-styled home and school in the African countryside.[70] Her mandate was 'not education in the general sense, it is not to educate the wives of merchants and planters, but of the future religious teachers and guides of the people', according to Board Secretary Nathaniel Clark. 'The time will come when you may be prepared to admit none but such as will pledge themselves to become the wives of native preachers or teachers of their own people for a term of years.'[71] Indeed, Inanda's aim to cultivate wives for an African clergy remained central to the mission's objectives over its first decade, as its leaders maintained that 'the present state of morals is such that it would be rash to ordain an unmarried man, either as a pastor of a church or an evangelist'.[72]

Inanda's mandate was the creation and perpetuation of exalted Christian domesticity: by producing exemplary Christian mothers, the school might salvage a struggling mission from the home outward. 'If the mothers make the men, this institution must be set above all price,' Lindley and colleagues rhapsodised upon Inanda's 1869 opening.

> Oh, how many times have we sighed to see, on our several stations, even one intelligent native mother, with a good degree of womanly refinement; one who would be a pattern to others in the keeping of her house, & especially in the instruction of her children; one whose cleanly habits & proper bearing would feel not to be above the attainment of a native woman. Some of us may live to see so great a sight, or at least a great improvement in those who will receive so much wise tuition & judicious training under Mrs. Edwards.

Alumnae influences upon 'the hundreds of children growing up in our day & Sabbath schools, & under the preaching of the gospel' would be key. 'It is impossible that these children should become a generation just like the heathen who live outside of such influences ... We feel sure that the body of them will, in ten thousand ways, spread the light they are receiving.'[73]

This focus on domestic transformation to ensure evangelical perpetuation was not unique. When the famous Cape Colony school at Lovedale opened a girls' department in August 1868, its headmistress stressed a similar impetus, declaring, 'The aim with which I started was not [to] turn out school-girls but women and with that aim in mind I tried to give the Institution not so much the air of a school as of a pleasant home ... the young women will never be able to make homes unless they understand and see what a home is.'[74] In the 1870s, the LMS had constructed a secondary school similar to Amanzimtoti, the Moffat Institution, for Tswana boys. As Jean Comaroff has described, its staff forbade students to visit their villages for fear of their contaminating 'heathen' influence; even parental visits to the institution were closely monitored, in 'an effort to make the scholars strangers to their own world; to enclose them in a total institution in which both formal and informal curricula were entirely controlled'.[75]

In the Americans' benevolent empire and in Natal, however, Edwards' position was remarkable. She was the first female appointee in the American Zulu Mission who was not the wife or daughter of an appointed minister; she was in the first cohort sponsored by the Board's new women's auxiliary; and the school to which she was assigned was the first of its kind in southern Africa. When Edwards' school opened in March 1869, few schools operated anywhere or for anyone beyond the primary level in the colony.[76] Through the 1870s, few white girls attended school beyond the primary grades. Those of some means studied the arts, needlework and other Victorian pursuits at 'dame schools' or 'ladies' academies' in towns, while others studied with governesses. After an unsuccessful first attempt by the Anglican Church at providing a liberal arts education for white girls, the Durban Young Girls' Collegiate Institution would open expressly for settlers' daughters in 1878, with guidance from American Zulu Mission personnel. The chairman of the school's founding committee was a frequent visitor to Inanda, and the school's founders took great interest in American missionaries' discussions of Mount Holyoke.[77] In the late 1870s through the 1890s, a growing number of white girls' schools would open in Natal, including public schools and a branch of the Huguenot Seminary, the Mount Holyoke-modelled school for whites in the Cape.[78] Alumnae from these schools, like Inanda alumnae, would later refer to themselves as 'Old Girls', suggesting a similar elite pride.[79]

Upon her arrival, Edwards could not have imagined her school's eventual prominence. She was too immediately overwhelmed. She was charged with launching this radically new sort of school by herself, and given authority over decisions that only male ministers had hitherto enjoyed – yet she could neither vote on mission business nor attend administrative meetings with her male peers, placing her at a disadvantage in securing support for her school within the mission.[80] Despite Rufus Anderson's initial reservations on the matter of language, she was to run an English-medium school; but she could speak no isiZulu, and few of her students could speak a modicum of English. She was to train young women on a Holyoke-inspired model; but in the school's early years, pupils included whomever she could entice to attend. And she was to prepare her students to transform the homesteads of their kin and neighbours in a period of profound flux, the causes and consequences of which Edwards did not grasp. Out of these challenges, Edwards would advance key elements of Holyoke education: her students would sustain a self-sufficient institution in which they cultivated self-sacrifice and self-discipline. But to navigate the constraints under which she worked, Edwards would introduce this modern institution through familial idioms of hierarchy and obligation that were remarkably similar to those that had long undergirded 'family schools'.

It is impossible to reconstruct the expectations that the seminary's first students harboured when, one morning in March 1869, they settled onto the pedestal chairs of the double desks that had come from Ohio along with their teacher. But Edwards left a breathless record of frustration:

> This is Thursday of the second week of school and this evening if I dared to I would engage passage on the first steamer homeward bound. Unless I can have help I am sure I shall not be here long. There are twenty girls, undisciplined, heedless . . . The truth is I am not fit to have charge of all these girls. I haven't strength to whip and not tact or patience to manage them without. But I was going to tell you that Helen, a great, fat, lazy girl, fifteen years old, an only and petted daughter has charge of the cooking this week, the corn has not been well cooked and I have been obliged – but what is the use of filling up a sheet with such stuff – 'suffice it to say' that I am thoroughly out of patience.

In the next line, as if exhaling, she conceded, 'The girls are generally well disposed and are obedient but need constant looking after, but then all children do. After all they are much better than I expected. This sheet is not to be "put on file" at the Missionary House. I am happier now than when I commenced writing.'[81] The next day, she assured the Board, 'I have had a delightful day, slept well after I told you my troubles and the scholars have been very good today – I will not leave this month.'[82] Even within a canon of some very disjointed, melodramatic and self-flagellating missionary reports, these and Edwards' other early letters stand out for their anxious stream-of-consciousness style, revealing a woman who felt rushed and alone, and for whom making contact with Boston was both burden and relief. More than once she backtracked or requested that the Board destroy her letters.[83]

Single women like Edwards were a novelty who struck many as noble but strange. 'Said a Christian Zulu: "I can understand how a missionary and his wife can leave friends & native land for a foreign field, but I wonder when I see young unmarried ladies leaving parents & friends & coming among strangers to live and labor. Only the love of Christ could induce them to do this!"' the men of the mission reported in 1871 – perhaps using this reaction to underscore their own ambivalence about the new women in their midst.[84] For while ministers generally welcomed women's work in schools and homes as a cost-saving and far-reaching evangelical strategy, many worried that they were appointing too many American women and local workers. Shortly after the mission's report of the amazed Zulu man, the Board observed that with fewer than a hundred American ministers and fifty single American women worldwide, 'we could only look for disaster' without the work of women or 'native agents'. But

> with all our admiration for the heroic spirit that has led so many unmarried ladies to go abroad, with all our gratitude for the Divine blessing on their labors, we cannot forget that there is work to be done that women cannot do. For the last year the record shows of new missionaries but four men and sixteen women, yet we do not disguise the fact that it is far more difficult for a woman to bear up against the peculiar trials and hardships of missionary life than for a man.[85]

Early on, the Board put Edwards through some 'peculiar trials' in their unwillingness to give her time to study isiZulu. She began threatening to leave as early as January 1870, exclaiming of her pupils, 'If I could but talk to them!'[86] In the first term, she had been unable to learn more than a polite modicum of the language, a limitation that would shape her pedagogy significantly. While students were supposed to work in English to master the tongue of both the benevolent empire and the British Empire, early pupils' ability to speak English was in fact far more limited than the school's ambitions to be an English-medium school would suggest. Although Edwards reported in April 1869 that 'all but three read easy books in English', she added that

Laurana Champion, 'one of the most advanced' students, 'understands English and speaks it a little' – revealing that Edwards could only speak with most students at great strain.[87] Despite this, Daniel Lindley opposed her suggestion to study isiZulu with James Dube and the Board denied her time to study isiZulu elsewhere.[88] Edwards complained, 'I cannot converse with them and do not attempt it with an interpreter. I am sure they would be glad to listen, the few times I have said anything, in English of course, some of them turned to Laurana with an earnest look saying *Nini? Nini?* [What? What?]'[89]

Edwards thus began to train Laurana Champion to take over. 'I sit by and tell them what to do if they seem at a loss. I was a good deal amused one day; Laurana Champion was hearing the primer class read, one little girl did not read to please her and she spoke decisively,' Edwards explained. 'I think she will make a good teacher, she keeps good order.'[90] In October she put Champion, Lucy Isaac and Helen Klasi – all daughters of prominent Inanda *kholwa* families – in charge of daily religious instruction, hoping 'the conversion of these girls does not depend upon my ability to speak the language'.[91] Throughout her first year, Edwards repeatedly asked the mission to send another teacher conversant in isiZulu to assist her. She wound up with a series of three teenaged daughters of missionaries. When the Board finally sent another single woman in mid-1871, Edwards took the opportunity to ask for a furlough, which the Board denied; this new colleague then departed for Amanzimtoti shortly after her arrival.[92] Edwards instead relied on student assistance. Their efforts yielded some success, as twenty-two of the forty-two girls enrolled in the first two years were confirmed.[93]

Edwards' reliance on her students kept her school afloat in its early years. From the start, advanced Inanda girls seem to have taught more than their peers at Amanzimtoti, as Inanda admitted a broader range of pupils. In 1873 and 1877, Inanda admitted more 'day scholars' from the surrounding area than boarders. While Inanda's boarders were themselves generally not academically advanced upon their arrival at the school, its day scholars were younger and almost all illiterate, and Edwards placed them in her more advanced pupils' charge.[94] In 1874, day scholars included the young sons of the African ministers James Dube and Benjamin Hawes and the children of Inanda's new resident missionaries, the Pixleys.[95] They also included the young sons of Chief Mqhawe, whom Edwards courted heavily in hopes that he might send his daughters.[96] By 1880, Edwards had acquired more young sons of Mqhawe and Chief Ndhlokolo, to whom her pupils taught the alphabet; Mqhawe's daughters had also come but could not stay as 'their mothers would not consent – they need them to take care of the babies or watch the mealie gardens or to dig'.[97]

To manage her growing 'family', Edwards delegated extensive campus tasks.[98] She informed a member of the Women's Board in 1876:

> The girls do all the work. Ten girls to cook, 8 girls for the dining room, 3 to carry water, one to sweep school room, one to sweep verandahs, one to keep the grounds clean, two to scour knives & forks, & one in each of the 5 rooms to keep them tidy & one is Stewardess, whose duty it is to see that each room is tidy, that the bells are rung at the right time. The girls do a good deal of work which is considered man's work at home. Transplanting trees, spading the garden, cutting grass with sickle, cleaning the paths etc. For this outside work we pay them one penny per hour & they buy their books in this way.[99]

Edwards – whose students called her 'Ma Edwards' and who styled herself 'their mother at Inanda' – and her colleague Martha Price saw themselves as overseers and maternal figures.[100] Price explained in 1881:

> Out of school they are with us, as children with their parents – they are noisy – what family of forty children would not be – they are constantly coming to us for medicine, for cotton, needles, for help in cutting and mending their clothes, etc. etc. When any of them are really sick, Mrs. E. takes them into her own room and cares for them night and day as if they were her own daughters. We think it is much better for the girls to be with us in this way than to be by themselves, indeed we could not have it any other way.[101]

Despite this familial arrangement, Edwards frequently found her position of responsibility without ultimate authority within the mission stressful.

After the Lindleys retired to the United States in April 1873, leaving the Inanda station under the charge of Edwards and her colleague James Dube, she decided she had borne enough responsibility. As soon as another American missionary couple replaced the Lindleys on the station, Edwards borrowed a hundred pounds from the mission treasury and boarded the next ship out. 'Please don't scold,' she wrote Clark from the shores of England in July 1874. 'I am on my way home, but I promise to return soon.'[102] The school's enrolment dropped precipitously during Edwards' self-declared furlough. That October, she confessed to the Women's Board, 'I secretly hoped some one would be found to take charge of the school and allow me to remain at home . . . I do not know the language and never will.'[103] Edwards stayed in Ohio the next year.[104] 'I can't feel that I acted honorably towards the Board or towards the school or Mission in Natal in remaining away or in leaving the school just as I did. But I sadly needed rest,' Edwards wrote Clark in December 1875.[105] The Board sought a replacement. When none was forthcoming, Edwards agreed to return, departing in May 1876.

Figure 3　Inanda principal Mary Edwards with student, n.d.
(Album B57-011, Campbell Collections, University of KwaZulu-Natal, Durban)

Mary Edwards would never return to the United States, dying in her bed at Inanda in 1927, at ninety-eight years old. But she would struggle to leave again. As early as 1873, she had been growing restless, contemplating trips with advanced pupils to begin new schools.[106] When Fannie Morris and Martha Price arrived from the United States in 1878, Edwards declared that she would leave the principalship to lead students in evangelical visits to the homesteads surrounding Inanda. The novice teachers were alarmed by her decision and shocked that the mission did not provide them with guidance in negotiating their position. Morris reported:

> Two or three days before time for school to begin, Mrs. E. surprised us all very much by saying, that she had come to the conclusion that it would be better for Miss Price and I to take the school, that we would do much better if she was away also, therefore consequently she would withdraw. This was a great trial both to Miss Price and me, and it was with difficulty that we restrained the feeling that our being sent from America was a mistake. So far at least it seemed only to have done harm, for we felt that our coming had driven Mrs. Edwards away from her home and work.[107]

To Edwards, her time 'among the kraals' was invigorating; with alumnae Talitha Hawes, Kumakwake Abraham and Esther Dube – all *kholwa* daughters – she set up a school amongst neighbouring homesteads, which the alumnae continued to visit each Sunday.[108] Morris found this work important, but she found her role within the mission frustrating. Women, she complained,

> can do . . . work among the women that it is impossible for a man to do, but until this fact is recognized by the brethren, it will be much better not to send any more single ladies, unless they are the daughters of the missionaries now in the field, for it tries one to the very soul, after having left a position at home where they felt they were doing acceptable work for the master to go where they thought there was a greater need, only to find that there was no recognized need.[109]

After this missive, Morris persuaded Edwards to return; Morris took over 'kraal work'.[110] With the increasing visibility of African and American Christian women in homesteads from the late 1870s, increasing numbers of other 'kraal girls' came to Inanda, as the next chapter explores. While some came with familial support, others ran away from home, often to evade marriages. In 1885, Inanda enrolled fifty daughters of *amakholwa* and eleven girls from traditionalist homes.[111]

Edwards' successor as principal, Fidelia Phelps, found upon her 1885 arrival that Inanda had been 'designed for the "higher education" of native girls, but that term "higher education" must not be understood to mean Greek, Latin, Psychology, Biology, etc. A fair knowledge of the elementary branches of learning is something far in advance of the majority of the girls of this race.' Phelps, a Holyoke alumna, had taught at the Huguenot Seminary from 1877 to 1880 and believed that while Huguenot was an effective 'outgrowth of Mt. Holyoke', Inanda was not:

> The design of the school is not strictly carried out for the reason that there are not as many girls on the stations anxious to go on with their studies after they have learned to read a little English & to do a little Arithmetic, as we wish there were, & because some girls from the kraals and a few from our stations not at all well-fitted, are so anxious to come that we cannot say 'no' to them.[112]

Indeed, while Inanda's curriculum also included lessons in geography and history (classical and modern, with an overwhelmingly European emphasis), most students in the period that this chapter covers would learn only enough English, scripture and arithmetic to teach primary school children. In contrast, Huguenot would receive official recognition as a full 'college' in 1898.[113] Despite Phelps' reservations, Inanda claimed some success in reproducing *kholwa* society: between 1869 and 1885, 216 students had attended, of whom at least sixty-six were teachers in Board schools and fifty-nine had married under Christian rites.[114]

The spaces of women's authority in an expanding benevolent empire

The epoch between Mary Edwards' 1868 arrival and her 1927 death on Inanda's campus was the high tide of American women's mission work, an era in which the enterprise was feminised and oriented towards institution building. As Patricia Hill has shown, it was American women's engagement in foreign missions that turned evangelisation from a minority pursuit into a broader social movement in these years. Since their mid-nineteenth-century Asian work, missionaries had imagined women to be uniquely capable of converting mothers and had seen maternal conversion as key to broader evangelisation. By the late nineteenth century, as women had elaborated professional niches for themselves in mission institutions, they claimed gendered authority in the science of domesticity.[115]

Their authority developed within a transnational public of texts, letters and meetings, where women elaborated a vision of domestic transformation in which female-led educational institutions and home visits figured prominently. The first American node in this public drew its inspiration from a British man who began the Society for Promoting Female Education in the East in 1834 and set out on an American speaking tour the next year to urge women to sponsor unmarried female teachers in the Americans' Asian missions. Over the 1840s, educated American women pushed the Board to open more girls' boarding schools, under female leadership. Unmarried women were particularly keen to lead schools: almost a fifth of Mount Holyoke alumnae between 1837 and 1850 never married, but they were quite fit for missionary service as teachers.[116] The utility of single women, 'in a measure free from domestic cares' such that 'they could devote themselves wholly to their work', did not escape the early mission to southern Africa.[117] Given the masses of children outside school and the calibre of women eager to teach them, (the unmarried) Mary Lyon opined in 1844, 'It is my humble opinion that the leadings of Providence should be decisive to justify our encouraging an unmarried female to go on a foreign mission.'[118] Over the opposition of the American Board's Rufus Anderson and other leading male missionaries, who worried about single women's safety in foreign 'fields', the non-denominational Women's Union Missionary Society was launched in 1861 to sponsor single women; it spawned New England and Midwestern branches over the next decade, provoking denominational boards to follow to keep 'women's work for women' under their control.[119] The Women's Board of Missions of the Congregational Churches became the first denominational board in 1868, followed by Methodist, Baptist, Presbyterian, Episcopalian and African Methodist Episcopal (AME) Church women's auxiliaries. While the AME was particularly concerned to send ' "representative" women of the race' to Africa, all took an interest in African women.[120]

But the early approaches of these boards were shaped indelibly by Protestant women's deeper history of preoccupation with 'Oriental' women, as Lisa Joy Pruitt has shown. American and British women across Asian missions had been prioritising evangelical home visits to their Asian counterparts since the 1850s. They were most invested in home visits in India, where high-caste women's *zenana* seclusion seemed a formidable impediment to evangelical success: missionaries believed that they could 'alter national feeling' only by converting high-caste families, and that they could best reach these families through their women.[121] American missionaries envisioned secluded women to have the same inherent maternal power as American Christian women did, but to be suppressed in their domestic 'slavery' from exercising it to morally elevating ends. Missionaries feared that, in their oppression, Hindu, Muslim and Armenian Christian women in a broadly defined 'Orient' stretching from South and East Asia through the Ottoman Empire were instead reinforcing 'backward', literally inward-looking social orders – by modelling female subservience and seclusion for their children and, more problematically, by guarding the traditions at the core of their societies that missionaries sought to access and alter. In the darkness of women's quarters, unconverted mothers and wives posed barriers to the work of missionaries convinced of the fundamental role of homes in shaping societies. Entering homes and interacting with women, missionary women in Asia carved out a role for themselves that was inaccessible to ordained men. But such home work could only go so far. It was a painstaking, intimate process in which missionaries grappled with language barriers and cultural constraints that they imagined local Christian women were more prepared to negotiate.

Thus, from their inception the women's auxiliaries looked to girls' boarding schools as a doubly promising evangelical approach: first, girls could be extracted from their mothers' apparently malevolent influence; then, they might return home to convert their mothers and those of their neighbours. The Women's Board of Missions of the Congregational Churches, which sponsored Edwards among its first cohort in 1868, thus began its first annual meeting the next year with a survey of the American Board's work in Turkey, where, as an American minister serving in Constantinople insisted, Muslim 'women not only stood in the way of their children, but of their husbands. If they had any suspicion that their husbands were about to read the Bible, or to turn Protestants, they knew how to step in, and make the house too hot to hold them.' They were at once 'servants and slaves' within their marriages and troublingly powerful in maintaining these 'degraded' homes. But, in altered domestic environments, 'it was abundantly proved that they were capable of elevation and education, and that the influence of the gospel upon them was exactly the same as upon the women of America'. Now, he insisted, more 'girls had to be gathered into the schools, of which many more were needed', in order 'to train up these girls for teachers, and to make them instrumental in gathering others into the kingdom of Christ' – under the guidance of unmarried American women.[122] Later that year in Bitlis, Turkey, American women began a day school where, 'as far as possible, we adopt Holyoke modes of teaching'. Explaining their plans to add a boarding facility, one reported that 'a strong reason for gathering girls together in a boarding-school is found in the fact that Christian influence is much more likely to become a saving power, than when, by a daily return to their homes, they hear the truth controverted and ridiculed'.[123]

By this logic, Inanda seemed poised to set off a series of transformations in another difficult field. Missionaries' concerns in southern Africa were not women's seclusion and marginalisation, but rather the centrality of women's productive and reproductive labour in the homestead economy. In Natal missionaries rued *ukulobola*, the foundational institution whereby a man gave cattle to his father-in-law upon marriage to solidify new affective and productive bonds, as bride-buying or even slavery, and they saw polygyny as male decadence since women performed most agricultural labour. But missionaries interpreted all non-Christian women's positions in the same basic terms: because all seemed oppressed within their homes and influential in shaping the moral orders of these homes, all posed both formidable obstacles to and essential conduits for evangelism. As Laura Bridgman put it bitterly:

> It is a sad truth in this as in other heathen lands that the women and girls are in a deeper degradation than the other sex. It is seldom that a heathen woman (unless she is very old and cast off by her husband) will give an ear to the truth ... she is wise in her own conceit and thinks the missionary is a fool and all his stories nonsense – really she is to herself her own greatest enemy and it is the mothers rather than the fathers who most often oppose the coming of their girls to school.[124]

At school, women in Africa, as in Asia, imagined they might reshape girls' obstinate domestic power into luminous Christian influence.

But in the new age of women's auxiliaries, increasing numbers of their teachers were not themselves mothers or wives. While they all sponsored married missionaries too, denominational women's boards followed the Women's Union Missionary Society in focusing on unmarried women. In its first decade, 60 per cent of the 103 Congregationalist Women's Board missionaries were single.[125] Married American churchwomen read of their experiences through periodicals and personal letters and supported them with funds, correspondence and promises of prayer. Single missionary women also kept in touch with one another within this public. Martha Price, for instance, came to Inanda in 1878 from Holyoke. Her college roommate also joined the Board, working at Oodooville Seminary in Ceylon, and she and Price shared strategies through their letters.[126] Fidelia Phelps, as we have seen, moved between Holyoke-inspired institutions in southern Africa.

The contours of their benevolent empire came into sharp relief when, in the middle of the second meeting of the Congregationalist Women's Board, one woman unfurled a 'moral map' that 'plainly delineated the moral condition and religious aspect of the world'. She guided her audience through its landscape:

Let us look at the eastern hemisphere: Asia is buried in the night of heathenism and Mohammedanism. Africa about equally divided between the same; Southern Europe is Roman Catholic; Eastern Europe is Greek Church, which also extends into Northern Asia; a sadly small portion of Northern Europe is Protestant. Turning to the western hemisphere, how large a portion of it we find still under the darkness of superstition! while the United States seems like a sun to scatter the moral darkness of the world. For this, God has opened the gates of mighty empires that had been shut during long ages.

And if Americans had a special burden to bear Christian light, American women bore it doubly:

To bear this to them is our privilege; and who that has been eye-witness to the deep degradation of our sex in heathen lands, – that has seen the highest and lowest type of womanhood side by side, and realised the broad moral gulf that lay between, – but would blush at our insensibility to the great needs of mothers and children, numbering four hundred millions, – tenfold the population of these United States.[127]

Their map depicted the United States as a golden icon, with only a few exceptional spots. Areas of American Board evangelism were marked with gold stars, but much of the globe was swathed in brown – for 'heathenism'. For the many members of the Women's Board who had come of age with American abolitionism, this was not the first 'moral map' they would have seen. Another had graced a widely circulated pamphlet of the American Anti-Slavery Society.[128] In that image, the darkness clouding the American South had signified not heathenism but slavery. The moral map implicitly referenced the country's recent past and situated missionaries' present labours within an unfolding narrative of women's reformism, in which American women bore a responsibility to protect and uplift women and children who had been literally or figuratively enslaved. Women's Board members' Americanness was wrapped up in their membership within a spiritual empire of women – whose work might follow upon or help precipitate the apparently divine opening of 'mighty empires' in Africa or 'the Orient'. All had come of age with the interlinked valorisation of American domesticity and national expansion, and they were acutely aware of 'their place in a global narrative' of women's reform.[129] They often worked in partnership with their British Protestant counterparts, whose own 'women's work for women' would advance, transcend and subvert imperial imperatives.[130] But they envisioned American Protestants as occupying the key role in global evangelisation.

The role women claimed in the global evangelical project grew over Inanda's first decade. Between Inanda's founding and 1910, the proportion of laypersons in the American and European missionary force climbed from 52 per cent to 70 per cent, reflecting a broader uptick in female participation.[131] By 1880, women constituted a majority of American missionaries.[132] They worked with a growing number of locally trained women, who hailed from a growing empire of women's schools: the American Board opened new women's colleges in Japan (1875), Spain (1881) and China (1882), and it expanded its Ottoman girls' schools into colleges.[133] In Natal, the Americans opened another boarding institution, the Umzumbe Home, in 1873, followed by the Ireland Home in 1894; both of these especially targeted the daughters of non-Christians. In all these schools, girls were to be 'brought under the most favorable influences to become fitted, as educated Christian women, to occupy important positions, and to illustrate the spirit and power of the gospel'.[134] As Rhonda Semple has observed, local women made Protestant missionary institutions possible, but their names and experiences are difficult to divine from the records their foreign supervisors left, as racism and status anxieties relegated assistants to the margins of their reports. But where 'single ladies' went, greater numbers of 'native teachers' joined them.[135]

In the Board as in peer missions, single foreign women were paid less than married foreign men, and local men were paid less than foreign men or women.[136] Local women, who generally taught when they were young and then were expected to marry, were paid least of all, enabling missionary institutions to proliferate through their essential but unrecognised labours. In the early 1880s, for instance, Inanda's African teacher Talitha Hawes earned a third of the salary that Edwards or Price earned, and together Edwards and Price earned less than married American couples – although individually each of these American women made more than any African minister.[137] Hawes' salary was greater than the pittance that 'pupil-teachers' received, which often included no more than lodging. Indeed, teaching could pay less than domestic service.[138]

The experiences of Talitha Hawes and another early student, Dalita Isaac, reveal the centrality of women's work to missionary institutions. Both may have been named after Dalida Dube, and because of their names Norman Etherington conflates their identities in one of the few accounts treating early Inanda graduates' experiences – fusing them into a symbol of *kholwa* women's disfranchisement.[139] The realities of their careers were more complex. Not only at the *bottom* of a mission hierarchy couched in familial idioms, these women also constituted the *basis* of the new sorts of families and institutions that grew out of mission schools – endowing them with a social influence that white women did not possess, although white women had more power within mission structures.

Talitha Hawes, daughter of early Inanda convert Thomas Hawes, was among Inanda's first pupils. While her sister Martha was an adolescent in 1869, Talitha Hawes fitted the school's ambitions less well. She was six years old, a 'little lame girl' who 'did not know the Alphabet and not one word in English'.[140] But Thomas Hawes was desperate for his disabled daughter to board, too; as Edwards put it, he 'begged me to take her', as he and his wife were 'so anxious to have her admitted that we could not refuse. They gave her to me.'[141] Talitha Hawes became Edwards' special charge. In 1875, while Edwards was in the United States, Hawes returned to her parents' home; when Edwards returned the next year, Hawes came back as a pupil-teacher. In 1877, Edwards paid for Hawes to undergo surgery in Durban and for an English housekeeper to tend to her recovery.[142] Hawes returned to teach and translate the Bible into isiZulu at Inanda, where she and Edwards were so close that they sometimes shared a bed.[143] Hawes considered Edwards 'not any less than a mother to me. I love her dearly.'[144]

Talitha Hawes' education proceeded through familial idioms much like those that had shaped her father's early trajectory at Inanda mission station. Thomas Hawes was the son of Joel Hawes, a charter member of the Inanda church who had changed his name from Goba in emulation of Joel Hawes, the prominent New England preacher who had presided over Daniel and Lucy Lindley's wedding in 1834.[145] Thomas Hawes' career trajectory shared much with that of James Dube. While Daniel Lindley had initially employed Dube as a teacher, Lucy Lindley had turned her attention to Hawes, who had been her servant before training as a teacher and preacher. Reflecting on his own progress from 'herd boy' to pastor in an 1873 Inanda speech, Hawes marvelled at his children, now 'in two fine, large boarding-schools: the one at Amansimtote, the other here at Inanda . . . See how we have increased. Our families are larger . . . Look into our houses; see what comforts: see our wagons and our cattle! Our cup is running over.'[146] For men like Hawes, schooling and generational progress were synonymous. Edwards, serving 'in the place of father and mother' for their daughters at Inanda, possessed great power.[147]

The costs of this power became clear as Talitha Hawes matured. She continued to work closely with Edwards, impressing her sufficiently such that in 1881 Edwards decided to enrol her in higher teachers' training courses at the Huguenot Seminary, Holyoke's 'daughter school' for white girls in the Cape.[148] Cognisant of the limits of their sisterhood, Edwards nonetheless inquired of Huguenot's principal whether 'they would make an exception since she is lame and will probably be a teacher all her life', but 'there was too much prejudice against color'. Instead, Edwards suggested to a supporter in the Women's Board, 'I hope some arrangement can be made by which she can go to Oberlin [College in Ohio]. What do you say? If I had money enough I would not trouble any one else but I cannot meet the expenses alone.' She affirmed that Hawes 'has had much to try her and she is old enough to have pretty well established her character'.[149]

If Edwards had indeed been able to send Hawes to Oberlin College in 1881, she would have been the first black South African to study in the United States. But this plan never came to fruition. Instead, John Nembula enrolled as a student at Oberlin in 1882. He then studied at Chicago Medical College, graduating in 1887 and returning the next year as the colony's first certified African doctor.[150] While extant evidence does not delineate the precise reasons for this course of events, the weakness of Edwards' and Hawes' gendered and racialised positions within missionary decision-making structures likely had much to do with it. The failure of Edwards' plan also derived from the structure of intimacies and institutional power in missionary institutions that made Hawes' educational future hinge on Edwards' personal idiosyncrasies. For, by the end of 1884, Edwards seemed to have forgotten her commitment to Hawes' education. Hawes, she told Clark, was still 'very anxious' to study in the United States, and had told Edwards that 'if she is to teach all her life she must study more'. But, Edwards claimed, 'I have never encouraged her going to America and supposed she had abandoned all thought of going until the arrival of Mr. and Mrs. Ousley' to serve in Mozambique as the first African American appointees in the mission.[151] The next year, Hawes announced that she had saved enough to pay her way to New York, but Edwards discouraged her, contending that the only 'preparation she needs is a baptism of the Holy Ghost'.[152] Hawes left Inanda Seminary in 1885.

When Talitha Hawes left her fictive kin, she returned to support her father's household. In 1889, she and her immediate family applied for and received exemption from the Natal Code of Native Law.[153] In 1895, she combined her savings with her brothers' earnings from mining in Johannesburg to buy her father a farm south of Port Natal.[154] There, at a mission they called Ebusisweni (the blessed place), the Hawes family began a church and school – the latter under Talitha's leadership.[155] She attained state certification and continued as a respected teacher.[156] She would die on the farm in 1927, six months before Edwards' death at Inanda. Talitha Hawes thus left the maternalistic mission fold. But from the perspective of Andile Hawes, great-grandson of Talitha's brother Lindley, she did not leave in defeat. She was a leading member of a 'very strong' family of 'fighters', whose members had sustained the Inanda community and carried Christian education beyond.[157] While disempowered by Edwards' vacillating affections, she forged a meaningful life in a transformative *kholwa* family.

Dalita Isaac was also the daughter of an early convert: Isaac Seme's children took his Christian name as their surname. Her younger brother, Pixley ka Isaka Seme, would graduate from Columbia

Figure 4 Thomas Hawes, n.d. (Album B48-099, Campbell Collections, University of KwaZulu-Natal, Durban)

Figure 5 Talitha Hawes, n.d. (Album B57-005, Campbell Collections, University of KwaZulu-Natal, Durban)

Figure 6 Dalita Isaac, n.d. (Album B57-004, Campbell Collections, University of KwaZulu-Natal, Durban)

University in 1906 and founded the South African Native National Congress with James Dube's son John in 1912.[158] In 1923, this organisation would change its name to the African National Congress. Despite Pixley Seme's later prominence, the family was quite poor. Dalita Isaac's older sister, Lucy, had been among Edwards' first students, and Edwards noticed Dalita Isaac's intelligence when she was a student in Inanda's day school; Edwards admitted her as a 'free pupil', who paid her own way through campus work. Dalita Isaac took a leading role in 'kraal visits' during her time as a student and pupil-teacher.[159]

After Dalita Isaac's 1881 graduation, she evangelised farther afield: in 1884, she went to Inhambane, Mozambique, to help launch a new American mission there. She worked as a translator, teacher and general assistant for Erwin Richards, his wife and the mission's first black American appointees, Benjamin and Henrietta Bailey Ousley and Nancy Jones.[160] The Isaacs knew the Richardses from their 1882–1884 term at Inanda, and Lucy had named her youngest son Erwin.[161] In 1887, Lucy joined Dalita in Inhambane.[162] Dalita also 'adopted' an ill little girl.[163] The personnel seemed ideal, with model *kholwa* sisters working beside model black and white American Christian couples.

In mid-1889, however, the Isaacs returned with the Richardses to Natal following political instability and illness in Inhambane. Back at Inanda, Dalita Isaac set to work translating the Book of Revelations into Xitsonga, prompting Phelps to exult, 'It does our hearts good to see one of our girls doing such good work, and sustaining such a pure character as she has thus far. There are so many that disappoint us.'[164] A few months after this assessment, Dalita Isaac gave her colleagues cause for concern. She confessed to Edwards 'that she had been guilty of gross sin, and immorality' with Erwin Richards in Mozambique.[165] Early the next year she made a self-flagelling apology to other missionaries.[166] The mission's leaders first suggested that Isaac should return to Inhambane while Richards should be quietly removed to another mission within the Board – lest other prospective African women mission workers or their families hear of the scandal, or lest prospective converts imagine that American missionaries practised polygyny.[167] But the mission ultimately decided to terminate its Inhambane operations altogether, and by 1893 they had relocated to

Mount Selinda in south-eastern Rhodesia. There, Cecil Rhodes offered tracts of land in a milder climate: as in the Americans' 1843 decision to stay in Natal, colonial concerns shaped policy.[168]

After leaving Inhambane, Isaac remained critical to the mission because her colleagues found her indispensable. Richards, on the other hand, was expelled from the Board but stayed on at Delagoa Bay, with the Methodist Episcopal Church.[169] Isaac returned to Inanda, where, Phelps reported, 'we know of no available former pupil, who can take Dalita's place. As a teacher she is invaluable. She interests her classes and has perfect control of them. In teaching beginners, she is especially good. She had adopted a method, largely original, of teaching reading, which is excellent. Some have learned to read Zulu quite well, in three months time under her instruction.'[170] The next year, she helped spark a religious revival after preaching on repentance: 'Dalita, our native teacher, has observed the increasing interest, and has been more instrumental in bringing it about, I believe, than any of us,' Phelps noted. 'Few native young women could manage the girls and the work as well as Dalita does. She is exceptionally mature and womanly for a Zulu girl.'[171] Despite her condescension, Phelps saw Isaac's gifts in making the gospel relevant for new converts and committed Christians – in a revival that extended the Board's appeal considerably at a time of growing African independent churches, like that of the Hawes family.[172] In 1897, Isaac extended her influence through a companionate marriage to Elijah Hlanti, an Adams man. They went to the American mission at Mount Selinda, where he preached and she taught.[173] They raised three sons, and she influenced generations of students.[174]

The first mission that Dalita Isaac had launched had floundered on political and health exigencies and a crisis of familial authority – a toxic blend of problems for a mission predicated on gendered and racialised divisions of labour. Inhambane's supervising minister, whose marriage was to serve as the luminous domestic example around which a new community would form, provided no such model, but rather abused his authority. Despite this scandal, Isaac continued within American Board institutions, leading an exemplary Christian life for the next four decades and keeping in touch with 'Mother Edwards'.[175]

Conclusion

American missionaries founded Inanda Seminary to save a fledgling mission by systematising the familial divisions of labour through which that mission had begun. From the mission's start, American wives were to undergird and parallel the work of their minister husbands. With the introduction of Amanzimtoti and Inanda, *kholwa* wives were to undergird and parallel *kholwa* men's evangelical and educational labours. In this missionary ideal, American ministers would exercise an ultimate paternal influence over their stations, and their wives would operate in a corresponding maternal role. African women and men would be their daughters and sons, preparing for some always-distant day of majority. The men of the mission envisioned Amanzimtoti and Inanda specifically to institutionalise these roles – to train young men and women within boarding schools structured as homes. At the same time that they did so, they supported the formation of a women's auxiliary, charged to expand women's work for women within the American Board's extant gendered logic. But as the Women's Board of Missions of the Congregational Churches and peer groups looked increasingly to expand and professionalise the work of American women – particularly single American women – in schools and other social institutions, the mission's gendered dynamics began to shift. Women's work came to comprise the bulk of evangelical labours.

In line with the hierarchical contours of 'native agency', local women in Natal and elsewhere remained junior partners in the mission, and they were paid the least. But they enabled missions to build institutions that would otherwise be impossible for them to sustain. As there was little official investment in social welfare in colonial Natal, these early institutions would be the first and for many years the only such institutions available to *amakholwa* and to the rising number of non-Christian Africans who sought access to literacy, numeracy and other benefits of schooling to advance themselves in colonial society. For these reasons, between the school's founding and the 1910 formation of the Union of South Africa, colonial officials regarded Inanda's development with growing interest. It is to the complex engagements between Inanda, the families and institutions its graduates forged, and officials that the next chapter turns.

CHAPTER TWO

Domestic Revolutions and the Feminisation of Schooling in Natal
1885–1910

In 1894, Native Schools Inspector Robert Plant concluded of Inanda that he had 'nothing but praise to give. The modesty, cleanliness, good behaviour, general intelligence, and industry shown by the girls generally is most creditable both to themselves and the ladies in charge.' He added that Inanda's enrolment evinced 'the popularity which it has deservedly gained amongst the Native people'; it was 'as near the ideal Native girls' school as it seems possible to get'.[1]

Such sunny appraisals appear throughout official reports from the 1885 appointment of the first inspector of African education through the early twentieth century, suggesting alignment between missionaries' and officials' visions. But Inanda missionaries were also combative visitors in the offices of magistrates. There they fought unsuccessfully to keep students from non-Christian homesteads – whom they called 'kraal girls' – in school against their fathers' protests. By 1893, the American Zulu Mission was sufficiently troubled by its lack of authority over such students that it organised a petition 'on behalf of kraal girls'. With missionaries of other denominations, they wielded testimony from runaway girls. Through these plaintive appeals, missionaries hoped to persuade colonial authorities 'that a great injustice is being done to native girls and women, involving the life destiny of individuals, and the moral, social and educational development of the race'.[2] To address this, they urged that the state revise women's protections under the African Marriage Law of 1869,[3] empower them to reject oppressive guardians and facilitate their access to schools. In effect, they asked to weaken fathers' claims on their daughters and strengthen those of missionaries – an increasing number of whom were unmarried women.

Colonial officials opposed these demands for such redefinition of the boundaries of patriarchal authority, confining the pupils of this 'ideal Native school' to those whose male guardians condoned – or at least did not legally challenge – their attendance. This decision was entirely in keeping with the gendered and generational basis of colonial conquest and governance in Natal – what Jeff Guy has termed an 'accommodation of patriarchs'.[4] First codified in 1878 and made legally binding in 1891, the Natal Code of Native Law formalised an interlocking set of patriarchal relationships. Under the ultimate authority of the 'Supreme Chief' of the colony – the governor – hereditary and colonially appointed chiefs would control the homesteads of subjects within colonially defined bounds. Within each homestead, patriarchs were endowed with authority over 'minors' – including all unmarried women present, as well as the homestead head's wife or wives. Under Section 289 of the Code of Native Law, children were also specifically forbidden to run away from their guardians. African men's authority in their homes was thus juridically inscribed, as an encroaching colony eroded homesteads' economic autonomy.

Yet at the same time that the legal exigencies of patriarchal colonial governance circumscribed the educational options of girls whose fathers opposed their schooling, the head of Natal's nascent educational bureaucracy argued that African girls' education in Western domesticity would be essential in creating different sorts of families with different sorts of needs. In monogamous families, Robert Plant argued, husbands and sons would be taught to 'want' enough to impel them to labour – but they would also be sufficiently satisfied by their domestic comforts to avoid political unrest. Thus, even as officials clamped down on African boys' curricula – attempting to restrict their schooling to the barest preparation for unskilled labour – they allowed missionaries autonomy to educate girls whose fathers did not challenge their schooling. Educated women's roles in the social reproduction of governable families seemed a benefit to the colony.

Crises of social reproduction in homesteads and Christian homes

Young women were at the heart of the homesteads that missionaries, following settler nomenclature, called 'kraals' – an Afrikaans term that properly referred to a cattle enclosure.[5] In isiZulu, homesteads are in fact *imizi* (singular, *umuzi*). The *imizi* that spread across the hills of Natal and Zululand in the late nineteenth century were concentrically arranged; both enclosed and expansive, they included the *umndeni* (family) of an *umnumzane* (homestead head) within a dynamic unit that grew and contracted through marriage. While not all African men would be able to gather sufficient *ilobolo* – gifts of cattle to their brides' fathers upon marriage – to marry multiple wives, polygyny represented the ideal domestic form, which secured the homestead's productive and reproductive well-being. Wives had daughters, whose *ilobolo* provided the *ilobolo* necessary to marry off their sons; sons' unions would enable them to move off their fathers' homesteads, extending the lineage. At the core of each homestead remained the *indlunkhulu*, the 'great house' – associated with the homestead head, with his mother and with his ancestors – around which the family's other houses were hierarchically arranged, encircling the actual cattle kraal, *isibaya* (which women were forbidden to enter, making the term 'kraal girl' ironic). To be *ekhaya* – to be at home – meant not only to reside in an *indlu* within an *umuzi*, but also to live in cognisance of one's place within the *umdeni*, which included ancestors who were ever invoked and involved.

This reality did not remotely accord with Protestant visions of the ideal family, each member connecting individually with God. Nor did marriage rites of *imizi* accord with missionaries' visions. Marriage was 'a long journey' known as *umendo* – a protracted transition from a woman's paternal homestead into that of her husband, completed only when her soul joined her husband's ancestors. Women's productive and reproductive labours were central to the sustenance of their fathers' and husbands' homesteads, and *ilobolo* and *umendo* comprised recognition of that centrality. 'Kraal girls' bore integral power within homesteads structured by a gendered and generationally ordered logic of encompassment, reproduced through *imfundiso* (children's socialisation, in which women took critical roles in teaching youth about religion and ritual).[6] In return for their work in sustaining *imizi*, women and unmarried men expected the *umnumzane* to provide land, cattle and protection. Belonging entailed entitlements and obligations, and when patriarchs or dependants failed to realise their responsibilities, conflict ensued.[7]

From the Americans' arrival in Natal through the early twentieth century, colonial demands for taxes, labour and land generated new conflicts in *imizi*. These conflicts drove increasing numbers of young people who had grown up through *imfundiso* to pursue *imfundo* – Western schooling, in which women also assumed integral roles. The British annexation of Natal in 1843 introduced the young 'diplomatic agent to the native tribes' Theophilus Shepstone. Over the next three decades, as Mahmood Mamdani has described, Shepstone ruled through a system of 'decentralized despotism' that successors in Natal and elsewhere in Africa would mimic and extend.[8] While Shepstone worked to make chiefs juridically subservient to colonial officials, he relied upon homestead heads as mediating authorities between their dependants and co-opted chiefs.[9] His encroachment on homestead heads began in 1849, with the new 'hut tax' placed upon each house in *imizi*; in effect, this was a tax on wives, and therefore an indirect tax on the basis of production and reproduction: women's labours.[10] Shepstone's immediate hopes for this tax were that it would raise revenue for an unpromising colony, in which the British government was willing to invest little, and compel African men to work for wages to pay it. In the long term, he avowedly hoped that a tax on wives might discourage polygyny. This latter promise fulfilled Victorian imperialists' self-styled 'civilising mission'. More practically, if homestead heads had fewer wives, *imizi* could no longer be so self-sufficient; African men and women would become workers and consumers in an expanding colonial economy.[11] But even as the Shepstone system anticipated the eventual demise of polygyny and therefore of *imizi*, the exigencies of administering a colony made up overwhelmingly of Africans in polygynous homesteads with the barest support from London demanded that Shepstone rule his subjects through extant networks of patriarchal authority. Homestead heads became effective tax collectors within their families, and through the

1860s most would pay their hut taxes to their chiefs by selling surplus grain, cattle and their labour.[12] As long as Africans retained access to land, this 'hut tax' was not catastrophic – prompting complaints from settlers who believed Africans to be 'rich and independent, in a great degree owing to the polygamy and female slavery that prevails'.[13]

What ultimately doomed the economic autonomy and social integrity of *imizi* were colonial land policies. After 1864 the 'native locations' (or the 'reserves') first delineated in 1846 were not expanded, although population growth accelerated and an additional 7 000 Africans went from Zululand to Natal.[14] About half of these came to work for settlers, and the other half came hoping for their opportunities to improve under British rather than Zulu rule. Between the 1840s and 1870s, Natal's African population had tripled: by the 1870s, there were some 300 000 Africans in the colony, nearly half of whom lived on the generally poor lands that had been parcelled out in 1846.[15] By then, reserves were thoroughly overcrowded and overworked, and residence on land controlled by whites was prohibitively expensive in rent, labour and taxes. After the Anglo-Zulu War of 1879 and the ensuing eight years of Zulu civil war, Zululand became a Crown Colony in 1887 and was incorporated into Natal in 1897. By 1907, Africans across the expanded colony were struggling to maintain *imizi* under these conditions: more than half the land was under white ownership, and white population density in rural Natal and Zululand was one settler to every 184 acres of land, whereas for Africans the ratio was just one to eight.[16] It became difficult to maintain cattle, and to produce a surplus to satisfy demands for taxes and rent.

To address this shortfall, Africans worked – as officials and settlers hoped they would. By 1864, David Welsh has claimed, '20,000 annually engaged themselves in hired labour'.[17] The majority of these workers were young men. After the opening of diamond mines in Kimberley in the late 1860s, men began to pursue work farther afield. After the 1886 discovery of gold on the Witwatersrand, migrant labour boomed, with some 25 000 men receiving passes to go from Natal to Johannesburg in 1894; homestead heads were paying taxes in gold coin – suggesting that sons working on the mines paid taxes for their father's wives.[18] Sons were in fact taking on an increasing number of their fathers' burdens by the 1890s. Men also began to gather their own *ilobolo* for their first marriages, due to the Marriage Law's legal restriction on the value of *ilobolo* and the opportunities engendered by the mineral revolution. But at the same time that patriarchs were becoming more economically reliant on their dependants, the Natal Code endowed them with more legal authority over these dependants than they had hitherto possessed. After 1891, fathers could take sons to court if they refused to pass their wages to their fathers. The law granted them authority, but this was authority to concretise a relationship that contravened the core expectation that fathers would provide the means of production and reproduction for sons.[19]

Crises in *imizi* became more pronounced after a biblical succession of agricultural catastrophies in the 1890s: a plague of locusts in 1894, drought two years later and, in 1896 and 1897, the rinderpest epidemic, which decimated the colony's cattle population. African herds declined by 85 per cent. As a consequence, the annual number of African marriages declined by half between 1896 and 1899, and by 1902 the marriage rate had not recovered to 1896 levels.[20] Rinderpest destroyed patriarchs' key resource – their command of which had already been weakened by their sons' capacity to pay their own *ilobolo*. The Anglo-Boer War of 1899 to 1902 made matters worse for *abanumzane*, as young men found more opportunities for wage labour and as the colony increased the hut tax, stretching sons' wages further. Some young men, resentful of this obligation, began to drink heavily at *utshwala* (beer) parties, to fight and to wind up in colonial courts, much to the embarrassment of their fathers. When, in 1905, the colony tried to levy a 'poll tax' or 'head tax' on all men, some in these strained *imizi* joined the Bambatha Rebellion against colonial authority. This rebellion was brutally crushed, claiming the lives of as many as 4 000 Africans and culminating in the arrest of Zulu king Dinuzulu in 1907 and his death in exile six years later.[21]

As some young men rebelled, their sisters fled to mission schools, most prominent among which was Inanda. There girls met *kholwa* daughters who also came from homes straining under colonial policies. *Kholwa* struggles stemmed from their status between customary and civil law, and between the domestic orders that justified each legal regime.

Natal officially had a non-racial, property-based, male franchise from 1856. But after settlers' exertions to put every obstacle in the way of a black person seeking the franchise, the colony settled upon a tortured policy of 'exemption' – which in theory delineated the process by which an African man might secure the vote, but in practice made it nearly impossible for anyone to ever succeed. Officials decreed that African men needed not just money or elite status, but also a more concrete attachment to a specific mode of production and domestic life to earn the franchise. A pair of 1865 laws established that *kholwa* men who had rejected polygyny and went through a series of bureaucratic procedures could secure 'exemption' from customary law, although they were subject to other discriminatory statutes and taxes. After seven years with this status, and after meeting a slew of other property requirements and securing white character witnesses, an African man could theoretically vote in Natal. An African woman (like Talitha Hawes, discussed in the previous chapter) could apply for exemption, provided she secured a white 'guardian' to vouch for her. As the Lieutenant Governor assured legislators in 1865,

> If this scheme of exemption was likely to throw a large number of Native voters on the colony, so as to really influence any election, I should be the first to oppose it, but this, owing to the deeply rooted and exceptional domestic institutions prevailing among the Natives, cannot be for generations to come, and certainly not before the Colony will have become densely peopled by white inhabitants.[22]

In the event, no one was exempted before 1876, and by 1891 only 851 had been. When Natal attained 'Responsible Government' in 1893, the electorate was almost exclusively white and male. By 1904, exempted Africans had increased to 5 000 (of some 100 000 *amakholwa* and 900 000 Africans), but only three African men had gained the vote. By 1907, six Africans and 150 Indians could vote, in Natal's electorate of 24 000.[23]

Natal *amakholwa* thus lived in a state of anxiety, mingled with hope and ambition. They were a growing community, in an increasingly

Africanised mission. Missionary activity and conversions had both increased steeply since the Anglo-Zulu War, such that by 1911, 7.5 per cent of the world's Protestant missionaries would work in the Union of South Africa, while some 26 per cent of Africans were Christian. By 1910, 85 per cent of all Protestant missionary ministers, evangelists and teachers – and 95 per cent of American Board personnel – would be black, although most foreign missions remained under white executive authority.[24] Natal *amakholwa* suffered the indignities of their legal position acutely. Generally subject to customary law, as well as other discriminatory laws and taxes assailing people of colour, they were also marrying under Christian rites, living on mission stations and making claims to civil rights commensurate with their 'civilised' self-conceptions.[25] Like their counterparts in *imizi*, *kholwa* fathers complained of their children's insubordination, as they joined the labour force by teaching and preaching as well as by working on the mines, on farms or in domestic service. *Amakholwa* complained of their daughters' resistance to parental restraints and uncertain marriage prospects – making Inanda an appealing site.[26]

Girls from *imizi* encountered Inanda through the 'kraal visits' of students and staff.[27] And by the early 1880s, Inanda sustained five 'kraal schools', with an annual grant of almost a hundred pounds.[28] In 1881, Inanda's principal Mary Edwards reported that two runaways had come after the parents of one had barred her from attending the local 'kraal school'. Edwards sent an African preacher to ask the girls' parents to let their daughters stay at Inanda, to no avail. One of their mothers came to plead with Edwards, who insouciantly maintained, 'I did not call the girls and I should not send them away, if they could persuade them to return with them I should say nothing.'[29] This was disingenuous, as Inanda women's presence encroached on parents' efforts to structure their daughters' coming-of-age. In 1885 the mission called for more 'kraal schools', recognising them as an integral evangelising strategy.[30] When an African preacher suggested that it was impolitic for Inanda to keep so many runaways, Edwards said: 'Go and tell their fathers and brothers to hire a teacher and keep up the school and I will send them home; but if they refuse to do this, then I will not send them away.'[31]

Figure 7
'Missionary Lady Entering Hut',
1915. (Karl Robert Brueckner
Papers, File 4, Campbell
Collections, University of
KwaZulu-Natal, Durban)

Figure 8
'Group Portrait of Zulu Girls
at Inanda', n.d. (Album B48-
116, Campbell Collections,
University of KwaZulu-
Natal, Durban)

Beginning in 1891, a majority of Inanda students hailed from *imizi*. Only in 1905 would enrolment in upper classes match that in the primaries, in which all 'kraal girls' began their schooling.[32] The American Board's Umzumbe Home, which had opened for 'kraal girls' in 1873, and the Ireland Home, which had opened in 1894 for the same purpose, did little to relieve this pressure, as both were far south. After the rinderpest epidemic of 1896–1897, Inanda's primaries swelled more (see Table 2).[33]

Table 2 Inanda Seminary enrolment, 1885–1909

Year	Students from Christian parents	Students from non-Christian parents	Total enrolment	Average attendance
1885–1886	48	12	60	47
1886–1887	At least 33	At least 20	More than 53	53
1888–1889	Majority	Minority	98	67
1890–1891	More than 44	More than 24	More than 68	6
1891–1892	54	59	113	73
1892–1893	46	78	124	108
1893–1894	73	108	181	112
1894–1895	83	114	197	118
1895–1896	More than 34	More than 76	More than 110	110
1896–1897	Minority	Majority	More than 168	168
1897–1898	63	145	208	161
1898–1899	Minority	Majority	185	150
1899–1900	Minority	Majority	244	151
1900–1901	Minority	Majority	301	164
1901–1902	Minority	Majority	132	125
1902–1903	Minority	Majority	222	136
1903–1904	Minority	Majority	244	148
1904–1905	Majority	56 in second term	225	130
1905–1906	Majority	Minority	154	135
1906–1907	Majority	Minority	More than 136	136
1907–1908	Majority	Minority	160	145
1908–1909	Majority	Minority	234	144

Sources: Fidelia Phelps, Inanda, to Judson Smith, Boston, 5 February 1887, American Board of Commissioners for Foreign Missions: African Missions Records (ABC), Series 15.4, Volume 11; Inanda Seminary reports to the American Board, 1890–1899, ABC, Series 15.4, Volume 13; Inanda Seminary reports to the American Board, 1900–1909, ABC, Series 15.4, Volume 23; Frederick Bernard Fynney, 'Report of the Inspector of Native Education for 1886', Colonial Secretary's Office Series (CSO),Volume 1121, Reference 1887/727; Robert Plant, 'Report of the Inspector of Native Education for 1889', 3, CSO, Volume 1253, Reference 1890/1603; Robert Russell, 'Report of the Superintendent of Education for the Year 1901', Inanda Seminary Papers, File 30; and Agnes Wood, *Shine Where You Are: A History of Inanda Seminary, 1869–1969* (Alice, South Africa: Lovedale Press, 1972), 3.

In both exalted and prosaic terms, missionary correspondence highlighted some of the factors impelling girls to come to Inanda. One of the school's most celebrated 'kraal girls' was Ntoyi Nxaba. She came in 1879 as a ten-year-old, reportedly 'attracted to the school by hearing the girls recite their simple lines of poetry in English and sing their English hymns, when she came one day with a little bag of mealies on her head to sell'.[34] She stayed for eight years as a model pupil and teacher; she converted her family, and her brother later enrolled his daughter at Inanda. Upon her graduation, she married a Christian but was left a widow after less than a year of marriage; thereafter she taught 'kraal girls' in Inanda's primaries, in evangelical visits and at the Umzumbe Home, while raising her son. Of her work at Umzumbe, Nxaba avowedly felt that 'some of these kraal girls show a very nice spirit. They are very fond of me and I feel quite responsible for them. My desire and prayer is that I may be shown just how to lead them to Christ.' She emphasised, 'I never felt so responsible for anybody's soul as I am for the girls. I see the reason of this. It is because I am the only one who can speak Christ in words' – that is, in isiZulu.[35] In 1894 Nxaba applied for exemption, reportedly after reading *Uncle Tom's Cabin* and feeling that she was as good as enslaved: her Christian marriage would not be recognised under Native Law, as *ilobolo* had not been given, and she feared that her late husband's father would take her small herd of cattle, her cash savings or her child. The next year, Nxaba and Edwards opened a hostel in Durban for other African women evading their own domestic dilemmas.[36]

Another runaway came in 1888 to evade marriage to a non-Christian because, in Edwards' account, 'the Holy Spirit told her she could never see the face of God in peace if she married this young man and was so overwhelmed with the sense of her danger that she fell to the floor'.[37] Edwards' colleagues suspected some just came for the dresses they provided. But in any event, their presence seemed providential, 'the work of the Spirit'.[38] These accounts are, of course, selective, and subject to exaggeration and elision, as the point of missionaries' correspondence to Boston was to engender American support, in the form of money as well as prayer.

The context in which girls sought schooling suggests that they did so in large part to escape the tensions within *imizi* that accompanied colonial taxation, customary law, land alienation and young men's wage labour. In the 1890s, young women were performing more work on *imizi* to compensate for absent male migrants. As their labours became more indispensable to homestead heads, John Lambert has suggested that patriarchs monitored female actions more closely, engendering tensions that could lead in extreme cases to girls' abandonment of their homes.[39] At the same time, Benedict Carton has pointed out, homestead heads were running out of garden plots to dispense to women in return for their work, in contravention of the expectations that governed the social relations of encompassment.[40] Immediate crises around *ilobolo* and *umendo* seem to have driven most of Inanda's runaways to the point of flight. *Ilobolo* and *umendo* represented respectability and maturity to young women on homesteads – the entitlements they could expect in recognition of their value to their families of birth and marriage. The rinderpest epidemic of 1896 and 1897 pushed the institution of marriage into an acute crisis. Some fathers grew so desperate to replenish their herds of cattle that they pushed their daughters to marry whomever could supply *ilobolo*, against young women's protests about their partners.[41] Many others tried to persuade their daughters to agree to a wedding without the immediate payment of *ilobolo*, which both contravened the Marriage Law and violated women's sense of social security.[42] Both scenarios could push young women to school. Heather Hughes has also suggested that, in the aftermath of rinderpest, some families might have supported their daughters' schooling because they could not afford to keep them at home and could not or did not want to arrange for their marriages.[43] While she does not substantiate this claim, it bears consideration as an explanation why most parents ultimately allowed their daughters to stay at Inanda, even if they initially disapproved.

As the number of African marriages declined by half between 1896 and 1899, Inanda thus presented young women with an alternative site of community and a temporary space of security, although the long-term advantages of their time at school were unclear. Some girls may have seen their time at school as a new stage in their preparation for marriage and motherhood. Missionary Frances Colenso suggested that runaway girls to the famous Anglican mission outside Pietermaritzburg in the 1860s came to school explicitly as a precursor to their more serious matrimonial journeys. While they claimed solace at the school ostensibly to escape unwanted unions, 'within a few weeks they all elected to return home and marry the very men on whose account they fled'. Colenso realised that the school had been incorporated into young women's courtship strategies, as 'their escapade was rather for the sake of attaching a little additional importance to the surrender of their freedom, than from any real objection to the marriages proposed for them'.[44] Young women who came to and then ran away from Inanda later in the century may well have been doing the same. But whether a young woman intended her time at school to comprise a brief episode in her *umendo* or whether she saw herself as entering on a fundamentally new life path, Carton argues that in running to missionaries a 'kraal girl' went from one regime of patriarchal authority to another. Speaking of the American Zulu Mission in particular but also of nineteenth-century missions in the region more generally, Carton contends that they offered a 'substitute patriarchy': while women performed an increasing bulk of evangelical labours, often within all-female institutions, ministers retained administrative authority, and their congregants appealed to a patriarchal faith.[45]

But American missionary women saw their roles as divinely ordained and transformative. And many fathers, and mothers, regarded their daughters' movement with alarm. Mothers, as legal minors, could only battle with missionaries on a personal basis. They did so with frequency and force from the school's early years, as did young women's brothers, kith and kin.[46] But only patriarchs could take matters to colonial magistrates. As their substantive power was crumbling from within and without, homestead heads challenged missionaries' right to educate their daughters, and they were usually successful in garnering the support of colonial officials in their struggle.

Struggles between 'mercenary guardians', missionaries and magistrates

Tellingly, it was in 1891 – the year that the Natal Code legally codified patriarchal authority – that Inanda received its first visit from a police officer. While fathers had successfully appealed their daughters' school attendance to magistrates before, this was the first time that an officer forcibly removed students. Two runaways were returned to their homes in that sweep. 'God give us Christian magistrates, and righteous laws,' Edwards' successor as principal, Fidelia Phelps, prayed in the incident's aftermath.[47] The next year, four other girls were forced to return to their homes, occasioning further police visits, and Edwards grew unwilling to tolerate such intervention on her campus.[48]

When Susiwe Bhengu, the daughter of the Ngcolosi Chief Dhlokolo, came to Inanda in August 1892, Edwards took special pains to protect this royal runaway. Since the mid-1880s, Bhengu and her younger sister had repeatedly come to Inanda from their home some fifteen miles away, and their brothers and other subjects of their father had consistently come to retrieve them. The sisters had first become interested in schooling and Christianity because some of the other children in their homestead attended day school. But their father discouraged their attendance, as he planned for them to marry well. When Bhengu was still quite young, her father arranged her betrothal to Khumalo Chief Bhulutshe, an elderly man with several wives. She refused, reportedly because of his unwillingness to embrace Christianity; she delayed the marriage so long that Bhulutshe died during the *ilobolo* negotiations. She was then to marry his son, who, Bhengu told the missionaries, 'would take me as he did the other things of his father'.[49] As she had done before, Bhengu ran to Inanda to escape the constraints of her homestead. Her father sent for her several times. Edwards unsuccessfully appealed to the magistrate, the governor and finally the Secretary of Native Affairs for Bhengu's protection. In a chance encounter with Chief Dhlokolo, Edwards finally gave him 'the idea that we had succeeded in getting help for our side', and he made no subsequent attempts to retrieve his daughters. Both became members of the *kholwa* community, and Susiwe married into the prominent Seme family.[50]

After this symbolic victory, Edwards believed that she had been able to achieve a fragile peace. 'The parents have come to the conclusion that they might as well let them remain. We have had no policeman since I wrote to the Magistrate that I should not send the girl with the policeman,' she reported in October 1893. 'We think the higher officials have instructed the magistrates not to require the return of the girls.'[51] This case has entered into Inanda lore. In long-time missionary Agnes Wood's history of the school, in which her treatment of Edwards is generally hagiographic, Edwards appears as a martyr for the cause of Bhengu and other runaway girls. 'Your Honour, I have brought my nightdress and toothbrush with me and am ready to go to jail, but I will not give up this girl,' she reportedly announced to the Verulam magistrate.[52] While this story may be apocryphal, it remains so resonant that it figured in a student play about the school's history at Inanda's 140th anniversary celebrations in March 2009. Students portrayed Edwards – complete with nightdress and toothbrush – and the magistrate – complete with pith helmet.

But despite Edwards' bravado, her actions would not offer a solution to the problem of juridical intervention in schooling. Other missionaries also struggled with this problem, prompting the Americans to coordinate an ecumenical appeal to officials.[53] In April 1893, they had dispatched a letter asking missionaries to relate difficulties that 'oppressed kraal girls' at their stations had experienced in trying to reject marriages or to remain in school, to submit to the Legislative Council of Natal. While the Americans did not explicate their goals in this letter, their dissatisfaction with the Natal Code was clear: 'In some parts of Natal there is at present a manifest and widespread wish on the part of heathen girls, for the advantages of school and Christian training. The law, as at present administered, discourages this desire, and favours continued heathen debasement rather than emancipation from it.'[54] To substantiate their disdain, they needed statements showing 'the inability of kraal girls to control their destiny, in matrimonial matters, or in the way of religious, intellectual or civilized, self improvement'.[55]

Inanda missionaries contributed thirty-two cases of young women who had come to evade 'forced marriages' to the petition committee, which by August 1893 was working under the Natal Missionary Conference. A list of these cases indicates the name, 'owner' (as missionaries referred to legal guardians), chief, locality, the year of arrival at Inanda and the final outcome. In eighteen of these cases, young women were 'forced to marry' by colonial magistrates. Five cases were still pending, and one girl had reportedly killed herself, according to her friend Susiwe Bhengu. Of the other eight cases, six had persuaded their families to allow them to stay at school for some time, after which some of them had already married other men by traditional rites. Only two, Susiwe Bhengu and Nomnyaka Lushingityi, appeared to remain at Inanda in 1893. Their depositions, as well as those of a score of other students, lay at the core of a draft petition that was verbose, inflammatory and wildly ambitious. It described the current system as one of 'mercenary guardianship' and requested no less than the abolition of polygyny, *ukulobola* (the payment of *ilobolo*) and Natal Code laws of inheritance; extension of elementary education to 'every native child'; and a 'majority' age for women.[56]

The final 'Petition on Behalf of Kraal Girls' arrived at the Colonial Secretary's office in June 1894. It was abridged: missionaries barraged officials with just seventeen cases, including eight from Inanda. But the petition retained its original ambitions. The injustices young women suffered under the Natal Code, the petitioners maintained, required 'not only the alteration of the law, but a different system of administering it'. They requested that the colony radically reverse its stance on *ukulobola* and polygyny, the domestic institutions on which the logic of Native Law and exemption hinged: 'While polygamy and ukulobolisa are sanctioned by law or allowed by custom, so long will the evils complained of continue, and, until they are made illegal, kraal girls must continue to fight against fearful odds in any effort made by them for mental, moral, or social improvement.'[57] Pointedly, they asserted that the Natal Code was unjust because it misappropriated authority over young women. They believed that young women should 'control their own destinies' – but that missionaries were the ideal guardians under whom they should define their life goals. This appeal was predicated on liberal assumptions of free choice, as well as their claims to be experts on the lives of girls in *imizi*: 'It is the custom of missionaries, on demand made by parents and guardians, to persuade the girl to return with them. The girl usually declines to go and Your petitioners refuse to employ force to compel her to do so, unless satisfied that she has wrongly left duties to which she ought to attend.' Missionaries, they claimed, were best placed to defend girls' interests, as 'only those living among the natives are in a position to know of the cruelties to which kraal girls are subject'.[58]

Missionaries made a case for young women's authority over their personal mobility, and for their authority over these women. These were not causes for which officials evinced sympathy. After testimony from Edwards and other missionaries, the Colonial Secretary and the Attorney General ruled that new legislation to protect African women was unnecessary, as their protection was assured by Native Law's prohibitions against coercion. The Secretary of Native Affairs concurred, concluding that these requests were unthinkable because 'legislation in regard to *lobolo* would imply a revision of native law'.[59] After the petition's failure, Inanda continued to be 'largely a refuge for kraal girls', with transient students.[60] This transience seemed due as much to girls' own inclinations to leave school as to parental and state interventions. As Phelps ruefully put it, 'We cannot but remark that in some cases they are as anxious to go home when the desire seizes them, as they are not to go when we wish to send them.'[61] During planting season of 1897, demands for labour increased.[62] While staff allowed girls to return home to work, in the first half of 1898 nineteen left 'without our consent or knowledge', for reasons that remained unclear to Phelps.[63]

In this less than promising context, Inanda missionary teacher Martha Price's battles with colonial magistrates weighed heavily. In late 1897, Price was summoned to appear before the Ndwedwe magistrate on charges of having prevented a student from returning home with her father upon his request. The student, Nokwasi, had run away to escape an arranged marriage while her father was working in Johannesburg. Upon his return, he found to his dismay that she was at Inanda. He went to the magistrate and received a letter to deliver to Price, with official instructions to return his daughter, which Price refused to honour. Soon after, a police officer came to summon Price to Ndwedwe, to which she travelled with an indignant Edwards. That magistrate decided that Nokwasi's father should be tried for forcing her to marry without consent; the Stanger magistrate found him not guilty of forcing his daughter into marriage, after Nokwasi's mother and sister claimed she had shown consent. But Nokwasi was able to remain at Inanda because the sister who had testified agreed to marry the man instead.[64] In 1903, the Umzinto magistrate charged the Umzumbe Home with harbouring four runaways and summoned a missionary there to court.[65] Two years later, Phelps reported that Inanda's proportion of 'kraal girls' had declined. This, she surmised, was due in part to the opening of more schools and to the labour needs of families. But frustratingly,

> [t]he attitude of our present magistrate may also have something
> to do with it. Although he is a Christian man and friendly to
> mission work he seems to think that a girl is never justified in
> coming to us without her father's consent. If her father or another
> owner (for every girl and woman has an owner) goes to the
> magistrate and complains that his daughter is in school against
> his wishes, the magistrate gives a letter to us, saying that if the
> girl refuses to go home she must go to him on a certain day. She
> has to obey, of course; if she goes to the magistrate, as she usually
> chooses to do (though we tell her it is of no use) he hears her
> story, but always tells her to go home, sometimes adding, that if
> she runs away again she may be put in prison, and that we may
> be also for keeping her. He has sent home nine girls in this way.[66]

But at the same time, Inanda maintained a firm position as one of the
favourite institutions of educational bureaucrats. Inspector of Native
Education Robert Plant was assuredly a 'warm friend of our school',
Phelps asserted – in the same report that complained of their
unfriendly magistrate.[67]

This contradiction obtained because of the gendered multivalence
of African schooling. Although Inanda offered a sanctuary for 'kraal
girls' and therefore seemed a socially transformative space to
missionaries and *amakholwa*, Plant saw its potential as a source of
social order in a context in which settlers were growing hostile about
African men's schooling. To understand how this contradiction played
out, we must first turn to the tenuous educational partnership between
missions and the colonial state. Natal's educational policies had been
influenced theoretically by Cape Governor George Grey's demand
for a system of state-run industrial schools that trained African men
in trades such as carpentry, masonry, printmaking, blacksmithing,
shoemaking and tailoring and that trained African women for domestic
service and housewifery.[68] But these visions were constrained by the
austerity of Natal's governance. Colonial officials delegated almost all
black education to missions – allowing them grants from one-fifteenth
of the annual tax revenue collected from Africans, beginning in 1856,

but also regulating curricula and developing state exams.[69] Neither officials nor missionaries were ever comfortable with their lack of control in this arrangement.

Officials watched the Americans' pair of seminaries as they developed and sought to assert influence through grants. Before Inanda opened, Superintendent of Education Warwick Brooks urged Shepstone to support it.[70] When, in 1868, the mission requested a hundred pounds per annum each for Amanzimtoti and Inanda, 'in the aid of secular and industrial education of natives', Brooks urged: 'They are sought to be established with the object of imparting more advanced knowledge and of fitting girls to became suitable wives for educated and more advanced young men – I am inclined to think that these objects are more deserving assisting than the industrial schools as carried on at some of the stations.'[71] In 1870, Inanda was granted a hundred pounds, and Amanzimtoti twice that. But Brooks regarded these seminaries with trepidation, cautioning:

> The results of this curious experiment to raise up among the natives a caste of (comparatively speaking) learned men with learned wives who can also wash, and sew, and dress themselves and cook food in our fashion, have yet to be seen. Whereas the plan of missionaries has been, and still is, to draw the kaffir from his kraal to the school and church at the station, the object of the American missionaries is to plant the school and the church in the kraal. It is perhaps to be regretted that this attempt (so far as it concerns supplying schools and teachers to the kraals) could not have been made by the Government, rather than by a religious body.[72]

Missionaries appreciated this support, but they were aggrieved that the support did not increase as their schools grew. While their grants were huge in terms of Natal's minuscule spending on African education, they remained fixed until the late 1880s. In 1872, Amanzimtoti's principal William Ireland drew Brooks' attention to the fact that Lovedale received an annual grant of 500 pounds from the Cape – then the value of Amanzimtoti's total administrative costs.[73] After a visit to Inanda, the headmistress of Lovedale's girls' division concluded that its 'rooms altogether are poverty stricken compared with ours'.[74] Edwards put their situation bluntly in an 1877 letter to Board Secretary Nathaniel Clark: 'You ask what are the Christian men and women of the Colony doing? My dear Dr. Clark distance lends enchantment and it is far more agreeable to send funds to the home land to support the benevolent enterprise set on foot for the poor and degraded than to "help the heathen at our doors",' she complained. 'Christian Kaffirs don't make such servants as the Eng. like and money expended for any other purpose is worse than thrown away' from settlers' perspectives, she explained.[75] In 1882, Ireland called for a Superintendent of Native Education to aid missionaries and introduce state-sponsored model schools, like those that had just opened for whites and Indians.[76]

The Native Education Law of 1884 appointed a new Inspector of Native Education to ensure that all aided African schools provided instruction in 'elements of industrial training' and 'in Girls' Schools, sewing or plain needlework', along with reading and writing (in English and isiZulu) and basic arithmetic.[77] Under the terms of the new law, officials also opened the Zwaartkop Native Industrial School for boys in 1886, but it closed as an unpopular, expensive failure in 1892, after being rejected by the community. Traditionalists insisted that they would not send their sons to school without their chief's support for the institution, while *amakholwa* preferred to send their children to mission schools.[78] Africans were right to be suspicious, as education and economic subjugation were becoming coterminous for officials. Inspectors evaluated schools on their 'means taken to encourage conformity with European habits' and time-work discipline.[79]

Robert Plant, who assumed his post in 1888, became the most influential voice on native education policy. Plant, who had come to Natal from London as a child and had fought in the Anglo-Zulu War, would spend the next two decades working to expand Africans' access to schooling that would make them good wage labourers, taxpayers and consumers. His 1889 'Minute on Native Education' made these objectives clear. He emphasised the financial benefits of entrusting education to missionaries who were 'constantly, both by example and precept, urging upon the Natives in their home life the advantages of a better state of things'. But schooling was reaching too few youth, and the state was missing an opportunity to mould better subjects:

'Assuming that the argument, "it is the duty of the State to educate the people," is based on the fact that a man or woman is made more useful to the State by the sharpening of intellect that is the result of education – assuming this, and the instincts alike of Humanity, Political Economy, or Christianity suggest that every possible effort should be made to give all our Natives these advantages.' He did not aim to educate Africans for citizenship:

> The fact must not be lost sight of that in this matter we are dealing with a barbarous and ignorant people, and that it will be better to lay a broad foundation, covering as wide a surface as possible, even though we have to build somewhat slower, than to force an unnatural growth in two or three years. What I think ought to be aimed at is a general low average of excellence, rather than the distinction of a few. What should the scope of our educational work be? I would define it as being able to qualify the Native youth for the effective discharge of their probable duties in life. These, for the present generation of school children, are those concerned with the stable, kitchen, nursery, wagon, or farm. A few will rise higher than these things, will become teachers, mechanics, clerks, &c.; ample provision for the more advanced instruction these will require already exists.

Plant thus advocated a growing network of schools for Africans, rather than 'a few advanced and showy centres' like Zwaartkop – from which, much to officials' embarrassment, all of the boarders had recently run away. These schools would be under white supervision but would rely on the work of low-paid African elementary school graduates; they would gather students by home visits, appeals to chiefs and, he hoped, a new mandate requiring basic school attendance as a prerequisite to employment. At the same time as the state was opening new 'model schools' for white children and starting less-well-endowed schools for Indians, Plant argued for rural schools for Africans that would be much like 'kraal schools' – but they were to teach not 'industries', but rather 'industry'.[80]

As white farmers who took offence to anything inimical to African rural labour dominated Natal's Legislative Council in the late nineteenth century, industrial education that facilitated marketable skills became increasingly impossible.[81] From 1895, Natal refused grants to schools where Africans made products that might 'compete with general trade', or which were 'in any way responsible for or associated with the printing and publishing of any Native newspaper'.[82] Exacerbating these restrictions, officials provided insufficient aid for most schools to maintain expensive industrial facilities like wood shops at all. The 1884 Act promised higher grants to institutions that developed industrial training programmes, but most institutions were too poor to launch these programmes without more aid than colonial officials would provide. Although Inanda's annual grant doubled to match Amanzimtoti's in 1888, staff struggled to support the majority of students who could not pay fees, requiring them to grow their food.[83] But Inanda was one of the more financially secure schools, because girls' industrial training was cheap: 'So far as the girls are concerned, it is not difficult to meet the requirements of the Law, by giving them instruction in needlework,' the Inspector of Native Education acknowledged.[84] Schools serving young men faced steeper unfunded mandates.

Figure 9 'Energy and Industry' (wood shop at Adams Training School), n.d. (Album B48-049, Campbell Collections, University of KwaZulu-Natal, Durban)

Political perils of African men's schooling

Missionaries at Amanzimtoti (then also known as Adams Training School) chafed under these restrictions. As principal Herbert Goodenough said, after 'Responsible Government' in 1893, 'the marking of grants for Industrial Schools became a burning question for the white artisans of the Colony. They had votes. We had none, and the natives had none.' He contended that the state's vision of industrial training as preparation for servitude or unskilled labour, 'and the whole system of native education, of which it is a part, are a reproach to the Colony'. This system, he pointed out, was one where per-pupil expenditure was eight times greater for white students than for blacks, and where the vast majority of black students had no access to schooling at all.[85]

African men also pushed against the limitations of this system. Officials were most suspicious of John Dube, who returned from a trip to the United States in 1899 to find himself followed by detectives.[86] The son of Inanda minister James Dube, he studied at Amanzimtoti and Ohio's Oberlin College before succeeding his father in Inanda's pulpit. He married an Inanda alumna and teacher, Nokutela Mdima, with whom he launched the Zulu Christian Industrial School (also known as the Ohlange Institute) on the Inanda mission reserve in 1901, with boarding facilities for young men and a day school for boys and girls. With the support of black American educationalist Booker T. Washington, the Dubes began their school 'to instruct Zulu and other Bantu youths in industrial trades and in the elements of all sciences, and to fit them to practice their trades and professions independently and skilfully, and to instruct them in the doctrines of the Word of God, that they may carry and spread the Light of the Gospel wherever they go throughout Africa'.[87] The Dubes sought to foster 'native agency', but under black leadership based in transatlantic ties; and they stressed professions beyond teaching and preaching. 'Such a school is necessary, because a religion whose teachings would enable him to build a two-room house, manage a plough, make a wagon, raise tea and coffee, grow sugar-cane, and do many other things which now they know not how, is a potent argument to show the Zulu the superiority of Christianity,' John Dube avowed.[88] The school

Figure 10 Promotional material for Ohlange Institute, n.d. (circa 1899). (American Board of Commissioners for Foreign Missions, African Missions Records, Series 15.4, Volume 14, Houghton Library, Harvard University)

became a site of settler anxiety, as John Dube began the Natal Native Congress in 1901 and the newspaper *Ilanga Lase Natal* in 1903. In 1912, he became the first president of the South African Native National Congress (later called the African National Congress). His activism and newspaper made his school ineligible for aid; students were barred from state exams.[89] But he attracted students who saw him as an icon of empowerment, as he did not mince words about their plight: 'The reason that the Christian native has a bad name, among the lower classes of Europeans especially, is that he does not submit to being treated as a dog.'[90]

Colonial officials blamed missionaries for fostering such boldness in their former pupils. In 1902, Undersecretary of Native Affairs S.O. Samuelson declared bluntly that missionaries 'cannot but exercise a seditious influence on the loyalty and affection of our natives'.[91] Americans seemed most suspect due to the African American influences to which they might expose their students. African Methodist Episcopal missionaries were banned outright from Natal in 1900.[92] While the American Zulu Mission was likely allowed to remain in no small part because its missionaries were almost uniformly white, it aroused suspicion because it had sent several of its most promising male students, such as Dube, to American universities.

In 1906, Adams' principal felt compelled to demonstrate that 'the educated natives are not filling up our prisons'. Most of his graduates were 'reliable men, a credit to the school and to the church'. From their employers, he had heard 'not a word about disrespect or about being spoiled because of their education'.[93] This 1906 defence of 'educated native' men was addressed to a white population for whom the Bambatha Rebellion had kindled long-standing suspicions of the colony's *kholwa* elite, and particularly of American Board and African independent church members. Most Christians in fact had not participated in the uprising, given their belief that education and political organisation could yield more gains than armed struggle against a vastly more militarised opponent. But Christians had also been far less willing to assist in putting down the anti-colonial insurgency than they had been during the Anglo-Zulu War of 1879. During British conquest of the Zulu kingdom, most *amakholwa* had supported the colony because their families and chiefdoms had come to Natal explicitly to evade Zulu authority. But as life under British rule became starker in the 1880s and 1890s and as annexation of the Zulu state rendered once formidable royals figureheads, the Zulu kingdom came to embody an alternative locus of power, prompting Bambatha rebels from an array of chiefdoms to consider themselves amaZulu.[94]

African women's schooling, social order and social mobility

For all of settlers' anxieties about educated African men like John Dube, girls made up the majority of African students from the early 1890s (see Table 3). This was a different balance from that amongst white and Indian children in Natal; amongst whites, slightly more boys than girls were students, while nearly five times more Indian boys attended school than Indian girls in 1896.[95] In addition to the greater variety of escape routes available to boys in stressful domestic situations, girls were better able to integrate schooling with their domestic and agricultural responsibilities; as herders or wage labourers, boys had less flexible schedules.[96]

Table 3 African school enrolment in Natal, 1885–1909

Year (June–June)	African females	African males	Total African enrolment	Percentage of students who are female
1885–1886	1 409	1 480	2 889	49%
1887–1888	1 420	1 482	2 902	49%
1890–1891	2 155	1 871	4 026	54%
1891–1892	2 157	1 739	3 896	55%
1893–1894	2 939	2 125	5 064	58%
1895–1896	4 104	2 945	7 049	58%
1897–1898	6 040	4 208	10 248	59%
1900–1901	6 568	4 503	11 071	59%
1908–1909	7 306	5 178	12 484	59%

Sources: Frederick Bernard Fynney, 'Report of the Inspector of Native Education for 1886', Colonial Secretary's Office Series (CSO), Volume 1121, Reference 1887/727; Fynney, 'Report of the Inspector of Native Education for 1888', CSO, Volume 1215, Reference 1889/1651; Robert Plant, 'Annual Report of the Inspector of Native Schools for 1891', Inanda Seminary Papers (ISP), File 29; Plant, 'Annual Report of the Inspector of Native Schools for 1892', ISP, File 29; Plant, 'Annual Report of the Inspector of Native Schools for 1893–1894', ISP, File 29; Robert Russell, 'Report of the Superintendent Inspector of Schools for the Year 1896', ISP, File 29; Russell, 'Report of the Superintendent of Education for the Year 1898', ISP, File 30; Russell, 'Report of the Superintendent of Education for the Year 1901', ISP, File 30; and David Welsh, *The Roots of Segregation: Native Policy in Colonial Natal, 1845–1910* (New York: Oxford University Press, 1971; 1973), 271.

This disparity may also have reflected the extent to which settlers and officials found educated African women less threatening than educated African men. While settlers and colonial officials worried about the political and economic implications of young men's industrial curricula, they found promise in girls' education for domesticity. As long as girls' schools did not alienate African patriarchs to an unmanageable extent, these schools might engender colonial order – by preparing women, whose productive labours had been crucial to *imizi*, to compel their husbands to pursue modest lives of wage labour, or to enter into wage labour themselves. In these respects, perhaps no institution held more promise for colonial officials than Inanda.

Inanda offered a more 'bookish' curriculum than did peers like the Benedictine Catholics' Mariannhill, which focused almost exclusively on physical labour and prayer.[97] This was an emphatically British colonial education: Inanda stressed reading and translating (using anglophone texts like the *English Royal Reader*) and world history (with a stronger British focus in this period than in the school's early years, likely in compliance with official concerns), as well as geography, physiology and arithmetic.[98] Along with its imperial curriculum, Inanda's values of self-reliance, self-discipline and self-sacrifice; its emphases on order, piety and chastity; and its goals to produce model wives, mothers and teachers thrilled school inspectors. While magistrates refused to push schooling on unwilling patriarchs, Native Schools Inspector Robert Plant approved heartily of the school's influence on girls whose fathers did not battle their attendance in court – and he hoped that graduates' influence would contribute to the erosion of independent *imizi* and encourage African incorporation into the colonial labour market.

Plant paid his first visit to Inanda in 1889. He told Phelps that he was impressed with the 'constancy of duties', commenting that 'Satan finds some mischief still for idle hands'.[99] Students were busy from dawn through dusk, on a rigorous schedule marked by bells. Plant raved of Inanda, 'This is by far the best school of its kind in the Colony', in which girls learned 'the dignity of labour, the advantages of education, and the excellence of Christianity'. He was struck that within the school's 'home-like' environment, the girls completed so much work:

In addition to ordinary school work these girls cultivate (even to the ploughing) about 12 acres of different kinds of food, sowing, clearing, and reaping it as the season goes round; washing, ironing, sewing, fancy work of different kinds; the making of bread, jams, jellies, and preserves of excellent quality – (the bread made by one of the girls the morning I was with them was, both in appearance and taste, first rate) – together with all the necessary details of house cleaning, go to form an apprenticeship to 'better things' that will be a life-long blessing to the girls.[100]

What were the 'better things' to which Inanda's home industries provided an 'apprenticeship'? Inanda missionaries never claimed to be training servants for settler homes in the colonial period. Edwards disavowed any engagement in placing graduates in domestic service. When the 1902 Lands Commission inquired whether Inanda had received many applications for servants, she replied, 'Yes. We have many applications. We reply that we have no right to send servants.'[101]

Archival sources do not explicitly substantiate or disprove Edwards' claim that Inanda did not send servants. But Inanda pupils – especially those who did not go far in their schooling – certainly went on to work for settlers, because they found few occupational outlets with which to support themselves or their families: they could teach, they could marry or they could work for wages on farms or in town. Their options were similar to those facing mission-educated girls around the region prior to 1910, many of whom pursued teaching and domestic work each for a spell, before and after marriage.[102] Inanda staff did, however, place the school into the service of settlers by taking in washing at a campus laundry, which opened in 1889 with the support of 'English colonists, interested in the work'.[103] The laundry made a profit through the 1890s; more important, it attracted an annual grant from officials, who looked with approval upon students' wage labour.[104]

While Plant approved of women's labour, he was as excited about their entrance into new sorts of families with new sorts of needs. He raved that Inanda

should form a first rate preparation, either for service amongst Europeans, to which many of the girls go on leaving school, or for their own home life as mothers of families. I am convinced that such education given to Native girls will go very far to solve the problem how to create 'wants' in the Native life; with a wife who has had such a training, a man will have to work to obtain the many things which his wife regards as absolute necessities. Cleanliness, order, industry, and happiness, are evident throughout the institution, and the most sceptical as to the advantages of Native education would probably leave the place with the conviction that the more schools of this kind that can be established in the Colony the better it will be for all parties.[105]

Schooling would thus take young women's labours out of their father's homesteads and onto their campuses, restructure these labours along more Western lines in their curricula and inculcate a new set of petty-bourgeois domestic desires in young women. Whether or not it impelled schoolgirls themselves to enter domestic service, schooling prepared women to enter a new social order and political economy. In the transformation from 'kraal girls' to schoolgirls, Plant envisioned no less than the production of manageable colonial subjects, perpetuating a chain of domestic transformations that would make Africans more dependent on wage labour. Women's schooling, then, would inculcate capitalist 'wants' in African men, turning them into heads of orderly homes that were dependent on the settler economy. As Plant concluded of African men in his 1891 report,

> Most of those who have attended school for any length of time go out into the world with a much higher aim in life than the ordinary Native has, and if only for this, that education leads them to seek the acquisition of immoveable property, and thus gives them a monetary interest in the peace and well-being of the Colony, it is worthy of increased support. I do not think that education will benefit the ordinary labour market – nothing short of the abolition of polygamy will effectually do that – but in the course of a few years we shall have a large body of Native men who are both intelligent, industrious and law-abiding, as the result of the too much decried station school work going on in our midst.[106]

To support what he perceived as Inanda's particular contribution to this cause, Plant gave the school some of the colony's largest African educational grants.[107]

As Senior Inspector of Native Schools in the first decade of the twentieth century, Plant presided over the expansion and feminisation of African schooling. Like missionaries, he believed that increased numbers of schools would promote a wave of popular enthusiasm for schooling, through which children would lead their elders to embrace new modes of social life. Plant envisioned runaway scholars as crucial actors in his vision of social transformation: 'Whilst the law is prepared to sanction the parental authority to the extent of requiring the missionary to give up the child, it positively refuses to allow the father to half-kill the child for leaving home. The child, knowing this, runs away to some more distant school, repeating the process until the father's persistence is worn down; and he eventually consults to the child's going to the nearest available school', whence that child would proceed to become a model student.[108] In his official capacity, of course, Plant was less interested in the perpetuation of Christianity for its own sake than in the state's broader goal of producing productive colonial subjects.

Ultimately, Plant contended in a 1905 treatise, the question of colonial governance hinged upon the intertwined questions of African domesticity and labour: 'Can we make them willing to work both for us and themselves in making their homes comfortable, clean, and healthy; work for us the more readily in that the wages so obtained can be used for home comforts? I think we can.' His suggested approach: to combat polygyny and *ukulobola*. 'While polygamy remains, it is sheer nonsense to hope for better morals, healthier or more industrious living, for pride in improved home surroundings, or for the development of individual self-respect,' Plant argued.

> With a plurality of wives, and all that is involved therein, the necessity for work at home is at once removed, and if some passing need leads a man to go work for a European, he will not remain away from home any longer than he is absolutely bound. The large family of children that polygamy brings him, brings him also an increased income, and very soon he will cease to work at all. The subject is a delicate one, but the stern fact is that the cause of the native's unwillingness to work is not his laziness so much as the uxoriousness.

Inversely relating men's labour power and governability to the labour power and sexual temptations awaiting them in their homesteads, Plant warned that polygynous men would abandon wage labour as soon as 'someone has come from home with bewitching stories of amorous living, and up like the morning tide surges the hot, passionate blood, and there is nothing for them but home'.[109] Economic domination entailed the inculcation of new domestic desires. In this schema, girls' education in domesticity played a fundamental role.

Inanda missionaries were sometimes troubled by the differences between their objectives and those of the state. Students increasingly sought careers as teachers: as teacher Martha Lindley reflected in 1894, 'The best change I see is that they all say they hope to be teachers and some hope to be missionaries – in 1875, they would shrug their shoulders and say, "It is hard work to teach".'[110] Yet also in 1894, Phelps complained to the American Board that 'under the present system of grants no provision is made for training teachers. It is impossible for a pupil to give five hours a day to industrial work and at the same time, to get the training by study, and by teaching under supervision, that is essential for one who is to be a teacher.'[111] The state's overarching interest in students' 'industry' complicated missionaries' prevailing goal of sustaining their mission by training essential teachers and evangelists.

But missionaries at Amanzimtoti were more vocally indignant about official demands than their counterparts at Inanda, because state restrictions on industrial production and artisanal training more fundamentally challenged missionaries' male curricula.[112] Despite concerns like those of Phelps – a proud Mount Holyoke alumna – Inanda missionaries adapted to conform to state requirements. They managed to train advanced students as pupil-teachers on top of their onerous labour requirements, while stressing domestic labours, piety and chastity as key elements of Christian womanhood – attributes that appealed to missionaries and the state.

Inanda's core attributes also appealed to African families. Alumnae sent their daughters with alacrity.[113] Inanda and the Zulu Christian Industrial School further attracted parents from around the region. Bertha Mkhize's parents moved from a village south of Amanzimtoti to the Inanda area explicitly for their children's education. Mkhize attended the Dubes' day school in its opening year and then came to Inanda as a precocious twelve-year-old, to train as a teacher. While she preferred the more rigorous maths courses at the Dubes' school (which included algebra, unlike Inanda), Mkhize admired Inanda for its order and its emphasis on English, a skill that she hoped to acquire for social mobility. On whole, she later reflected, Inanda was where she became 'a person'. At sixteen, she began teaching at Inanda; she left in 1911, at age twenty-one, because she 'wanted to see the world'. She then taught at the Umzumbe Home and around Natal for a decade, followed by a brief stint teaching in Johannesburg. She returned to Durban, moved into the Native Women's Hostel, worked as a tailor and obtained exemption, before becoming a trade unionist and political activist.[114]

Mkhize was not the only alumna from this period to use her schooling to effect social mobility in a rigidly racialised society. Adelaide Tantsi attended Inanda in the 1890s before following her friend Charlotte Maxeke to Wilberforce University in Ohio, where Tantsi earned a bachelor of science degree in 1904. Upon her return, Tantsi began a school outside of Johannesburg, married John Dube's son Charles and moved with her husband to teach at the Dubes' school. In 1913, she became the first black female published poet in the region, when she contributed a powerful nationalist piece to *Ilanga Lase Natal*.[115] In 1904, Evelyn Goba earned the top score of all candidates for a new African teachers' examination; with four other Inanda graduates, she became one of Natal's first state-certified African female teachers that year.[116] Goba stayed on as a teacher at Inanda until 1912, at which point she left to marry a Presbyterian minister from the prominent *kholwa* family of Edendale, the Caluzas.[117] And in 1910, Inanda alumna Anna Victoria Cobela Ntuli became the first qualified African nurse in the Transvaal. She married Alfred Mangena – the first African barrister in southern Africa and a founding member of the South African Native National Congress.[118]

From Inanda, ambitious 'kraal girls' turned their personal mobility into the basis for a new family tradition of investment in education, but they did so in a time of diminishing opportunities for educated Africans. Lauretta Ngcobo, who attended Inanda from 1945 to 1949, remembers that her grandmother Agnes Mdladla 'always talked about Inanda Seminary'. A beautiful girl from the nearby Ndwedwe area, as Ngcobo recounted, Mdladla left her home in the 1880s with a group of friends to pursue schooling at Inanda. While she did not go far in her studies, she learned to read and write; Ngcobo recalls that 'she used to speak some English to us sometimes, which she had gathered from Inanda'. After her schooling, she married a young man who had grown up across the river and had put himself through school at

Figure 11   Agnes (Mdladla) Cele and
Nyoni Cele, n.d. (Courtesy of Lauretta
Ngcobo)

Lovedale in the Cape, and they settled at Inanda. Her husband worked
as a teacher and saved enough to buy a large farm with ten other
African men, just before the Natives Land Act of 1913 would make it
impossible for many others to do so. Mdladla sent her daughter Rosa
Cele to Inanda, from which she went on to teachers' training at the
Wesleyan school at Edendale; from Inanda, Lauretta Ngcobo went
on to attend university at Fort Hare and to become a teacher, exiled
political activist, acclaimed novelist and member of post-apartheid
Parliament.[119] Ngcobo carried her grandparents' proud portrait – he
with a pocket watch, suit and cane, she in a refined dress – with her
through exile: their visages were the vestiges of the ambition of
amakholwa.

Conclusion

While missionaries and officials argued between themselves and with Africans over the *content* of African men's curriculum, they fought over the *composition* of the African female student body. So long as African girls' presence in the classroom did not radically unsettle the patriarchal authority on which colonial rule hinged, their education in domesticity was relatively uncontroversial. Because of colonial officials' and missionaries' gendered consensus around the aims of African women's and men's schooling – the former would be oriented towards social reproduction and domestic activities, the latter towards production and public life – women's schooling seemed less dangerous to colonial order.

Ultimately, of course, neither men's nor women's education was politically innocuous. As an expanding class of educated Africans ran up against a thickening wall of constraints in segregationist South Africa, African nationalists premised a *political division of labour* upon the edifice of their gendered mission school curricula. Educated African women generally assumed powerful roles in social welfare groups, while men dominated legalistic political organisations. These divisions were never airtight, and they did not go uncontested. But critically, women's public authority issued from their assumed centrality to social reproduction. As critically, segregationist state officials did not tend to see educated women's public work as politically threatening, but rather as socially essential. It is to this ambiguous politicisation of women's roles in social reproduction in the segregationist Union of South Africa that the next chapter turns.

CHAPTER THREE

New African Women's Work in Segregationist South Africa
1910–1948

In honour of Inanda Seminary's seventieth anniversary, over 500 alumnae descended upon the campus in 1939. After a ceremony featuring Lucy Isaac, the oldest alumna, the women crowded into the chapel to hear the day's keynote speaker: alumna Ntombi Mndima Tantsi, who spoke on behalf of the more than 4 000 women who had attended Inanda since its founding. Tantsi was an apt representative. A third-generation Inanda Christian, she had worked for the American Board in Southern Rhodesia before she 'married into the African Methodist Episcopal Church' and, with her husband, went to evangelise in the Transvaal.[1] Her AME work would take her to the United States, but she never forgot her roots: she had named her daughter Inanda and later enrolled her there.[2]

'Wherever I go, I find here and there ex-students of Inanda Seminary holding their heads up in spite of the terrible environments that tend to pull them down,' Tantsi declared. 'You will find among them Sunday School Teachers, Day and Night School Teachers, Nurses, Business Women, Social Workers, Politicians and Missionaries. They need encouragement and support, for without the women the nation will never rise. But alas! their number is like a drop in the ocean compared with the masses of our less fortunate sisters! What can we do to help them? They need religion in their hearts, education in their minds and money in their pockets.' She urged, 'There is a transcendent power in example. We reform others unconsciously when we walk uprightly.' Exemplary womanhood entailed self-empowerment:

We must have money in our pockets in order to be good citizens. We must do something for ourselves and not expect luck from heaven to descend to us. Let the women form business clubs – Dressmakers organize their clubs and teach some of the girls the art of dressmaking and fancywork, and organize your money like the Municipalities organize money from the sale of beer in towns; and so on with the other business women. Have business clubs for girls, encourage them to put aside a certain amount of money at the end of each month, with which they may later start on some venture. Teach the children to save their pennies in order that they may help them to pay their college fees. Let the women have a vision and ambition, and then inject it into their children.

She concluded on an ominous and rallying note: 'The race is looking to you, women; if you fail then the whole black race will perish.'[3]

Tantsi mobilised Inanda women's traditions of transforming the lives of their 'less fortunate sisters' to call for female-led action to address the economic exploitation and political marginalisation facing all black South Africans. Her words were glowingly received by missionaries and by John Dube's newspaper *Ilanga Lase Natal*, which published a full transcript. The event's 'master of ceremonies' Albert Luthuli – Adams alumnus, spouse of an Inanda alumna, and Congregationalist minister – echoed Tantsi's call. He suggested that Inanda posed 'an inspiration to us at a time when we must do something for ourselves'.[4]

As Inanda became the leading African girls' school in the Union of South Africa, staff and students emphasised women's central roles in the social reproduction of an uplifting African elite. This was an ambiguous vision: Inanda remained under the control of white women, working for a patriarchal mission within a patriarchal state. As the state sought to ensure the reproduction of a black labour force on a shoestring, it increasingly relied upon the work of educated African women in the core social service professions of teaching, nursing and social work. While women like Tantsi envisioned their labours as acts of self-empowerment, officials saw them as fonts of self-help that enabled their general neglect of black social welfare. As educated African women asserted their social leadership with growing force in the 1930s and 1940s, officials did not see any political peril in their decision to delegate core duties of a state to these women – enabling educated women's social labours to expand on the eve of apartheid.

The politicisation of social reproduction in the making of a national elite

Racial uplift as an object of education was not new in southern Africa. Inanda missionaries had called for the education of 'kraal girls' as a matter of 'the moral, social and educational development of the race', and the Dubes' Ohlange Institute and AME schools had drawn upon various transatlantic black educational models for racial advancement. The American Zulu Mission itself had begun as a sort of racial project: aimed at converting a 'Zulu nation', the mission retained its name although it served people who did not identify as Zulu from its start.

What was new in the period that this chapter covers was that Africans espoused the racially uplifting aims of education within a network of institutions that undergirded a self-consciously *national* African elite. This elite was tiny: in 1911, the Union's first census found that less than 7 per cent of the African population could read and write. While growing numbers of children were attending day schools, a slimmer minority went on to the secondary schools and teacher training colleges scattered throughout the country, due to the limited capacity of these schools and their relatively high costs. Between 1901 and 1934, only 253 Africans in the whole country passed matriculation (the highest school-leaving exam, which enabled university entrance). In 1915, Lovedale launched the first university for black students, the South African Native College at Fort Hare, but by 1935 just fifty-one students had received bachelor's degrees. By 1936, still just 12 per cent of the national African population of 6 500 000 were literate. And while schooling was feminised at the lower levels, African boys outnumbered girls in high school throughout this period.[5]

Attending high school, then, was a remarkable thing. By the 1920s, Africans with secondary schooling made up a recognisable group of teachers, ministers, health workers, entrepreneurs and clerks; alumni from Inanda, Adams College (as Amanzimtoti was more often known) and Ohlange dominated this elite in Natal, and they played leading roles in Johannesburg, too. The aforementioned were the most prominent secondary schools in Natal, together with the Catholic school at Mariannhill. Mariannhill had opened a girls' section in 1885, Adams added a girls' section in 1909 and Ohlange added a girls' hostel in 1917; but these were male-dominated institutions in the upper grades, generally with at least twice as many young men as women.[6]

Inanda was the most prestigious all-female school in the country.[7] From 1913 it offered education up to the level of the American ninth grade (Standard Seven), and from 1926 it offered an Academic High School course that culminated in the University of South Africa's Junior Certificate exam, which qualified girls for teachers' training or matriculation.[8] Graduates also began to attend nurses' training at the American Board's McCord Zulu Hospital in Durban, which opened in 1909 and offered a nurses' course from 1925. In the 1930s, as nursing became the consummate elite African women's profession, Inanda became widely acknowledged as the key institution from which to gain entry to the nurses' training programmes at McCord and King Edward VIII Hospital. The latter, Durban's first state-run 'non-European' hospital, opened in 1936 and commenced its nurses' training programme on Inanda's campus, attracting more than twice as many applications as there were spaces for trainees. This was the first state-run training programme for black nurses in the Union – a distinction for Inanda, and one that reflected the favour with which officials regarded the school.[9] In the 1940s, Inanda became the country's first school catering to African women to offer a matriculation course; the first eight matriculants passed their exams in 1946. All matriculants, principal Lavinia Scott announced in *Ilanga Lase Natal*, 'expect eventually to become teachers or nurses'.[10] Six entered teachers' training at Adams, one trained as a teacher at Fort Hare and one trained as a nurse at McCord.[11] Most would also marry and have children, prompting missionaries to call Inanda a 'school for homemakers', where 'Christian nurses, teachers, and wives for Africa' came of age.[12] Its multi-ethnic campus included students from all four provinces and from Basutoland, and from denominations other than the American Board.[13] By 1935 there were enough Johannesburg students to form a society, and in the 1940s students from Southern Rhodesia, Uganda and Kenya attended.[14] Instruction was in English, with isiZulu as a required additional language course. So, too, was Latin – until the early 1940s, when it was replaced as a requirement by domestic science; Latin would be removed from the curriculum entirely in the late 1940s, due to declining student interest and changing national examination standards.[15]

Graduates joined a class *between* – a class of what Nancy Rose Hunt has elsewhere termed 'hybrid middle figures' – both mediating and militating against state power.[16] In isiZulu, members of this class were identified by reference to the bases of their social position: their Christianity (*amakholwa* – believers), education (*izifundiswa* – learned ones) or legal status (*izemtiti* – those exempted from Native Law). Some traditionalists called them *amabuka* – traitors.[17] But in both isiZulu and isiXhosa, they were more often known as *amarespectable*. Their critics applied that moniker sardonically, revealing elite snobbery towards the majority who were neither Christian, school-educated nor exempted.[18] Critically for this analysis, the term *amarespectable* also reveals the gendered stakes of their position in a state premised on racialised public exclusions and transracial Christian domestic values. In the first half of the twentieth century, debates over the bounds of *women's* respectability flourished in the press and on the streets; although these debates were male-dominated, women participated as individuals, and as members of all-female political, religious and social service groups.[19]

Premised on the virtues of impeccable self-fashioning and unimpeachable manners, respectability was a public, racial discourse that hinged significantly upon private, familial conduct – reflecting the contradictions that had long structured *kholwa* domestic life. While the *amarespectable* continually evinced a deep faith in privacy, a sovereign home life had been impossible from the very start in the mission communities out of which their families grew. These communities had been predicated on missionary and *kholwa* couples' spectacles of domesticity – enacted both for local audiences of prospective converts and for the American supporters who regarded their tales of civilised home life with interest, prayers and money. If homestead life had been centrally premised on *ukuhlonipha* – respect – *kholwa* home life was centrally premised on maintaining respectability, within mission communities located ambiguously in a racially exclusive state. Maintaining a respectable home meant maintaining a home ready to confront the judgements of others: *kholwa*, missionaries and agents of the state, to whom the *amarespectable* appealed in vain for their land and for the vote. The respectable home thus stood upon a tenuous foundation of double-consciousness. From this foundation, women like Tantsi nurtured what Evelyn Brooks Higginbotham has termed a 'politics of respectability' in the African American context, and what Lynn Thomas has called 'racial respectability' in South Africa: the women of the *amarespectable* drew upon their pride in their upright conduct as a survival strategy – both to preserve their dignity, and to forge solidarity with whites and black men who had greater access to public fora than they possessed.[20]

In the Union of South Africa, the politics of the *amarespectable* took on urgency as the land on which African homes stood was pulled out from under them. In 1913, the Natives Land Act barred Africans from purchasing land within the 87 per cent of South Africa that the Act declared 'white' farmland, leaving only 7 per cent of the country part of the African 'reserves' and making African sharecropping on white land illegal. This passed after a petition campaign from the South African Native National Congress (SANNC), which had formed in 1912 to organise opposition. SANNC member Sol Plaatje, an intellectual based in the diamond-mining city of Kimberley, condemned the Act's effects on families forced onto reserves, struggling to 'lead respectable lives and to educate their children'.[21]

This critique should come as no surprise, as men of the *amarespectable* dominated the SANNC (known from 1923 as the African National Congress, or ANC). Its first president and treasurer general were the consummate *amakholwa* John Dube (trained at Amanzimtoti and Oberlin College) and Pixley ka Isaka Seme (trained at Amanzimtoti, Columbia and Oxford), while Plaatje was its first secretary general. They modelled the group on the Indian National Congress and the National Association for the Advancement of Colored People; they also included chiefs in an Upper House styled like the British House of Lords.[22] Despite its ambitions 'to maintain and uplift the standard of the race morally and spiritually, mentally and materially, socially and politically', the SANNC was riven by discord: in 1917, it ousted Dube for accepting segregationism, and he retreated to the Natal Native Congress.[23] It was only in 1943, after women's admission as full members, that the ANC advocated a universal franchise.[24]

Another key political movement dominated by men of the *amarespectable* was the Zulu cultural group Inkatha, in whose foundation Dube was also seminal after being ousted from the Natal Native Congress by more radical members in the mid-1920s.[25] While Dube's Zulu identity had posed a threat in the early twentieth century, it now signalled an appealing inclination to work within the logic of segregation to agents of the state and industry, in a context of rising activism.[26] A font of this activism was Amanzimtoti man George Champion's Industrial and Commercial Workers Union (ICU). In 1929, the ICU launched a beer hall boycott to combat the 'Durban system' of municipal funding through *utshwala* beer – a system that enraged women, its traditional producers.[27] This was the system Tantsi invoked when she called for women to organise their savings like 'the Municipalities organize money from the sale of beer in towns' – giving her call subversive implications. The boycott culminated in a white mob's attack and Champion's expulsion from Natal in 1930 – signalling the start of a nadir, in which white women gained the franchise to dilute the influence of the black male vote in the Cape; in 1936, the state abolished the Cape's non-racial franchise.

In this bleak context, elite men looked to African women – those most fully excluded from political power – to uplift their families and communities through personal and professional nurturance. The cultural nationalist Zulu Society exemplified these themes strikingly. Founded by Albert Luthuli, this group was led by men of the *amarespectable* – with the exception of the Inanda alumna (1910), former Inanda teacher (1915–1923) and American-trained social worker Sibusisiwe Makhanya, who served with John Dube as an 'adviser'. Its charter bemoaned the gendered crises that deepened political crises: 'Home Life is losing its time-honoured grip of discipline – homes, forsooth, where the children of our whole people are nurtured. If our women lose the dignity and the favour which are their national possession, then who will mother the future men of rank and the leaders and counsellors who will sustain the Zulus as a people

Figure 12 Sibusisiwe Makhanya, n.d. (circa 1928–1929). (Sibusisiwe Makhanya Papers, Photograph Album, Campbell Collections, University of KwaZulu-Natal, Durban)

forever?'[28] The Society's female adviser reminded her colleagues that good mothers could save the nation:

> Women of all classes and all of countries contribute very highly in the upbringing of their respective communities. Women are teachers of religion as they are the immediate example. They are the teachers of home discipline and self-respect. They are the ones who have brought up men and women who possess that great appellation 'UBUNTU' which is so indispensable in good citizenship. Women are the lilies of the veld in the houses, kraals, and communities.[29]

Zulu nationalists were hardly alone in looking to mothers to salve suffering.

Just after Tantsi's address, a pair of editorials, 'Women and Their Responsibility' and 'Failure of Responsibility', appeared in the women's section of *The Bantu World* of Johannesburg. The section was then under a male 'Editress', Ohlange and Adams graduate Rolfes Dhlomo; between his 1932 debut as Editress and assumption of *The Bantu World*'s editorship a decade later, Dhlomo regularly advised women on respectable conduct, and these editorials bear his didactic stamp.[30] The first proclaimed:

> 'The hand that rocks the cradle rules the world.' This refers to women, as it is they who bring in to being, nurse and nurture the infant, be it boy or girl, which must become the man or woman of to-morrow . . . The whole future, the whole form and destiny to which a race must be shaped lies, NOT in the hands of our politicians, NOT in the hands of our teachers and NOT in the powers of our ministers, but in the hands of the women of the race . . . 'The future of a race lies entirely in the hands of its women folk.'[31]

And, its companion piece stressed, women's responsibility was a mortal matter:

> A woman must be chaste, for by her chastity she insures well for the future of her progeny, and hence for the social and moral uplift and advance of her nation. If a woman fails to do this, then she spells ruination for her people, and hence she's a murderer and a traitor. A woman who indulges in foul talk or foul language is NOT shouldering her responsibility in life, indeed she is slaying her race, and has no business to be alive. I say so because she is sure to produce an offspring of swearing reprobates and brigands. Her progeny will be gaol-birds. A woman should be self-disciplined in order to impart this virtue to her offspring. Smoking and being 'too modern' by some of our too-clever-for-words young women is an intolerable eye-sore which must be put down or stamped out ruthlessly. For any woman to do this is but to ruin her race . . . A wild mother, a wild domestic environment must play a

potentially strong part in sowing the seeds of savagery in the poor innocent offspring. Thus for women to conduct themselves in an unseemly manner knowing well how, in virtue of their natural responsibility over their offspring and race, they have an unalterable influence, is, to put it straight, an open crime of 'murder' against human society.[32]

Such prose was extreme, but it embodied a broader fixation on 'responsibility'. As Dhlomo's brother Herbert (another Adams man) had written in 1930, 'Let us liberate our women folk from the thralldom and tyranny of custom, ignorance, subjection and the inferiority complex, and our progress will be accelerated. When we consider the high figures of juvenile delinquency, the spread of certain kinds of virulent diseases among the people, and the general moral laxity, we realise the danger that confronts us, and the tremendous responsibility which rests on our women. Liberation means responsibility.' New forms of public presence brought new challenges to respectability: 'In her old state of bondage and subjection, woman was kept pure and virtuous by prohibition; in her new position of freedom and equality she must keep pure and virtuous by inhibition.'[33]

In this context, some African men worried that women's education was contributing to a loosening of their morals, and they fretted particularly about the independence of unmarried young women working as nurses.[34] Against these critiques, others made the same argument for women's schooling that missionaries had made in launching Inanda initially: as missionaries had founded Inanda because 'the mothers make the men', these African men saw women as possessed of natural influence that, if not harnessed to uplift, could lead to catastrophe. One male-authored 1936 'Appeal for Educated Girls' in *Ilanga Lase Natal* argued:

A girl is more clever than a man, and if she has been highly educated she becomes the greatest asset to the man that she marries, for a girl with a trained mind knows well how to manage her household, to take care of the husband and the children. These days are days of intellectual capability, and not of dul[l]ness of intellect and idleness . . . When a girl is uneducated she is the greatest drawback in the family, and the family retrogrades, instead of progressing and generally the family does not attain any highest civilization as the case would be if she had been an educated girl. Educated girls are not bumptious and stubborn, as it is believed that they are. Educated girls are more reserved and very polite. Uneducated girls are very loquacious, very ill mannered and very backward in civilization. The Bantu girls are the very types of this class in Africa. Girls must be highly educated even above education which a man has, because she has great work to do in the family, more important than of a man . . . The girls are in reality involved in a great drama of human improvement. They are highly improved creatures in the world, and men must follow the best examples of these educated females . . .[35]

A male-authored *Bantu World* piece developed this theme of schooling for social reproduction, contending that women 'should be given higher education not because they make men's lives sweet but because they give birth to children and remain in closer relation with them than is the case with their fathers'.[36]

But at the same time that African men looked to educated women to uplift the race through their social influence, they were unwilling to include them within political decision-making structures. As Natasha Erlank has shown, this was in part a strategic move – black men demanded political inclusion on the basis of their willingness to forge a 'fraternal contract' with white male citizens. Erlank concluded that early 'black nationalist activity, therefore, was not only premised on the exclusion of women, but also relied on the exclusion of women for its own legitimation'.[37] Others have shown that women's official exclusion from male-dominated fora did not mean that they were absent from these spaces. Exceptional women such as Sibusisiwe Makhanya or Charlotte Maxeke – the first southern African woman to receive a bachelor's degree (in 1901, from Wilberforce University in Ohio), founder of the ANC-affiliated Bantu Women's League (1918) and first president of the National Council of African Women, an amalgamation of social welfare groups (1937) – were very visible at political conventions. Women such as Inanda affiliates Nokutela Mdima Dube, Angeline Khumalo Dube, Nokukhanya Bhengu Luthuli and Frieda Bokwe Matthews were essential helpmates without whom their activist husbands would not have been able to sustain their work.[38] But outside of the scope of existing scholarship remains a deeper question than the reasons for and extent of women's exclusion from male-dominated political organisations. What did women's marginality in these groups – but centrality in the realms of public and private social service – *actually empower them to do*?

These elite men and women envisioned that respectability should replace respect as the determining qualification for political authority. Within this paradigm, women bore social authority as *exemplary nurturers* – not only sustaining their families through their productive and reproductive labours, as African women had done long before the rise of *amakholwa*, but also using their homes to model new forms of sociality and racial pride. Women occupied fundamental roles in the social reproduction of a self-consciously uplifting class – and through these roles, men and women saw that women possessed potent roles in the making or undoing of the race. As black men confronted deepening political and economic exclusion, men and women of the *amarespectable* both asserted that women could, and must, advance the interests of the race on a different register – that of social reproduction. When women entered male-dominated political fora, then, it should not surprise us that they did so on the basis of their nurturing authority. Those exceptional women Maxeke and Makhanya justified their public roles upon their training as teachers and social workers. Maxeke also invoked her authority as a mother; Makhanya, unmarried and childless, devoted her life to domestic activism.

As women came together with increasing self-consciousness of their social responsibilities during the Second World War, accelerating African urbanisation and crises in the reserves fuelled militant strikes and boycotts. Women's social networks were central to these campaigns. Most notably, the Daughters of Africa, a group formed in Natal in 1932 by Lillian Tshabalala on the model of African American women's club movements, grew bolder in its mission after men lost the Cape franchise, calling for organisation of 'African Women into a National Movement of the economic life'.[39] Working in concert with male-dominated African nationalist groups, the Daughters were instrumental in the 1943 Alexandra bus boycott. Yet the public faces of a more militant ANC remained mission-educated men. In 1944, the leftist ANC Youth League formed under the leadership of Anton Lembede (Adams, class of 1935) and Jordan Ngubane (Adams, class of 1937), working with Nelson Mandela, Oliver Tambo and Walter Sisulu.

Herbert Dhlomo personified the spirit of the age with his figure of 'the New African'. Unlike the 'Tribal African', locked into a decaying regime, and the 'Neither-Nor African', who neither took pride in his heritage nor fully embraced the possibilities of African nationalism, the 'New African' was cosmopolitan and bold, working for an inclusive, progressive South Africa:

> The New African knows where he belongs and what belongs to him; where he is going and how; what he wants and the methods to obtain it. Such incidents as workers' strikes; organised boycotts; mass defiance of injustice – these and many others are but straws in the wind heralding the awakening of the New African masses. What is this New African's attitude? Put briefly and bluntly, he wants a social order where every South African will be free to express himself and his personality fully, live and breathe freely, and have a part in shaping the destiny of his country; a social order in which race, colour and creed will be a badge neither of privilege nor of discrimination.[40]

While Dhlomo represented the New African as a male figure, he suggested a female counterpart elsewhere. Just before this schematisation, he had published an article simply titled 'Woman' in *Ilanga Lase Natal*. Listening to 'a group of our local intellectuals discussing heatedly the subject of the role the modern African woman should play today, and also her merits and demerits', he wrote, 'I was not surprised to hear some condemning her as a devil and others endorsing her as a goddess as poets and thinkers of all races have done through the ages, because the point is that goddess or devil, you admit woman's boundless power.' Dhlomo concluded: 'Everywhere woman has played, is playing and will continue to play a master role in human affairs, whether or not we know or like it.'[41] While New African men embodied a bold political will, Dhlomo suggested that women embodied a foundational social power.

A central institution at which they developed this power was Inanda Seminary. Appropriately, Inanda was the site of a 1935 address by recent Fort Hare BA Pumla Ngozwana on 'The Emancipation of Women', which laid out the core vision of New African womanhood that Tantsi and her peers would echo. Ngozwana described her generation thus: 'Although in primitive Bantu society woman was free in that she was given her own sphere in which she moved and was her own mistress, the new Bantu woman realized that there was not sufficient scope for her to develop.' Now, she said, '[t]he Bantu woman, on account of her opportunities, has not attained to the same standard as her Negro and white sisters, but in spite of that she too has shown the world what she can do . . . Before the emancipation of women who ever heard of a woman leaving her home and going about giving lectures?' She emphasised the 'good examples of Bantu women who are devoting their lives to the service of their people', first among whom were Sibusisiwe Makhanya and Lillian Tshabalala. To emulate their example, she exhorted Inanda students to cultivate their minds and bodies, as 'these are the days of competition and only the fittest will survive'. In these Darwinian times, she suggested, women must be at the vanguard of developing 'race consciousness', overcoming tribalism and 'the feeling of inferiority, the feeling that white people do things because they are white'. Through their emancipation from the constraints of the homestead, she suggested, women's mobility in a new public sphere would foster their empowerment and thus the empowerment of their race. She closed with W.E. Henley's 1875 poem 'Invictus', culminating in the stirring lines, 'I am master of my fate / I am captain of my soul'.[42] That homage to self-possession, a favourite of Nelson Mandela and Marcus Garvey, resonated with New Africans' faith in the possibilities of individual and racial progress – a faith that enabled survival and expressions of militancy.[43]

Lessons in the social reproduction of an uplifting class at Inanda

The writing of Inanda students around the time of Ngozwana's address suggests that they were intensely cognisant of their position in the social reproduction of an uplifting elite. 'Boys and girls look forward to the time when they will be men and women of the nation, when they will take the place of those men and women we admire most at the present moment,' one graduating student wrote in *The Torchbearer*, a magazine published by Inanda and Ohlange students, in 1933. 'Whose place are you going to take?' she asked. 'Whose work are you going to complete?' Specifically, 'How many of us are going to take the teachers' places? How many of us are going to take the place of a minister? How many of us are going to take the place of nurses and doctors?'[44] As a 1935 graduate warned her peers:

> We are to face the world and its temptations. We are to find out if our character is like a house which is built on the sand, without any foundation, or a house with a firm foundation built on the rock, which when the wind comes to blow, it is not destroyed. We want to be like lights which are kindled and give light to all people. Our intention is to be the ladder of our race to climb up on us and be high as other nations. 'High ambitions' is our motto.[45]

A 1940 Junior Certificate recipient agreed:

> I wonder how many of us realize the difficulty of being a completer. It is a hard task indeed, because whatever one does, one should be a good example to others. Respect and responsibility in details are the most important things. When we go out to face the world, we want to be judged according to our good quality of manners and the way we behave ourselves, so that the people who are still uncivilized should understand the good of sending children to school.[46]

Inanda staff and students constantly invoked their campus motto, 'Shine Where You Are', in publications and school events. 'It is our ideal that every Inanda girl may be a bearer of light – a Torch Bearer – driving away the shadows and even the thick darkness of ignorance, poverty, sickness, sorrow, and despair, and spreading the light of knowledge, of better living conditions, health, joy, and hope, wherever she may go,' a *Torchbearer* editorial rhapsodised in 1940.[47]

Professionally, Inanda girls believed that they might best 'shine' as nurses and teachers, the most prestigious careers open to black women. South Africans believed that black women made ideal nurses for black patients because they already believed that white women made ideal nurses for white patients; both black and white men were seen as too 'clumsy' for a job that was styled as quintessentially nurturing and maternal.[48] For African women, nursing bore a remarkable degree of glamour, and it was the best-compensated profession open to black women. It also appealed to many parents because nurses' training programmes were less expensive than teacher training colleges. But nursing remained elite within limits. As Shula Marks has written of black nurses in the 1930s, 'Their salaries were far lower than those of their white counterparts, barely a handful reached senior levels, and conditions were even more difficult than they were for the white probationers, but black nurses were still better off than the majority of African women.'[49] In this difficult context, some saw their calling as both religious and political. As a McCord hospital trainee urged her peers in a 1940 *Torchbearer* piece, 'Girls of our race, let us come to this course when there is a call. The black race is calling us in its darkness. I now imagine how many people have died through ignorance. So let us therefore be leaders of our race in the midst of all tumults, help our nation, so that we will have fine growing young men and women.'[50] Herbert Dhlomo called African nurses 'God's stethoscope'.[51]

Due to missionaries' fiscal concerns and African women's assertions of their maternal authority, teaching was also an accessible occupation for girls, although a less prestigious one than nursing, as Deborah Gaitskell has shown. The Anglican St Matthew's College in the Cape actually closed its teachers' training programme to men in 1945. By 1949, there would be 3 019 African women in teacher training colleges, but just 2 209 men.[52] Like nursing, teaching enabled women to exercise social leadership, albeit within racialised and gendered limits.

Inanda's own staff revealed these limits vividly. It remained controlled by white, unmarried missionary women. No African attained a position of authority until the apartheid years. Inanda's missionaries chafed under men's continuing control of the mission and prioritisation of Adams College, prompting them to defend their expert knowledge in black women's schooling.[53] At the same time, they battled to justify their presence in the face of African women who also claimed such expertise.[54] The most troublesome of these women was Sibusisiwe Makhanya, who during her 1929 training at Columbia University's Teachers College told Inanda principal Margaret

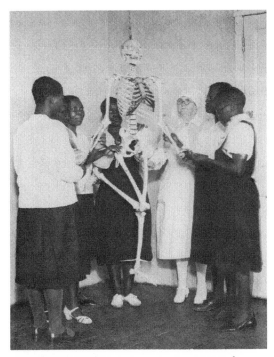

Figure 13 Preliminary nurses' training for King Edward VIII Hospital, Inanda Seminary, 1936. (Photograph Collection, Inanda Seminary Campus Archive)

Walbridge that 'she definitely would not be "tied down" when she returned to Africa, apparently meaning to school routine and under someone like myself', as Walbridge complained, concerned her 'unrest would be contagious'.[55] Makhanya's assertion of independence was dramatic. She had been sent to South Carolina by the Phelps-Stokes Fund in 1927 to train at a black industrial school as a 'Jeanes' teacher: an African version of the black women who visited rural homes across the American South with the support of the Anna T. Jeanes Foundation, preaching the gospels of modern hygiene and agricultural methods for overworked bodies and lands. Makhanya quickly broke with her sponsors, paying her way north by working as a domestic and lecturing on Zulu culture.[56] But Makhanya was successful in maintaining influence in mission circles: amidst her rebellion, she remained such a powerful figure that Walbridge used her image on a promotional brochure. Makhanya was, after all, 'native agency' embodied, a Christian woman spreading the gospel of domesticity across the countryside. But while Inanda's missionaries celebrated her successes publicly, these successes threatened to make white missionary women redundant. After Makhanya launched her own rural social work centre at Umbumbulu, another Inanda missionary fretted that in their gardening skills, 'the women here can't come up to Miss Makanya's women all at once. And Miss Makanya, by the way, is probably one reason the Carnegie grant for me won't go through; my work is too much like hers.'[57]

Although her struggle was exceptionally public, Makhanya was not the only accomplished African woman to part ways with Inanda's white staff. Inanda's first two African teachers with BA degrees left the school shortly after graduating. Inanda alumna Gertrude Ntlabati left at the end of 1929, a year after her triumphant return from Fort Hare in cap and gown as the first African woman to earn a BA there – reportedly on account of a 'nervous condition'.[58] Clarissa Mzoneli, who received her BA in 1939, left in 1940, also after apparent stress.[59] Her American colleague Minnie Carter complained that Mzoneli was 'erratic and has not made good contacts with the other African staff members. She has chosen to have her meals by herself, thinking it a waste of time to go to the staff dining room.'[60] Mzoneli resigned because, as Carter put it, 'we were not progressive enough for her. Next we heard that she had taken a position at Ohlange. Now we hear that she has resigned there. She has great personal possibilities if she could only hold steadily to her highest ideals and be content to make progress slowly.'[61] No archival or published accounts explicate Mzoneli's 'highest ideals'. But the only published reference to her suggests that she was committed to an egalitarianism that was not a reality within white-controlled institutions of her time: a Fort Hare classmate's memoir relates how Mzoneli refused to take tea with a teacher whom she had seen speaking abusively towards black staff.[62] In this light, her refusal to take meals 'with the other African staff members' at Inanda suggests not merely antisocial behaviour, but also possibly a rejection of the fact that taking a meal with Inanda's African staff meant taking a meal separately from her white colleagues. Dining and lodging were racially segregated at Inanda, and they would remain

Figure 14 'Inanda Electric Light Leaflet, Inanda Seminary, Natal, South Africa', n.d. (circa 1929). (American Board of Commissioners for Foreign Missions, African Missions, Box 15.4, Volume 48, Houghton Library, Harvard University)

so until Inanda missionaries' horror at apartheid forced them to confront segregation on their campus in the 1960s. Refusing to 'make progress slowly' may have entailed rejecting white colleagues' distance and condescension.

At Inanda and other missionary institutions, salary scales were differentiated by race and gender – a scale in which black women landed at the bottom, no matter their qualifications.[63] Women other than white single women (known in this era as 'unappropriated blessings') were assumed to have access to a matrimonial supplement that would keep them afloat as teachers or enable them to leave the profession.[64] Given the racially constrained salaries available to African teachers' prospective husbands, however, this supplement would generally be small, compelling most African women to continue working after their marriages.

Marriage, Inanda girls learned, was about more than financial security. Staff sought to show students how they might uplift their own families and, by example, those of the race through companionate relationships with men. From the early 1920s, students hosted weekly 'Student Nights' of debates, concerts and literary society meetings, often inviting young men from the neighbouring Ohlange. Walbridge introduced these nights to 'help school spirit' and to promote 'sane and healthful social relationships' on Inanda's campus.[65] These relationships included intellectual comradeship: Inanda girls debated Ohlange boys on issues such as 'boys should receive a higher education than girls' (Ohlange took the affirmative position), and Inanda girls often won.[66] Ohlange boys praised Inanda as 'the cultivator of our young Native girls who are uplifted by the school which shows the progress of what is done'.[67] From the 1920s, Ohlange and Adams boys also playfully referred to Inanda as 'the Zoo' because Inanda girls were so well guarded.[68] For at the same time that Inanda staff prepared their students to be self-confident women, they impelled them to guard their sexuality fiercely. Makhanya's Purity League, which she founded as an Inanda teacher in 1919, was a key early forum in which girls learned that respectable womanhood demanded sexual restraint. Some two-thirds of Inanda's students were members of the group by the mid-1920s; from the late 1920s, the Student Christian Association, a Girl Scouts-like group called the Wayfarers and Makhanya's co-educational Bantu Youth League filled similar roles.[69] Staff read all of students' mail to guard against 'love letters', a habit in which they were not unique. Mariannhill indicated in its 1925 prospectus for its female branch that 'in spite of continual warnings every year scholars must be dismissed on account of love affairs. Those who do not want to devote all their time to becoming educated and better should stay away.'[70] At Adams College, too, girls' behaviour was carefully policed.[71]

These concerns about protecting young women were not irrational: parents and staff bemoaned rising numbers of premarital pregnancies from the 1920s through the 1940s, a trend that many *amarespectable* and traditionalists attributed to the decline of pre-colonial rites of passage and the failure of new institutions to replace them.[72] Older girls in southern Africa had long provided counsel to their younger peers on matters of romance, marriage and childbearing. But ironically, Christian silences and disavowals around sexuality left girls cognisant of a structural link between their sexual inhibition and social prominence, but mystified by the complexities of desire and the mechanics of reproduction. To remedy this, the Purity League insisted that romance should occur only after an engagement and should be 'public'.[73] From 1937 through 1957, missionary Dora Phillips reinforced this message with annual talks on 'sex hygiene' at Inanda. After her first round of talks, one student reflected, 'If mothers of our days were as careful in telling their children the correct ways of doing things, we should be much better than we are now, doing things without knowledge.'[74] But the impact of this new structure of sexual guidance remained unclear: 'Some of the girls tell her that her ideal is right but unattainable,' Scott indicated in 1940, prompting Scott to engage African women for further talks.[75] These women were likely members of the Daughters of Africa, as sexual education lay within their social and economic uplift objectives and as a number of the group's leaders hailed from Inanda.[76] Then two students and an unmarried African teacher became pregnant; the next year, so did two more students.[77] To pre-empt further reproductive crises, an elderly John Dube preached about 'purity', comparing girls to rosebuds – some of whom would be 'eaten in the bud' before blooming. Constance Miriam (Dlomo) Koza, who attended Inanda from 1941 to 1945, took in Dube's sermon avidly and would communicate his lesson as Inanda's principal in the 1980s.[78]

All students and unmarried staff who became pregnant left school, and the spectre of pregnancy was a central preoccupation of Inanda women, given the tremendous blow to a woman's respectability that motherhood outside of marriage conferred. In contrast, sources are entirely silent about the matter of sexually intimate relationships between Inanda women in this period – either students or staff. This silence is surprising, given the alacrity with which missionaries discussed heterosexual relations between and amongst students and staff at other institutions, and given missionaries' concerns about homosexual relations between African men in Johannesburg.[79] It suggests that anxieties around the shame and burden of an unplanned pregnancy – more than guilt around unsanctioned intimacies more broadly – haunted Inanda women.

Caroline Sililo – who attended Inanda from 1934 to 1936, trained as a teacher at Adams, and returned to teach at Inanda from 1943 to 1950 – and her former student Faith (Nomvete) Nyongo – who attended Inanda from 1943 to 1945 before training as a nurse at McCord Hospital – remember these anxieties well. Nyongo confessed to me, 'We used to fear males.' Nyongo believed that Inanda's environment had improved when her daughter attended in the early 1980s because of the infusion of male staff. 'It made a difference that girls must not fear males, they must know that they are human beings and not animals,' Nyongo said, as Sililo nodded. Sililo, a diffident woman, said, 'My shyness became worse when we were not allowed to mix with boys, we were not allowed to talk to them. I don't think girls' schools are good enough.' Nyongo added, half-joking, 'Yes, because you know they made girls once they are out to be wild!' Sililo then insisted that we discuss Inanda's concerts with Ohlange boys 'because we used to get very excited'. Nyongo agreed, 'That was very exciting, ja. And then the boys will sit on the other side and then girls will sit on the other side.' Both women laughed. Nyongo described: 'And then when the concert was over they said [clapping her hands and taking on a high-pitched voice], "Okay, you can talk to each other! Woo!" And you see the excitement! The boys will come to the girls and the girls will come to the boys!' Sililo added ruefully, 'Inanda Seminary was called "The Zoo".' Sundays offered the rare treat of a trip off campus, to the Inanda mission church down the road. 'I used to like it,' Nyongo recalled. 'Because, you know, we were locked in. We used not to go out of bounds. We were locked in.' This was not strictly true. But, 'a big, big dog' called Khumbula (isiZulu for 'remember') guarded campus and would 'go wild' if he saw a man.[80]

Despite these anxieties, Inanda girls found pride in their school's long trajectory of enlightening women. In a 1940 essay contest, Inanda students submitted pieces commemorating 'old girls' who had 'brought help, inspiration, and uplift[ment] into unnumbered homes and communities'.[81] The prize-winning entry commemorated Talitha Hawes – founder of the school that the author and her siblings had attended.[82] Second prize went to Lauretta (Gwina) Ngcobo, who attended Inanda from 1945 to 1949 before training as a teacher at Fort Hare and becoming an anti-apartheid activist and internationally acclaimed novelist. She described how her grandmother, Agnes Mdladla Cele, and her husband 'were the copy on the blackboard, because everything they did was copied by their neighbors'.[83] To Gwina, her grandmother was a living 'encyclopedia' who 'remembers even the trees' of Inanda. A third essay discussed Constance Khumalo Makhanya, an Inanda-trained domestic science teacher and McCord-trained nurse-midwife who ran a clinic at Umbumbulu, where, as the journalist Jordan Ngubane elsewhere described it, her 'results began to tell. Fewer and fewer mothers died in childbirth. The numbers of rickety children fell; plump little human beings, with a lusty enjoyment of life, could be seen everywhere.'[84] On a shoestring, Makhanya thus laboured for the physical and social reproduction of a community whose needs the state had long ignored. Officials were not blind to the value of such contributions, giving the clinic modest grants from the Department of Native Affairs and the Department of Public Health.

'A steadying influence over more unstable elements': official views of educated women

Indeed, as colonial officials had long delegated core social welfare work to missions, the segregationist state was entrusting this work to African women. The Phelps-Stokes Fund – Sibusisiwe Makhanya's erstwhile benefactors, and a dominant philanthropic influence in African and African American schooling in the 1920s and 1930s – played a pronounced role in shaping Natal policies in this dimension.[85] When the Phelps-Stokes African Education Commission toured African schools in 1920 and 1924, Natal educational official Charles Loram eagerly accompanied. Loram was multiply linked to Americans, and especially to Inanda: he received his PhD at Columbia University's Teachers College, and in the 1930s he would teach Walbridge's successor Lavinia Scott at Yale University.[86] The Phelps-Stokes Fund itself was closely tied to Inanda: its administrator, Anson Phelps Stokes, was the grandson of the woman who had endowed Inanda Seminary's first building, and he was married to the granddaughter of Inanda mission's first minister, Daniel Lindley.[87] Loram and the Commission also shared core ideas about the significance of women's schooling with many at Inanda. 'The woman not only presides in the dwelling, directs or controls the beginnings of life, but also holds the vital forces that make or unmake the social group,' the Commission opined in 1925.

> Tragic results will follow if the education of the African woman does not develop on parallel lines and simultaneously with that of her husband. Together they must advance to the full development of civilized life in all its phases. The influence of ignorant and uncivilized wives and mothers upon semi-educated men and boys can do nothing but hamper and delay the development of civilization.

The ideal professions for African female 'leaders', the Commission declared, were teaching and nursing. But these were professions into which they should be guided under the 'essential' counsel of 'European' woman missionaries, 'as civilization progresses'.[88]

As their emphasis on white guidance suggests, the Commission did not see women's schooling as a mode of racial empowerment. Rather, it seemed an efficient route to self-help, hastening the inexpensive incorporation of Africans as subjugated workers in the segregationist state. The Phelps-Stokes model of schooling was loosely based on Booker T. Washington's Tuskegee Institute in Alabama, with all of the empowering political potential that the Dubes had seen in the late nineteenth century emptied out. It advocated a low standard of schooling in 'character development, health and hygiene, agriculture and gardening, industrial skill, knowledge of home economics and wholesome recreation' for the 'Negro masses'.[89] The goal of mass education was to teach children that 'they are part and parcel of a community for whose standards and ideas they are largely responsible', emphasising the values of 'perseverance, thrift, temperance, self-control, reliability, honesty and respect for parents'.[90] Elite men and women would receive training in the 'disciplines which white civilization has found valuable' – but in local rather than foreign schools, so that they would 'become accustomed to the conditions with which they will have to cope later in life'.[91]

Inanda's emphasis on training students to serve society fit well within this framework, in two dimensions. First, Phelps-Stokes' advocates hoped to develop a modern form of 'kraal visits' – conducted by black 'home demonstrators' and agricultural instructors trained by white missionaries, and modelled on the African American Jeanes teachers.[92] The contributions of Inanda graduates met these objectives – even if women like Sibusisiwe Makhanya and the Daughters of Africa emphasised their independence from missionary imperatives more strongly than whites found ideal. Secondly, Inanda's administrators recalibrated their position on training students for domestic service in the 1920s. At Loram's urging, Inanda systematised its domestic training, opening an Industrial Class in 1917 and a Domestic Arts High School in 1919.[93] Missionaries proclaimed that domestic science at Inanda and Adams would be 'a boon to many a Zulu girl, and through her, to the homes of both native and colonist'.[94] In 1923, the American Board conceded, 'Changing economic conditions and the increasing competition for the available positions as teachers indicates that many girls will be compelled to make their living in domestic service.'[95] While Mary Edwards had opposed training girls for service, as the previous chapter discussed, Walbridge placed eleven girls in employment in white homes during her first year as principal.[96]

Inanda's prospectuses in both 1923 and 1929 stated frankly that the industrial course provided 'suitable training to girls who wish to become Home-makers, Dressmakers, or Cooks. Training for Household Service is emphasized, and satisfactory students are assisted in finding suitable positions.'[97] Agnes Wood, the American head of the industrial course between 1931 and its termination three decades later, claimed later that 'the aim of the Industrial Course was to raise the standard of living of the girls and through them of their homes, to give some training in making salable articles and – of first importance to the Government Education Department – to train them for domestic service in European homes'.[98] She maintained that 'few of the girls ever went into service'.[99] Certainly the school's public reputation was of a more elite stature.

Yet domestic service was economically necessary for many women of a class with elite ambitions and shrinking access to capital. The career of Lucy Twala exemplifies this well. During her schooldays at Inanda, Twala was an accomplished actress who performed in Herbert Dhlomo's plays at the Bantu Men's Social Centre in Johannesburg during her holidays and served as a correspondent for *The Bantu World*.[100] But she left Inanda without the Junior Certificate because her parents, struggling to make ends meet in Johannesburg, could not afford to support her; she then went into service in a white home, the most lucrative option. In 1937, Twala founded the Bantu Domestic Service Association in Johannesburg, a union aimed at guarding the respectability of 'the elite group of ex-boarding school students to which she belonged', as Iris Berger has characterised it.[101] The elite base of Twala's group suggests that a considerable number of such girls were going into service. Indeed, domestic service then composed the widest category of formal employment for African women around South Africa: in 1936, at least 80 per cent of 'economically active' African women were domestic workers.[102] Twala's preoccupation with their respectability reveals the perils women and their families found in the profession.[103]

As important as women's work as helping professionals and domestic workers seemed for the segregationist state, women's labours in their own homes still bore deep official appeal. A 1922 event at Inanda made this clear. To celebrate the opening of a new building, Sibusisiwe Makhanya presided over an event that attracted over 800 alumnae.[104] It also drew Natal's Chief Native Commissioner, C.A. Wheelwright, who opined that Inanda was essential for its 'training of good and useful Native women who will exercise in this generation, and even more in the future, an influence for good in the future of So. Africa, a future in which both White and Black must play a recognized and important part'. To the alumnae before him, he stressed, 'I trust that each of you who have been trained in this Institution will exercise yourselves through your husbands, and most of all through your children, a steadying influence over more unstable elements. Remember always what you yourselves owe, and what your children owe, to White civilization and Christian sacrifice.'[105] On one level, like Natal educational official Robert Plant (discussed in the previous chapter), Wheelwright sought to harness women's influence to induce men to be manageable subjects. He was admittedly concerned that 'education should aim at training the Native to become a better citizen; by a better citizen I mean a better worker'.[106] But Wheelwright added new emphasis on women's roles as interracial ambassadors – working under white women to stabilise the state.

The gender of student 'disturbances' in the 1940s

Surprisingly, given the ambiguities under which they grew up, students on Inanda's campus evinced little organised dissent during and after the Second World War. The school was in this respect markedly different from major co-educational institutions. In March 1946, Lavinia Scott reported:

> Adams has had a sad time, as some of the boys went on strike and smashed up the school store room, taking lots of supplies and causing a good deal of loss. Apparently the cause was an increase in fees, and the substitution of mealie meal for bread at one meal! Probably there were a few trouble-makers at the back of it all, and I hope they will be discovered and expelled; but I don't know just what is happening about that. Our girls (and the Adams girls, too) show no signs of wanting to strike![107]

In August 1946, as Scott boasted in *Ilanga Lase Natal* of Inanda's first matriculants, their peers in the Cape's most prestigious high schools were attracting attention for their participation in boycotts and riots. At Lovedale, 157 young men were arrested after stoning staff and police and burning buildings and equipment on their campus; in the days that followed, both male and female students boycotted classes and church. Inspired by their peers, students at the Methodist secondary school Healdtown set fires and tried to organise a boycott.

Enraged over their food rations, manual labour on campus and the subjugation of African staff, student unrest revealed a broader spirit of African nationalism and resistance to missionary authority sweeping elite mission institutions after the Second World War. Between 1945 and 1947, similar disturbances wracked institutions around the country; over the next decade, conflicts would continue, as well as conflicts between students of different ethnicities and between rural and urban students.[108] These students were following national and international developments and identifying with politically outspoken teachers and family members.

While most of these disturbances were initiated and led by older male students, some girls demonstrated solidarity. In 1945, the day after young men at St Matthew's in the Cape called for the appointment of an African housemaster and torched a hostel to underscore their point, 'the girls refused to eat their lunch, turning their anger inward in an act of self-denial', as Anne Mager has described.[109] At other moments, female students organised outward expressions of their anger over their racialised and gendered marginality: at St Matthew's in 1949, girls rose in fiery protest against a white male warden who had been suspected of sexual impropriety towards older female students. High school girls and teacher trainees pelted the warden – a priest – with rocks and burned the housemistress' home and car. In Mager's view, the girls had proceeded 'to follow the long-established tradition of rebellion by male students' to articulate their gendered concerns. Male students at St Matthew's and at Fort Hare expressed their solidarity with what a female staff member termed the 'girls' war', expressing disgust with the warden's 'deflowering our African women students'. Similarly, when nurse trainees affiliated to Lovedale went on strike to reject its hierarchical environment in 1949, Fort Hare men supported them with food and counsel.[110] The Disciplinary Committee of the South African Nursing Council fretted that the men of the ANC Youth League found 'the nurses fruitful soil to work on'.[111]

While these episodes of female students' forceful unrest have attracted rich historical analysis, archival evidence suggests that they may have been exceptional. The 1947 Commission of Enquiry into Disturbances at Native Educational Institutions mentioned female participation in only eight incidents, out of fifty-two documented cases of indiscipline. In twelve cases, the Commission emphasised that girls 'took no part in the unrest'. In no co-educational school did the Commission stress that boys took no part. Half of the documented incidents of female indiscipline took place at St Matthew's: in addition to the 1945 incident, girls rose up in 1939 and 1940 against a white housemistress for her 'harsh treatment of [a] hysterical girl' and united with their male peers to demand an African housemaster in 1941. In addition to refusing food, they started a fire in the assistant housemistress' room and threw stones at white staff. Two of the incidents occurred at Emfundisweni in the Cape: in 1940, girls fought off drunken male classmates who invaded their dormitory, and in 1945 girls and boys united to protest the poor teaching of English on campus. The remaining incidents were a 1942 male and female boycott at Emmarentia-Geldenhuys in the Transvaal, after a teacher called the Standard Six (Grade Eight) class 'kaffirs' and 'sat in [the] field directing "Manual" [work] with gun over shoulder', and a 1944 fight between students from Natal and the Transvaal at St Hilda's, an all-girls school in Natal. Girls expressed racialised, gendered and regional grievances, but they do not appear to have taken central roles in student unrest.[112]

Inanda students manifested a more subtle form of unrest that was internalised and bodily. They suffered periodically from '*ufufunyana*', 'hysteria' or 'nervous breakdown'.[113] These conditions manifested in refusals to eat, thrashing or screaming, irrational speech, exhaustion or loss of consciousness. Staff and students variously attributed these conditions to witchcraft, interpersonal tensions or overwork. We might also see these afflictions as expressions of the distress accompanying the burdens of respectable girlhood in an unjust society.[114] In the same letter in which Scott asserted that her students showed no signs of striking, for example, she wrote of a student's fit just after McCord's doctor Alan Taylor came to conduct physicals. Four students had syphilis. Another showed signs of smallpox, which occasioned great fear given insufficient access to health care: 'There is no place at present in Durban for African smallpox cases, as the isolation hospital is being remodeled.' During study hall that evening, Scott said,

> The largest girl in school suddenly went hysterical and fell flat on the floor in her classroom, screaming. I happened to be nearby, and dashed in; and we managed to get her up, but she flung us off after a struggle, and ran outdoors. We caught her and, with the help of sal volatile and five or six people, finally got her to the Hospital and onto the top of a bed. She was ill, with a temperature, for nearly a week after that, but I don't know just what the reason for all the violence was. Of course, she was quite out of

her mind – and she apologized to me afterward, rather shame-facedly, for doing such funny things! She is a nice girl, anyway, and one of my Sunday School teachers.[115]

To suggest that Inanda girls did not engage in political protest and may have instead internalised their frustrations does not imply that they were apolitical or inarticulate.

Far from it. Students read newspapers in Inanda's library, which then held over a thousand books; it had opened in 1927, one of the country's first libraries open to blacks.[116] In 1937, Inanda began a tradition of democratic discussion, with students and staff convening on Fridays to discuss current events.[117] Inanda, Ohlange and Adams students debated the topic, 'Resolved, that the coming of the White people has improved the mass of Bantu'. Inanda and Ohlange took the negative and won, by staff judgement.[118] In another match, Inanda and Ohlange debated, 'Resolved, that the African people are responsible for the slum conditions in Urban areas'; Inanda took the negative and won.[119] In 1940, Inanda argued, 'Africans should be allowed to have their own government without Europeans', losing narrowly to Adams.[120] The *Torchbearer* and its successor, Inanda's *Ezakwamah-Edwards* ('at Mother Edwards' place'), also served as critical fora. In 1940, a female Ohlange student urged her peers to 'know their rights' before and after marriage.[121] In 1948, an Inanda student examined her school as a democracy: 'It is the government of the school by the school. Both teachers and students have a share in it.'[122] Students engaged with visitors from King Solomon kaDinuzulu to black American social worker Max Yergan (in his radical phase).[123] Lauretta Ngcobo recalls that Scott 'used to awaken us to what was expected in us' by inviting speakers such as a

> young woman doctor, the first African woman doctor . . . Those talks, when you link them up with the stories you hear at home – we were absolutely, we had never been face to face with these situations, but we knew that life as it had been lived before was changing fast, for the worse. And so they conscientized us really, I remember well.[124]

Figure 15 Inanda principal Margaret Walbridge and King Solomon kaDinuzulu, 1926. (Album B48-164, Campbell Collections, University of KwaZulu-Natal, Durban)

Despite these glimpses into a lively public sphere, Faith Nyongo, class of 1945, assured me that students 'were not allowed to speak about politics at all'. In the next breath, she made clear that such a claim was not incompatible with the world discussed above: Inanda girls understood that they were not to be activists, but rather informed members of society. She recalled her teacher Charlotte Goba, who emphasised, 'You must know about politics, but you must not be active, *ja*. You must know. You must read your papers, you must know what is going on. But don't take an active part, *ja*.'[125]

Nomangcobo Sibusisiwe Bhengu, who attended Inanda between 1949 and 1951 and trained as a teacher at Adams, and Dorcas Sibusisiwe (Gumbi) Meyiwa, who attended from 1944 to 1948 and trained as a teacher at Adams, emphasised that they had 'a good teacher, Miss Khumalo', who 'knew history from beginning to end' without opening a book and 'would give us articles about what was going on in Parliament'.[126] Bhengu, Meyiwa and their friend Melodious (Blose) Gumede, who attended Inanda between 1944 and 1946 before training as a nurse at King Edward, more vividly recall lessons in respectability. Meyiwa found, 'A girl from that school was just a different girl in the community. Because you knew you had a role to play in your community. You had to be exemplary in all ways. In your speech, in your behavior.' Gumede added, 'You have to shine where you are!' They recounted their teacher Margaret Nduna's guidance excitedly, rushing to finish one another's sentences:

Gumede: Mama Nduna. Mama Nduna.

Meyiwa: Oh yes!

Bhengu: All the advice that she gave us, all that, oh my, oh my.

Gumede: That one really made us ladies.

Bhengu: Yes, and know who you are.

Meyiwa: With a smile.

Bhengu: Each time you take a step, you must know who you are.

These lessons resonated with the history they had received at home: Meyiwa and Bhengu were both named for Sibusisiwe Makhanya, who had been taught by Meyiwa's grandmother and taught Bhengu's mother at Inanda.[127]

Conclusion

As respectable girls developed into New African women, officials did not seem to have noticed. As elsewhere in colonial Africa, they were more concerned to use education policy to divert threats to white governance emanating from political groups led by educated men.[128] But because a female educated elite existed and the profession of teaching was feminising in South Africa by the Second World War, the expansion of schooling to address threats issuing from men would imply an expansion of professional opportunities to women. At the same time, policymakers were planning a national health care scheme, expanding nursing services to answer the crises in labourers' health that threatened to limit the expansion of modern secondary industry.[129] After the Second World War, then, black women's schooling in South Africa seemed poised for expansion.

New Africans and their allies worried that apartheid would halt women's opportunities. As Lavinia Scott confided to her family just after the National Party's May 1948 election on an apartheid platform, 'their idea of "Apartheid," or Separation, is an impossible one, for they want the labor of the Natives and they simply cannot have that and make any kind of progress while trying to set up two distinct civilizations in South Africa . . . We fear that there will be far less progress in African education and welfare than there has been in recent years.'[130] But ironically, the professions of teaching and nursing would grow unprecedentedly during apartheid. While African men's schooling was a prime site of official concern, women's schooling appeared to officials as a site of still-untapped stabilising potential.

CHAPTER FOUR

Education Policy and the Gendered Making of Separate Development
1948–1976

In late 1956, Adams College held its last service. During a storm that pelted the iron-roofed chapel with ominous force, a full congregation tearfully sang 'God Be with You until We Meet Again'. 'Two Native women students in the choir stopped singing because they were overcome with emotion. Male students silently bowed their heads as they realised that "the final blow had fallen",' the *Natal Daily News* reported.[1] 'As scores of rich, meaningful Bantu voices rose to the crescendo of the last Amen in the Adams College Mission Church yesterday afternoon, more than a century of Christian endeavour came to an end and the political era of the Bantu Education Act came to the College,' the *Natal Mercury* declared.[2] Adams' principal and his family left the country. The high school continued as the Amanzimtoti Zulu Training School: it was sold to the state on condition that the name 'Adams' not be used.[3] Students staged a boycott the next year.[4]

Adams has since served as a metonym for possibilities apartheid foreclosed.[5] Under Bantu Education, the state nationalised or closed most mission schools, of which Adams – alma mater of doctors and lawyers, and of the founders and the then president of the African National Congress – was among the most prestigious.

With less ceremony, the American Board retained control of its other major educational institution. In late 1957, Inanda Seminary received official permission to continue as a private high school, under which status it would operate through the apartheid years. Although the American Board had struggled to maintain control over its pair of flagship schools – founded the century before as a matched set to create transformative African Christian families – the state was only willing to tolerate Americans' continued authority at their all-female institution. This chapter examines the reasons for, and meanings of, Inanda's trajectory by situating it within the gendered framework of apartheid education.

Scholars have shown that the Bantu Education Act of 1953 sought to bring volatile mission institutions under state control and to bring the majority of Africans who were not in school into state-controlled classrooms: it was a modernising project of racialised state-building and subject-making through a model of mass schooling that left little space for the mission schools where an elite few had previously received training. As growing numbers of African students would attend Bantu Education schools, students classified as 'coloured' or Indian would go to their own ethnically demarcated schools; for no black pupils was education free or compulsory, and it was in fact grievously underfunded, resulting in overcrowded classrooms staffed by overworked teachers.[6]

Consumed by the overarching racialised indignities of apartheid education, scholars have neglected how it was also a gendered project. As Bantu Education sought to limit student unrest – unrest that was, as the previous chapter pointed out, most often associated with young African men – it also sought to educate masses of semi-skilled workers – in classrooms that were increasingly headed by young African women. By this gendered logic, the state nationalised most teacher training colleges and restricted their male enrolment.[7] By this same gendered logic, officials tolerated Inanda's continued operation as an elite, all-female institution that prepared young women for careers in teaching and nursing, even as the state consolidated its control over the vast majority of Inanda's peers in the 1950s. On the eve of apartheid, Inanda had been both a calm and academically thriving institution – unlike many other leading mission institutions, as the previous chapter has shown. And Inanda graduates represented some of the best students at the new post-secondary institutions of the apartheid state in the 1960s. During the 1970s, KwaZulu homeland leader Chief Mangosuthu Gatsha Buthelezi saw Inanda as an institution that could cultivate skilled teachers, health workers and secretaries – a black bourgeoisie who could make separate development work for black people. Inanda's role in nurturing black professional women thus obviated the need to nationalise Inanda, even as it became a site that nurtured opposition to apartheid.

The apartheid state's crises of social reproduction

The platform of apartheid – separateness – on which the National Party came to power in May 1948 was an answer to crises of the social reproduction of a divided society that Afrikaner nationalists perceived. The policies of cheap black labour on which the mineral revolution had been premised had introduced a series of unmanageable contradictions for Jan Smuts' United Party: the rapid expansion of secondary industrialisation along with an underdeveloped consumer economy, deterioration of rural reserves, rapid black urbanisation and rising black militancy.[8] The United Party and its rival National Party agreed that a more expansive, interventionist state was necessary to manage these contradictions and facilitate economic development that would profit white elites. But while the United Party's Fagan Commission had concluded in February 1948 that complete racial segregation was economically and politically untenable, and that black urbanisation was an inexorable modern trend, the National Party espoused a more thoroughly racialised developmental state that would answer the demands of its populist Afrikaner base.

Elsewhere on the continent, developmental colonial states sought partially to answer and therefore to manage the demands of Africans emboldened by the transformations of the Second World War, while making empire pay.[9] The apartheid state also sought to manage African demands through development, but it refused to accede to black calls for enfranchisement – as British and French officials did, to varying extents, in colonies that did not include significant white settlement in the late 1950s and 1960s.[10] Apartheid officials instead elaborated farcical schemes for 'separate development' in ethnic 'homelands' (known as Bantustans), from which workers would travel to 'white' South Africa.[11]

This was a cynical 'internal decolonization' in which Africans over age sixteen had to carry passes indicating their racially defined places of residence and employment at all times.[12] Until the abolition of the pass laws in 1986, the state sought to control spatially the social reproduction of African families – within a framework which, building upon the colonial tradition described in Chapter 2, legally valorised patriarchy and economically undermined men's control of their lives and those of their families. Pass laws compelled most African women to sustain households in rural or peri-urban homelands to subsidise men's migrant labour, while the state tolerated small numbers of women, mostly domestic workers, to meet labour needs in 'white' areas.[13]

Officials saw immediately that youth would need to be educated to fit into this system. They had inherited anxieties about the lack of a mass black schooling system from their United Party predecessors; as Jonathan Hyslop has shown, both governments were concerned with 'urban youth – how to control and train them'.[14] The old system of delegating black schooling almost wholly to missionaries would not do – not only because mission schools were regularly exploding into unrest, but also because most Africans had little to no formal schooling due to the missions' limited scale.

The Commission of Enquiry into Native Education thus convened from 1949 to 1951 to address the future of African schooling. The commission, under chairman W.W.M. Eiselen, adjudged that mission schools neither separated students into their proper ethnic units nor prepared them to develop the reserves or to labour in semi-skilled industrial jobs.[15] The system evinced 'vagueness of objectives', an 'uncertainty as to the future of development of Bantu Culture', a 'lack of a clear-cut economic policy' and a 'lack of holding power'.[16] In 1946, the Commission reported, just 42 per cent of Africans between ages seven and sixteen were in school in the Cape, the province with the longest history of schooling and highest enrolment; only 27 per cent of this population attended school in Natal, where Zululand had few facilities.[17] Of pupils, three-quarters were in the first four years of school, while fewer than 3 per cent were in high school: 'The school life of a Native pupil, under a system of voluntary attendance, is relatively short, averaging about four years.'[18] The Commission found that few Africans were 'school-conscious': the only parents who reliably sent their children to school for extended periods were 'teachers, clergymen, evangelists, policemen, clerks, etc. – the intelligentsia of the Bantu population'.[19] Moreover, these educated few were too often 'subjected to foreign ideologies and doctrines'.[20]

Mission education was 'creating a modern and extremely undesirable phenomenon, viz. that group of people who break away too rapidly from the views and habits of their own people and sometimes act against their own people': in the Commission's view, the prototypical educated African 'does not contribute to building up his own people'.[21]

The Commission was particularly concerned about the developmental limitations of mission high schools. It complained that 'the present Bantu schools, though following the curricula set for European schools, are in reality vocational schools for the preliminary training of teachers and nurses', and they were failing at this task.[22] Nearly half of African secondary students were young women in the first two years of high school, most of whom pursued these careers (see Table 4).[23] Standard Eight (equivalent to the American Grade Ten) then culminated in the Junior Certificate, the prerequisite to train as a nurse or higher primary teacher.

Table 4   African students in South African high schools, 1949 (19 901 total)

Percentage and number of female students		Percentage and number of male students	
Lower secondary	**Higher secondary**	**Lower secondary**	**Higher secondary**
48.5% (9 647)	1% (201)	45.5% (9 042)	5% (1 011)

Source: Union of South Africa, *Report of the Commission on Native Education, 1949–1951 – U.G. No. 53/1951* (Pretoria: Government Printer, 1951), 122.

But too few students were passing their Junior Certificate exams, resulting in a shortage of African teachers in all provinces but the Cape and an acute shortage of African nurses across the country.[24] Matriculation then comprised the prerequisite to train as a secondary school teacher, and very few students completed Standard Ten.

Beyond high school, the situation was bleaker still. Just 400 African students in the country were attending university in 1948. 'There does not seem to be an overproduction of university graduates,' the

Commission stated dryly. 'The importance of university education for the Bantu cannot be over-emphasized, both to provide general education for leaders and to provide high-grade technical men for their future economic and social development.'[25] Only by radically expanding African access to schooling could this state of under-development be remedied. The Commission advised that the state double the number of pupils and train two and a half times as many teachers.[26]

The Commission often spoke of 'the Bantu' in neutered terms, or as male. But it did acknowledge the considerable presence of young women amongst African students in a section entitled 'Unequal Demand for Education', which dealt largely with the failure of the masses to be 'school conscious'. The Commission observed that 'the Bantu girl up to a certain stage, which varies according to the Province – from Std. VIII in Natal to Std. IV in the O.F.S. – stays longer at school than the boy'. It explained young women's apparently greater avidity for education in terms of their household economy:

> According to Bantu tradition the female is excluded from any participation in cattle farming: the daughter is accordingly valueless to the parent as a cattle-herd, while the boys have to herd the cattle and therefore cannot attend school. The Bantu are aware of the fact that education raises the economic value of the girls – as nurses or teachers they can contribute considerably to the family exchequer. The prospects of marriage are better for the educated girl as she may marry a salaried man.[27]

Apartheid officials would soon attempt to capitalise on young women's interest in schooling to advance broader developmental agendas.

As the Bantu Education Act applied its core recommendations, most Africans preparing to be teachers were female (see Table 5). It rapidly became clear that officials sought to entrust further the teaching of African children to African women. In a June 1954 parliamentary statement, Minister of Native Affairs Hendrik Verwoerd called for an African teaching workforce that was 70 per cent female. He based this argument first on maternalistic assumptions: 'Since a woman is by nature so much better fitted for handling young children and as

Table 5 African students in South African teacher training colleges, 1949 (5 228 total)

Percentage and number of students	
Female	Male
58%	42%
(3 019)	(2 209)

Source: Deborah Gaitskell, '"Doing a Missionary Hard Work . . . in the Black Hole of Calcutta": African Women Teachers Pioneering a Profession in the Cape and Natal, 1880–1950', *Women's History Review* 13, no. 3 (September 2004): 407–425, p. 421.

the great majority of Bantu pupils are to be found in the lower classes of the primary school, it follows that there should be more female than male teachers in the service.' The Department of Bantu Education would henceforth 'declare the posts of assistants in lower and, perhaps to a certain extent in higher primary schools, to be female teachers' posts. Such posts as fall vacant will not be filled by males again. At the same time a quota will be laid down for training schools to regulate the relative number of male and female candidates which may be admitted to courses.' Verwoerd was not being sentimental about women's nurturance. Like the missionaries that had pioneered women's training as 'native assistants', Verwoerd saw females as cheap labour. Employing more women – including married women – would enable the state to 'admit more children to school without a corresponding increase in the taxation of the Bantu. Male teachers receive not only a higher basic salary but also, in the case of married persons, a much higher cost of living allowance than female teachers,' Verwoerd explained.[28] Following this logic of cost efficiency, the Department of Bantu Education would 'do away entirely with the European teacher in Bantu primary schools', although whites would continue in secondary and post-secondary schools.[29] Moreover, as Anne Mager has argued, feminising teaching depoliticised it:

Young women were to be subordinated to the control of school committees, dominated by chiefs – often illiterate, government-appointed lackeys with a rigid, ethnicized mind-set. The combined patriarchal forces of the state's ethnic controls effectively ensured the disempowerment of female teachers both as women and as professionals.[30]

At the same time as Bantu Education demanded the feminisation of teaching, the state's broader developmental imperatives would demand a larger workforce of African nurses to undergird more rigidly segregated hospitals and clinics.

The black nursing workforce trebled between the mid-1940s and the mid-1950s – in response to increasing numbers of training opportunities and state hospital beds, the solution to official concerns about the health of black labourers, particularly in urban slums. In 1956, when some 3 000 black nurses were working around the country, a Select Committee vetted a proposed Nursing Amendment Bill to ensure that black nurses were not too empowered by their opportunities. Eiselen, who participated as Secretary for Native Affairs, maintained that in matters of the body as in matters of the mind, it was essential that women serve their state-defined communities. 'My Department holds the view that as far as possible there should be separate hospitals for different races. As the Bantu are the largest group, it should, in most cases, be possible to have separate hospitals for them, at any rate. Where it is uneconomic for the smaller towns to have separate units, however, the subdivisions should be clearly separate,' Eiselen stated. 'Bantu patients should be attended by Bantu nurses,' he emphasised, as 'Bantu nurses are there to perform an essential service for the Bantu community'. He adjudged that African nurses should be paid less than whites – lest an African nurse's equitable salary 'estrange her from her own community'. Nurses, like teachers, ought to serve people of their 'tribal' group in reserves.[31]

Missionaries saw their control over African social institutions eroding, giving way to a racialised developmental state. The Bantu Education Act declared that a mission school could only exist where, in the view of the Minister of Native Affairs, it did not 'preclude, retard, or render impracticable' a state school.[32] The next year, the state declared that it would nationalise all teachers' training institutions in the reserves, and that it would close those located outside.[33] In 1955, officials added that state subsidies for private schools would stop altogether in 1957.[34] Schools were not allowed to charge tuition above nominal fees for boarding or supplies, making it impossible for many to continue. At the dawn of apartheid, Inanda derived nearly half of its annual operating budget from the state, a dependence that was not atypical.[35] Many mission schools thus shut down or passed control to the state out of economic necessity. Others were forced to close for occupying a 'white spot', in contravention of the Group Areas Act.[36] By 1957, two denominations other than the American Board controlled schools. The first was the Seventh-Day Adventist Church, a minor player in African schooling that was avowedly non-political and not reliant on state aid.[37] The other was the Catholic Church, which maintained its empire of institutions by relying on its deep pockets and appealing to the respect for religious difference of the Dutch Reformed Church-dominated state.[38]

As 'separate development' unfurled following Verwoerd's 1958 ascension as prime minister, apartheid schemes of social reproduction quickly multiplied apartheid's critics – among which American Board affiliates were prominent. Albert Luthuli, an Adams man, Congregationalist preacher and Inanda father, assumed the African National Congress presidency in late 1952. Following the national Defiance Campaign Against Unjust Laws, paid-up ANC members increased from 7 000 to 100 000 between 1951 and 1953; in 1955, the ANC united with other anti-apartheid organisations in the Congress Alliance.[39] The ANC sought to confront Bantu Education with a national boycott of primary schools that began in April 1955.[40] But most young people were not prepared to risk dropping out of the state school system, as Verwoerd warned that boycotting students would not be allowed to attend state schools in the future and as the ANC did not offer a viable alternative. For parents, Luthuli saw, the choice was 'almost an impossible one – they do not want Bantu Education and they do not want their children on the streets'.[41] By late 1956, the campaign had ended in what Jonathan Hyslop has called an 'absolute and crushing defeat': during the latter half of the 1950s, enrolment in fact rose from fewer than one million children to more

than one and a half million across the country, ⟨
compulsory.[42] As the boycott folded, the Congress ⟨
massive siege from the state: 156 Congress activis
trial for treason in December 1956. The group incl⟨
most of whom, including Inanda alumna Bert⟨
members of the Federation of South African Wom⟨.., ⸺ ⟩
in August 1956 organised a march of some 20 000 women on the Union
Buildings in Pretoria against the national extension of pass laws to
African women. Other American Board affiliates among the
defendants included Z.K. Matthews, Adams' first African head in the
1920s; A.B. Ngcobo, Adams graduate and husband of Inanda alumna
Lauretta Ngcobo; and M.B. Yengwa, fiancé of Inanda alumna and
teacher Edith Sibisi.[43] After an accelerating anti-pass campaign and a
massacre of activists in March 1960, the ANC and other opposition
groups were banned – moving underground for the next three decades.

Struggles over African men's political leadership and the end of Adams College

This political context explains why Adams held the emotional final
service with which this chapter began. Adams was deeply associated
with anti-apartheid politics, and officials were plainly concerned to
neutralise the threats to apartheid order that its graduates posed, as
events preceding its takeover reveal.

Adams principal Jack Grant, a white Trinidadian, and his white
South African wife, Ida Russel Grant, had been vocal critics of apartheid
since their 1949 arrival.[44] Early in 1954, six officers came to Grant's
home with a search warrant, seeking treasonous materials – Grant
surmised that they did so on account of Luthuli's visits to Adams and
Grant's voluble criticism of the Bantu Education Act.[45] Secretary for
Bantu Education F.J. de Villiers then warned that Grant was
'endangering the future of the institution by his attitude'.[46] By the
year's end, Grant had closed Adams' teachers' training division rather
than pass it to state control. But Grant continued to pursue registration
to operate Adams' academic and industrial high schools as private,
state-aided institutions. De Villiers encouraged him to rethink that
position sometime in early 1955, around the same time that a meeting
of the chiefs and headmen of the Umlazi Magistracy condemned the
closing of the teachers' training institution at Adams and demanded

at it be reopened under state control. Grant suspected that District Inspector of Education S.R. Dent, who had been present at the meeting, persuaded the council to issue this statement. Whatever in fact occurred at this meeting, W.W.M. Eiselen – in his new capacity as Secretary for Native Affairs – told Grant in May 1955 that because of that statement, the state could not provide Adams with any further subsidies. Eiselen did extend to Grant a final option: 'Should it still be your aim "to run the two schools as entirely private schools," notwithstanding the attitude of the Bantu community and notwithstanding the desire of the Department to use this institution for teacher-training, you are, in accordance with the regulations, entitled to apply for registration as such.' Notwithstanding the dubiousness of this offer, Grant applied.[47]

In December 1955, representatives of the Native Affairs Department visited the Adams campus to discuss the school's future. Five officials were greeted by a thirteen-member delegation from the Council of Governors of Adams College – the white-dominated but interracial group that had run the school since 1940. All of the council members present were white male American Board personnel, except for Inanda teacher Agnes Wood, former Head of Adams High School Dr Donald M'timkulu and Reverend Alphaeus Zulu. Zulu had publicly condemned the Bantu Education Act upon its passage, maintaining that it 'should have been called the Bantu Development and Training Scheme Act. All it was designed to do was to teach the African that he was born to be the slave of the European.'[48] Officials refused to shake hands with M'timkulu and Zulu or to dine with them, making for an awkward visit. The visitors' words were not encouraging. Member of Parliament and chairman of the Permanent Commission of Native Affairs W.A. Maree informed Grant that applications for private schools could only be considered if 'special reasons could be presented' – for example, he suggested, it would be best that Catholic schools continued to serve Catholic children, for purely religious reasons. When Reverend Zulu and Dr Alan Taylor of McCord Hospital suggested that Adams could play a similar role as an ecumenical Protestant institution, officials dismissed this suggestion, arguing that 'Bantu community' and state schools would also have a Protestant character. The state visitors suggested, moreover, that Adams presented a threat to fundamental tenets of apartheid that the Catholic Church would not. While the Catholics agreed to comply with official restrictions on staff racial hierarchies, Maree noted with concern that Adams had previously posted Africans like M'timkulu in positions of authority over whites and that Grant avowed plans to increase African authority.[49]

Ultimately, officials objected to the facts that Adams was insufficiently segregationist in its administrative structure and insufficiently tribalist in its student base, and that it had a tradition of educating outspoken political leaders. The officials asked whence Adams' students came, and Grant indicated that just half were from Natal, provoking official concerns about Adams' service to the local 'Bantu community' – i.e., to local isiZulu-speaking Africans. It could not have helped matters that Adams graduates included politically prominent Africans not only in South Africa, but also in Bechuanaland (Seretse Khama) and Southern Rhodesia (Herbert Chitepo, Joshua Nkomo, Stanlake Samkange). Maree voiced special concern about the school's relationship with Luthuli, who had long been a member of Adams' Governing Council, about the political implications of a 'Christian and liberal education', and about Grant's views on Bantu Education, of which he admitted he fundamentally disapproved. Most seriously, officials expressed concern over recent statements of Adams College Alumni Association member Manasseh Moerane, who had circulated a letter emphasising Adams' commitment to a liberal, interracial society as a key tenet of its Christianity. Moerane epitomised the politically engaged Adams alumnus: a member of a prominent Cape family, Moerane had been a founding member of the ANC Youth League and an instrumental activist in pushing the Natal branch of the ANC leftward in the 1940s and 1950s.[50] As president of the Natal African Teachers' Union, he had condemned the Eiselen report as a 'terrifying' and 'sinister' document, and had declared that apartheid would 'divorce not only Education but the whole of the common life of the African, divorce it from the rest of South African life and shut it up in a stifling, congested bottle-neck too fantastic even to conceive'.[51] Council members tried to distance themselves from Moerane's letter – but officials found their attempts 'very unsatisfactory'.[52]

The state commission reported unfavourably on their visit and recommended that Adams' registration for private school status be rejected. De Villiers explained to Grant the rationale behind this decision in July 1956. Pragmatically, he said, the state could not operate a training school next to a missionary-run high school. On a deeper level, officials took exception to the cosmopolitanism of Adams' students. Verwoerd, De Villiers explained,

> appreciates the [Adams Governing] Council's views in connection with preparing students for responsible leadership, but considers that leaders for any particular Bantu community should be produced from within by the community itself, in relation to its needs. A heterogeneous collection of students from all over the country at any particular boarding institution must needs be unrelated to the development of community interests.[53]

The next month, De Villiers elaborated the state's rationale in a meeting with Inanda principal Lavinia Scott and American Board Africa Secretary John Reuling. As Scott's minutes described:

> Mr. de V. – The only schools refused (besides Adams) are new ones started up in opposition to the Bt. Ed. Act. Some schools have employed, even as principals, teachers who had been named under the Suppression of Com'm Act.
> Ques. – What about Adams?
> de V. – Mr. and Mrs. G. were very active in criticism of Bt. Ed. Act (earlier, not recently).
> LS – But they did not use the school as a center of opposition. It was in their personal capacity as citizens.
> de V. – Well, there is such a thing as being too liberal.
> JAR – This sounds like Thought Control. Is any criticism of Gov't ruled out? Or considered subversive?
> de V. – You must remember that we are dealing with African people, who are still largely primitive. We must be careful what they are taught.[54]

Ida Grant's screed in the liberal journal *Contact* suggested the tenor of the American Board's attitudes towards nationalisation: 'It is true that the Government intends to come in like a hermit crab to inhabit the empty shell and run its own institution on the premises, but Adams College as we have known it, will cease to be.' The piece closed with her admonition, 'Whenever again Christian principles such as truth, justice, mercy, freedom and love are sacrificed to the Moloch of Apartheid, remember that Adams was sacrificed. REMEMBER ADAMS!'[55]

Gendered consensus over African women's social service and Inanda's resilience

The American Board decided to 'remember Adams' in part by attempting to continue its traditions at Inanda: in September 1956, Scott prepared an application for Inanda to continue as an unaided private institution. Just as she was finalising the application, S.R. Dent, now Regional Director of Bantu Education, appeared at her door. As Scott reported, Dent urged her 'to reconsider our decision to apply for registration as a private school – because he thinks that we are in grave danger of being refused, and that it would be tragic for Inanda to die. He urged that the Mission should retain the hostels, and let the Government run the school.'[56] Scott informed her colleagues on the Mission Council of his counsel, but they agreed to proceed as they had planned. Dent assured her that she might still lease the school to the state and retain control of the hostels and thus some influence over the students' extracurricular life, and Scott was willing to entertain that possibility if the application was rejected.

Dent's intervention here, in a time of extreme official hostility towards missions generally and Adams in particular, reveals an openness towards missionaries at Inanda that demands explanation. Educational scholar Lynette Hlongwane has suggested that Scott's 'non-confrontational' approach enabled her to maintain this working relationship.[57] Archival evidence reveals that Scott indeed used gentler language in her official interactions than did Grant, and she encouraged other missionaries to avoid impolitic words as well.[58] But Scott had also openly opposed the Bantu Education Act since its inception, issuing a public denunciation as chair of the Natal Native Education Advisory

Board.[59] She was a close friend to Luthuli and his family.[60] Scott thus tried to maintain cordial official relations, but that cannot explain her success in maintaining control over Inanda; as a missionary who expressed ideals of non-racialism, she was inherently a political figure.

To understand Inanda's resilience, we must instead look to Inanda's and Adams' traditions of cultivating different sorts of leaders, traditions that the previous chapter explored. Adams alumni had been at the forefront of African nationalist political groups since their advent. While some Inanda alumnae had also been active in political mobilisations, the school was in the 1940s and 1950s primarily renowned for producing teachers and nurses, and Christian wives and mothers. Although it had long been co-educational and trained significant numbers of teachers and nurses, Adams was strongly associated with politically influential male alumni like Luthuli. While Adams could not exist within the society apartheid officials imagined, Inanda advanced a critical dimension of apartheid education policy: it trained women to serve in the feminised professions that sustained a divided state. Reuling foregrounded this role in a July 1954 letter to Verwoerd, affirming that Inanda

> has made a valuable contribution to the civilising and Christianizing of African home and family life, and that it has helped to establish Christian standards of life and character in the African people. Many hundreds of girls, after receiving their high school or domestic science training at Inanda, have gone on to become teachers, nurses, and home makers, and have helped to meet the great needs of their people.[61]

Scott suspected the appeal would resonate, anticipating that

> we are in a safer position than Adams, also, because we have only girls. The Gov't prefers separate education of the sexes, and also it is not likely to be so concerned about the teaching of girls as of boys. I think it quite likely that we will be ignored, or at least permitted to go on, for some time.[62]

Scott was astute in her predictions: in November 1957, Inanda received approval to continue as an unaided, private institution, and compared with state-controlled institutions it was relatively ignored.[63]

The state did police the institution, predicating Inanda's registration on the terms that 'no student will be encouraged or influenced in any direct or indirect manner to disobey or disregard any Statutory Act or section of any such Statutory Act or regulations published thereunder thus fostering disobedience to the laws of the State'.[64] Officials also required that Inanda not charge tuition beyond boarding fees and that state inspectors could examine the Inanda campus at any time. They sought to require all non-examination subjects (including religious instruction) immediately to be taught in isiZulu, with isiZulu gradually introduced in examination subjects as well. Scott worried that all of these, particularly the last, infringed upon missionaries' administrative autonomy and would complicate the American Board's already challenging task of filling missionary posts.[65] But by November 1958, Bantu Education officials withdrew their calls for Inanda to teach in isiZulu on the grounds that they were 'not yet feasible'.[66] This was a critical concession, ensuring that Inanda could continue as an English-medium institution through the apartheid years. Its excellent English instruction enabled its pupils to sit for the same school-leaving examination that white candidates took, the exam of the Joint Matriculation Board of the University of South Africa (Unisa).

Inanda's curriculum became unprecedentedly elite under the state's neglect. In 1961, after years of declining interest and staff concerns that it did not produce 'potential leaders', Inanda closed its 'technical course' – the track from which girls had married, become domestic science instructors or gone into domestic service.[67] From the early 1960s, maths and science courses became more advanced – and 'homecraft', which had been required of all students since it had replaced Latin in the late 1940s, became elective.[68]

Inanda continued to prepare many students to enter nurses' or teachers' training programmes, but increasingly students sought more. By 1965, for instance, Inanda's 324 pupils included a matriculation class of twenty-nine, who informed a delegation of the South African Association of University Women that they harboured 'ambitions for higher education and tend to the medical side – doctors, physiotherapists, radiographers, social workers, and nurses'.[69] Inanda girls who hoped to become doctors had two alumnae role models. Dr Mavis Mbambo, who had attended Inanda and the University of Natal Medical School, had received her MD in 1958.[70] Dr Vida Mungwira, who had attended Inanda, Fort Hare and Bristol University in the 1950s, became the first African female doctor in the Central African Federation in 1961.[71] Despite these predecessors, Inanda students held remarkable ambitions. In 1969, just 342 African girls in all of South Africa matriculated – less than a tenth of all African matriculants.[72] That year, matriculation became more attractive, as the South African Nursing Council made it mandatory.[73] In 1970, thirty-five Inanda students matriculated.[74]

Although state officials appeared not to notice, Inanda was also profoundly cosmopolitan. Students represented a range of religious backgrounds and came from urban and rural areas across South Africa's four provinces. The majority of Inanda students spoke isiZulu as their home language, but Inanda also continued to admit students of other ethnic backgrounds as well – unlike state schools, which segregated students on ethnic as well as racial lines, assigning children to different schools on the basis of their surnames or first languages. Staff, too, represented members of multiple ethnic, religious and national groups. African, white, Indian and 'coloured' South African staff joined with American and European appointees. Protestants and non-religious social justice activists worked alongside Catholics – including a handful of novice nuns in the late 1960s and 1970s.

But at the same time as Inanda was an island of diversity in apartheid society, it was sending some of the best-trained young women in the country into apartheid-run institutions. Inanda survived because the state depended on its graduates to help effect its plans for separate development, even as their school contravened core tenets of apartheid. Mabel Christofersen, an American missionary teacher who worked at Inanda between 1946 and 1980, argued this point in a 1979 interview. 'Ours was not such a threat because we were not training boys,' Christofersen said of the difference between Inanda's and Adams' fates. 'It was evident in some of the things that were said that they [officials] felt that the boys would be the leaders of the country. Of course we feel that the girls can do as much as the men. But that was really the reason at that time, that we weren't as much of a threat. Also by that time we were already sending enough girls to the university. The proportion of Inanda girls at the university was pretty high . . . In order to get [apartheid state-created University of] Zululand started, they sort of needed our girls. So they weren't stupid,' Christofersen said, laughing scornfully.[75] In 2008 – before stumbling upon this interview – I posed the same question, and she replied that Inanda had survived 'because we were only girls'. And, she added later in our interview, Inanda graduates were better prepared for university than their peers in state schools.[76] Roger Aylard, Inanda principal from 1970 to 1973, agreed that state officials tolerated Inanda because 'it was a girls' school . . . Girls weren't that important in the eyes of the male chauvinist pigs in the South African government', while 'Adams was really overtly political'. His former wife, Darlene Woodburn, who served as Inanda's choir director during his tenure, also emphasised that 'the goal of the school was to get those girls into university'.[77]

Indeed, Inanda's top students would comprise some of the first and best-qualified female students at the state's flagship black universities. These schools were necessary evils from the point of view of apartheid officials: while the state aimed to train small cohorts of professionals to keep state and society afloat, it desperately sought to avoid the reproduction of an assertive educated elite. As occurred elsewhere in racialised societies, this would prove an impossible balancing act: students got just enough education to enrage them that the state denied them more – tensions that would ignite in the Soweto students uprising of 1976 and the states of emergency that followed, as the next chapter explores. In the 1950s, however, apartheid officials still saw university schooling as both a promising site for social control and a mode of propaganda to hold up to a decolonising international society. Until white institutions opened admission to black students in the late 1970s, Inanda staff and students were sceptical but generally willing to make the most of apartheid-created black institutions.

When the Non-European Medical School of the white University of Natal opened in 1951 to produce black doctors for black patients, Scott observed, 'We suspect that part of the motive is to give a good example of "Apartheid" at its best – but at any rate, it's an excellent thing in itself.'[78] Dr Alan Taylor of the American Board's McCord Hospital served as its dean.[79] However 'excellent' the Natal Medical School's existence, access to medical training would remain tightly limited for black South Africans, and particularly for black women. The Natal Medical School would be the only medical training institution open to black South Africans between 1960 and 1978, and its students thus made up a tiny elite.[80] Between 1957 and 1975, just 612 students graduated from the institution. Of these, only eighty-eight were women; just thirty of these women were African.[81] Extant sources do not indicate how many of these hailed from Inanda. But significantly, the first African woman to qualify as a doctor there was Mavis Mbambo, who had matriculated from Inanda with a first-class pass in 1950.[82]

Inanda made greater contributions to the University College of Zululand, which opened in rural Ngoye in 1960 as an affiliate to the correspondence-only Unisa.[83] Its first class consisted of forty-one students. Five of these students were women, and four of these women were Inanda alumnae.[84] Other students hailed from Catholic schools, prompting Muriel Horrell of the South African Institute of Race Relations to opine that 'had these schools (which the Government refuses to subsidize) not existed, the new university colleges would have had pitifully few students'.[85] In 1964, Horrell indicated, 'Most of the women students at the University College of Zululand are from Inanda Seminary. The majority of those who do not go to this college take up nursing as a career.'[86] By 1969, at least sixty-three alumnae had attended Zululand; twenty-three were then enrolled on the male-dominated campus of 400.[87] A 1971 Inanda brochure boasted, 'The majority of recent woman graduates of the University of Zululand received their high school education at Inanda. Inanda students have become doctors, matrons, nurses, teachers, social workers and outstanding community leaders throughout Southern Africa.'[88] Through the 1960s, social service professions remained common career tracks for Inanda graduates.

These professions were growing steadily in the apartheid state: between 1946 and 1970, according to census data, the proportion of women in the African teaching force increased from 46 per cent (of some 14 000 teachers) to 62.5 per cent (of some 42 000 teachers).[89] As sociologist Leo Kuper observed scathingly in 1965, the teaching profession would soon be dominated by state-trained 'herd girls shepherding the new generations into the Bantustan kraals'.[90] Verwoerd's 1954 demand for a 70 per cent female African teaching force was nearly realised in a generation. Similarly, as a white nursing leader observed in 1965, 'no single factor contributed more to the rapid development of the non-White nursing services than the policy of separate development'.[91] While for black patients access to health care remained woefully insufficient, it was growing, and it was growing through the labours of African women: from just 800 registered nurses in 1948, there would be some 5 000 in 1960, and nearly 25 000 in 1971 – almost all women.[92] These professions nonetheless remained elite – in 1970, a third of all African women active in formal economic sectors were domestic workers, while teachers and nurses represented only 2 per cent of all formally employed women.[93]

Inanda's centenary (1869–1969) brochure, distributed at a celebration that included state officials, made a telling self-portrait of an institution that flouted apartheid ideologies yet worked openly within the state – and that resolved these contradictions through its commitment to women's education for nurturing professions. The brochure featured photographs of former ANC president Albert Luthuli addressing the campus (he had died in 1967, under circumstances for which many blamed the state); black and white children of staff smiling beside one another; liberal icon Alan Paton and a member of the Gandhi family with Inanda schoolgirls; and the multiracial staff. The brochure's sketch of Inanda's history quoted a 1959 statement from Scott affirming the school's independence. Lest the brochure's bravado alienate officials, it ended with an affirmation of Inanda graduates' social usefulness. 'The Fruit of Inanda's Teaching' listed alumnae's personal and professional roles – from being 'teachers and nurses' and 'wives and mothers', to serving as 'domestic servants, dressmakers, clerks, factory employees, and in other useful occupations'. It closed with a breathless invocation of their range of work:

'Time would fail me' to tell of Nokukhanya Luthuli, 'good
companion' to her husband Chief Albert Luthuli through many
years; of Sister Zamazulu Nkosi, first African Matron of the large
Polyclinic at Kwa Mashu; of Edith Yengwa, B.A., first African
Head Teacher at Inanda Seminary; of Nokutula Gasa, Victory
Nomvete, and Ferriel Ngcobo, Christian Education workers in
the Bantu Congregational Church; of Mrs. Ntombikaba Tantsi,
gifted wife of a leading Minister of the African Methodist Episcopal
Church; of Evelyn Lebona, B.A., wife of Dr. Lebona and a
YWCA worker with training in the United States, and now
Chief Guide in Lesotho; of Dr. Mavis Mbambo; of Sister Mavis
Xulu, Sister Hilda Gcabashe; of Matron Doris Cele of Dundee
Hospital; of Winnie Ngcobo, now studying for her Ph.D. in
Psychology at the University of Chicago; of Faith Gcabashe, B.A.,
and hundreds of other teachers steadily carrying on the work of
education at Inanda and many other schools.[94]

These contributions, it implied, justified the space officials had granted
Inanda.

Figure 16 'Life of Inanda
through the Years', in 'Inanda
Seminary: One Hundred Years,
1869–1969'. (Inanda Seminary
Campus Archive)

Figures 17 and 18 'The Present Day' and 'The Staff - 1968', in 'Inanda Seminary: One Hundred Years, 1869–1969'. (Inanda Seminary Campus Archive)

Figures 19 and 20 'The Fruit of Inanda's Teaching' and alumnae, in 'Inanda Seminary: One Hundred Years, 1869–1969'. (Inanda Seminary Campus Archive)

Manpower and 'woman-power': women's schooling and development in KwaZulu

Inanda's centenary celebrations also underscored a more direct connection between Inanda Seminary and the nascent KwaZulu Bantustan: a photograph from the event features Chief Mangosuthu Gatsha Buthelezi, absorbed in conversation with J.H. Dugard, Regional Director of Bantu Education.

Figure 21 Chief Mangosuthu Gatsha Buthelezi and J.H. Dugard, Inanda, 1969. (Photograph Collection, Inanda Seminary Campus Archive)

In 1970, Buthelezi became 'Chief Executive Officer' of KwaZulu – the non-contiguous conglomeration of African reserves within the province of Natal that apartheid planners envisioned as the home for amaZulu. That year, the Black Homelands Citizenship Act revoked Africans' national citizenship to render them 'citizens' of ethnic Bantustans. Inanda Seminary and the surrounding reserve, which was transforming into an exurban slum, joined KwaZulu.[95]

Buthelezi's engagement with Inanda posed ambiguities for American missionaries concerned with guarding their school's autonomy. In 1975, he would revive the Inkatha movement as a latter-day Zulu cultural and political organisation. Between 1976 and 1994, he would utterly dominate KwaZulu as Chief Minister of the homeland and head of Inkatha; from 1979 to 2001, he would also serve as chancellor of the University of Zululand. Like John Dube, Buthelezi came from a doubly elite background: Buthelezi was both Zulu royalty and an Adams College alumnus, attending Fort Hare briefly before being expelled for his agitation as a member of the ANC Youth League. Also like Dube, Buthelezi would have a falling-out with his erstwhile ANC colleagues: upon Inkatha's conception, most in the ANC supported the movement as an entrée to a popular anti-apartheid movement within KwaZulu, but in 1980 the ANC would publicly repudiate its support, and most anti-apartheid activists within and outside South Africa considered Buthelezi an unforgivable state collaborator.[96] Finally, like Dube, Buthelezi had familial ties to Inanda: his daughters Phumzile, Mandisi and Lethuxolo attended in the 1970s.

Inanda's operation depended increasingly on Buthelezi's patronage in the early 1970s because apartheid's 'internal decolonization' coincided with American missionaries' decolonisation of their 'benevolent empire' of Christian social institutions. The latter process was quickening in the 1960s due to the political pressures of the American civil rights movement and global decolonisation, and to the financial constraints facing foreign missions in the increasingly secular United States. From 1964, all American Board-founded institutions in South Africa became institutions of the local Bantu Congregational Church, supported by New York's United Church Board for World Ministries (UCBWM); in 1967, the Bantu Congregational Church united with the churches of the London Missionary Society and the Congregational Union of South Africa to form the United Congregational Church of Southern Africa (UCCSA). To fulfil this localising impulse at Inanda, its 'major institution in South Africa', the UCBWM passed control of Inanda's operations to a majority-black Governing Council in 1964.[97] From 1972 through 1978, Buthelezi would serve on that council.[98]

Buthelezi's influence lay in the decolonising UCBWM's unwillingness to provide the funds necessary to keep Inanda operating at the level missionaries envisioned.[99] In August 1971, the press reported that Inanda would likely close: it needed a new sanitation system and water supply, as the school had suffered a hepatitis outbreak and lacked running water. Scott's successor as principal, Roger Aylard, insisted that Inanda had no plans to close and called for support from beyond the UCBWM.[100] Buthelezi then stepped in. As chairman of Inanda's

Fundraising Sponsorship Committee, Buthelezi persuaded Mobil Oil to fund a student centre at Inanda. He presided over the building's dedication in September 1972, an opportunity he used 'to impress upon the American visitors the importance of enlightened investments in South Africa such as the new student centre'. He reflected upon his recent American tour, during which he had confronted calls for divestment, and he opined, 'Corporations such as Mobil, which felt "troubled by apartheid," had scope for helping Africans by giving money for schemes such as that at Inanda.'[101] Thanks in large part to Buthelezi's personal exertions, Inanda garnered hundreds of thousands of US dollars in donations in the early 1970s. Donors included other American corporations working in South Africa (IBM, Ford, General Motors and Coca-Cola), the South African unit of Unilever, the South African banks Barclays and Standard Bank, and the Natal Sugar Association Trust.[102] This support enabled Inanda to remain afloat at a time when Catholics were losing control over their schools to the state, for lack of funds.[103] As Inanda secured a sounder financial base, KwaZulu officials encouraged Aylard to expand enrolment first to 350 and later to 500 students.[104] This was wise, given demand: in 1971, Inanda administrators reported over 1 900 applications for eighty-six openings.[105] In 1972 and 1973, applications reportedly topped 2 000.[106]

But Buthelezi assured donors Inanda would eventually be handed over to KwaZulu; some donations, UCCSA officials observed critically, were 'conditional on this being done'.[107] In 1973, to secure the 'broad base of continuing support' necessary for expansion, Inanda's Governing Council planned to 'consult with leaders of KwaZulu regarding the School's relationship to the Territorial Authority and the possibility of its ultimate incorporation into the KwaZulu educational system'.[108] UCCSA leaders warned:

> Inanda is at present commendably so very much an alternate society in our apartheid structured national life. The enrollment reflects a cross-section of the entire country. As far as staff is concerned, it is uniquely multi-racial and without parallel. There are now five Coloured members of staff whereas previously it was only whites and Africans. Ecumenically, there has been at

Inanda the hitherto unprecedented incorporation of both Catholic staff and students. At this time when former missionary societies are withdrawing from several countries, Inanda is still able to involve both American and S.A. Churches. There is a definite fear that State Control and restrictional conformity to Nationalist Policy will follow if the school is handed over to local territorial authority – and thus end our distinctive Christian witness and stance against the segregatory structures in the state.[109]

Yet the UCCSA did not extend funding to help Inanda avoid closer homeland ties. Thus Inanda administrators discussed the possibilities of subsidies with KwaZulu officials in 1973 and 1975.[110]

Even as KwaZulu took over many of the homeland's Catholic schools, Buthelezi did not push Inanda administrators into KwaZulu governance structures in the latter half of the 1970s.[111] Buthelezi's campus engagements suggest that he came to respect Inanda's autonomy because he believed that the school was making a major contribution to 'woman-power' in KwaZulu – developing the Bantustan while costing it nothing.[112]

KwaZulu officials saw schooling for both men and women as essential to homeland development, as the 1973 'Education Manifesto of KwaZulu' revealed. Education, in KwaZulu officials' view, should provide for 'high-level manpower in modern societies': this demanded 'entrepreneurial, managerial, and administrative personnel in both public and private establishments, including educational institutions'; 'professional personnel such as scientists, engineers, architects, agronomists, doctors, veterinarians, economists, lawyers, accountants, journalists, artists, etc.'; ' "qualified" teachers, defined as those who have had a minimum of twelve years of education themselves'; 'subprofessional technical personnel such as agricultural assistants, nurses, engineering assistants, technicians, senior clerks, supervisors of skilled workers, the highest level of skilled craftsmen, and skilled clerical workers such as stenographers'; and 'top-ranking political leaders, labour leaders, judges, and officials of police and the armed forces'. But as Bantu Education instead provided the majority of KwaZulu residents with training for unskilled or semi-skilled labour, it ensured 'educational bankruptcy' in the homeland. The manifesto called for KwaZulu to provide free compulsory schooling to Standard Ten; for the restriction of isiZulu instruction to the lower primary grades, after which it would be replaced by English or Afrikaans, the languages of the labour market; and for a 'differentiated' educational system that would fulfil 'the manpower needs of KwaZulu'.[113]

The next year, Buthelezi revealed the economic stakes of 'woman-power' in a speech at the opening of Inanda's new Secretarial School, a project funded by IBM's South African branch and the Department of Bantu Education. Buthelezi was critical in mobilising support for the school, the country's first such institution for African women, and in his speech he invoked the gendered opportunities that it heralded. 'It seems more true in African Society than in any other that if you educate a man you are educating an individual, but if you educate a woman you are educating a Nation,' Buthelezi began, invoking the classic trope of missionaries, African nationalists and apartheid bureaucrats alike. But he added a twist, reflecting the changing dynamics of schooling in KwaZulu:

> Our women folk are miles ahead of our male population as in every sphere they seem to be taking to education as a duck takes to water. The only snag that one can point out has been the fact that our girls have been too confined in their ambitions. This mainly not through their own fault. The women folk have tended to seize with both hands most of the openings available to them. We boys have tended to succumb too easily to the temptation to fritter away the rather scarce opportunities available to us.

After gesturing towards women's potentially expansive professional roles, Buthelezi returned to a stereotypical invocation of women's powers – gesturing now not towards their maternal prowess, but towards their feminine allure. 'Female Secretaries apart from being the best in this field, are important as they brighten up any place wherever they are with their natural charm. Most male Secretaries can only twist arms, which is quite masculine, but crude. Female Secretaries can only make all comers wilt away before their charm and this makes a big difference,' Buthelezi added. 'I am sure our friends of IBM will confirm this from the world-wide experience of IBM!' His appeal to an international gendered consensus around women's roles in development and suitability for secretarial work complete, Buthelezi stressed the 'unlimited' openings for secretaries in homeland governments and the private sector.[114]

Figure 22 Chief Buthelezi and Inanda secretarial teacher Carroll Jacobs, opening of Inanda Secretarial School, 1974. (Inanda Seminary Campus Archive)

Buthelezi was exaggerating when he claimed that women were 'miles ahead', but he had a point that increasing numbers were 'taking to education' (see Table 6). Most African high school students in South Africa were then girls in the first two years of high school, at a time when they could train as primary teachers after two years of high school.[115]

Developmental discourses on education in KwaZulu, and the role of corporate capital in new programmes like the Secretarial School, reflect the broader gendered context of apartheid educational reforms in the 1970s. White capitalists and homeland leaders looked to schooling to make separate development work – entailing growing opportunities in feminised professions.[116]

Table 6 High school students in KwaZulu, 1972–1976

Year	Percentage and number of female students		Percentage and number of male students		Total high school students
	Lower secondary	Higher secondary	Lower secondary	Higher secondary	
1972	49.5% (13 124)	3.5% (899)	41.5% (10 970)	5.5% (1 502)	26 495
1973	50% (15 291)	4% (1 153)	41% (12 710)	5% (1 648)	30 802
1974	49% (17 294)	4% (1 487)	41% (14 436)	6% (2 078)	35 295
1975	49.5% (23 659)	4% (1 901)	41% (19 580)	5% (2 609)	47 749
1976	51% (39 350)	3% (2 522)	42% (32 379)	4% (3 027)	77 278

Source: C.T. Verwey, P.D. Carstens and A. du Plessis, with E.B. Gumbi, *Statistical Review of Education in KwaZulu, 1979–1984* (Bloemfontein: Research Institute for Education Planning, University of the Orange Free State, 1985), 2.

'We felt like we were citizens of the world': the possibilities of women's schooling in apartheid South Africa

But if officials believed that these educated women would subsidise the social costs of reproducing an ethnically divided society, Inanda students hoped to reproduce the world of possibilities that the New Africans discussed in the previous chapter had envisioned, and which apartheid was labouring to foreclose. Women who became the most forceful rebels against apartheid in the 1960s entered school expecting to become teachers, nurses or social workers, following their families' example or advice. Political activist, doctor and anthropologist Mamphela Ramphele has aptly summarised the expectations of most black South Africans then: 'Most people in our village assumed that one automatically became a teacher or nurse if one did well at school, or a policeman or labourer if one did not.'[117] Their rebellion came out of their engagement in the politicised institutions that were the necessary evils of apartheid governance: elite high schools and post-secondary institutions.

The University of Fort Hare was a core site of politicised nostalgia, where students commemorated the litany of New Africans who had studied at their school in the years before apartheid by resisting nationalisation at every step.[118] In the 1950s and early 1960s, young women from Inanda who went on to Fort Hare found that it completed the incipient 'conscientisation' that they had cultivated in high school. Lauretta Ngcobo, a third-generation Inanda student, attended Inanda (1945–1949) and the University of Fort Hare (1950–1954) to train as a teacher – like her mother and grandmother, as the previous chapter described. But at Fort Hare, she encountered a world of cosmopolitan students, engaging in rollicking debates: 'I will never forget how penetrated my mind was by these discussions. I was meeting intellectuals for the first time. It was a most exhilarating time,' she told me, with passion in her voice. 'I got my political education at Fort Hare.' As the first woman from her rural village to attend university, and one of relatively few women at the male-dominated university, she asserted herself in these discussions, despite an initial sense of gendered intimidation. After receiving her BA, she married A.B. Ngcobo, a Pan-Africanist Congress activist, with whom she went into exile in London in 1962; she became an activist, a teacher and later an author of feminist anti-apartheid novels.[119] During the nationalisation of Fort Hare in 1959 and the banning of major political parties in 1960, Inanda alumnae encountered a more radicalising climate, as administrators clamped down on this world of debate Ngcobo described.[120] Manto Tshabalala-Msimang (known at Inanda as Edmie Mali), daughter of an alumna and a descendant of a member of Inanda's first class, and Ivy Matsepe-Casaburri, the daughter of teachers, came to Fort Hare from Inanda in 1959 to prepare for teaching careers.[121] Matsepe-Casaburri taught at Inanda from 1961 to 1963 before joining the ANC in exile (working with the Women's League) and earning a PhD in English at Rutgers University in New Jersey.[122] Tshabalala-Msimang joined the ANC in 1963, trained as a doctor in the Soviet Union and worked in military camps.[123]

From personal or family backgrounds in nursing and social work, young women also found possibilities for personal and political transformation. Bongekile (Makhoba) Dlomo attended Inanda (1951–1952) and then nurses' training at McCord Hospital (1953–1957) to fulfil the dreams of her semi-literate parents, who worked as subsistence farmers, and her grandfather, who worked on the Johannesburg mines. Her grandfather had seen the material benefits of schooling in the lives of mine clerks, many of whom were proud Ohlange men. Dlomo herself dreamed of becoming a nurse, the most useful and prestigious profession she could envision: 'I always wanted to be a nurse. I liked looking after people. As a child I had always admired how nurses carried themselves, their smart uniforms.' Dlomo's politicisation followed directly from her nursing career and marriage to ANC stalwart Albert Dlomo: she attended meetings in opposition to the new racialised nursing registers in 1957 and joined her husband in London in 1972, where she worked as a nurse and as an ANC Women's League leader.[124] Her turn from nursing to activism was not unique. Dudu Mfusi, for instance, matriculated from Inanda in 1957 and then trained as a nurse at King Edward Hospital before joining Umkhonto we Sizwe, the ANC's armed wing, in 1961.[125] ANC activists Albertina Sisulu and Adelaide Tambo also trained as nurses, while Winnie Mandela took a post as a social worker at Soweto's Baragwanath Hospital in the 1950s.[126]

Barbara Masekela attended Inanda (1956–1960) on the recommendation of her mother, who had trained as a social worker at the American Board's Hofmeyr School. Masekela studied at Inanda during a time of deepening staff and student politicisation. Her isiZulu teacher, Edith Sibisi Yengwa, gave covert lessons in ANC history; she would become Inanda's first black Head Teacher in 1966 and go into political exile soon thereafter.[127] As school chairperson, Masekela provided cover for classmates such as Joyce Sikhakhane to sneak off campus on weekends for Durban meetings of the African Students Association, which opposed apartheid schooling.[128] Sikhakhane, who, like Masekela, was from Johannesburg, had participated in the ANC's Bantu Education boycotts and became a pioneering journalist in the early 1960s.[129] Masekela and Sikhakhane refused to attend apartheid universities, pursuing schooling abroad and working with the ANC.

While these women took on the state by joining exiled political movements, others remained in South Africa and joined a class of nurturing professionals – a class with a history, and a class that they believed would be critical in helping themselves, their families and their communities survive apartheid. Their acute senses of self-efficacy, rooted in expansive understandings of their roles in social reproduction, more subtly challenged a racialised patriarchy. Lindiwe (Gumede) Baloyi attended Inanda (1960–1964) in the footsteps of her aunt Emmeline Gumede, who had graduated from Inanda in the mid-1920s to become a teacher, school inspector and pillar of her family. Aunt Emmeline, who never married, instead stayed in her father's house as 'an engine that was really driving everybody': she had subsidised the education of her six siblings, supported her brother through medical school in the United Kingdom and even helped to contract her nephews' marriages – assuming a male role in her *kholwa* family, whose home became a gathering place for ANC political meetings during Baloyi's childhood. Baloyi came to appreciate the 'independent' spirit that Inanda fostered in her as well. Studying debate and history with Matsepe-Casaburri, Baloyi came to 'understand more of politics'. Her teacher 'had a very broad vision of how the political climate is and what it is and looking at other countries and also encouraging us to read about other places'. When Matsepe-Casaburri left Inanda in 1963 to fight with the ANC in exile, Baloyi did not follow her. She instead trained as a social worker at the University of Zululand and worked in child welfare services in Durban, carrying on in her aunt's tradition of social leadership. But with her salary, Baloyi asserted herself in her personal life, sending her children to historically white schools as soon as they opened to black students in the 1980s. She saw herself as both living up to her ancestors' values and charting her own course: 'I do what I want, any time, and I bring up my children the way I was brought up and that basis was because I went to a very good school, a powerful school that could make me stand on my own two feet.'[130] Gloria (Mbalula) Malindi attended Inanda (1962–1964) following the example of her own influential aunt. The intellectual curiosity that Malindi developed as a student pushed her to train as a nurse at the state-run Baragwanath Hospital (1965–1968). Her schooling gave her 'self-dependence' and the 'self-esteem and self-confidence to say, "Don't be reliant on the male component"' in her personal and professional life.[131]

Compared with participation in the liberation struggle, the development of such qualities may seem a small achievement. But the sense of self that Baloyi and Malindi described was precisely the object of student politics in the late 1960s. The career of Steve Biko reveals how students beyond Inanda also used the educational space that apartheid policy allowed to think their way out of apartheid, a move that they recognised as deeply political. 'Born shortly before 1948, I have lived all my conscious life in the framework of institutionalised separate development,' Biko wrote in 1970. 'My friendships, my love, my education, my thinking and every other facet of my life have been carved and shaped within the context of separate development.'[132]

Indeed, Biko's formal schooling took place within the limited elite spaces that apartheid allowed: he attended high school at St Francis College, Mariannhill – the Catholic institution in Natal – and went on to the University of Natal Non-European Medical School in Durban. It was in these classrooms – and at meetings of the University Christian Movement, which formed in 1967 as a multiracial, ecumenical group, and which officials tolerated because it was a religious rather than overtly political organisation – that Biko and his peers began to cultivate a new political subjectivity they called Black Consciousness. Rejecting the values of black inferiority that undergirded separate development, they refashioned themselves as agentive beings with 'faith in themselves and in the promise, ultimately, of a future', as Daniel Magaziner has eloquently summarised.[133] As Biko put it, they realised that the first step to political transformation was

> to make the black man come to himself; to pump back life into his empty shell; to infuse him with pride and dignity, to remind him of his complicity in the crime of allowing himself to be misused and therefore letting evil reign supreme in the country of his birth. This is what we mean by an inward-looking process. This is the definition of 'Black Consciousness.'[134]

Black Consciousness expanded through a student-generated institutional framework: the first meeting of the all-black South African Students' Organisation (SASO) convened at Mariannhill in December 1968, and Biko became the group's first president; SASO soon attracted black university students from around the country. Core principles of Black Consciousness – that African, Indian and multiracial South

Africans should think critically about the racial hierarchy in which they lived, reject their non-white statuses for a unifying 'Black'-ness and position themselves as agents for change – fast attracted high school and primary students.

Black Consciousness was at its inception a male-led project, in which the black agent of change was presumed male in the first instance, and in which female SASO activists endured casual sexism from their male comrades in their personal encounters and in the pages of SASO's newsletter.[135] But male activists believed that their project of resurrecting black men could not take place if black women did not inculcate Black Consciousness at the grassroots – prompting men to encourage women's public health, educational and economic development work, in a gendered division of political labour that would have been familiar to New Africans.[136] And as Black Consciousness ideologies spread, female students engaged actively in local groups. In Soweto, Clive Glaser found that '[g]irls participated widely in student politics during the 1970s (if only very rarely in leadership positions). This was not altogether surprising given the greater numbers of girls at school and their relative confidence within school, as opposed to street, culture. School was the most important collective environment for teenage girls.'[137]

Male SASO activists Saths Cooper, Strini Moodley and Barney Pityana visited Inanda regularly in the late 1960s and early 1970s, guiding students in writing and performing to help them become 'aware' of their world and their place in it, as alumna Thoko (Mbanjwa) Mpumlwana recalled.[138] From 1969 to 1972, SASO was headquartered on the Durban campus of the University of Natal Medical School (known as the Black Section from 1970), facilitating opportunities for aspirant doctors to combine premedical training with politics. The 1969 alumna Nozizwe Madlala-Routledge, for instance, worked with Biko through the medical school's programme at the Gandhi Settlement; she enrolled at the medical school, and later became an ANC and South African Communist Party activist.[139]

Inanda administrators nonetheless refused to allow SASO to begin a branch on campus: 'If you got your name on a government list, there was no way you would get into the University of Zululand, which was the only African university really open to them, and our goal was to get the girls into university,' explained Darlene Woodburn, Inanda teacher and choir director (1968–1973).[140] When Inanda students formed a Black Consciousness group called the Junior African Students' Congress in June 1971, administrators banned it and expelled its leaders.[141] But Roger Aylard, Inanda principal from 1970 to 1973, recalled a cordial relationship between activists and Inanda staff. He claimed that when students threatened to boycott state exams,

> I had Steve Biko come over and talk to them, and explain, you know, what we were about, and the fact that they would lose everything, the government would not allow them to take an exam, if they boycotted. That is was going to hurt them more than anything they could do to solve the problem of examinations in South Africa.[142]

Aylard's successor, Dumi Zondi, also did not encourage political organisation on his campus. But he deepened Inanda students' links to Black Consciousness activists at the University of Natal during his tenure (1974–1976). With Fatima Meer, the first black woman lecturer appointed at a white university in South Africa, Zondi founded a Black Consciousness research group called the Institute for Black Research at the University of Natal. Zondi regularly brought his students to sit in on Meer's sociology courses. Meer was impressed, Zondi recalled, at how Inanda girls 'took over' discussions. 'What do you do to these girls? They almost took over the meeting, the leadership,' Meer said to him. Zondi suggested that Inanda students displayed such leadership outside their campus because his staff allowed them 'the freedom to say what they want and how they feel'.[143] In early 1976, Zondi contributed an article about Inanda to a new journal of the Institute for Black Research, in which he underscored Inanda's diversity: 'The teaching staff is racially integrated and salaries are paid according to qualification and not colour of one's skin.' He hoped that Inanda's student base might become more diverse, too: 'Inanda hopes that in the near future she will be able to admit black students of other black groups.'[144] That journal also featured articles by Winnie Mandela and Maurice Lewis, who would succeed Zondi as principal.

It would not survive to produce a second issue – Meer, Mandela and other members of the editorial would be banned after June 1976.[145]

While continuing to prepare students for state-run institutions, other staff covertly incorporated 'conscientisation' into the curriculum. Carohn Cornell, a young white graduate of the University of the Witwatersrand, came to Inanda through her connection with the liberal, ecumenical Grail movement.[146] She taught English at Inanda from 1968 to 1970, seeing that Inanda students' pursuit of an elite, English-medium education 'was essentially political'. As she explained to me, 'The way it worked was, it was us – staff and students – against them – Bantu Education authorities. Because it was a private school, but it was still under inspection by the Bantu Education inspectors, who were white and hostile.' She recalled students singing a praise song to commemorate Bantu Education ideologue Hendrik Verwoerd's 1966 assassination, as 'Verwoerd was personally hated'. Cornell built upon and sought to deepen not only her students' political consciousness, but also their self-confidence, through dramatic role play. 'When you are in a role as Verwoerd, or you know, the pigs in *Animal Farm*,' Cornell found, 'you can just come into your own, and be anyone's equal there.' Such role-playing prompted furtive action on the occasion of an unscheduled, and terrifying, visit of a state school inspector. 'Suddenly, there was this man who was coming to inspect my classroom. And I had to walk with him across campus to my classroom, remembering that the walls were papered with things about freedom, because we'd been doing *Animal Farm* as an extra, it wasn't on the syllabus,' Cornell recalled. 'And we came up the stairs and into the classroom, and the walls were clear – everything, the kids had taken everything down, and I launched into a lesson we had done previously, which was about something completely innocuous. And they played along like you wouldn't believe, as if it were new to them, just played along.' She showed me these and other yellowed quotations with which she had decorated her classroom: ' "The Dream Deferred", things like this hung up all over the place. These are probably the ones that students pulled down before the inspector came ... What you see is a sort of religious-political thing running through.' Cornell also 'did a whole theme on "black is beautiful" ', during which she distributed 'articles against skin lighteners'.[147] She was not alone in this campaign: her student Nozizwe Madlala confirmed, 'Many of the girls, like most black girls in South Africa at the time, used skin lightening creams in pursuit of a white skin, even if it was just your face. Our teachers were concerned about this and wanted us to see why it was not right.'[148]

In such classrooms students developed expansive subjectivities, capable of situating the indignities of apartheid within broader analytical frames – even if most did not revolt overtly against the state. Cornell's student Khosi Mpanza, who came from rural Natal to Inanda from 1964 to 1969, best summarised their position: 'We felt like we were citizens of the world. Nothing could keep us back,' she told me boldly. Yet, she added in the next breath, 'I doubt that in those years we really thought we would go far out into the world – apartheid, in a way, always made it just about possible, not quite.' But by reading extensively – poring over materials from banned books by African novelists and on the American civil rights/Black Power movement, to newspapers and magazines from South Africa and the United States – Inanda students readied themselves intellectually for an uncertain future. 'Inanda Seminary allowed you to open your mouth and say something, just open your mouth and say something. And we learned a lot, because in the course of that freedom, that flexibility, we tested out ideas,' she emphasised of her favourite classes, world history and English. 'So in a sense you learned to be critical and be criticised.'

Students applied these skills in debate tournaments amongst themselves and with other schools. Most memorably, 'one school was Kearsney Boys School, all white, and we beat them!' Mpanza emphasised that she and her classmates knew that 'we could hold our own, against anyone. It's a pity that we were growing up in a situation that was just loaded against us, you know, so we always had to limit our aspirations.' She recalled her classmate Baleka Mbete, a committed student of anti-apartheid politics, constantly reminding her, 'Ooh, the world is not an island like Inanda Seminary. There is a whole world out there and you are going to see what is happening.' Mbete joined the ANC in exile after graduating. But Mpanza trained as a teacher and librarian at the University of Zululand, a male-dominated apartheid institution where she had to draw on Inanda's lessons in self-possession and resilience – in what she called the 'stillness' that teachers like Cornell sought to instil in them. Mpanza returned to work as Inanda's librarian from 1974 to 1978, empowering her students through reading and debate. She explained:

> Nobody ever thought, you know, apartheid would end. But we were preparing ourselves, we were preparing to know how to maneuver, you know, and manipulate – we were not even going to manipulate the system, but we were going to survive the system, you know, we were going to survive the system, we were amassing a lot of personal weaponry – what do you know, what are you going to give when you get to the world out there? So by that time we understood apartheid, we understood its viciousness, but we also realised that the only way is to be educationally prepared.[149]

Inanda students' writing reveals that they were not only cognisant of the world beyond their campus, but also believed that they could change it. In her 1966 application, Baleka Mbete described this goal in old-fashioned terms: 'I like education devotedly, and am determined to continue my education as much as I possibly can. I want to encourage my people (Africans) and uplift them. I pray God to use me as an instrument for improving his people. There are some who are still in the dark, who need me to show them the way.'[150] In Inanda's campus newspaper in 1971, matriculant Faith Duma articulated a more expansive role of women's potential. 'Women have been considered as feeble inferior beings who either chain themselves to what their families need or become a nurse, a secretary or any of the "feminine" occupations,' Duma complained. 'I, being a woman, can be a mother of the nation, but, due to birth control, I should be aware of the gift of time which modern medicine has conferred on me. When my children are at school, what is there for me to do in a home besides cleaning it? I think I will have to go out and put my knowledge and skills to the service of my community. Through this, women see the need of being educated.' Duma's screed – which combined a homage to second-wave Western feminism with language of upliftment that would have been familiar to New Africans – concluded with a challenge to patriarchy:

As the slogan 'Men Only' is dying, some men try by every means to stop women from contributing to society, especially to the working part of it. They belittle their professional abilities – glorify their role as wives and mothers – which is quite good of course – and use various other means to undermine women's careers. By this, they do not realise that they are compelling women to go on contributing to society, to prove how good they really are. I, as a woman, should not believe that I have no separate identity, for my knowledge and skills are needed in the development of my society.[151]

Through education, other Inanda students agreed, young women might effect greater control over their own future, and that of South Africa.

They belied the assumptions of separate development by assuming responsibility for their *own development* and for that of the *world* beyond their campus. As Head Prefect Khathija Phili reflected, 'Inanda has made me a woman. Inanda has taught me to think. It has made me realise that I have a role to play in society; that as a woman I have rights to fight for; that I have the world to be responsible to and perhaps even for. Most of all, I have been brought to face the stark reality of our country.'[152] Nomvuyo Qubeka, a Secretarial School student, thought through the implications of these responsibilities in a bold article on 'The Place of Women's Liberation in Society', which began with a quote from Samora Machel on women's double subordination under 'reactionary traditions' and capitalism. Qubeka contended:

Never has it been proved that women are less intelligent than men, the only reason for women occupying less high positions is that they have not completely overcome their initial belief that they are inferior to men. Women not only form half the oppressed people, but they are the most humiliated and exploited beings in society. Women's Liberation in society aims at stimulating awareness in females' locked-up ideas . . . Liberation does not mean liberated in action only, but also in the mind. People should be what they are, men should be free from female domination. Women's Liberation deals with problems affecting the whole structure of society.

Qubeka invoked women as diverse as prime ministers Indira Gandhi and Golda Meir, African American federal judge Constance Baker Motley, and South Africa's lone opposition parliamentarian, Helen Suzman, as exemplars of women's 'intelligence' and 'high status, some higher than that of men and others at the same level with them'.[153]

These critical attitudes caused students difficulty in apartheid institutions. When Mpanza's classmate Esther (Cele) Sangweni entered the University of Zululand in 1970, she became 'very angry, for a long time'. She explained to me that Inanda was an 'island', and after leaving that island students 'realised that the life you had lived at Inanda wasn't real. Many of us were traumatised when we got out, because life wasn't as it was at Inanda . . . Whereas at Inanda, we were encouraged to express ourselves, we were encouraged to be independent. Now the South Africa of the 1960s, 1970s, 1980s, did not want that. You couldn't express yourself at all.' She became 'very angry with the Seminary, in that they didn't expose us' sufficiently to the gendered and racialised challenges that alumnae would confront. 'We didn't know anything about boys! We didn't know anything about the fact that we were second-class citizens!' Inanda, she said,

taught us to be independent, to be able to think independently – although, for some time, we couldn't use that. Especially at university. At university, no one wanted to know what your opinion was, about anything. So we just sat there and took whatever the lecturers gave us. But of course those lessons had already been learned, so that when we came out of university, we could be ourselves again. So we had that advantage over the other students, in that they had been groomed from small to be subservient, not to express themselves, whereas we knew how to express ourselves, even though for four years we were not allowed to.

She returned to Inanda as an English teacher from 1974 to 1979, teaching her students about the low expectations that they would need to transgress beyond Inanda's bounds. She later became a professor of English at the University of Zululand, communicating similar lessons.[154] As Sangweni's classmate Kho (Nduli) Zimu recalled, Inanda 'used to give us very high standards, *ehhe* [yes], and we were aware that was the demand, out there. Unfortunately, when we came out, we did not find that. We were the epitome instead. *Hawu!* [No way!] Instead of being led by people to get up to those high standards, no, we were the ones to bring up the others.'[155] After graduating from the University of Zululand, Zimu also returned to Inanda to teach, helping to connect younger students to the realities that confronted them.

Cecilia (Mvelase) Khuzwayo, who attended Inanda from 1966 to 1970, also found the University of Zululand to be a shockingly repressive climate. But at Inanda, '[t]he American missionaries and the South African staff both made us believe in who we are. They taught me that God made me a human being equal to any other human being made in this world, I am made in God's image, therefore I cannot be less than anyone.' She found that her education made her receptive to Black Consciousness student groups at Zululand: 'When they said "Black man, you are on your own", that fitted in very nicely with the teachings I had at Inanda that I am made in the image of God, so I am equal to anyone.' She quickly joined SASO, as well as a local consciousness-raising group that would 'teach each other about what was happening in the rest of Africa. We realised that we were being cut off from the rest of the world.' Her lecturers were 'very conservative' and particularly hostile to female students in the commercial track, which Khuzwayo pursued:

> Since I was eleven years old I had an aspiration to be an African manager, because I saw that there were not many. It was difficult for me in Zululand. We had reached a climax at Inanda; when we went to Zululand we took a dive. The education there wasn't as good as at Inanda; the lecturers came out of Bantu Education schools, and the attitude of the professor was that we were going to fail Economics; his attitude was, "We are going to fail this girl". But Inanda made a difference – at Inanda they told me nothing is difficult, if I put my head to it, so I did not believe that Economics was difficult.

She excelled in her courses, landing jobs in finance and management with Anglo American and Unilever in the 1970s and 1980s. She maintained a defiant sense of self-efficacy: 'Once I went to Inanda, nobody could tell me I'm inferior because I'm black, and I was not willing to take any nonsense from anyone in terms of logic. I had a number of spates with some policemen.'[156]

As alienated as Inanda students felt due to their unique experiences, their *ambition* for education as a route to personal and social transformation was not unique. Students who had been 'groomed from small to be subservient' in state schools could hold similar visions.[157] Mamphela Ramphele's life vividly shows how young women perceived the limited spaces for elite professional achievement that apartheid allowed, and from those spaces pushed against the boundaries of separate development. Ramphele grew up in the northern Transvaal, where she attended a Dickensian state-controlled boarding school in which she 'felt intellectually under-stimulated most of the time' from 1962 to 1964.[158] Although all but one of the other young women at her school pursued teacher's training, and her sister chose nursing, Ramphele harboured an ambition to become a doctor, which she fulfilled at the University of Natal Medical School (graduating in 1972): 'The little I had heard about doctors suggested that medicine could offer me the greatest professional freedom and satisfaction. It was not the desire to serve which influenced my career choice, but the passion for freedom to be my own mistress in a society where being black and woman defined the boundaries within which one could legitimately operate.'[159] She nonetheless found that as a black female professional, '[o]ne's entire life becomes dedicated to national service'.[160]

Conclusion

The expansion and feminisation of African schooling constituted a central goal of apartheid education policy, as apartheid ideologues believed that women played critical roles in the social reproduction of a divided society. The feminisation of schooling was not, as scholars have recently claimed, 'an ironic effect of Bantu Education', which 'unintentionally addressed gender inequalities by producing high participation rates by African girls'.[161] Rather, like missionaries before them, apartheid planners believed that developing women as nurturing professionals would enable them to effect profound societal transformations on a shoestring and therefore encouraged increasing numbers of young women to train as teachers and nurses. This was a key reason that Inanda avoided nationalisation in the 1950s and 1960s: Inanda staff were fulfilling apartheid planners' goals of producing teachers and nurses so well that the state was never compelled to take it over. As Inanda grew more elite in the 1970s, Bantustan officials and corporate philanthropists saw educated women as fulfilling their efforts to make separate development work. The gendered irony of Bantu Education lay in its upshot: as schooling expanded and feminised, educated women grew unwilling to fulfil the narrow roles that apartheid bureaucrats had imagined for them. These ironies would accelerate at Inanda and around South Africa after 1976.

CHAPTER FIVE

Educated African Women
in a Time of Political Revolution
1976–1994

In June 1976, Sikose Mji was training as a secretary at Inanda, in the course that had been launched with funding from American corporations avoiding divestment and with the support of KwaZulu leader Mangosuthu Gatsha Buthelezi. But Mji was not interested in using her schooling to sustain the society that existed beyond Inanda, a society that capitalists and elites like Buthelezi structured. She came from a political family, who had sneaked her into 'coloured' schools and to Lesotho for a decade of schooling; her father was a doctor and had been a pioneering member of the African National Congress (ANC) Youth League, and her brother was a South African Students' Organisation (SASO) leader. Mji chose Inanda to 'become broad minded as well as to be more able to understand the people with whom we live in everyday life'.[1] She soon declared her ambition to replicate her campus in the world beyond, in a searing poem in Inanda's newspaper:

> Living in a world of their own
> you'd think they're the happiest in the world
> not knowing that they suffer
> suffer during their holidays . . .

> . . . Outside Inanda is the real world
> a world that challenges the African girl
> a world that challenges humanity
> a world outside Inanda Seminary

So permanently you're faced with reality
permanently you have to fight
and permanently you are faced with
a challenge
a challenge of building another Inanda Seminary
but this time outside Inanda
for the world of Inanda is not your world.[2]

Inanda gave Mji the political space to articulate a critique of the social order to which her training was supposed to contribute. But making this critique was not enough: she abandoned her studies shortly after this poem appeared to join in the Soweto student protests, after which she joined the ANC and studied in Zambia.[3]

The Soweto protests, through which Mji sought to create a new world beyond Inanda's bounds, emerged directly out of the rapid expansion of black schooling, through which apartheid ideologues had believed they could develop a divided society. Mass schooling created volatile new public spheres, in which students demanded real education, in line with Black Consciousness ideals. On 16 June 1976, police opened fire on Soweto students marching in protest against Afrikaans-language instruction and the broader system of Bantu Education, leading to bloody riots that left at least 600 people dead in Soweto and a schools boycott that stretched into 1977. By the South African spring of 1977, a quarter of a million students around the country were on strike and some 600 teachers in Soweto had resigned. Steve Biko was murdered by the police in September 1977 and SASO was banned the next month. Demands for divestment and sanctions grew; as South Africa's pariah status deepened, the country sank into an economic morass.[4]

Official investigations into the Soweto uprisings noted young women's participation, but, as Clive Glaser observed, evidence on the forms of and reasons for their involvement remained 'extremely thin and impressionistic'.[5] Scholars are only beginning to explore young women's roles in the Soweto unrest and ensuing protests, and to ask why these roles have been silenced in official and popular narratives.[6] As we ask new questions about female participation in student politics, we must also ask a more basic question: why, in this time of intensifying unrest, were rising numbers of young women staying in school? This question has seldom been asked or answered, but it demands explanation: we must understand young women's educational visions to understand what they sought to achieve by participating – or not participating – in student protests and boycotts.[7]

This chapter situates young women's strategies within the context of the volatile late-apartheid state, within which their access to education expanded dramatically. The tentative reformist measures that Pretoria bureaucrats and 'homeland' rulers had pursued from the early 1970s deepened after 1976, as these leaders extended reforms with one hand and repression with the other. As officials granted new benefits to teachers and nurses from the late 1970s, and as historically white schools and corporate professions opened to a male and female black elite in the 1980s, the most educated African women seized these reforms to push for transformations in their lives, and in their country. Yet at the same time that the African educated elite feminised, schooling was becoming a site of political crisis and gender-based violence was becoming epidemic – as young men at many schools responded to apartheid's dehumanisation by asserting their control over women. Schooling promised new degrees of personal and social mobility for the most successful female students. But many were bitterly disappointed, as they came of age amidst the implosion of the racialised patriarchy that was apartheid.

The post-1976 expansion of African women's schooling

Enrolment figures suggest that young women found compelling reasons to stay in school in a time of revolution. Female students in the final high school grades rose after 1976 – absolutely and relatively, in an era of the 'massification' of schooling.[8] But access remained limited, with just 38 per cent of fifteen- to nineteen-year-old African girls in high school in 1980 (see Tables 7 and 8).[9]

Only 5 per cent of all African adults had matriculated in 1985, compared to 52 per cent of white women and 59 per cent of white men.[10] As late as 1991, less than half of the African population had a Grade Six (Standard Four) education.[11] But African matriculants rose

Table 7 African female students in South Africa, 1975–1985

| Year | Percentage and number of female African students | | | |
	Lower primary	Higher primary	Lower secondary	Higher secondary
1975	48.7% (1 151 100)	52.5% (532 000)	55.3% (161 000)	39.2% (10 700)
1980	48.9% (1 386 600)	52.2% (640 200)	55.7% (359 800)	50.1% (64 100)
1985	48.8% (1 597 100)	52.2% (807 200)	55.4% (513 700)	54.5% (145 200)

Source: Elaine Unterhalter, 'The Impact of Apartheid on Women's Education in South Africa', *Review of African Political Economy* 48 (Autumn 1990): 66–75. Based on census figures.

Table 8 High school students in KwaZulu, 1975–1984

| Year | Percentage and number of female students | | Percentage and number of male students | | Total high school students |
	Lower secondary	Higher secondary	Lower secondary	Higher secondary	
1975	49.5% (23 659)	4% (1 901)	41% (19 580)	5% (2 609)	47 749
1976	51% (39 350)	3% (2 522)	42% (32 379)	4% (3 027)	77 278
1977	50% (49 905)	3.5% (3 457)	42% (41 703)	4% (3 960)	99 025
1978	49% (60 690)	4% (5 109)	42% (51 873)	4% (5 242)	122 914
1979	47% (64 696)	6% (8 014)	41% (56 170)	6% (8 009)	136 889
1980	45% (67 547)	8% (11 475)	40% (59 112)	7% (10 697)	148 831
1981	43.5% (70 148)	10.5% (17 007)	37% (59 932)	9% (14 065)	161 152
1982	41% (76 120)	13% (24 457)	35% (64 957)	10% (18 487)	184 001
1983	42% (83 618)	12% (24 200)	36% (71 425)	9% (18 103)	197 346
1984	42% (87 427)	13% (27 002)	36% (74 914)	10% (20 752)	210 095

Source: C.T. Verwey, P.D. Carstens and A. du Plessis, with E.B. Gumbi, *Statistical Review of Education in KwaZulu, 1979–1984* (Bloemfontein: Research Institute for Education Planning, University of the Orange Free State, 1985): 3–4.

tenfold over the 1970s: from fewer than 3 000 in 1970, to over 30 000 in 1980. Nearly three times as many African students (about 87 000) matriculated in 1984.[12] Growing numbers of students were continuing on to university (see Table 9).[13]

Table 9 African female university students in South Africa, 1977–1985

Year	Percentage and number of female students	
	Universities	Teacher training colleges
1977	27% (2 902)	63% (10 388)
1981	40% (8 131)	64.5% (9 213)
1985	44% (19 025)	55% (10 335)
1990	53% (50 323)	64.2% (22 987)

Sources: M. Saleem Badat, *Black Student Politics, Higher Education, and Apartheid: From SASO to SANSCO, 1968–1990* (Pretoria: HSRC Press, 1999), 202; and ANC Women's League, *Status of South African Women: A Sourcebook in Tables and Graphs* (Marshalltown, South Africa: ANC Women's League Policy Division, 1993). Teachers' training figures for 1977 exclude Transkei; for 1981, Transkei, Venda and Bophuthatswana; and for 1985 and 1990, all of the 'independent' Bantustans.

Young women's rising school attendance after 1976 was remarkable. Schooling was not compulsory for Africans, and school strikes were sweeping the country. Most alarmingly, many schools were sites of gendered violence. As Robert Morrell and Relebohile Moletsane have described, 'Township youth in and out of school were reported to be engaging in rape. No longer a feature of one-on-one encounters, rape often became a social, peer-approved action designed to affirm masculinity in an extreme physical, heterosexual manner.'[14]

This violence grew out of the gendered crises characterising late-apartheid patriarchies, and it fuelled the incipient HIV/AIDS epidemic. As Mark Hunter has pointed out, 'the unravelling of both apartheid and the male-led family were inextricably linked'.[15] Although state policies had been undermining men's authority over their lives and those of their families since the coming of colonial capitalism, apartheid was predicated on absent male migrants' roles as heads of their family homes in ethnic homelands.[16] But marriage rates fell steadily as 'separate development' unfolded (see Table 10).

Table 10   The apartheid-era decline
in marriage rates

Year	Percentage of Africans over age fifteen who are married
1960	57%
1970	49%
1980	42%
1991	38%
2001	30%

Source: Mark Hunter, Love in the Time of AIDS: Inequality, Gender, and Rights in South Africa (Bloomington: University of Indiana Press, 2010), 93. Based on census data. Rates for 1980 and 1991 exclude 'independent' homelands: Transkei ('independent' 1976), Bophuthatswana (1977), Venda (1979) and Ciskei (1981). While Hunter does not provide raw numbers of marriages in each year, these rates declined amidst population growth.

In the late 1970s, as South Africa's economic crisis drove rising unemployment, young men saw that provider roles would be more impossible than ever to fulfil. As patriarchal apartheid policies exploded, exposed as the fictions that they were, young men cultivated 'struggle masculinities', violently asserting their control over young women.[17] In this fraught context, young women sought mobility – not only to attend school, but also to live and work in peri-urban areas in the homelands and in 'white' cities – to provide for themselves and their families.[18]

To understand the allure of schooling for young women despite the perils of school attendance, we must first examine the strategies with which a desperately reformist state tried to incentivise youth to stay in school. Like the architects of the Bantu Education Act of 1953, late-apartheid officials often spoke of black subjects in male or neutered terms. As the Minister of Justice said in July 1976, for instance, officials were concerned that 'blacks should be given enough to make them believe in separate development, so that they have too much to lose' by protest.[19] But, as the previous chapter demonstrated, black female teachers and nurses were key mediating figures in apartheid officials' developmental visions.

After 1976, teachers and nurses also became targets of the reformist state's efforts to co-opt a black elite. In 1978, the Department of Bantu Education became the Department of Education and Training and its budget increased by a third; this improved black teachers' salaries, in a bid to reduce class size.[20] Over the next decade, the number of African teachers doubled, from some 66 000 to 146 000, a majority of whom were women.[21] But as the state sought to co-opt teachers, it cracked down on their political dissent. Teachers' raises and new job openings were accompanied by official surveillance of their political engagements.[22] Similarly, while making nurses' strikes illegal in 1978, the state allowed breaches in nursing apartheid. That year, there were 20 000 registered African nurses, and about 32 000 African enrolled nurses and nursing assistants – almost all women.[23] The number of registered African nurses would increase to some 29 000 by 1985, and to 38 000 by 1991.[24] Faced with the choice 'between Black nurses and dead [white] patients', the state had declared in 1976 that black nurses could work in white private hospitals.[25] The Minister of Health couched this opening in terms that were both racist and economically empowering: black nurses could assume these jobs only if whites were not available, if patients did not object, and 'as long as they were paid the same salaries as whites and the hospital was not saving money'.[26] Shula Marks has shown that the state sought to maintain black female nurses' *general* status as exploitable labour –they were systematically paid less than whites in public hospitals, although they had new access to supervisory positions, and private posts were rare – while creating enough space for *personal* mobility to limit racial solidarity and to keep the health system functioning.

Marks' study of nurses speaks to the broader ambiguities facing educated black women. Social mobility existed – *particularly* in professions where black advancement did not centrally challenge white male economic hegemony. Sociologist Owen Crankshaw concluded: 'The advancement of Africans into traditionally white occupations during the apartheid era was by no means even. Although there was significant advancement into semi-professional and routine white-collar occupations, the extent of this advancement was not matched in the skilled trades.'[27] Key 'semi-professional' occupations were teaching and nursing, while 'routine white-collar occupations' encompassed clerical positions.[28] But black women remained systematically underpaid. Making their marginalisation more vivid, elite black women witnessed the depravities of apartheid and homeland officials' repression at close range – in the social institutions in which many of them worked, and in their own families. Expanding educational and occupational access plainly did not remove them from a revolutionary time.

Nurses and teachers pushed at the bounds of a reforming and repressive state, demanding real transformation. Student nurses at Soweto's Baragwanath Hospital went on strike in November 1985, introducing South African troops into the hospital and inaugurating a revolt by members of the helping professions.[29] Aiming to quell protests, the state racially equalised nursing salaries in 1986, but white privilege was preserved through promotion policies. Strikes against the conditions of black nurses in particular, and black South Africans generally, deepened in the late 1980s, finally prompting the Minister of Health to end racial segregation in state hospitals in 1991.[30] Teachers' militancy followed a similar course. In the 1980s, younger teachers splintered off from established professional groups, forming new unions. These groups often aligned with the United Democratic Front (UDF), a coalition of some 400 anti-apartheid community groups and trade unions that formed in 1983 to push for a non-racial democracy that would fulfil the demands of the ANC's 1955 Freedom Charter. After the intensification of educational protests in 1985 and 1986, the state also racially equalised teachers' salaries. But promotion policies still disadvantaged black teachers, and salary scales would remain differentiated by gender until 1992 – giving rise to continuing demands on a reformist state.[31]

As the previous chapter demonstrated, some of the most educated young women sought to transcend the feminised professions. After 1976, high school graduates encountered an unprecedented number of alternatives to teaching and nursing. Medical training expanded in 1978, with the opening of the Medical University of Southern Africa (MEDUNSA).[32] Even as officials clamped down on protest, African students at 'English' universities jumped from fewer than 500 in 1977 to nearly 3 000 by 1985, to over 7 000 in 1990.[33] The state and corporations such as Anglo American extended scholarships to black students; corporations created training programmes to create a tiny new black professional contingent.[34] As student protests deepened in the 1980s, so did repression and reform. To students chanting 'Liberation now, education later!' during the 1985 wave of strikes that helped to make South Africa ungovernable, officials both declared martial law and conceived of new strategies to co-opt a black bourgeoisie. In 1986, the Private Schools Act solidified the right of private schools to admit black students; following the Education Affairs Act of 1988, black students could also attend state-aided, mostly white institutions known as 'Model C' schools in the early 1990s.[35]

In KwaZulu, where officials feared militancy against Bantu Education as a challenge to their validity, students in state schools were encountering a more toothless version of educational reform – accompanied by deepening repression. Buthelezi had avowed opposition to Afrikaans instruction at a March 1976 meeting in Soweto – for which he had donned an atypical 'Che Guevara-style guerrilla's outfit'.[36] But he could not countenance ungovernability. In August 1976, he called for vigilante groups to combat rioting students.[37] The KwaZulu legislature formally repealed Bantu Education in the homeland in 1978, but they promptly replaced it with a pro-Inkatha curriculum that valorised Zuluness and discouraged protest.[38] In 1980, Inkatha brutally repressed student protestors in KwaMashu, followed by a 1983 crushing of dissent at the University of Zululand, in which five supporters of the UDF were killed and a hundred injured. Public school teachers, as KwaZulu civil servants, were forced to sign a pledge of loyalty to KwaZulu in 1987, limiting their activism. Violence between Inkatha and UDF-aligned students deepened over the 1980s – culminating in the death of some 20 000 people between 1990 and

1994, with the apartheid state providing furtive military aid to Inkatha.[39]

Inkatha sought to draw women into its visions for homeland development, with some success. Inanda served as the site for the first meeting of the Inkatha Women's Brigade in May 1977, which promoted Zulu women as fonts of development. The Brigade's founder was S'bongile Daphne Bhengu-Nene: Inanda class of 1959, recipient of the University of Zululand's first BA degree in social sciences and a University of Zululand lecturer.[40] At its first meeting, the Brigade praised four 'Unsung Heroines of the Zulu Nation'. Three were affiliated with Inanda: long-time teacher Margaret Nduna, alumna Nokukhanya Luthuli and Daughters of Africa member Angeline Dube. The fourth was Buthelezi's mother, Constance Magogo kaDinuzulu.[41] The Women's Brigade described them as 'the power behind the throne'.[42]

Buthelezi also affirmed the place of Inanda in his political visions in a February 1978 address to a delegation of visiting IBM executives at the Secretarial School. 'The whole black Community of South Africa appreciate the role such an organisation as Inanda has played in the development of our Community and of South Africa. Inanda having been founded by Missionaries from the United States, stands today as a monument to all missionary endeavor in this part of Africa. Most of us who went through Missionary institutions are almost overwhelmed when we visit here by a nostalgia which is often too difficult to bear,' Buthelezi said – emphasising the particular appeal of an elite, historic mission institution to an Adams man. 'We are therefore most grateful that Inanda has in spite of her difficulties, been able to continue to operate. We are aware that this would have been impossible if we were not so fortunate to have a few benefactors who have made it possible for Inanda to survive, such as our friends from IBM.' He then claimed that educational philanthropy was both apolitical and an aid to the anti-apartheid struggle. Countering advocates of complete American corporate disengagement from South Africa, Buthelezi emphasised to the IBM executives that education was 'a non-controversial area. I cannot see how such assistance to Blacks can contaminate the donors.' Turning to the students present, however, he urged:

I have children too, some were educated here and there is one who has been here only for a couple of days. One thing that strikes me more and more each day is that very few of our children who are at school, let alone in a school like Inanda, appreciate this fact as a blessing . . . We need you in the field of preparation that black people need in order to consolidate for the final onslaught against apartheid and oppression. This you can only do efficiently if you bear your difficulties for a few years, in order to acquire your education. Do remember that we form the majority of the poor in South Africa. Do therefore remember the sacrifices of your parents.[43]

But no archival or oral evidence suggests Inanda students generally embraced Inkatha. 'Inkatha came to us at the wrong time, because we were quite aware of who we were, we were quite conscientized, and we were perceived as being protected out there,' Khanyisile Kweyama (1976–1980) recalled. 'Inkatha was non grata . . . Inkatha tried to come to have some kind of presence at our school as at government schools in KwaZulu-Natal. That was a good excuse for us not to get involved. We were not a government school, so we didn't have to do what they told us.'[44] When Inkatha leaders visited, Mamsie Ntshangase (1977–1981) said, 'The students out-debated them and it was very, very embarrassing for them.'[45] Nozizwe Maneli (1981–1985) found that Inkatha's Zuluness felt provincial on Inanda's campus, which was only about half Zulu: 'Some of us who were from the Joburg area were like, "Why should we get involved in this Zulu thing?"' she recalled.[46] Inanda students appreciated their education as preparation to confront the world beyond – but evidence suggests that they did not envision this preparation to be in the service of KwaZulu development.

The resilience of New African ideals of schooling after Soweto
Interviews with Inanda alumnae suggest broader possibilities that education continued to hold for African girls at the upper echelons. In the decade after Soweto, Inanda remained a beacon of protection and possibility for daughters of an embattled black bourgeoisie, as well as for girls who had grown up in abject conditions in rural and urban areas. The fourteen women I interviewed who attended Inanda

between 1976 and 1986 came from around South Africa: while half were from KwaZulu, three came from townships near Johannesburg and Pretoria, and four came from the Eastern Cape. Their reflections on the meanings of schooling suggest the resilience of not only early Black Consciousness ideals, but also New African ideals of education as a source of pride and self-efficacy after 1976 – amongst Inanda students, and in the communities whence they came.

Visions of boarding school as an ideal site for coming-of-age ran deep in some African families, particularly those with elite histories. Daniel Magaziner has pointed out that SASO's leadership 'was stocked with graduates of the country's shrinking array of mission schools', as 'parents with the means to do so tried to circumvent the system as best they could'.[47] Although schools like Amanzimtoti (co-educational), Lovedale (all male under apartheid) and the formerly Anglican St John's in the Transkei (also all male) were state-controlled in the 1970s, their roots in the years before apartheid endowed them with an imprimatur of political nostalgia.[48] Rebekah Lee has also noted that for working-class African families in Cape Town, boarding schools run by Transkei homeland authorities 'represented a viable alternative to urban-based education primarily during the 1970s until about 1990', as sites of protection from violence and preparation for social mobility.[49] These aspects of boarding schooling – and the sexual protection and academic preparation represented by girls' schooling – resonated with Inanda families. Khanyisile Kweyama was born in a township outside of Pretoria to a graduate of the old Adams College, who sent two daughters to Inanda and one of his sons to Amanzimtoti. Although the latter was state-run, 'it was his alma mater', and maintained his sentimental allegiance. 'For my parents, most importantly, Inanda Seminary was a girls' school, and it had a reputation that it was an excellent school. The so-called white schools were not an option at the time I went to school.' Her parents enrolled her youngest brother in a historically white school in Pretoria just after she graduated from Inanda. Her parents' goals, Kweyama suggested, were to protect their children, to enable their mobility and to transcend apartheid's limitations: 'The rest of the country is burning, and our parents have protected us in this little enclave because they could afford to protect us there. Even though June '76 was a turning point, it didn't start with '76. Our parents were probably thinking ahead,' she said. Her father, a medical technician, hoped that Kweyama would become a doctor.[50]

Ndo Nyembezi (1975–1980), the daughter of a lawyer and niece of a professor who sent their daughters to Inanda, also emphasised her elite schooling as a 'family thing'. But as she put it, 'Soweto changed everything' about Inanda. When she first arrived, Inanda remained the 'island' that alumnae of the 1960s had described. 'We weren't part of the community, we weren't part of the society, we lived in this high-faluting world of books and drama and debate, and the people we debated with and played with often weren't black schools,' Nyembezi recalled. 'We were twilight kids. We're neither fish nor fowl.' As unrest first spread,

[w]e weren't part of the world who said you have to be schooled in Afrikaans. It was a them–us thing, there was a fair amount of that I think. But as it progressed and people started dying, it stopped being them and us, and it became clearly black–white – except even then it was a demarcated white. Our teachers were fine. The people we had a problem with were more Afrikaans than just white. And the school was amazing, because the announcements in chapel in the morning started to include, as part of the agenda, an update on what was happening, the State of Emergency.

The uprisings hit many students close to home, including Nyembezi; her brother, a University of Zululand activist, was imprisoned.[51] Kweyama similarly described the personal dimensions of the national unrest that followed the Soweto uprisings: her brother, an Amanzimtoti student activist, began a year in solitary confinement in 1976, and her boyfriend left for ANC military training in Angola in 1979. To make sense of this political climate, Kweyama relished conversations with her prefect, Sikose Mji; the school nurse Mina Ngubane, whose ANC activist husband was on Robben Island; her maths teacher, former University of Natal Medical School student activist Jabulani Sithole; and her English teacher, David Brown, a white 'hippie' from the University of Natal who sneaked copies of the banned literary magazine *Staffrider*.[52]

Despite students' political engagements, parents were right to imagine that Inanda would protect their daughters from political violence and prepare them academically. In 1976, thirty-five students matriculated; the next year, seven of these matriculants enrolled at the University of Natal Medical School, five went to the University of Zululand and five attended Fort Hare. There were over 2 000 applicants to Inanda in 1977, many of whom were fleeing township schools.[53]

Nonhlanhla Khumalo (1979–1982), who grew up in Soweto, 'was thrown into boarding school because of the 1976 riots'. Her mother had taught at and her brothers had attended Orlando High School, one of the institutions at which the Soweto uprisings began. In 1977, her parents sent her to school with her grandmother in the Transvaal countryside to avoid the urban warfare surrounding her parents' home, and to continue her schooling. Her parents, both teachers, believed fervently in education, and sent all of their children to boarding school in KwaZulu: Khumalo had a sister at Amanzimtoti and a brother at the state-created Dlangezwa. She reflected:

> I think, for me, Inanda was the best experience that any girl could ever expect. Especially at the time. Because, I mean, we grew up at a time when – I mean, I had just been through 1976. Now you have to imagine the scene. You are ten years old. People are being shot at like flies. I mean, people are just dying all around you. And there's a funeral this Saturday, and you know, that as you are going to the funeral, there will be another funeral the following weekend. And your friends, your brother's friends, someone is dying. I mean, it was just mayhem in Soweto, you know?

She vividly remembers her first train ride from Johannesburg to Durban, a journey she made with other Inanda students:

> What happened, right from the moment you arrived, was that people started saying 'members'. 'Come here, member. Come

here, member.' And it was the most phenomenal thing . . . You're feeling threatened, you've left home, but all of a sudden you're being welcomed into this camaraderie that you know nothing about . . . I also fit, I also belonged.

Inanda offered her a sense not only of belonging, but also 'that I could accomplish anything' – that 'you can stand up to any man, you can match up to anyone, you are just as good as anyone'.[54]

Figure 23 Nonhlanhla Khumalo and her teacher Karen Roy, with Khumalo's future husband, Bongani Mayosi, n.d. (circa mid-1980s). (Courtesy of Karen Roy-Guglielmi)

Khumalo's connections with Inanda's multiracial staff kindled this feeling. She noted that when she first arrived,

I hated white people, like a passion. Because the only white people that I really saw closely were the soldiers carrying guns in the township. There weren't any other white people that I knew closely. So I associated white people with evil, and death, and cruelty, and all those negative feelings.

Her American maths teacher, Karen Roy, was the first white person she trusted. But the most remarkable individual she encountered was

Constance Koza, Inanda's first black woman principal (1980–1986):

> I'd come out of Soweto, okay. Out of – you know – an environment that said white people were better than you were. Then you come to Inanda and you get a multiracial staff, with a black principal. What a lady. What a lady. Wow. Firstly, she was extremely articulate. She was very confident, you know. And she was just – I think, to this day, I am struggling to find a lady who dresses better than MaKoza. *Eish*. Smart, hey?[55]

Figure 24 Inanda principal Constance Koza, n.d. (circa early to mid-1980s). (Courtesy of Karen Roy-Guglielmi)

A proud Inanda and Fort Hare alumna, Koza emblematised the ideals of New African womanhood discussed in Chapter 3, pointing to the promises of missionary modernity as an antidote to the depravations of apartheid. Karen Roy recalled:

> Of course, she was educated long before apartheid. So there was a worldliness about her experience and exposure that brought good things to Inanda. She invoked the history, particularly from that perspective, from its founding as a mission. I think that she knew that Inanda had been influential in her life and she wanted it to be influential for everyone who crossed those gates. That was clear.[56]

Khumalo emphasised:

> Her thing was, your chest must stand upright. Your head must be held high. This is who you are. You are an Inanda girl. And this is how you walk. And when you talk, you lift your head up and look people in the eye. She was amazing, you know. And it was wonderful to see a black woman command that amount of respect.[57]

Vuyo Ncwaiba (1984–1985) also underscored 'how Mrs. Koza would make an issue of the way that you would stand, even in chapel. You cannot be leaning against the chairs, even if you're dying. Little things like that, you know. You must stand tall, and be proud.' Ncwaiba had come from East London, where students boycotted school in 1980 and 1983. 'My dad felt, you know, this township thing is a waste of time. So we must find you a school, a good girls' school where you'll be locked in, and study, and focus, and, so that's how I got to know about Inanda.' She felt that

> leaving Inanda you could almost feel you could conquer the world and do everything and anything that you wanted to do. You had the mentality that there were no limitations. You must just fly to whatever. I think also, looking at people that came before us, you would always find a member . . . You would go out there, and you would feel like, 'You know what? I come from Inanda, and I'm going to make this happen'.[58]

When I asked Thandeka (Zama) Dloti (1982–1986) about her political consciousness, she replied, 'We all knew the leaders that the school had produced.'[59]

'MaKoza. I think she opened up our minds to a whole lot of possibilities,' Nomsa Makhoba (1981–1985), who came from a village in northern KwaZulu, concurred.

> I think the one value or culture I took out of Inanda was the spirit of excellence. Just wanting to be the best that I could be. In fact I never look at myself as a woman. I look at myself in terms

of abilities and limitations. So if I have an opportunity, I'll go
... with my opportunities to see what I can and cannot do. But
I never say, 'I am a woman, and therefore – because it's a man's
world.' I don't look at myself that way.[60]

Her classmate Pamela Dube (1980–1984), from Natal's South Coast,
suggested the meanings of such a sense of self-efficacy for young women
from rural areas. Her childhood in KwaMakuta 'had a big impact on
my actually having really been so grateful that a school like Inanda
exists. Because there were some, you know, expectations for a girl
child to grow a certain way, and you already had people thinking,
you know, you were going to be their future wife or something.' At
age ten, she wore a headscarf to town so that men would assume she
was married and leave her alone. Then one day she met a distant cousin,
who 'looked like a young lady ... she looked very special,' Dube
recalled. 'And when she talked about the school where she goes called
Inanda Seminary, and that it's not far from Durban and all that, I
thought, my goodness, everything she said about this place, I thought,
this is where I want to go.' Her mother, a nurse and the family's main
breadwinner, sacrificed to fulfil her goal. At Inanda, Dube felt
privileged to be among girls with 'similar aspirations about becoming
something, about contributing to the world'.[61]

Epitomising Koza's insistence that her students see themselves as
the equals of anyone was the 1982 matric ball. To escort her students,
Koza invited none other than the senior boys of Hilton College,
Kearsney College and Michaelhouse – Natal's most prestigious, mostly
white boys' schools. 'They all accepted and all arrived. The girls looked
stunning, the young men looked rather dashing in their school
uniforms, trousers' seams pressed to a knife edge. Their manners were
faultless,' recalled Inanda teacher and school secretary Carroll Jacobs
(1972–1974; 1981–1984). 'The irony was that at the height of apartheid
in South Africa, Inanda Seminary gave a matric dance where 99% of
the young men who partnered our girls were white!'[62] While some
colleagues found Koza's emphasis on discipline and flair for statements
such as the matric ball dramatic, she was living testimony to the limits
of apartheid.

Figures 25 and 26
Inanda Seminary
matriculation ball,
1982, with guests from
Hilton College,
Kearsney College and
Michaelhouse.
(Courtesy of Karen
Roy-Guglielmi)

But students chafed under Koza's emphasis on sexual shame and discipline – also direct inheritances from New African women's experiences. The spectre of pregnancy still haunted elite young women's educational ambitions, as their success remained structured by their respectability. Koza recited the sermon that John Dube had delivered to her generation of Inanda students when an Inanda student became pregnant, comparing Inanda girls to 'a garden full of roses' and sexually active girls as buds that failed to blossom. She recalled Dube's stark words to me in our interview: 'You will find them in your garden, hard, dry, hollow. They did not develop. Before they could even sprout, the inside was already finished, eaten by ants and worms.'[63] Nozizwe Maneli recalled her words as an effort to 'protect us', but as unduly harsh: 'It was like, "You know what? You are terrible people. You look like innocent kids, but you are full of worms inside. You are like a flower that is all closed up, and it's being eaten by worms. You are rotten. You must just go now and pray for your sins." '⁶⁴ About two students a year became pregnant in the first half of the 1980s, and each pregnancy was an occasion for school-wide anxiety. Pamela Dube recalled:

> If there was someone who was suspected of being pregnant after the holidays, we would be subjected to the whole school – everybody – the whole school would be subjected to an examination. I didn't have a boyfriend, I didn't even engage in these things, but I guess I had seen enough to know at home – where I came from, the worst thing to do was to get pregnant. But the only place where I felt safe and I felt we had the opportunities to be guided in a different way, it was just as bad, and in fact worse. And that used to really frustrate me.⁶⁵

The stigma around pregnancy was so acute that 'there were also a few instances where there were fetuses found in the drain', Siphokazi Koyana (1981–1985) said. 'There was a man who was a groundsman, who took care of drains, and I understand there were reports that he had found – not often – fetuses, and all would be called into chapel and criticized, "You're all rotten apples inside".'⁶⁶ Girls who were discovered to be pregnant or to have had abortions were summarily expelled. Nonetheless, students experimented with sex on campus and on vacations, and sometimes boasted about it.⁶⁷ Sexual pleasure thus enabled escape from and resistance against the strictures of respectable girlhood – but pregnancy bore steep consequences.

Given these tensions, some found that 'MaKoza was very arrogant and very fresh and very authoritative', as Mamsie Ntshangase put it. She and other students had organised a strike against her in 1980, after which they were expelled – leaving them feeling 'very beaten'. While she and most of the students apologised and were readmitted, others went to state schools, where 'it was quite a shock to their systems because there was just no schooling happening'. While Koza was 'a darling once you really get to know her', she kindled a 'fractious relationship' with more rebellious students.⁶⁸ Koza's sense of pride also left an ambiguous impression on people outside the campus. Mandisa (Mesatywa) Zungu (1978–1982) married a man from the neighbouring KwaMashu township who grew up thinking of Inanda girls as 'these black girls speaking English in West Street, in the main streets of Durban'. When I asked her to elaborate on his ideas of Inanda girls, she erupted in laughter, and replied: 'Colonized. I mean, colonized, you can't tell anything to an Inanda girl, stubborn. When my husband says I'm being stubborn, it's "MaKoza". He doesn't even know MaKoza. "A typical MaKoza girl." Stubborn, you know, all those things. Very independent, hey. Clever.'[69]

This sense that Inanda girls were 'colonized' – a little too elite, too close to white culture – haunted other interviewees' recollections. Khanyisile Kweyama, who joined the ANC in exile in the mid-1980s, recalled, 'While I was in exile, I did hear some things like, "You had it nice, you went into private school".'[70] Lungi (Mkhize) Kwitshana (1976–1980), whose father was a clerical worker in a township in the Natal Midlands, recalled, 'The minute people heard that you were attending Inanda you were perceived as being upper-class.'[71]

As a consequence of their rarified and precarious opportunities, Mamsie Ntshangase believed, 'We could not afford to fail. Failure was not an option for any of us.'[72] Inanda students saw the expanding range of careers open to black women, and they worked hard to avail themselves of these opportunities. Medical careers exerted the strongest appeal. Thuthula Balfour-Kaipa (1976–1980), whose mother had earned her MD from the University of Natal during her childhood, believed that hers was 'the biggest class of doctors'.[73] Thembi (Ndlela) Msane (1980–1984) remembers an intensely competitive environment, where maths and science were held in the highest esteem and where she regularly rose before five in the morning to study. Her time at Inanda enabled her to fulfil the dreams of her father, a municipal employee in rural northern KwaZulu who

was very ambitious. He started talking to me about education, about being a professional, at seven years. He would sit me down and say, this year you will be this age, and you will be doing this . . . 'In the year 2000, you will be thirty-four years, and you must have worked for these companies. When you are eighteen, you will be done with school, you will be going to university.' He never used to talk about anything else except university.[74]

Inanda women seizing late-apartheid reforms

Inanda's implicit and explicit curricula converged to prepare its graduates from the latter half of the 1970s and the first half of the 1980s to seize the meagre but expanding opportunities available to black women in late-apartheid society – and to push for more. The models of New African female leadership that faculty like Koza presented were matched by strong emphases on English, maths and science, oriented towards college and career: for instance, the 'homecraft' course, which had replaced Latin in the late 1940s, was tellingly replaced with an accountancy course in 1976.[75]

University attendance was the universal goal for Inanda students after 1976, and most fulfilled it. But their experiences were uneven, revealing the changing terrain that educated women occupied in the late-apartheid cycle of revolution, repression and reform. After graduation, half of my fourteen interviewees from the classes of 1976–1986 enrolled at black state universities, and half enrolled at white universities. Those who attended black universities experienced frustrations that would have been familiar to alumnae from an older generation, described in Chapter 4. Those who attended white institutions also faced challenges – they were underestimated, and treated as tokens – but they generally left feeling empowered to forge a non-racial society.

My three interviewees who attended Fort Hare were most frustrated by their university experiences. Two were expelled. Khanyisile Kweyama began to study medicine at Fort Hare in 1982, despite the fact that her father had gone to the University of Natal Medical School. She explained her choice as a political one:

> There was a lot of anti-[Ciskei leader Lennox] Sebe sentiment at the time. But there was a lot of history there as well. There was an expectation for us to continue living that. A lot of leaders had come from Fort Hare. But it was a 'Bantu university', run by the national government. There was a contradictory history at Fort Hare. We were able to keep the Ciskei police out, because the university was South African property. And there was a very rich history of activism there.

She found her time there stressful, as Fort Hare remained a male-dominated institution. She recalled:

> If Mother Edwards had not only come and built a high school, but had built a university so that we could leave high school and go to that university, our time would not have been wasted. Inanda made life after school difficult, in terms of coping with guys. There was a spirit that Inanda Seminary gave me, an assertiveness, and I'm pretty sure of who I am. My developmental years were in a place where excellence was preached, excellence was rewarded, and that's where excellence happened. If Inanda Seminary had a university, I wouldn't have wasted those years. But Fort Hare also made me who I am in life.

At Fort Hare, Kweyama's commitment to ANC politics deepened. After she was expelled the next year, during the national student strike wave that hit Fort Hare hard, she left the country to act as a courier for the ANC in Swaziland. Kweyama later studied management and emerged as a powerful executive in post-apartheid South Africa.[76] Although her classmate Lungi Kwitshana was 'not a political leader', she was also involved in the Fort Hare strike, in which she was injured. 'I had a rubber bullet wound, and I couldn't go to the hospital because the police were waiting there. I felt vulnerable and unprotected compared to where I was coming from,' she recalled. After her expulsion from Fort Hare, she struggled to pursue her medical studies, later training as a microbiologist at the University of Natal.[77] Mandisa Zungu studied mathematics at Fort Hare, where she confronted her lecturers' racist assumptions. 'For people who went into B.Sc. like myself, it was hell. We had hell, we had hell. Because they didn't want us to do B.Sc. in mathematics, so we were taken all over the place, this way and that way.' Realising that 'you must have nerves of steel and just push', she earned her degree and went into finance. 'South Africa let us down. It still continues, in many ways, unfortunately.' She went on to say:

> The unfortunate part of that is that South Africa seems not to be ready for such women. Black women who know what they are

about, you know? Who can do things . . . It's almost like – you know, there's this thing that apartheid did – so the assumption is that every black person, you know, was therefore not educated, whatever. So to find these women mushrooming all over the place, with all the background that they have, it's like, do they actually really exist? Can they really contribute? This also goes I think for women in general, from other schools as well.[78]

The alumnae I interviewed who attended predominantly white universities related fewer disappointments about their university experiences, emphasising that Inanda – in the attitudes it imparted, and in the English fluency and maths skills it developed – prepared them to equal or better their white classmates' achievements. Ndo Nyembezi suggested that some Inanda alumnae of her generation saw academic excellence as their brand of politics: 'We used our thinking skills and sassiness to open doors . . . The guys kind of figured politics was their thing. The girls from Inanda didn't understand that . . . So I think the guys sometimes were a bit wary of us.'[79] For Nyembezi and her older sister Nonkululeko (a genius who, in 1977, had been the highest-scoring student in South Africa on her Junior Certificate exam), challenging racialised patriarchy meant struggling to win access to universities beyond the 'bush universities' and excelling there. The Nyembezis succeeded: Nonkululeko by winning an Anglo American scholarship to study in Britain, followed by engineering graduate school at the California Institute of Technology, and Ndo by selecting a drama programme that was not available at black universities. After testifying before Parliament about her desire to study drama, she was admitted to the University of Cape Town. When she arrived in 1981, she was one of two black students in the programme. Although she had to live off campus, in line with UCT's status as a 'white' area, Nyembezi made a place for herself, befriending a number of Jewish and gay male students. She drew upon the self-confidence she had cultivated at Inanda, emphasising that if

you come in, and your focus isn't on the negatives, if you don't see them, they just don't exist, they don't push your buttons. I was just so excited to be on my own, at drama school, learning to smoke, you know, I had a blast, I had friends, we used to hang out, I was being introduced to a world I had never been exposed to, and people would say, ah, you should worry about the disparaging racism. Should I?

Nyembezi did not pursue the feminised professions, but went into a corporate career.[80]

Inanda graduates were also among the first cohorts of African students at Howard College, the 'white section' of the University of Natal, in the mid-1980s, pursuing careers in business and academia. Many of their peers came from Bantustan institutions that had just made mass expulsions; they joined together with black medical school students and white leftists to push the university for deeper reforms.[81] Most black Howard College students, such as Thembi Msane, boarded with the medical school students, in the politicised Alan Taylor residences.[82] Pamela Dube, who enrolled in Howard College in 1985, was told outright that she was placed in the white students' dormitories 'as an experiment to see if we could stay', because her English was so strong. She studied psychology and sociology, earned a PhD in comparative literature in Germany and returned to post-apartheid South Africa to work for the Department of Education.[83] Dube was not alone in her pursuit of foreign schooling: Siphokazi Koyana left to attend Smith College in Massachusetts in 1986, earning an MA in African Studies from Yale University and a PhD in English from Temple University before returning as an English lecturer at the historically white Rhodes University. At Smith,

[I]t was just an older group of Inanda girls, they were just white. Again, it was that same spirit of women being excellent, without having to please any man. Just being able to discover who you are as a woman, and grow into your own self, in a very protected and safe environment where you are encouraged to excel and to break boundaries.[84]

Notably, none of my fourteen interviewees became teachers or nurses. Eight pursued corporate careers, three became medical doctors, one became a medical researcher and two went into higher education.

Although previous generations of women's work in the helping professions had made Inanda's survival possible, they seized the widening opportunities of a reformist apartheid state to transcend the gendered limitations that those professions implied.

This was not the only irony in Inanda's experiences in the late-apartheid state. For the very openings that enabled elite women to escape the feminised professions also made Inanda seem increasingly obsolete to the elite. As alumnae pursued new opportunities, their younger relatives generally rejected Inanda for historically white high schools, if they had sufficient money or talent to do so. Thuthula Balfour-Kaipa remembers some of her friends – like her, children of doctors in the Transkei – abandoning Inanda for a white Catholic school in Pietermaritzburg, in the early 1980s. She explained their move simply: 'At that time, we only had cold water. That was a very important feature really, which must not be forgotten, because it determined who went there.'[85] In other words, Inanda was elite within apartheid's limits, and by the 1980s it was hard-pressed for funding to maintain its facilities. Nonetheless, the high price and low admission rates of white schools meant that Inanda still enrolled 450 students in early 1985, at which time Koza noted that the school had 'never been subjected to such a high rate of applications with parents using so much pressure to get their children into Inanda Seminary. The selection is becoming more and more difficult, as most of the people who apply, meet the criteria but are too many.'[86] In 1985, however, Inanda's surrounding township exploded into riots following the assassination of a UDF activist and a school boycott, during which Inanda shut down for ten days.[87]

Koza left Inanda in 1986. The institution floundered thereafter, as it had largely been through her personal fund-raising efforts that Inanda stayed afloat.[88] Beginning in 1984, Koza had also secured an annual grant from the KwaZulu Department of Education; this move engendered acute hostility from the United Church Board for World Missions (UCBWM) in New York, whose members saw Buthelezi as an apartheid stooge.[89] But missionary networks had so attenuated that New York did not notice Inanda was receiving a Bantustan grant until late 1987.[90] Inanda's Governing Council was nonplussed by the Board's sudden interest, suggesting that Inanda had appealed to

KwaZulu because support from the UCBWM was not forthcoming – explaining that all private schools in South Africa were then receiving some form of state subsidy but that Inanda drew only 10 per cent of its budget from KwaZulu.[91] The UCBWM's response to this explanation was to complete its decolonisation of the benevolent empire in apartheid South Africa: the UCBWM would henceforth delegate all funding decisions about Inanda to the United Congregational Church of South Africa (UCCSA), which was to fund Inanda at its discretion from the grant that the UCBWM paid to the UCCSA each year.[92] A diminishing funding base combined with the volatile atmosphere across KwaZulu to provoke unrest on Inanda's campus, capped with students forcing the bursar off campus to protest a fees hike in 1992.[93] An accidental 1993 fire destroyed Edwards Hall, a building at the centre of campus that honoured Inanda's founder.[94]

Principal F.G. Mhlambo described Inanda's plight plaintively in a letter appealing for aid from the new government in June 1994:

> With the relaxation of restrictions which debarred Blacks from attending White Government Schools, and the movement of Black families from the townships to live in White suburbs, our enrolment tumbled to a record low of 315 this year. We really find that the school can no longer continue to function without State intervention.[95]

When state aid was not forthcoming, Mhlambo accepted day scholars from the surrounding community to attract revenue. But by early 1997, the school was on the brink of closure, prompting a small scandal. 'Ex-Inanda girls have distinguished themselves in almost all spheres of life. They are a living testimony of the equality or even superiority of women to men,' a letter to the editor in the *Daily News* exhorted. 'How can they sit back when their alma mater is in such a terrible state of disrepair?'[96]

Conclusion

Inanda's fate over apartheid's final decade emblematises the broader contradictions accompanying educated black women's growing achievements. While the black elite feminised, most women – like the day scholars from Inanda's surrounding community – were still left behind. On the one hand, if educated women's labours as teachers and nurses had initially made separate development possible, their rejection of apartheid's core visions helped make it unsustainable. On the other hand, some women's empowerment within male-dominated political and professional realms coincided with many women's deepening disempowerment. Given these contradictions, what possibilities might Inanda's model of schooling bear for post-apartheid society? The Epilogue offers some preliminary answers, as it opens up further inquiries for historical investigation.

Epilogue

Post-apartheid educational transformations will hinge on concurrent transformations in the economy and society – which remain characterised by striking degrees of progress towards gender and racial equity in some dimensions, but limited by deepening class divisions and the violence that widespread poverty generates. Young women make up a majority of all students at secondary and university levels; their enrolments now outpace those of men even at medical schools.[1] Yet their pay and promotions tend to trail those of men.[2] The feminisation of the labour force has coincided with feminisation of unemployment, poverty and disease.[3]

As the then Minister of Education Naledi Pandor put it in 2005, 'Not only do girls and women dominate in terms of numbers, they also have a different attitude to learning to boys and men. They appear to be more flexible, equipped to cope with different modes of teaching and assessment. Yet although girls do better at school in previously male-dominated subjects, such as science and maths, proportionately fewer of them take these up to degree level. In other words, the gender gap is perpetuated at another level.'[4] In this regard, she suggested, South Africa's 'hidden face of gender inequality' resembles that facing many societies. In 2005, a majority of higher education students were female in all regions of the globe except for sub-Saharan Africa and Asia. But globally, female students cluster in education, health, humanities and social science courses and face a pay gap.[5]

South Africa, site of the world's most pervasive crises of sexual violence, poses a particular paradox. It features '[h]igh numbers of girls completing school with excellent grades (in many areas, outperforming boys); widening labour market access for women, with unparalleled opportunities available at professional and managerial levels for the best qualified; escalating levels of violence, much of it hinging on questions of gender; and the ravages of HIV and AIDS, where gender identities and power relations in relation to sex and sexuality figure prominently'.[6] Some have claimed that this violent climate is one of post-apartheid 'backlash'.[7]

This history of women's schooling reveals that these gendered tensions and possibilities of education have deeper roots: they emerged out of the politics of social reproduction that made the apartheid-era expansion of African women's schooling possible. In the years before apartheid, the first three chapters of this book demonstrated, women's empowerment and marginalisation were coeval. Both were shaped by women's centrality to processes of social reproduction in an interlocking set of patriarchies: those of African families and the colonial and segregationist states, with missionaries playing key intermediary roles. On the one hand, women's association with the nurturance of children and workers justified their increasing presence in the growing fields of educational and health work, where they cultivated social leadership. On the other hand, women's roles in social reproduction justified their exclusion from male-dominated political organisations and gave rise to intense anxieties about their gendered propriety. While social reproduction became intensely politicised within African nationalist circles, however, officials did not seem to regard women as threatening political actors.

In the apartheid years, Chapters 4 and 5 demonstrated, women's seemingly apolitical association with social reproduction encouraged officials to enact policies that enabled a growing elite to join the feminised professions of teaching and nursing. But the same assumptions that had opened up space for more young black women to attend high school under apartheid – that they would tend to the social reproduction of a divided society, by sustaining children, families and ultimately a racialised labour force – justified most black women's legal relegation to barren homelands until 1986 under the pass laws. Educated African women were bitterly cognisant that they were elite within racialised and gendered limits. Premised on official assumptions that women would undergird a divided society socially without threatening it politically, women's schooling had opened new spaces from which to think their way out of racialised patriarchy. After 1976, growing numbers of high school and university educated African women pushed against the constraints to which their gender and race subjected them. Their struggles contributed to the gendered cycle of revolution, repression and reform, through which the interlocking patriarchies underpinning apartheid – those of households and homelands – fell apart.

Schools remain haunted by the history of inequities that produced them. As structural unemployment constrains both male and female students, young men feel their loss of patriarchal status acutely, while young women strain to fulfil modern expectations of independence in the midst of a plague.[8] In this context, South African leaders are voicing a sense of nostalgia for the elite world of missionary boarding schools in the 1930s and 1940s – for an imperfect but hopeful world in which dreams of social mobility and political equality seemed more readily within reach than they do today, amidst global economic crisis and a pandemic that has hit South Africans mercilessly. And many South African students and their parents see in girls' single-sex boarding schooling a way out of the poverty and gender-linked violence that many continue to face. Inanda's model of schooling thus suggests a solution to post-apartheid crises of social reproduction.

* * *

A few months after accounts of Inanda's impending closure appeared in Durban newspapers, alumnae took their school back. Three of my interviewees – Bongekile Dlomo, Khosi Mpanza and Esther Sangweni – and other graduates from the past half-century organised a co-ordinating committee. With the support of a newly formed Inanda Seminary Old Girls Association (ISOGA), this committee registered as a non-profit group and negotiated with the United Congregational Church of South Africa to transfer control from the church to themselves. On 1 January 1998, the committee announced that Inanda would continue as a low-fees-paying private school – thanks to aid from a government in which alumnae like Ivy Matsepe-Casaburri (then Free State premier) and Baleka Mbete (then Deputy Speaker of Parliament) also avowed their personal support.[9] As Sangweni put it at the time, 'The girls took control', hiring a new staff and overhauling the curriculum.[10] In 1999, Inanda was named a national heritage site and merited visits from President Nelson Mandela and Deputy

President Jacob Zuma, as well as Inanda's old supporter Mangosuthu Gatsha Buthelezi (now Minister of Home Affairs).[11] Mandela successfully solicited corporate donations to improve Inanda's infrastructure. The next year, Inanda welcomed an American minister, Susan Valiquette, as its chaplain. ISOGA members Kho Zimu (class of 1969) and Cynthia Mpati (1967) served as principal, followed by the 2003 appointment of Judy Tate, granddaughter of an Inanda teacher, who continues in this role today.

ISOGA members emphasised the possibilities Inanda's traditions posed in a society in which most black women still suffered deep marginalisation. 'The school was founded so that black women did not get left behind the wave of education by missionaries who had come to Natal,' Mpati wrote in 2001.

> In the early 1960s, when the struggle for liberation of the black people of South Africa intensified, Inanda Seminary, very quietly behind the gum trees, identified with all those who fought for respect of all races in the country and elsewhere in the world. This fight was not only by word of mouth, but by actions as well. Women who were educated at the Seminary found themselves in an environment that opened a small window, so that black and white people on campus could experience normal non-racial life – an oasis indeed, in an otherwise bitterly racist bigger society.[12]

Now Inanda's low fee structure enabled it to offer preparation and protection to less affluent students: 'Behind the tall gum trees, a strong fence and heavy gate, Inanda Seminary is therefore not a prison and shelter from the realities of the world out there.'[13] As Sangweni explained, 'It is our heritage; it has been a beacon of light in our community for over 130 years, and we felt very strongly that what the school stands for cannot be allowed to die. And we felt that the school needed to continue to give young African women what we gained from it, because we feel that is what has made our lives different, that is what has made our lives worthwhile.'[14]

Inanda is beginning to attract the daughters of the black bourgeoisie back to its campus, as some young women and their families see

Figure 27 Inanda Seminary Old Girls Association members, n.d. (circa 1998). (Inanda Seminary Campus Archive)

Figure 28 Alumnae and current students at Inanda Seminary's 140th anniversary, March 2009. (Photograph by the author)

attending Inanda as a 'tradition type of thing'.[15] Given the range of educational options now available to young black women, and the continuing poverty of its surrounding community, Inanda is unlikely ever to be as elite as it was during the apartheid years. But it boasted a matriculation pass rate of 100 per cent in 2010, and students go on to South Africa's best universities. Inanda's status approximates that of a historically black college in the United States, as the school foregrounds its tradition of black achievement at campus events and in its public persona. In 2010, Scott Couper, husband of the school chaplain and a historian with a doctorate from the University of KwaZulu-Natal, became Inanda's Development Manager, working to publicise its heritage further.

Inanda seems to have been more successful in its efforts to revitalise itself through an appeal to its history than peer institutions that were taken over by the apartheid state. But other institutions are also working with the post-apartheid government to resume a proud position, and they have made progress. The Historic Schools Restoration Project (HSRP), an initiative of the South African Department of Arts and Culture, was launched in 2006 as 'part of a wider national movement to revive a culture of learning but also to revitalise African culture and reclaim parts of our African heritage that were ignored and marginalised during the apartheid years'. As the project description puts it, 'Christian missionaries and the institutions they established became the principal bearers of modern education among South African Africans in the late nineteenth and early twentieth centuries . . . the incubators of the African elite and the breeding grounds for an African intelligentsia.'[16] Inanda and five other schools were pilot sites.[17] President Thabo Mbeki, Lovedale alumnus, celebrated the schools in a 2008 address at Healdtown, his father Govan Mbeki's alma mater. After an opening laced with fond, rambling jokes about Lovedale–Healdtown sports rivalries and a 'tippling' science teacher, Mbeki emphasised the project's objectives simply: 'The HSRP project is very dear to the heart of the government, and the reason why we have given it financial backing is because we believe that these schools and those who went to them are in a position to give us a particular perspective on the high standard of education they achieved before apartheid policies destroyed them.'[18]

As Mbeki's clubby remarks make clear, the HSRP is a nation-building exercise led by African educated elites, promoting nostalgia for a time when this elite's confidence in its capacity to uplift and unite 'the race' was far firmer than it is today – Govan Mbeki's hopeful schooldays in the late 1920s and 1930s, not Thabo Mbeki's own bitter schooldays in the 1950s, during Lovedale's transfer to state control.[19] The project invokes New Africans' ambitions to address the limits of national liberation – suggesting that through self-discipline and self-empowerment, a new generation of young Africans might lead what Mbeki has elsewhere termed the 'African Renaissance', revitalising South Africa's moral, socio-economic and political order to revitalise the continent. Mbeki's catastrophic AIDS policies, neoliberal economic plans, questionable foreign dealings and aloof attitude culminated in his ouster from the presidency shortly after his address at Healdtown.[20] But the HSRP continues, adding more 'schools that had played a meaningful role in the struggle for democracy', including Lovedale and Mariannhill.[21]

In a time of growing class cleavages amongst Africans, historic institutions aim to prepare young people from a diversity of socio-economic backgrounds to lead an expanding African elite that sees its interests in *national* terms. The project provides full scholarships for some and assures low fees across all of the schools. Its Educational Trust is aptly named for ANC activist Z.K. Matthews – a Lovedale graduate, the first African to earn a bachelor's degree in South Africa upon his 1923 graduation from Fort Hare and the first African head of Adams College in 1925. Matthews embodies the project's visions: 'His lifelong quest for knowledge and unwavering selflessness in serving the cause of political freedom and a better life for all South Africans stands as an exemplar for the vision of the HSRP: *To nurture future African leaders of calibre and integrity, who are able to meet the critical needs of community and country, in a values-based, transformational environment.*'[22]

Resuscitating mission schools cannot, of course, close the gaps between affluent blacks who have availed themselves of widening opportunities in post-apartheid South Africa and the majority, who continue to suffer in an economy that has been plagued by catastrophic unemployment for three decades. But by offering models of achievement that include a sense of national consciousness and responsibility, these institutions offer the promise of social mobility within a moral framework that avoids narrow individualism and excessive consumption – which many regard as a plague in one of the world's most unequal countries.[23] As Nonhlanhla Khumalo (1979–1982), a passionate ISOGA member, told me, 'The problem with the younger generation is, kids who haven't experienced apartheid are taking the freedoms that they have so for granted . . . They think they are all of a sudden equal with whites, and everything is perfect – nothing is perfect. Until the people in rural Transkei and rural Zululand have got access to facilities and opportunities, we are not yet equal.' Turning to two recent Inanda alumnae whom she had invited to our interview, Khumalo exhorted, 'I mean, those people are dependent on you guys! You guys are the people who are going to go back, and give those people opportunity. You mustn't be satisfied that you're wearing high heels and speaking English and sitting in bars.' Her classmate Mandisa Zungu added, laughing derisively, 'Smoking cigars.'[24]

Inanda also offers a distinct appeal, as the only all-female Historic School. Post-apartheid students and staff have suggested that Inanda's single-sex environment exerts the *strongest* appeal for students and their families.[25] Inanda empowers young women to pursue academic tracks that remain male-dominated – such as computer science, which a recent graduate told me she pursued at the University of Cape Town 'firstly because I felt as though, well, there were only like three girls who did it, and that ticked me off, and there were only like five black people who did it as well, so I sort of wanted to break the stereotype'.[26] Graduates of girls' schools around the world have cited a similar sense of empowerment, although the long-term effects of single-sex schooling remain debatable.[27]

In South Africa, as Robert Morrell has argued, all-female schools might also play a critical role as sites of protection from the gender-linked violence that pervades many schools.[28] Yet poor and working-class women generally lack access to South Africa's small number of all-female schools, most of which were established to serve a white elite and now mostly serve a multiracial elite. Despite recommendations of a national Gender Equity Task Team to establish more all-female schools in the late 1990s, institutions targeting non-elite students have not proliferated. But in early 2007, a new player came onto the scene:

the Oprah Winfrey Leadership Academy for Girls opened near Johannesburg, built with forty million dollars of the African American talk-show tycoon's own funds to provide single-sex, boarding schooling for girls with family incomes of less than 700 dollars per month. Declaring that hers would be the 'best school in the world', Winfrey attracted applications from more than 3 500 students for 152 openings; her interviews with finalists were broadcast in a tear-jerking American television special.[29] Like the Historic Schools, the Leadership Academy aims to produce nationally conscious leaders, 'who are able to navigate a variety of social and cultural contexts throughout the world, but who remain committed to the development of South Africa and the African continent'.[30] Inanda's past suggests that all-female schooling, particularly with strong female role models as leaders, can be as personally empowering for some students as Winfrey has hoped. But as revitalised mission institutions will not, on their own, bridge the profound divisions in post-apartheid society, neither can all-female schools resolve the contradictions that have accompanied South Africa's feminisation of schooling.

*   *   *

Ultimately, to understand the possibilities and limits accompanying South African women's roles in social reproduction, we must think more critically about the categories on which their location in processes of social reproduction has hinged – the 'public' and 'private', the 'national' and the 'familial'. By tending to the multivalence of women's roles in social reproduction, this study has demonstrated what the *instability* of these categories enabled women to do in the domain of schooling. It has revealed the political space that, ironically, women's association with the social opened up. To understand how to effect real gendered, racial and class transformations for students in post-apartheid South Africa, scholars and activists need a better handle on the historical links between women's power and marginality in other domains of South African society – from households to political organisations. Through the analytical framework of the politics of social reproduction, this study offers a way into these fundamental questions.

Notes

Introduction

1. Baleka Mbete, keynote address, 140th anniversary, Inanda Seminary, 7 March 2009, notes in author's possession.
2. Besides dozens of biographies of Nelson Mandela, exemplary texts include: Tim Couzens, *The New African: A Study of the Life and Work of H.I.E. Dhlomo* (Johannesburg: Ravan, 1985); Mark Gevisser, *A Legacy of Liberation: Thabo Mbeki and the Future of the South African Dream* (New York: Palgrave Macmillan, 2009); and Heather Hughes, *First President: A Life of John L. Dube, Founding President of the ANC* (Auckland Park, South Africa: Jacana, 2011).
3. Published scholarly works on Inanda are all articles: Scott Couper, 'Fearing for Its Future: Bantu Education's Threat of Closure to Inanda Seminary', *Journal of Gender and Religion in Africa* 17, no. 1 (July 2011): 74–95; Meghan Elisabeth Healy, ' "To Control Their Destiny": The Politics of Home and the Feminisation of Schooling in Colonial Natal', *Journal of Southern African Studies* 37, no. 2 (June 2011): 247–264; Healy, ' "Like a Family": Global Models, Familial Bonds, and the Making of an American School for Zulu Girls', *Safundi: The Journal of South African and American Studies* 11, no. 3 (July 2010): 279–300; Heather Hughes, ' "A Lighthouse for African Womanhood": Inanda Seminary, 1869–1945', in *Women and Gender in Southern Africa to 1945*, ed. Cherryl Walker (Cape Town: David Philip, 1990), 197–220; Khosi Mpanza, 'Schooled for Success', *Agenda* 21 (1994): 43–46, on apartheid-era alumnae's reflections. Missionary Agnes Wood's out-of-print *Shine Where You Are: A History of Inanda Seminary, 1869–1969* (Alice, South Africa: Lovedale Press, 1972) is based on her archival research and personal reflections. Unpublished work includes Hughes' student Lyndsay MacDougall's 1990 University of Natal honours thesis, 'Inanda Seminary, 1950–1980: Educating a Nation'; and alumna Lynette Hlongwane's analysis of Inanda as a model for post-apartheid schooling, 'The Role of Inanda Seminary in the Education of African Girls in South Africa: A Report of Graduates' Views' (PhD diss., Teachers College, Columbia University, 1998).

4. Mark Hunter, 'Beneath the "Zunami": Jacob Zuma and the Gendered Politics of Social Reproduction in South Africa', *Antipode* (February 2011): 1–25, p. 3. This explicitly emphasises the reproduction of people and of social relations, refining Karl Marx, *Capital: A Critique of Political Economy* (New York: Vintage, 1977; first published in German, 1867; first published in English, 1887), 711: 'Every social process of production is at the same time a process of reproduction.'

5. Monica Wilson, *Reaction to Conquest* (London: Oxford University Press, 1936), 175–177; Wilson, 'Co-operation and Conflict: The Eastern Cape Frontier', in *The Oxford History of South Africa*, Volume 1, eds. Wilson and Leonard Thompson (Oxford: Clarendon Press, 1969), 233–271, p. 262.

6. Wilson, 'Co-operation and Conflict', 262.

7. Jacklyn Cock, 'Domestic Service and Education for Domesticity: The Incorporation of Xhosa Women into Colonial Society', in *Women and Gender in Southern Africa to 1945*, 76–96, p. 95. See also Cock, *Maids and Madams: A Study in the Politics of Exploitation* (Johannesburg: Ravan, 1980).

8. Claire Robertson, 'Women's Education and Class Formation in Africa, 1950–1980', in *Women and Class in Africa*, eds. Iris Berger and Claire Robertson (New York: Africana Publishing, 1986), 92–116, p. 96. Deborah Gaitskell also notes that girls made up the majority of students in the future Union of South Africa from the late nineteenth century – but she does not explain why: see Gaitskell, 'Race, Gender and Imperialism: A Century of Black Girls' Education in South Africa', in *'Benefits Bestowed'? Education and British Imperialism*, ed. J.A. Mangan (New York: Manchester University Press, 1988), 151–173, p. 151. On the general pattern of male domination of schooling, see Marianne Bloch, Josephine A. Beoku-Betts and B. Robert Tabachnick, eds, *Women and Education in Sub-Saharan Africa: Power, Opportunities, and Constraints* (Boulder, CO: Lynne Rienner, 1998).

9. Elaine Unterhalter, 'The Impact of Apartheid on Women's Education in South Africa', *Review of African Political Economy* 48 (Autumn 1990): 66–75; Unterhalter, 'Can Education Overcome Women's Subordinate Position in the Occupation Structure?' in *Education in a Future South Africa: Policy Issues for Transformation*, eds. Unterhalter, Harold Wolpe and Thozamile Botha (Portsmouth, NH: Heinemann, 1991), 65–84; Unterhalter, 'Remembering and Forgetting: Constructions of Education Gender Reform in Autobiography and Policy Texts of the South African Transition', *History of Education* 29, no. 5 (2000): 457–472; and Unterhalter, 'The Schooling of South African Girls', in *Gender, Education, and Development: Beyond Access to Empowerment*, eds. Christine Heward and Sheila S. Bunwaree (London: Zed, 1999), 49–64.

10. Robert Morrell, Debbie Epstein, Elaine Unterhalter, Deevia Bhana and Relebohile Moletsane, *Towards Gender Equality: South African Schools During the HIV and AIDS Epidemic* (Pietermaritzburg: University of KwaZulu-Natal Press, 2009), 29; Morrell and Moletsane, 'Inequality and Fear: Living and Working inside Bantu Education Schools', in *The History of Education under Apartheid, 1948–1994: The Doors of Learning and Culture Shall Be Opened*, ed. Peter Kallaway (New York: P. Lang, 2002), 224–242, p. 238.

11. Shula Marks' remarkable work on one schoolgirl's experiences in the early years of apartheid has been widely cited to illustrate the promises and dangers of schooling: see Marks, *Not Either an Experimental Doll: The Separate Worlds of Three South African Women* (Bloomington: Indiana University Press, 1987). Anne Mager also developed these themes: see Mager, *Gender and the Making of a South African Bantustan: A Social History of the Ciskei, 1945–1959* (Portsmouth, NH: Heinemann, 1999), 208–213. But little has been written on girls' investments in schooling after 1976, during the greatest expansion in their enrolment – a startling lacuna.

12. See Shula Marks, *Divided Sisterhood: Race, Class, and Gender in the South African Nursing Profession* (Johannesburg: Wits University Press, 1994); Deborah Gaitskell, ' "Doing a Missionary Hard Work . . . in the Black Hole of Calcutta": African Women Teachers Pioneering a Profession in the Cape and Natal, 1880–1950', *Women's History Review* 13, no. 3 (September 2004): 407–425.

13. For classic examples of early scholarship, see I.B. Tabata, *Education for Barbarism: Bantu Education in South Africa* (Durban: Prometheus, 1959); Muriel Horrell, *African Education: Some Origins, and Development until 1953* (Johannesburg: South African Institute of Race Relations, 1963); and Horrell, *Bantu Education to 1968* (Johannesburg: South African Institute of Race Relations, 1968).

14. Peter Kallaway's introduction to his pioneering 1984 volume character-istically drew upon Antonio Gramsci, Frantz Fanon, Albert Memmi, Nicos Poulantzas and Paulo Freire: see Kallaway, 'An Introduction to the Study of Education for Blacks in South Africa', in *Apartheid and Education: Education of Black South Africans*, ed. Kallaway (Johannesburg: Ravan, 1984), 1–44.

15. For a typical ancillary note, see Pam Christie, *The Right to Learn: The Struggle for Education in South Africa* (Johannesburg: Ravan, 1985), 75–77.

16. For a sophisticated account that nonetheless pays minimal attention to gender, see Jean Comaroff, 'Reading, Rioting, and Arithmetic: The Impact of Mission Education on Black Consciousness in South Africa', *Bulletin of the Institute of Ethnology, Academia Sinica* 82 (Autumn 1996): 19–63.

333333333333

17. On the role of 'intersectional' analyses, inspired by the work of African American feminist scholars and by South African scholars' concept of women's 'triple oppression', in South Africa, see J. Maki Motapanyane, 'The Politics of Feminism in South Africa: Gender Consciousness and Political Agency in the Twentieth Century' (PhD diss., York University, 2009).
18. Belinda Bozzoli, 'Marxism, Feminism, and South African Studies', *Journal of Southern African Studies* 9, no. 2 (1983): 139–171, p. 149.
19. See Harold Wolpe, 'Capitalism and Cheap Labour Power in South Africa: From Segregation to Apartheid', *Economy and Society* 1, no. 4 (1972): 425–456.
20. Bozzoli, 'Marxism, Feminism, and South African Studies', 151.
21. Bozzoli, 'Marxism, Feminism, and South African Studies', 155.
22. See Linzi Manicom, 'Ruling Relations: Rethinking State and Gender in South African History', *The Journal of African History* 33, no. 3 (1992): 441–465; Sean Hanretta, 'Women, Marginality, and the Zulu State: Women's Institutions and Power in the Early Nineteenth Century', *The Journal of African History* 39, no. 3 (1998): 389–415; Jeff Guy, 'Analysing Pre-capitalist Societies in Southern Africa', *Journal of Southern African Studies* 14, no. 1 (October 1987): 18–37; Guy, 'Gender Oppression in Southern Africa's Precapitalist Societies', in *Women and Gender in Southern Africa to 1945*, 33–47; Guy, 'An Accommodation of Patriarchs: Theophilus Shepstone and the System of Native Administration in Natal' (seminar paper, Colloquium on Masculinities in Southern Africa, University of Natal, Durban, 1997); Guy, 'Tradition in Transition: The Gendered Origins of Our Time' (seminar paper, History and African Studies Seminar, University of KwaZulu-Natal, Durban, 2010); and Marks, *Divided Sisterhood*.
23. Hanretta, 'Women, Marginality and the Zulu State', 392–393.
24. Barbara Laslett and Joanna Brenner, 'Gender and Social Reproduction', *Annual Review of Sociology* 15 (1989): 381–404, p. 383.
25. See Carole Leathwood and Barbara Read, *Gender and the Changing Face of Higher Education: A Feminized Future?* (New York: Open University Press, 2009); Khayaat Fakier and Jacklyn Cock, 'A Gendered Analysis of the Crisis of Social Reproduction in Contemporary South Africa', *International Feminist Journal of Politics* 11, no. 3 (September 2009): 353–371; and Meg Luxton and Kate Bezanson, *Social Reproduction: Feminist Political Economy Challenges Neo-liberalism* (Montreal: McGill-Queen's University Press, 2006).
26. On the value of family history, see Rebekah Lee, *African Women and Apartheid: Migration and Settlement in Urban South Africa* (New York: I.B. Tauris, 2009).

27. See Deborah Mindry, ' "Good Women": Philanthropy, Power, and the Politics of Femininity in Contemporary South Africa' (PhD diss., University of California–Irvine, 1999), 101–109.

28. This method follows Susan Geiger, *TANU Women: Gender and Culture in the Making of Tanganyikan Nationalism, 1955–1965* (Portsmouth, NH: Heinemann, 1998), 16. On life histories, see also Belinda Bozzoli, *Women of Phokeng: Consciousness, Life Strategy, and Migration in South Africa, 1900–1983* (Portsmouth, NH: Heinemann, 1991), 1–15; Heidi Gengenbach, 'Truth-Telling and the Politics of Women's Life History Research in Africa: A Reply to Kirk Hoppe', *The International Journal of African Historical Studies* 27, no. 3 (1994): 619–627; Kathleen Weiler and Sue Middleton, eds, *Telling Women's Lives: Narrative Inquiries in the History of Women's Education* (Buckingham, UK: Open University Press, 1999); and Luise White, Stephan F. Miescher and David William Cohen, eds, *African Words, African Voices: Critical Practices in Oral History* (Bloomington: Indiana University Press, 2001), 8–9.

29. As Jean Comaroff has discussed, this attention to micro- and macro-level contradictions makes vivid the whole culture of schooling – within which multiple 'disjunctions' fuel informal and formal student politics. See Comaroff, 'Reading, Rioting, and Arithmetic'. In Inanda's case, the 'hidden curricula' has included implicit instruction in practices that not only *enable individual advancement* in white-dominated, capitalist society – preference for speaking in English, as the most conspicuous example – but also *trouble the collective categories* which structure that society – socialising with white people on a basis of equality, for example. For a cogent exploration of how another 'hidden curriculum' enables visions of 'modernity' that both reinforce and trouble existing power relations, see Vandra Masemann, 'The "Hidden Curriculum" of a West African Girls' Boarding School', *Canadian Journal of African Studies* 6, no. 3 (1974): 479–494.

Chapter One

1. Henry Bridgman, Ifumi, Natal, to Rufus Anderson, Secretary, American Board of Commissioners for Foreign Missions, Boston, 18 January 1864. In American Board of Commissioners for Foreign Missions: African Missions Records (henceforth ABC), Series 15.4, Volume 6, Houghton Library, Harvard University, Cambridge, Massachusetts.

2. The 'benevolent empire' encompassed the network of evangelical institutions – 'churches, schools, and moral and evangelistic societies of every kind' – that began to flourish in the United States following the Second Great Awakening of the early nineteenth century, and which

expanded through the American foreign missions movement over the next century. See Margaret Lamberts Bendroth, *A School of the Church: Andover Newton across Two Centuries* (Grand Rapids, MI: William B. Eerdmans, 2008), 25. For the meanings of the benevolent empire in South Africa, see Richard Elphick, 'The Benevolent Empire and the Social Gospel: Missionaries and South African Christians in the Age of Segregation', in *Christianity in South Africa: A Political, Social, and Cultural History*, eds. Elphick and Rodney Davenport (Cape Town: David Philip, 1997), 347–369.

3. Amanda Porterfield, *Mary Lyon and the Mount Holyoke Missionaries* (New York: Oxford University Press, 1997), 124–127.

4. Elizabeth Alden Green, *Mary Lyon and Mount Holyoke: Opening the Gates* (Hanover, NH: University Press of New England, 1979), 264.

5. See Thomas Woody, *A History of Women's Education in the United States* (New York: Octagon Books, 1966), 458; and Porterfield, *Mary Lyon*, 97–98.

6. See Gertrude R. Hance, *The Zulu Yesterday and To-day: Twenty-nine Years in South Africa* (New York: Negro Universities Press, 1916; 1969), 129; Porterfield, *Mary Lyon*, 127; and S.E. Duff, ' "The Right Kind of Ambition": Discourses of Femininity at the Huguenot Seminary and College, 1895–1910', in *Girlhood: A Global History*, eds. Jennifer Halgren and Colleen A. Vasconcellos (New Brunswick, NJ: Rutgers University Press, 2010), 234–249. Huguenot College offered university courses from 1898.

7. See Porterfield, *Mary Lyon*; and Lisa Joy Pruitt, *A Looking-Glass for Ladies: American Protestant Women and the Orient in the Nineteenth Century* (Macon, GA: Mercer University Press, 2005), 110–111.

8. See Dana L. Robert, *American Women in Mission: A Social History of Their Thought and Practice* (Macon, GA: Mercer University Press, 1996), 97.

9. Mary Lyon, 1839, cited in Robert, *American Women in Mission*, 97.

10. See Paul William Harris, *Nothing but Christ: Rufus Anderson and the Ideology of Protestant Foreign Missions* (New York: Oxford University Press, 1999), 4.

11. Robert, *American Women in Mission*, 104–105.

12. See Patricia Grimshaw, *Paths of Duty: American Missionary Wives in Nineteenth-Century Hawaii* (Honolulu: University of Hawaii Press, 1989), 5–7.

13. Anderson, Boston, to the American Zulu Mission, Natal, 24 December 1865, American Board Mission Collection (ABMC), File A/2/16, National Archives of South Africa, Pietermaritzburg, KwaZulu-Natal.

14. See Ussama Makdisi, *Artillery of Heaven: American Missionaries and the Failed Conversion of the Middle East* (Ithaca: Cornell University Press,

2008), 61–71; and William R. Hutchinson, *Errand to the World: American Protestant Thought and Foreign Missions* (Chicago: University of Chicago Press, 1987), 43–61.

15. Hutchinson, *Errand to the World*, 45.
16. See John Andrew, 'Educating the Heathen: The Foreign Mission School Controversy and American Ideals', *Journal of American Studies* 12, no. 3 (December 1978): 331–342, p. 331.
17. S. Worcester, 'Report of the Prudential Committee: Foreign Mission School', *The Missionary Herald* 17, no. 1 (January 1821): 2. By 1821, pupils comprised nineteen Native Americans, seven Asians and three local whites. See Rufus Anderson, *Memorial Volume of the First Fifty Years of the American Board of Commissioners for Foreign Missions* (Boston: American Board, 1862), 330.
18. See Andrew, 'Educating the Heathen', 335–342.
19. American Board Annual Report of 1825, cited in Anderson, *Memorial Volume*, 331.
20. American Board, *Brief Sketch of the American Ceylon Mission* (Jaffna, Ceylon: American Mission Press, 1849), 4–5.
21. American Board, *Brief Sketch of the American Ceylon Mission*, 8. Marriage later became a more integral goal of the Ceylon schools: in 1855, the Board censured education beyond the Bible in its Asian missions, worrying that they were losing too many graduates to secular pursuits. Oodooville and the men's seminary were suspended that year and reopened with Tamil-medium curricula. And Oodooville's mandate was revised: no more was it to train teachers, but it would expressly cultivate Christian wives. Enrolment was reduced by half, to correspond precisely with the number of eligible Tamil bachelors in the mission. See Royal Gould Wilder, *Mission Schools in India of the American Board of Commissioners for Foreign Missions* (New York: A.D.F. Randolph, 1861); and Anderson, Boston, to the American Zulu Mission, Natal, 24 December 1865, ABMC, File A/2/16.
22. See Pruitt, *A Looking-Glass for Ladies*, 99–104.
23. 'New Mission to Western Africa', *The Missionary Herald* 29, no. 11 (November 1833): 399–403, p. 402.
24. 'Extracts of a Letter of the Rev. Dr. Philip, of the London Missionary Society', *The Missionary Herald* 29, no. 11 (November 1833): 414–420; 'Proposed Mission on the Eastern Coast of Africa', *The Missionary Herald* 29, no. 8 (August 1832): 291.
25. 'New Mission to Western Africa', *The Missionary Herald* 29, no. 11 (November 1833): 399–403, p. 399.

26. See William Ireland, *Historical Sketch of the Zulu Mission in South Africa, as Also of the Gaboon Mission, in Western Africa* (Boston: American Board of Commissioners for Foreign Missions, n.d., circa 1865), 25–32.

27. See Norman Etherington, 'An American Errand into the South African Wilderness', *Church History* 39 (1970): 62–71; and Heather Hughes, 'Politics and Society in Inanda, Natal: The Qadi under Chief Mqhawe, c. 1840–1906' (PhD diss., University of London, 1995), 160.

28. See John Wright, 'Reflections on the Politics of Being "Zulu"', in *Zulu Identities: Being Zulu, Past and Present*, eds. Benedict Carton, John Laband and Jabulani Sithole (Pietermaritzburg: University of KwaZulu-Natal Press, 2008), 35–43; and Norman Etherington, *The Great Treks: The Transformation of Southern Africa, 1815–1854* (New York: Longman, 2001).

29. In southern Africa, the Board apparently did not feel compelled to appoint any African Americans, and in fact it would not until it sent Benjamin Ousley, his wife, Henrietta Bailey Ousley, and a single black woman, Nancy Jones, to serve the Board's new mission to Mozambique in 1884. See Sylvia M. Jacobs, 'Give a Thought to Africa: Black Women Missionaries in Southern Africa', in *Western Women and Imperialism: Complicity and Resistance*, eds. Nupur Chaudhuri and Margaret Strobel (Bloomington: Indiana University Press, 1992), 207–230, pp. 209–210. See also Etherington, 'An American Errand', 70. As racial divisions congealed, the mission maintained a de facto policy of appointing only whites to Natal.

30. On the Grout women, see Porterfield, *Mary Lyon*, 116.

31. For the foregoing biographies, see Edwin W. Smith, *The Life and Times of Daniel Lindley, 1801–1880* (London: The Epworth Press, 1949), 52–54; and D.J. Kotze, ed., *Letters of the American Missionaries, 1835–1838* (Cape Town: Van Riebeeck Society, 1950), 11–12.

32. See Ireland, *Historical Sketch of the Zulu Mission*, 16–17.

33. See 'Extracts of a Letter of the Rev. Dr. Philip, of the London Missionary Society', 416.

34. See Ireland, *Historical Sketch of the Zulu Mission*, 17–19.

35. See Daniel Lindley, Umlazi, to Anderson, 4 December 1847, ABC, Series 15.4, Volume 4; and David Welsh, *The Roots of Segregation: Native Policy in Colonial Natal, 1845–1910* (New York: Oxford University Press, 1971; 1973), 12–14.

36. See Hughes, 'Politics and Society in Inanda, Natal', 52–80 and 151; and Heather Hughes, 'Doubly Elite: Exploring the Life of John Langalibalele Dube', *Journal of Southern African Studies* 27, no. 3 (September 2001): 445–458, pp. 450–451.

37. Lindley, Inanda, to Anderson, 16 November 1855, ABC, Series 15.4, Volume 4.
38. Inanda was among the largest of twelve mission reserves, totalling some 90 000 acres. The American Board controlled more land than any other mission in Natal. See Heather Hughes, ' "A Lighthouse for African Womanhood": Inanda Seminary, 1869-1945', in *Women and Gender in Southern Africa to 1945*, ed. Cherryl Walker (Cape Town: David Philip, 1990), 197-220, p. 200; and Welsh, *The Roots of Segregation*, 47.
39. See Etherington, 'An American Errand'; and Etherington, *Preachers, Peasants, and Politics in Southeast Africa, 1835-1880: African Christian Communities in Natal, Pondoland, and Zululand* (London: Royal Historical Society, 1978).
40. See 'Extracts of a Letter of the Rev. Dr. Philip, of the London Missionary Society'; and 'Proposed Mission on the Eastern Coast of Africa'.
41. See Hughes, 'Doubly Elite', 449-450.
42. So maintained guests at her funeral. See G.A. Gollock, *Daughters of Africa* (New York: Longmans, Green, and Co., 1932), 83. On the Dube family, see also Heather Hughes, *First President: A Life of John L. Dube, Founding President of the ANC* (Auckland Park, South Africa: Jacana, 2011), 1-19.
43. Etherington, *Preachers, Peasants, and Politics in Southeast Africa*, 24.
44. Etherington, *Preachers, Peasants, and Politics in Southeast Africa*, 27.
45. See Ian Booth, 'Natal and Zululand: The Work of the American Board Mission', *Changing Frontiers: The Mission Story of the UCCSA*, ed. Steve de Gruchy (Gaborone, Botswana: Pula Press, 1999), 80-92, p. 88; and Gerald J. Pillay, 'Community Service and Conversion: Christianity among Indian South Africans', in *Christianity in South Africa: A Political, Social, and Cultural History*, 286-296, p. 289. Americans would maintain that Zulu speakers would 'become His messengers of love and mercy to all the Bantu tribes on the seaboard and interior up to and across the Zambezi'; see Frederick Bunker, Amanzimtoti, 'Dear Friends', November 1898, ABC, Series 15.6.2, Volume 1. In contrast, Indians 'compete sharply with both the white colonists and the native Zulu', but 'they do not affiliate with the Zulus. Christian work for them cannot be conducted in conjunction with the established work of our mission'; see 'Report of the Deputation to Africa', 1903, ABMC, File A/4/51. See also Joy Brain, *Christian Indians in Natal, 1860-1911: An Historical and Statistical Study* (Cape Town: Oxford University Press, 1983), 228-229.
46. See Etherington, 'An American Errand', 66.
47. 'Annual Letter of the American Zulu Mission to the Prudential Committee of the ABCFM for the Year Ending Dec 31st 1858', ABC, Series 15.4, Volume 4.

48. David Rood, Lewis Grout et al., Amanzimtoti, to Anderson, Boston, 5 June 1865, ABC, Series 15.4, Volume 6. Lovedale opened to boys in 1841, adding a girls' section in 1868: R.H.W. Shepherd, *Lovedale, South Africa: 1824–1955* (Alice, South Africa: Lovedale Press, 1971), 15; and Graham A. Duncan, *Lovedale: Coercive Agency* (Pietermaritzburg: Cluster, 2003).

49. Lindley to Anderson, Boston, 24 June 1864, ABC, Series 15.4, Volume 6. See also Hughes, 'Politics and Society in Inanda, Natal', 184–185.

50. Lindley, Grant et al., Durban, to Anderson, Boston, 23 May 1864, ABC, Series 15.4, Volume 6.

51. 'The Female Boarding School in Foreign Missions', December 1866, ABMC, File A/2/16.

52. Smith, *The Life and Times of Daniel Lindley*, 281.

53. See Myra Dinnerstein, 'The American Board Mission to the Zulu, 1835–1900' (PhD diss., Columbia University, 1971), 44–45; and Dinnerstein, 'The American Zulu Mission in the Nineteenth Century: Clash over Customs', *Church History* 45, no. 2 (June 1976): 235–246, p. 236. Labour extraction also accompanied education at the Wesleyan station in Edendale, where converts 'apprenticed' their children to missionaries in the 1840s and 1850s: see Sheila Meintjes, 'Family and Gender in the Christian Community at Edendale, Natal, in Colonial Times', in *Women and Gender in Southern Africa to 1945*, 125–145, pp. 129–133.

54. 'General Survey of the Missions of the American Board of Commissioners for Foreign Missions, Presented at the Annual Meeting at Brooklyn, October 4, 1870', ABMC, Box D/1/90.

55. Henry Bridgman, Ifumi, to Anderson, Boston, 22 June 1864, ABC, Series 15.4, Volume 6.

56. On American women's expanding educational opportunities in the 1860s, see Robert, *American Women in Mission*, 92–93; and Nancy Cott, *The Bonds of Womanhood: 'Woman's Sphere' in New England, 1780–1835* (New Haven: Yale University Press, 1977), 121.

57. See 'General Letter of the American Zulu Mission for the Year July, 1909, to June, 1910', ABC, Series 15.4, Volume 29; and Agnes Wood, *Shine Where You Are* (Alice, South Africa: Lovedale Press, 1972), 5.

58. See Smith, *The Life and Times of Daniel Lindley*, 384–385. The most important benefactor, Caroline Phelps Stokes, was the wife of banker James Phelps Stokes; their daughter, also named Caroline Phelps Stokes, endowed the Phelps-Stokes Fund, the major philanthropic player in African and African American schooling from its 1911 founding through the interwar years. The fund's administrator was Dr Anson Phelps Stokes (grandson of the Caroline who endowed Inanda's first building, and nephew of the Caroline who endowed the Phelps-Stokes Fund). Dr Anson

Phelps Stokes married Daniel Lindley's granddaughter Caroline Mitchell in the early twentieth century – producing yet another Caroline Phelps Stokes and binding Inanda more tightly to this philanthropic family. See also Mabel Emerson, Boston, to Anne Brookings, Inanda, 7 November 1932, ABC, Series 15.4, Volume 45.

59. See Rood, Grant et al., Amanzimtoti, to Anderson, Boston, 5 June 1865, ABC, Series 15.4, Volume 6; 'Home Proceedings: Embarkations of Missionaries', *The Missionary Herald* 44, no. 11 (November 1848): 403; and Ireland, 'First Annual Report of the Amanzimtoti High School', 1866, ABC, Series 15.4, Volume 6.

60. 'Annual Tabular Views and Estimates, 1860–1871', ABC, Series 15.4, Volume 6.

61. Ireland, 'Second Annual Report of the Amanzimtoti High School', 1867, ABC, Series 15.4, Volume 6.

62. Ireland, 'Fourth Annual Report of the Male Seminary of Amanzimtoti', 1869, ABC, Series 15.4, Volume 6.

63. Ireland, 'Fifth Annual Report of the Amanzimtoti Male Seminary', 1870, ABC, Series 15.4, Volume 6.

64. Ireland, 'Twelfth Annual Report of the Amanzimtoti Seminary', 1877, ABC, Series 15.4, Volume 8.

65. See Etherington, *Preachers, Peasants, and Politics*, 124–127 and 148–149. On the critical economic importance of transport-riding for peasants in the Cape, see Colin Bundy, *The Rise and Fall of the South African Peasantry* (Berkeley: University of California Press, 1979), 76–77.

66. Ireland, 'Twelfth Annual Report of the Amanzimtoti Seminary', 1877, ABC, Series 15.4, Volume 8.

67. Herbert Goodenough, Amanzimtoti, to J.O. Means, Boston, 6 July 1882, ABC, Series 15.4, Volume 9.

68. Goodenough, 'Annual Report of Amanzimtoti', 21 May 1887, ABC, Series 15.4, Volume 9.

69. Debra L. Duke, 'From True Woman to New Woman: Mary Kelly Edwards, Single Woman Missionary to Natal, South Africa, 1868–1927' (PhD diss., Princeton Theological Seminary, 2004), 95.

70. See Mary Edwards, Lawrence, Kansas, to Clark, Boston, 7 May 1868, ABC, Series 15.4, Volume 6; and Wood, *Shine Where You Are*, 16.

71. Nathaniel Clark, 1868, quoted in Duke, 'From True Woman to New Woman', 102.

72. Elijah Robbins, 'Report of the Amanzimtoti Theological School', 1876, ABC, Series 15.4, Volume 8.

73. Daniel Lindley, Lewis Grout et al., Umvoti, to Clark, Boston, 23 May 1869, ABC, Series 15.4, Volume 6.

74. Jane Waterston, quoted in Robert Young, *African Wastes Reclaimed: Illustrated in the Story of the Lovedale Mission* (London: J.M. Dent and Company, 1902), 14.

75. Jean Comaroff, 'Reading, Rioting, and Arithmetic: The Impact of Mission Education on Black Consciousness in South Africa', *Bulletin of the Institute of Ethnology, Academia Sinica* 82 (Autumn 1996): 19–63, p. 44. On these themes, see also Dana L. Robert, 'The "Christian Home" as a Cornerstone of Anglo-American Missionary Thought and Practice', in *Converting Colonialism: Visions and Realities in Mission History, 1706–1914*, ed. Robert (Grand Rapids, MI: William B. Eerdmans, 2008), 134–165; Deborah Gaitskell, 'At Home with Hegemony? Coercion and Consent in African Girls' Education for Domesticity in South Africa before 1910', in *Contesting Colonial Hegemony: State and Society in Africa and India*, eds. Dagmar Engels and Shula Marks (London: British Academic Press, 1994), 110–128; Modupe Labode, 'From Heathen Kraal to Christian Home: Anglican Mission Education and African Christian Girls, 1850–1900', in *Women and Missions: Past and Present Anthropological and Historical Perceptions*, eds. Fiona Bowie, Deborah Kirkwood and Shirley Ardener (Providence, RI: Berg, 1993), 126–144; Karen Tranberg Hansen, ed., *African Encounters with Domesticity* (New Brunswick, NJ: Rutgers University Press, 1992); and Jean Comaroff and John Comaroff, 'Mansions of the Lord: Architecture, Interiority, Domesticity', in *The Dialectics of Modernity on a South African Frontier*, Volume 2, *Of Revelation and Revolution*, eds. Comaroff and Comaroff (Chicago: University of Chicago Press, 1991), 274–322.

76. See Hughes, ' "A Lighthouse for African Womanhood" ', 197–198.

77. See Sylvia Vietzen, *A History of Education for European Girls in Natal with Particular Reference to the Establishment of Some Leading Schools, 1837–1902* (Pietermaritzburg: University of Natal Press, 1973), 184.

78. Vietzen, *A History of Education*, 249.

79. See *Girls Collegiate School, 1878–1989* (Pietermaritzburg: Girls Collegiate School, 1989); and S.M. Moran, *The First 100 Years, 1882–1982: Durban Girls' Model School and Durban Girls' High School* (Durban: S.M. Moran, 1982).

80. See Duke, 'From True Woman to New Woman', 212–213.

81. Edwards, Inanda, to Clark, Boston, 11 March 1869, ABC, Series 15.4, Volume 6.

82. Edwards, Inanda, to Clark, Boston, 12 March 1869, ABC, Series 15.4, Volume 6.

83. See also, for instance, Edwards, Inanda, to Clark, 20 December 1869, ABC, Series 15.4, Volume 6; Edwards, Inanda, to Clark, 19 January 1870,

ABC, Series 15.4, Volume 6; and Edwards, Inanda, to Chapin, Boston, 19 May 1870, ABC, Series 15.4, Volume 6.

84. Pixley et al., Umtwalume, to Clark, Boston, 3 June 1871, ABC, Series 15.4, Volume 6.

85. 'General Survey of the Missions of the American Board of Commissioners for Foreign Missions, Presented at the Annual Meeting at Salem, October 3, 1871', ABMC, Box D/1/90.

86. Edwards, Inanda, to Clark, Boston, 7 January 1870, ABC, Series 15.4, Volume 6.

87. Edwards, Inanda, to 'My Dear Young Friends', 12 April 1869, ABC, Series 15.4, Volume 6.

88. See Edwards, Ifumi, to Clark, Boston, 15 June 1869, ABC, Series 15.4, Volume 6; and Duke, 'From True Woman to New Woman', 191–192.

89. Edwards, Inanda, to Clark, Boston, 17 September 1869, ABC, Series 15.4, Volume 6.

90. Edwards, Inanda, to Clark, Boston, 17 September 1869, ABC, Series 15.4, Volume 6.

91. Edwards, Inanda, to Clark, Boston, 18 October 1869, ABC, Series 15.4, Volume 6.

92. Edwards, Inanda, to Clark, Boston, 20 July 1871, ABC, Series 15.4, Volume 6.

93. See Edwards, Inanda, to Clark, Boston, 22 May 1871, ABC, Series 15.4, Volume 6.

94. See Edwards, Inanda, to Mrs Hume, Boston, 13 October 1873, ABC, Series 15.4, Volume 49; and 'Report of Inanda Seminary, 1877', ABC, Series 15.4, Volume 49.

95. Edwards, Inanda, to Clark, Boston, 16 March 1874, ABC, Series 15.4, Volume 8.

96. Edwards, Inanda, to Mrs Lawson, Boston, 13 November 1876, ABC, Series 15.4, Volume 49.

97. Edwards, Inanda, to Clark, Boston, 16 June 1880, ABC, Series 15.4, Volume 49. See also Josiah Tyler, 'General Letter of the American Zulu Mission', 15 June 1877, ABC, Series 15.4, Volume 9.

98. Edwards, Inanda, to Mrs Hubbard, Boston, 18 March 1873, ABC, Series 15.4, Volume 49.

99. Edwards, Inanda, to Miss Dorn, Boston, 30 October 1876, ABC, Series 15.4, Volume 49.

100. See Edwards, Inanda, to Clark, Boston, 14 June 1869, ABC, Series 15.4, Volume 6.

101. Martha Price, Inanda, to Means, Boston, 5 August 1881, ABC, Series 15.4, Volume 11.

102. Edwards, 'On Board the "Danube"', to Clark, Boston, 16 July 1874, ABC, Series 15.4, Volume 8.

103. Edwards, Troy, Ohio, to Mrs Hume, Boston, 27 October 1874, ABC, Series 15.4, Volume 49.

104. See Edwards, West Milton, Ohio, to Clark, Boston, 14 June 1875, ABC, Series 15.4, Volume 8; Edwards, West Milton, Ohio, to Clark, Boston, 2 November 1875, ABC, Series 15.4, Volume 8.

105. Edwards, West Milton, to Clark, Boston, 13 December 1875, ABC, Series 15.4, Volume 8.

106. Edwards, Inanda, to Clark, Boston, 14 October 1873, ABC, Series 15.4, Volume 8. See also Edwards, Inanda, to Clark, Boston, 27 September 1877, ABC, Series 15.4, Volume 8.

107. Fannie Morris, Inanda, to Clark, Boston, 11 July 1879, ABC, Series 15.4, Volume 8.

108. Edwards, Inanda, to Clark, 9 July 1879, ABC, Series 15.4, Volume 8. The term 'kraal', an Afrikaans term that properly referred to a cattle enclosure, was widely used by colonial settlers, officials and missionaries to refer to the African homesteads that had constituted the region's productive and reproductive basis prior to the coming of colonial capitalism. On 'kraals' and 'kraal girls', see Chapter 2 of this study.

109. Morris, Inanda, to Clark, Boston, 11 July 1879, ABC, Series 15.4, Volume 8.

110. Morris pursued her task with personal, unseemly zeal. She confessed, 'I've been wanting a little girl ever since I came to Natal, but had almost given up finding one, for girls are property here . . . so there are no homeless orphans.' Morris nonetheless persuaded an ill five-year-old to live with her. The girl's father was reportedly interested in Christianity and her mother agreed to send her 'away from the kraal before she learned the bad customs of the people', although the appeal of medical treatment may have been more compelling. Morris then took in another girl, assembling 'quite a little family'. See 'Extracts from Miss Morris' letter', Inanda, 16 November 1879, ABC, Series 15.4, Volume 49.

111. 'Report of Inanda Seminary for the Year 1885', ABC, Series 15.4, Volume 9.

112. Fidelia Phelps, Inanda, to Emerson, Boston, 30 July 1885, ABC, Series 15.4, Volume 49.

113. Vietzen, *A History of Education*, 131.

114. Price, Inanda, to Smith, Boston, 28 February 1885, ABC, Series 15.4, Volume 11.

115. See Patricia R. Hill, *The World Their Household: The American Women's Foreign Mission Movement and Cultural Transformation, 1870–1920* (Ann Arbor: University of Michigan Press, 1985), 1–5.

116. See Robert, *American Women in Mission*, 108; Duke, 'From True Woman to New Woman', 77–81; and Harris, *Nothing but Christ*, 32. From the 1820s, single women had gone in small numbers to Hawaii, including an African American woman who ran a school; in the 1840s, a handful taught at Oodooville; in 1843, a Holyoke alumna ran a girls' school in Persia modelled on her alma mater; and nearly a quarter of the more than 400 missionaries sent to work with Native Americans by 1860 were single women.

117. George Champion, American Zulu Mission, 1836, cited in Norman Etherington, 'Gender Issues in Southeast African Missions, 1835–1885', in *Missions and Christianity in South African History*, eds. Henry Bredekamp and Robert Ross (Johannesburg: Wits University Press, 1995), 135–152, p. 140.

118. Cited in Pruitt, 'A Looking-Glass for Ladies', 104.

119. Pruitt, 'A Looking-Glass for Ladies', 167. On Anderson's attitudes towards single female missionaries, see Duke, 'From True Woman to New Woman', 81.

120. James T. Campbell, *Songs of Zion: The African Methodist Episcopal Church in the United States and South Africa* (New York: Oxford University Press, 1995), 93.

121. Pruitt, 'A Looking-Glass for Ladies', 144–176; and Joan Jacobs Brumberg, 'Zenanas and Girlless Villages: The Ethnology of American Evangelical Women, 1870–1900', *Journal of American History* 69, no. 2 (September 1982): 347–371.

122. 'Annual Meeting', *Life and Light for Heathen Women* 1, no. 1 (March 1869): 7–8.

123. See 'Letter from Bitlis', *Life and Light for Heathen Women* 1, no. 3 (September 1869): 83–86; and 'The Boarding School', *Life and Light for Heathen Women* 1, no. 4 (December 1869): 119. See also Barbara Reeves-Ellington, 'A Vision of Mount Holyoke in the Ottoman Balkans: American Cultural Transfer, Bulgarian Nation-Building and Women's Educational Reform, 1858–1870', *Gender and History* 16, no. 1 (April 2004): 146–171.

124. Laura Bridgman, Umzumbe, to 'Dear Friends', 10 July 1874, ABC, Series 15.4, Volume 49.

125. Brumberg, 'Zenanas and Girlless Villages', 350.

126. See Price, Inanda, to Miss Child, Boston, 20 May 1884, ABC, Series 15.4, Volume 49.

127. *Life and Light for Heathen Women* 1, no. 5 (March 1870): 165–166.

128. Frontispiece in *The Legion of Liberty! and Force of Truth, Containing the Thoughts, Words, and Deeds, of Some Prominent Apostles, Champions, and Martyrs* (New York: American Anti-Slavery Society, 1847; 1837).

129. Lori D. Ginzberg, 'Global Goals, Local Acts: Grass-Roots Activism in Imperial Narratives', *The Journal of American History* 88, no. 3 (December 2001): 870–873, p. 871. See also Jane H. Hunter, 'Women's Mission in Historical Perspective: American Identity and Christian Internationalism', in *Competing Kingdoms: Women, Mission, Nation, and the American Protestant Empire, 1812–1960*, eds. Barbara Reeves-Ellington, Kathryn Kish Sklar and Connie A. Shemo (Durham, NC: Duke University Press, 2010), 19–42; Amy Kaplan, 'Manifest Domesticity', in *No More Separate Spheres!* eds. Cathy N. Davidson and Jessamyn Hatcher (Durham, NC: Duke University Press, 2002), 183–207; and Ann Laura Stoler, 'Tense and Tender Ties: The Politics of Comparison in North American History and (Post) Colonial Studies', in *Haunted by Empire: Geographies of Intimacy in North American History*, ed. Stoler (Durham, NC: Duke University Press, 2006), 23–70.

130. See Elizabeth E. Prevost, *The Communion of Women: Missions and Gender in Colonial Africa and the British Metropole* (New York: Oxford University Press, 2010); Patricia Grimshaw and Peter Sherlock, 'Women and Cultural Exchanges', in *Missions and Empire*, ed. Norman Etherington (New York: Oxford University Press, 2005), 173–193, pp. 184–185.

131. Hutchinson, 'Errand to the World', 101.

132. Pruitt, 'A Looking-Glass for Ladies', 145.

133. 'The Higher Educational Institutions of the American Board', n.d. (circa 1887), ABMC, Box D/1/90.

134. 'General Survey of the Missions of the American Board of Commissioners for Foreign Missions, Presented at the Annual Meeting at Brooklyn, October 4, 1870', ABMC, Box D/1/90.

135. See Rhonda Semple, 'Ruth, Miss Mackintosh, and Ada and Rose Marris: Biblewomen, *Zenana* Workers, and Missionaries in Nineteenth-Century British Missions to North India', *Women's History Review* 17, no. 4 (September 2008): 561–574.

136. See Etherington, 'Gender Issues', 140.

137. See Edwards, 'Native School Return for 1880', ABC, Series 15.4, Volume 9; Price to Means, 5 August 1881, ABC, Series 15.4, Volume 11; and 'Tabular View, Inanda Seminary', 1869–1884, ABC, Series 15.4, Volume 9. Hawes was only eighteen in 1880, but she had served as a pupil-teacher since she was thirteen and was by that point teaching full-time, as well as working as a translator. Hawes earned thirty pounds per year, while the American women each earned ninety pounds. In 1883, Hawes and another recent Inanda alumna, Dalita Isaac, together earned sixty-one pounds per year. According to Etherington (*Preachers, Peasants, and Politics*, 148), the highest salary paid to any African by Christian missions in Natal in 1876 was just seventy-five pounds, and the American Zulu Mission did not

appear to exceed this amount by the mid-1880s. This salary paled in comparison to what men might make in trade, and so ministers like James Dube tended to supplement their pastoral pay with earnings from transport-riding and other enterprises. Young African women, and many African men who worked as local evangelists rather than ordained ministers, did not have the time or opportunity to engage in other significant income-generating activities and so relied largely on their paltry wages from the mission.

138. See, for example, Edwards, 'Report of Inanda Seminary, 1877', ABC, Series 15.4, Volume 49, which reports on a recent Inanda graduate's decision to leave domestic service to teach at a rural school: 'She could only be promised half the salary there which she has received as a servant, but she remarked that she could not stop for thinking of the children.'

139. See Etherington, 'Gender Issues', 149–150. Their first names are variously spelt in missionary and state records and in published accounts. Here I use the spellings that the women used in legal documents and personal correspondence as adults.

140. Edwards, Inanda, to Miss Lawson, Boston, 13 November 1876, ABC, Series 15.4, Volume 49. My estimate of Hawes' age comes from the birthdate of 26 September 1862 in all state records.

141. Edwards, Inanda, to Clark, Boston, 11 March 1869, ABC, Series 15.4, Volume 6; Edwards, Inanda, to 'My Dear Young Friends', St Johnsbury, Vermont, 12 April 1869, ABC, Series 15.4, Volume 6.

142. Edwards, Inanda, 27 September 1877, to Women's Board, Boston, ABC, Series 15.4, Volume 49.

143. See Edwards, Inanda, to Mrs Barnes, Boston, 30 August 1880, ABC, Series 15.4, Volume 49.

144. Talitha Hawes, Inanda, to Mrs Hume, Boston, 28 January 1879, ABC, Series 15.4, Volume 49.

145. Smith, *The Life and Times of Daniel Lindley*, 55; Andile Hawes, descendant of Thomas Hawes and Hawes family historian, interviewed by the author, 21 March 2009, Inanda, Inanda Seminary Oral History Project (ISOHP). Joel Hawes was not the only head of a *kholwa* lineage to be baptised on American lines. Nembula Makhanya had been baptised Ira Adams Nembula in 1847 after he left one of his two wives and married the other under Christian rites; he was named for Newton Adams' brother, and his wife was baptised Laura after Adams' sister. Laura's brother George Champion, another charter member of the Inanda church, was baptised after the missionary George Champion.

146. Quoted in Smith, *The Life and Times of Daniel Lindley*, 419.

147. Edwards, Inanda, to Clark, Boston, 8 May 1869, ABC, Series 15.4, Volume 6.

148. See Edwards, Inanda, to Clark, 28 September 1876, ABC, Series 15.4, Volume 8.

149. Edwards, Inanda, to Mrs Haskett, Boston, 16 April 1881, ABC, Series 15.4, Volume 49.

150. Robert Vinson and Robert Edgar, 'Zulus, African Americans and the African Diaspora', in *Zulu Identities*, 240–249, p. 243.

151. Edwards, Inanda, to Clark, Boston, 8 December 1884, ABC, Series 15.4, Volume 9.

152. Edwards, Inanda, to Smith, Boston, 6 April 1885, ABC, Series 15.4, Volume 9.

153. Talitha E. Hawes, 'Petition under the provisions of Law No. 28, 1865, "For relieving certain persons from the operation of Native Law"', 25 March 1889, Secretary for Native Affairs Series (SNA), Volume I/1/113, Reference 1889/327, National Archives of South Africa, Pietermaritzburg, KwaZulu-Natal. On exemption, see Chapter 2.

154. 'Estate of the Late Talitha Emily Hawes', 10 June 1927, Master of the Supreme Court, Estates Records (MSCE), Volume 12298/12304, Reference 12299, National Archives of South Africa, Pietermaritzburg, KwaZulu-Natal; 'Death Notice of Thomas Hawes', 10 November 1921, SNA, Volume I/1/278, Reference 470/1897.

155. Hawes, ISOHP.

156. 'Examinations for Teachers' Certificates', 1905, Inanda Seminary Papers (ISP), File 30, Campbell Collections, University of KwaZulu-Natal, Durban.

157. Hawes, ISOHP.

158. See Richard Rive, 'The Early Years', in *Seme: The Founder of the ANC*, eds. Richard Rive and Tim Couzens (Braamfontein, South Africa: Skotaville, 1991), 9–35; and Hughes, *First President*, 12.

159. On the foregoing, see Edwards, Inanda, to Mrs W.H. Fairchild, New Haven, 26 May 1888, ABC, Series 15.6.2, Volume 1.

160. Dalita Isaac, Mongwe, to Edwards, Inanda, 2 June 1888, ABC, Series 15.4, Volume 12.

161. 'Translation of a Letter Written to Mrs. Edwards by Lucy Mgceki', Mongwe, 20 September 1885, ABC, Series 15.4, Volume 49.

162. Lawrence Gilley, 'Mozambique: The Work of the American Board Mission in Inhambane', in *Changing Frontiers*, 93–106, p. 96.

163. See Dalita Isaac, Mongwe, to Edwards, Inanda, 1 June 1889, ABC, Series 15.6.2, Volume 2.

164. Phelps, Inanda, to Miss Dunn, Boston, 26 August 1889, ABC, Series 15.6.2, Volume 2.

165. Pixley, Inanda, to Smith, 25 December 1889, ABC, Series 15.4, Volume 11.

166. See Isaac, Inanda, to Mr and Mrs Bates, Adams, 6 January 1890, ABC, Series 15.4, Volume 15.
167. See Francis Bates, Inanda, to Smith, Boston, 1 January 1890, ABC, Series 15.4, Volume 15; and Bates, Adams, to Smith, Boston, 21 January 1890, ABC, Series 15.4, Volume 15.
168. See Patrick Harries, *Butterflies and Barbarians: Swiss Missionaries and Systems of Knowledge in South-East Africa* (Athens: Ohio University Press, 2007), 89.
169. See Harries, *Butterflies and Barbarians*, 89.
170. Phelps, Inanda, to Smith, Boston, 3 May 1895, ABC, Series 15.4, Volume 17.
171. See Phelps, Inanda, to Smith, Boston, 16 October 1896, ABC, Series 15.4, Volume 17.
172. See Robert Houle, 'Mbiya Kuzwayo's Christianity: Revival, Reformation and the Surprising Viability of Mainline Churches in South Africa', *Journal of Religion in Africa* 38 (2008): 141–170, although he misidentifies the 'Dalita' referenced in missionary reports as Talitha Hawes.
173. Phelps, 'Inanda Seminary Report, July 1897 to June 1898', ABC, Series 15.4, Volume 13.
174. 'Ukufa Kuka Mrs. Dalitha Elijah Hlanti', *Ilanga Lase Natal* (16 January 1937): 8.
175. See Dalita Hlanti, Mount Silinda Mission Station, to 'Mother Edwards', Inanda, 30 April 1925, ABC, Series 15.4, Volume 40.

Chapter Two

1. See Robert Plant, 'Annual Report of the Inspector of Native Schools for 1893–94', in Inanda Seminary Papers (ISP), File 29, Campbell Collections, University of KwaZulu-Natal, Durban.
2. 'To the Honourable Legislative Assembly of Natal, A Petition on Behalf of Kraal Girls', n.d. draft (circa 1893), ISP, File 1a; see also Henry Dale, Natal Missionary Conference, 'Petition on Behalf of Kraal Girls', to the Colonial Secretary, Pietermaritzburg, 5 June 1894, Secretary for Native Affairs Series (SNA), Volume I/1/186, Reference 650/1894, National Archives of South Africa, Pietermaritzburg, KwaZulu-Natal.
3. The Marriage Law taxed marriage; it also required registration of marriages and compelled women to consent to unions in the presence of a chief-appointed (colonially approved) witness. See Michael R. Mahoney and Julie Parle, 'An Ambiguous Sexual Revolution: Intragenerational Conflict in Late Colonial Natal, 1879–1906', *South African Historical Journal* 50 (2004): 134–151.

4. Jeff Guy, 'An Accommodation of Patriarchs: Theophilus Shepstone and the System of Native Administration in Natal' (seminar paper, Colloquium on Masculinities in Southern Africa, University of Natal, Durban, 1997).

5. The term came into Afrikaans from the Portuguese *curral* (corral): see Kathleen K. McCormick, 'Code-Switching, Code-Mixing, and Convergence in Cape Town', in *Language and Social History: Studies in South African Sociolinguistics*, ed. Rajend Mesthrie (Cape Town: David Philip, 1995), 216–234, p. 214.

6. See Absolom Vilakazi, *Zulu Transformations: A Study of the Dynamics of Social Change* (Pietermaritzburg: University of Natal Press, 1962), 123–125.

7. See Harriet Ngubane, 'Marriage, Affinity and the Ancestral Realm: Zulu Marriage in Female Perspective', in *Essays on African Marriage in Southern Africa*, eds. Eileen Krige and John Comaroff (Cape Town: Juta, 1981), 84–95; Jeff Guy, 'Analysing Pre-capitalist Societies in Southern Africa', *Journal of Southern African Studies* 14, no. 1 (October 1987): 18–37; Guy, 'Gender Oppression in Southern Africa's Precapitalist Societies', in *Women and Gender in Southern Africa to 1945*, ed. Cherryl Walker (Cape Town: David Philip, 1990), 33–47; and Adam Kuper, 'The "House" and Zulu Political Structure in the Nineteenth Century', *The Journal of African History* 34, no. 3 (1993): 469–487.

8. See Mahmood Mamdani, *Citizen and Subject: Contemporary Africa and the Legacy of Late Colonialism* (Princeton, NJ: Princeton University Press, 1996), 62–108.

9. See Thembisa Waetjen, *Workers and Warriors: Masculinity and the Struggle for Nation in South Africa* (Urbana: University of Illinois Press, 2004), 33–36; and Benedict Carton, *Blood from Your Children: The Colonial Origins of Generational Conflict in South Africa* (Charlottesville: University of Virginia Press, 2000), 22–25.

10. See Guy, 'Women in Labour: The Birth of Colonial Natal' (seminar paper, History and African Studies Seminar, University of KwaZulu-Natal, Durban, 2009).

11. See David Welsh, *The Roots of Segregation: Native Policy in Colonial Natal, 1845–1910* (New York: Oxford University Press, 1971; 1973), 23.

12. Shula Marks, *Reluctant Rebellion: The 1906–8 Disturbances in Natal* (Oxford: Clarendon Press, 1970), 119.

13. 'Report of the 1852 Natal Commission of Inquiry', quoted in Welsh, *The Roots of Segregation*, 34.

14. Marks, *Reluctant Rebellion*, 121–122; and Welsh, *The Roots of Segregation*, 32.

15. John Lambert, *Betrayed Trust: Africans and the State in Colonial Natal* (Pietermaritzburg: University of Natal Press, 1995), 71.

16. Marks, *Reluctant Rebellion*, 121.

17. Welsh, *The Roots of Segregation*, 33.

18. See Lambert, *Betrayed Trust*, 95.

19. See Carton, *Blood from Your Children*, 50.

20. See Mahoney and Parle, *An Ambiguous Sexual Revolution*, 140; and Lambert, *Betrayed Trust*, 153–161.

21. See Carton, *Blood from Your Children*, 53–65; and Marks, *Reluctant Rebellion*.

22. Cited in Welsh, *The Roots of Segregation*, 62.

23. The Cape had a propertied franchise in which 5 per cent of 142 000 voters were African and 10 per cent were 'coloured' men by 1909. See Welsh, *The Roots of Segregation*, 236–259; Julie Evans and David Philips, ' "When There's No Safety in Numbers": Fear and the Franchise in South Africa: The Case of Natal', in *Law, History, and Colonialism: The Reach of Empire*, eds. Diane Kirkby and Catharine Coleborne (Manchester: Manchester University Press, 2001), 91–105; and 'South African Native Affairs Commission Report of 1903–1905', ISP, File 31.

24. See Richard Elphick, 'The Benevolent Empire and the Social Gospel: Missionaries and South African Christians in the Age of Segregation', in *Christianity in South Africa: A Political, Social, and Cultural History*, eds. Elphick and Rodney Davenport (Cape Town: David Philip, 1997), 347–369.

25. See Welsh, *The Roots of Segregation*, 244.

26. See Norman Etherington, *Preachers, Peasants, and Politics in Southeast Africa, 1835–1880: African Christian Communities in Natal, Pondoland, and Zuluand* (London: Royal Historical Society, 1978), 137–141.

27. See Talitha Hawes, Inanda, to Mrs Hume, Boston, 28 January 1879, American Board of Commissioners for Foreign Missions: African Missions Records (henceforth ABC), Series 15.4, Volume 49, Houghton Library, Harvard University, Cambridge, Massachusetts.

28. See Mary Edwards, Inanda, to Miss Orcutt, Boston, 15 July 1881, ABC, Series 15.4, Volume 49.

29. Edwards, Inanda, to Orcutt, Boston, 15 July 1881, ABC, Series 15.4, Volume 49.

30. Stephen Pixley, Inanda, to Smith, Boston, 13 June 1885, ABC, Series 15.4, Volume 11; Fidelia Phelps, Inanda, to Judson Smith, Boston, 5 February 1887, ABC, Series 15.4, Volume 11.

31. Edwards, Inanda, to the Women's Board of Missions, Boston, 21 February 1886, ABC, Series 15.6.2, Volume 1.

32. See Phelps, 'Report of Inanda Seminary, June 1907–June 1908', ABC, Series 15.4, Volume 23; and Agnes Wood, *Shine Where You Are: A History of Inanda Seminary, 1869–1969* (Alice, South Africa: Lovedale Press, 1972), 63.

33. See Heather Hughes, 'Politics and Society in Inanda, Natal: The Qadi under Chief Mqhawe, c. 1840–1906' (PhD diss., University of London, 1995), 246.

34. Phelps, Inanda, to Mrs Buffum, Providence, 7 June 1894, ABC, Series 15.4, Volume 49.

35. Ntoyi Nxaba, quotes in Phelps, Inanda, to Mrs Buffum, Providence, 7 June 1894, ABC, Series 15.4, Volume 49.

36. On Nxaba: see Price, Inanda, to Smith, Boston, 28 February 1885, ABC, Series 15.4, Volume 11; Edwards, Inanda, to Smith, Boston, 7 August 1886, ABC, Series 15.4, Volume 9; Edwards, Natal, to Mrs Fairchild, New Haven, 26 May 1888, ABC, Series 15.6.2, Volume 1; Agnes Bigelow, Umzumbe, to Women's Board of Missions, Boston, 27 March 1893, ABC, Series 15.6.2, Volume 1; Bigelow, Inanda, to Miss Fay, Boston, 2 October 1895, ABC, Series 15.6.2, Volume 1.

37. Edwards, Inanda, to Smith, Boston, 27 August 1888, ABC, Series 15.4, Volume 9.

38. See Price, Pietermaritzburg, to Smith, Boston, 25 October 1893, ABC, Series 15.4, Volume 17.

39. Lambert, *Betrayed Trust*, 135.

40. Carton, *Blood from Your Children*, 68.

41. Hughes, 'Politics and Society in Inanda, Natal', 246.

42. See Carton, *Blood from Your Children*, 72.

43. See Hughes, 'Politics and Society in Inanda', 246.

44. Frances E. Colenso, *History of the Zulu War and Its Origin* (London: Chapman and Hall, 1880), 193–194.

45. Carton, *Blood from Your Children*, 72.

46. See Price, Pietermaritzburg, to Smith, Boston, 25 October 1893, ABC, Series 15.4, Volume 17. In most missionary accounts, in fact, mothers or brothers struggle to retrieve girls from school, not fathers. See Hughes, 'Politics and Society in Inanda', 246.

47. Related in 'Inanda Seminary, 1891–1892: Statistics', ABC, Series 15.4, Volume 13.

48. See 'List of Cases Illustrating the Forced Marriages of Native Girls', n.d. (circa 1893), ISP, File 1a; Herbert Goodenough, 'Nomnyaka's Case', 21 March 1893, ISP, File 1a.

49. Testimony of Susiwe Bhengu, in 'List of Cases Illustrating the Forced Marriages of Native Girls', n.d. (circa 1893), ISP, File 1a.

50. See Price, Pietermaritzburg, to the Women's Board of Missions, 27 December 1892, ABC, Series 15.6.2, Volume 2; and Hughes, 'Politics and Society in Inanda', 245.
51. Edwards, Inanda, to Smith, Boston, 23 October 1893, ABC, Series 15.4, Volume 16.
52. Wood, *Shine Where You Are*, 50.
53. On Catholics' contemporaneous struggles in Natal, see Risimati Samuel Khandlhela, 'Mariannhill Mission and African Education, 1882–1915' (master's thesis, University of Natal, 1993), 86–90.
54. Charles Kilbon, Edwards, Price et al., Amanzimtoti, 28 April 1893, ISP, File 1a.
55. Kilbon, Amanzimtoti, 'To Missionaries and Others in Natal', 12 August 1893, ISP, File 1a. German Lutherans of the Hermannsburg and Berlin Missions, Swedish Lutherans of the Church of Sweden, Anglicans of the Bethany Zulu Mission and Presbyterians of the Free Church of Scotland all replied with dramatic tales of court cases that upheld patriarchal authority: see H. Hormann, Emtombeni, 'To the Petition Committee of the American Zulu Mission', Amanzimtoti, 18 May 1893; G.A. Stielan, Noodsberg, to Kilbon, Amanzimtoti, 19 September 1893; and Mr and Mrs J.J. Haviland, Bethany Zulu Mission, Estcourt, to Kilbon, Amanzimtoti, 30 August 1893, all in ISP, File 1a.
56. See 'To the Honourable the Legislative Assembly of Natal, A Petition on Behalf of Kraal Girls', n.d. draft (circa 1893), ISP, File 1a.
57. See Dale, Natal Missionary Conference, 'Petition on Behalf of Kraal Girls', to the Colonial Secretary, Pietermaritzburg, 5 June 1894, SNA, Volume I/1/186, Reference 650/1894.
58. See Dale, Natal Missionary Conference, 'Petition on Behalf of Kraal Girls', to the Colonial Secretary, Pietermaritzburg, 5 June 1894, SNA, Volume I/1/186, Reference 650/1894.
59. See Circulation Paper, No. 2664/94: Note by Attorney General, 16 October 1894; note by Colonial Secretary, 7 November 1894; and note by Secretary of Native Affairs, 2 November 1894, SNA, Volume I/1/186, Reference 650/1894.
60. Phelps, Inanda, to Smith, Boston, 18 July 1894, ABC, Series 15.4, Volume 17.
61. Phelps, Inanda, to Smith, Boston, 3 May 1895, ABC, Series 15.4, Volume 17; see also Price, Inanda, to Smith, Boston, 5 February 1895, ABC, Series 15.4, Volume 17.
62. See Phelps, 'Inanda Seminary Report, July 1897 to June 1898', ABC, Series 15.4, Volume 13.
63. Phelps, 'Inanda Seminary Report, July 1897 to June 1898', ABC, Series 15.4, Volume 13.

64. See Phelps, 'Inanda Seminary Report for 1895–96', ABC, Series 15.4, Volume 13.

65. See Benedict Carton, ' "Get Thee to Church": Zulu Women and American Board Missionaries in the Early Twentieth Century' (seminar paper, Southern African Research Program, Yale University, 1991), 1–4; and 'Mrs. Malcolm, Umzumbe Mission Station: Arrest of Two Native Girls, Named "Dosie" and "Nobuhlungu," at Umzumbe, Under Section 289 of the Code', SNA, Volume I/1/301, Reference 1679/1903.

66. Phelps, 'Annual Report of Inanda Seminary', June 1905, ABC, Series 15.4, Volume 23.

67. Phelps, 'Annual Report of Inanda Seminary', June 1905, ABC, Series 15.4, Volume 23.

68. See A.L. Behr and R.G. Macmillan, *Education in South Africa* (Pretoria: J.L. van Schaik, 1966), 330–336; Khandlhela, 'Mariannhill Mission and African Education', 43–49; and Lindley to Anderson, 16 November 1855, ABC, Series 15.4, Volume 4.

69. See Welsh, *The Roots of Segregation*, 48–50; A.M.P. Kiernan, 'The Work for Education in Natal of Robert James Mann (1857–1865)', (master's thesis, University of Manchester, 1982).

70. Brooks to Shepstone, 24 June 1867, SNA, Volume 1/1/17.

71. H. Wilder, Umtwalume, to Shepstone, Pietermaritzburg, 24 February 1868, American Board Mission Collection (ABMC), File A/3/49, National Archives of South Africa, Pietermaritzburg, KwaZulu-Natal; Brooks to Shepstone, 27 February 1868, SNA, Volume 1/1/18.

72. Brooks, 'Native Schools', 1870, 2–3, SNA, Volume 1/1/17.

73. 'Extract from Native School Report', 1872, ABC, Series 15.4, Volume 8.

74. Jane Waterston, Durban, to James Stewart, Lovedale, 10 January 1872. In *The Letters of Elizabeth Jane Waterston, 1866–1905*, ed. Lucy Bean and Elizabeth van Heyningen (Cape Town: Van Riebeeck Society, 1983).

75. Edwards, Inanda, to Clark, 27 September 1877, ABC, Series 15.4, Volume 8.

76. Ireland, Adams, to the Natal Native Commission, 29 April 1882, ABMC, File A/3/49.

77. Law No. 1, 1884, 'For the Promotion of Elementary Education among the Children of the Native Population', in *Natal Ordinances, Laws, and Proclamations*, ed. Charles Fitzwilliam Kadiz (Pietermaritzburg: Government Printers, 1890), 1480–1482.

78. Plant, 'Report of the Inspector of Native Education for 1889', 3, Colonial Secretary's Office Series (CSO), Volume 1253, Reference 1890/1603, National Archives of South Africa, Pietermaritzburg, KwaZulu-Natal; and Plant, 'Report of the Inspector for Native Education for the Year Ending June 30, 1892', 3, ISP, File 29.

79. See Fynney, 'Report of the Inspector of Native Education for 1886', CSO, Volume 1121, Reference 1887/727; and Plant, 'Annual Report of the Inspector of Native Schools for 1893–1894', ISP, File 29.

80. See Plant, 'Minute on Native Education', in Plant, 'Report of the Inspector of Native Education for 1889', 42–44, CSO, Volume 1253, Reference 1890/1603.

81. See Marks, *Reluctant Rebellion*, 18–19.

82. Natal Superintendent of Education Russell, 1895, cited in Welsh, *The Roots of Segregation*, 270.

83. Edwards to Smith, 30 October 1888, ABC, Series 15.4, Volume 9. Students were tempted to down their hoes: 'They were very much hurt to know that we counted the meals they eat. They came in a body to say that they worked too much or too long and wished to go home.'

84. Frederick Bernard Fynney, Inspector of Native Education, 'Report of the Inspector of Native Education for 1886', 49, CSO, Volume 1121, Reference 1887/727.

85. H.D. Goodenough, 'Reply of the American Mission Reserve Trustees to Lands Commission Report: Mis-statements Exposed', n.d. (circa 1903), ABMC, File A/3/49.

86. See Marks, *Reluctant Rebellion*, 73–81.

87. John L. Dube, 'The Zulu Christian Industrial School and a Plan for the Evangelization and Civilization of Africa', n.d. (circa 1899), ABC, Series 15.4, Volume 14. See also Manning Marable, 'John L. Dube and the Politics of Segregated Education in South Africa', in *Independence without Freedom: The Political Economy of Colonial Education in Southern Africa*, eds. Agrippah Mugomba and Mougo Nyaggah (Santa Barbara, CA: ABC-Clio, 1977), 113–128; and Heather Hughes, *First President: A Life of John L. Dube, Founding President of the ANC* (Auckland Park, South Africa: Jacana, 2011), 93–99. Hughes points out the significance of the name 'Ohlange' on p. 93: 'The hilltop on which the school started to take shape was named Ohlange, deriving from the term *uhlanga*. Signifying the starting point of new growth, and hence the founder of a lineage or "stem" of a family, *uhlanga* had, under the very trying conditions of colonial rule in Natal, come to connote "indigenous people" who claimed a right to the land for themselves and their cattle, as opposed to incoming white and Indian settlers who were trying to snatch it away.'

88. Dube, 'The Zulu Christian Industrial School'.

89. See Welsh, *The Roots of Segregation*, 270.

90. Dube, 'A Native View of Christianity in South Africa', *Missionary Review of the World* 24 (1901): 421–426, p. 425.

91. S.O. Samuelson, 1902, cited in Marks, *Reluctant Rebellion*, 80.

92. James T. Campbell, *Songs of Zion: The African Methodist Episcopal Church in the United States and South Africa* (New York: Oxford University Press, 1995), 223.

93. A.E. LeRoy, *The Educated Native: Fact vs. Theory* (Dundee, Natal: Church of Sweden, 1906), 6–14, in Karl Robert Brueckner Papers (KRBP), File 3, Campbell Collections, University of KwaZulu-Natal, Durban.

94. See Michael R. Mahoney, 'Racial Formation and Ethnogenesis from Below: The Zulu Case, 1879–1906', *The International Journal of African Historical Studies* 36, no. 3 (2003): 559–583.

95. Russell, 'Report of the Superintendent Inspector of Schools for the Year 1896', ISP, File 29.

96. See Plant, 'Report of the Inspector of Native Education of the Government Aided Native Schools for the Year Ending June 30, 1891', 5, ISP, File 29; Plant, 'Report of the Inspector for Native Education for the Year Ending June 30, 1892', 5, ISP, File 29; and Claire Robertson, 'Women's Education and Class Formation in Africa, 1950–1980', in *Women and Class in Africa*, eds. Iris Berger and Claire Robertson (New York: Africana Publishing, 1986), 92–116, p. 96.

97. In 1889, an anonymous woman wrote a letter to the *Natal Mercury* defending 'book learning' as well as domestic training for African women, against the protests of Mariannhill mission's Father Pfanner that girls needed only to be trained to labour and pray. She substantiated her case by pointing to Inanda Seminary: 'Should the visitor consider that they are spoiled by this education, and taught to despise manual labour, let him, led by the cultured lady, who is herself an example of the dignity of labour, visit the broad acres of Inanda, cultivated by these "spoiled" girls under her direct supervision.' See S.L.H. from Mapumulo, 'Natives and Book Learning', *Natal Mercury*, 22 October 1889: 5.

98. See, for instance, Price, Inanda, to Smith, Boston, 28 February 1885, ABC, Series 15.4, Volume 11.

99. Phelps, Inanda, to Smith, Boston, 11 March 1889, ABC, Series 15.4, Volume 17.

100. Plant, 'Report of the Inspector of Native Education for 1889', 26, CSO, Volume 1253, Reference 1890/1603.

101. Quoted in Hughes, 'Politics and Society in Inanda', 249.

102. See Gaitskell, 'At Home with Hegemony? Coercion and Consent in African Girls' Education for Domesticity in South Africa before 1910', in *Contesting Colonial Hegemony: State and Society in Africa and India*, eds. Dagmar Engels and Shula Marks (London: British Academic Press, 1994), 110–128. See also Jacklyn Cock, 'Domestic Service and Education for Domesticity: The Incorporation of Xhosa Women into Colonial Society', in *Women and Gender in Southern Africa to 1945*, 76–96. Young

women were less likely to have entered domestic service in Natal (or in the Transvaal) than in the Cape or Orange Free State, because domestic service was a male-dominated profession in the former regions and a female-dominated occupation in the latter. But girls with a little schooling – enough to give them a smattering of English and some skills in Western housewifery – would likely be the most desirable domestic employees. By 1911, there were some 6 000 African female servants in Natal, but more than three times as many African men in domestic service. It would remain male-dominated in Natal until the Second World War. See Gaitskell, Judy Kimble, Moira Maconachie and Elaine Unterhalter, 'Class, Race and Gender: Domestic Workers in South Africa', *Review of African Political Economy* 27/28 (1983): 86–108.

103. S.C. Pixley, General Letter of the American Zulu Mission, 26 June 1889, ABC, Series 15.4, Volume 9; Phelps, Inanda, to Smith, Boston, 24 February 1890, ABC, Series 15.4, Volume 17.

104. Officials initially gave Inanda a grant for the laundry following Plant's advice that it would qualify girls 'for an especially useful branch of service', and it competed successfully with washermen in Durban until commercial laundry work grew in the early twentieth century. See Hughes, 'Politics and Society in Inanda, Natal', 248; Memo from Secretary of Native Affairs, 1 July 1889, SNA, Volume 1/1/112, Reference 27/1889; and Edwards, Inanda, to the Women's Board of Missions, Boston, 3 April 1893, ABC, Series 15.6.2, Volume 1.

105. Plant, 'Report of the Inspector of Native Education of the Government Aided Native Schools for the Year Ending June 30, 1891', 31, ISP, File 29.

106. Plant, 'Report of the Inspector of Native Education of the Government Aided Native Schools for the Year Ending June 30, 1891', 48–49, ISP, File 29.

107. In 1893–1894, for instance, Inanda received the largest grant in the entire colony – nearly 350 pounds. See Plant, 'Annual Report of the Inspector of Native Schools for 1893–1894', ISP, File 29.

108. Robert Plant, *The Zulu in Three Tenses: Being a Forecast of the Zulu's Future in the Light of His Past and His Present* (Pietermaritzburg: P. Davis and Sons, 1905), 105.

109. Plant, *The Zulu in Three Tenses*, 125–129.

110. Martha Lindley, Inanda, to Judson Smith, Boston, 31 May 1894, ABC, Series 15.4, Volume 17.

111. Phelps, Inanda, to Smith, Boston, 18 July 1894, ABC, Series 15.4, Volume 17.

112. See H.D. Goodenough, 'Reply of the American Mission Reserve Trustees to Lands Commission Report: Mis-statements Exposed', n.d. (circa 1903),

ABMC, File A/3/49; and A.E. LeRoy, *The Educated Native*, 6, KRBP, File 3.

113. See Lindley, Inanda, to Smith, Boston, 31 May 1894, ABC, Series 15.4, Volume 17.

114. The foregoing draws upon life history interviews with Mkhize in the Killie Campbell Audio Visual Collection (KCAV), Killie Campbell Oral History Programme (KCOHP), Campbell Collections, University of KwaZulu-Natal, Durban: Bertha Mkhize, interviewed at her home in Inanda by A. Manson and D. Collins, 14 and 22 August 1979, KCAV, 147, 151 and 180, KCOHP; and Bertha Mkhize, interviewed at her home in Inanda by Julia Wells and Heather Hughes, 27 August 1980, KCAV, 354, KCOHP.

115. Adelaide Charles Dube, 'Africa: My Native Land', 1913, reprinted with a note by Dorothy Driver and Esther Sbongile Sangweni, in *Women Writing Africa: The Southern Region*, eds. M.J. Daymond et al. (New York: Feminist Press at the City University of New York, 2003), 161–162.

116. See 'Examinations for Teachers' Certificates', 1905 (exams held in December 1904), ISP, File 30.

117. 'Late Evelyn Caluza (nee Goba)', *The Bantu World* (1 August 1936): 11.

118. T.D. Mweli Skota, *The African Yearly Register: Being an Illustrated National Biography Dictionary (Who's Who) of Black Folks in Africa* (Johannesburg: Esson, 1930), 182–183.

119. Lauretta (Gwina) Ngcobo, Inanda student (1945–1949), interviewed by the author, 19 March 2009, Durban, Inanda Seminary Oral History Project (ISOHP).

Chapter Three

1. Ntombi Tantsi, Wilberforce University, Xenia, Ohio, to the American Board Mission, Boston, 18 July 1940, in American Board of Commissioners for Foreign Missions: African Missions Records (henceforth ABC), Series 15.4, Volume 55, Houghton Library, Harvard University, Cambridge, Massachusetts.

2. Mabel Emerson, Boston, to Tantsi, Inanda, 13 April 1944, ABC, Series 15.4, Volume 55.

3. 'Address Given at Inanda Seminary 70th Anniversary Celebrations, May 6th, 1939, by Mrs. N. Tantsi of Pretoria: An African Woman', Lavinia Scott Papers (LSP), Box 4, Folder 15, Melville J. Herskovits Library of African Studies, Northwestern University, Evanston, Illinois. See also 'The African Woman: Mrs. N. Tantsi's Address at the Inanda Seminary, on the Occasion of Its 70th Birthday', *Ilanga Lase Natal* (27 May 1939): 6.

4. 'Inanda Celebrates 70th Birthday: Hundreds of Visitors at the Seminary, Brilliant Speeches from Platform', *Ilanga Lase Natal* (13 May 1939): 17.

5. See Alan Cobley, *Class and Consciousness: The Black Petty Bourgeoisie in South Africa, 1924-1950* (New York: Greenwood Press, 1990), 61-63; Lynn Thomas, 'The Modern Girl and Racial Respectability in 1930s South Africa', in *The Modern Girl Around the World: Consumption, Modernity, and Globalization*, eds. Alys Eve Weinbaum et al. (Durham, NC: Duke University Press, 2008), 96-119, p. 97; and Kenneth Hartshorne, *Native Education in the Union of South Africa: A Summary of the Report of the Commission on Native Education in South Africa - U.G. 53-1951* (Johannesburg: South African Institute of Race Relations, 1953), 17.

6. See E.G. Wyatt, 'Adams College Annual Report, Year Ending June, 1946', ABC, Series 15.4, Volume 52; see also 'Notes of Visits to Native Schools', 1949, pp. 34-37, in Native Education Commission Papers (NECP), BC 282, A 1.30, University of Cape Town Manuscripts and Archives; and Muriel Horrell, *African Education: Some Origins, and Development until 1953* (Johannesburg: South African Institute of Race Relations, 1963), 49.

7. See 'First Year High School Certificate Examination', 'Second Year High School Certificate Examination', 'Native School Leaving Certificate Examination' and 'Native Training College Bursaries', *Native Teachers' Journal* 5, no. 3 (April 1926): 88-89; 'Notes of Visits to Native Schools', 1949, pp. 34-35, in NECP, BC 282, A 1.30.

8. See Margaret Walbridge, 'Inanda Seminary Report for 1925', ABC, Series 15.4, Volume 39; 'Inanda Seminary Report', *Native Teachers' Journal* 6, no. 4 (July 1927): 201-204; and 'Miss M.E. Walbridge, B.Sc.', *The Bantu World* (12 December 1936): 11.

9. Lavinia Scott, 'Inanda Seminary Annual Report', 1 July 1937, ABC, Series 15.4, Volume 44. On nursing as the ideal respectable profession, and Inanda's role, see James B. McCord, with John Scott Douglas, *My Patients Were Zulus* (London: Frederick Muller, 1946; 1951), 240-241; Hilda Kuper, 'Nurses', in Leo Kuper, *An African Bourgeoisie: Race, Class, and Politics in South Africa* (New Haven: Yale University Press, 1965), 216-235; Margaret McCord, *The Calling of Katie Makhanya* (Cape Town: David Philip, 1997); and Shula Marks, *Divided Sisterhood: Race, Class, and Gender in the South African Nursing Profession* (Johannesburg: Wits University Press, 1994), 78-112.

10. Lavinia Scott, 'Promising Young Women', *Ilanga Lase Natal* (18 August 1946): 15.

11. Scott, 'Annual Report of Inanda Seminary, July 1, 1946', ABC, Series 15.4, Volume 52.

12. Missions Council of the Congregational Christian Churches, 'Three Coat Men: The Story of the American Board in Africa Today', 1945, American

Board Mission Collection (ABMC), File A/4/51, National Archives of South Africa, Pietermaritzburg, KwaZulu-Natal.

13. See Clarke, 'Inanda Seminary Report, 1919–1920', ABC, Series 15.4, Volume 39. See also Scott, 'Dear Friends', 30 July 1937, LSP, File 3, Box 11.

14. See Rachel Sibeko, 'Rand Students at Inanda', *The Bantu World* (27 July 1935): 12; Scott, 'Annual Report of Inanda Seminary, June 1943', ABC, Series 15.4, Volume 52; and Scott, 'Dear Friends', 10 May 1948, LSP, File 3, Folder 12.

15. See Minnie Carter, Inanda, to Emerson, Boston, 9 November 1940, ABC, Series 15.4, Volume 53; Charlotte Brenneman to Emerson, 17 February 1941, ABC, Series 15.4, Volume 53; Emerson, Boston, to Carter, Inanda, 4 March 1941, ABC, Series 15.4, Volume 53; Agnes Wood, Inanda, to Emerson, Boston, 18 March 1946, ABC, Series 15.4, Volume 55; Nomangcobo Sibusisiwe Zamakhosi Bhengu, Inanda student (1949–1951); Melodious (Blose) Gumede, Inanda student (1944–1946); and Dorcas Sibusisiwe (Gumbi) Meyiwa, Inanda student (1944–1948), interviewed by the author, 20 January 2009, Inanda, Inanda Seminary Oral History Project (ISOHP).

16. Nancy Rose Hunt, *A Colonial Lexicon of Birth Ritual, Medicalization, and Mobility in the Congo* (Durham, NC: Duke University Press, 1999), 12. See also Benjamin N. Lawrance, Emily Lynn Osborn and Richard L. Roberts, eds, *Intermediaries, Interpreters, and Clerks: African Employees in the Making of Colonial Africa* (Madison: University of Wisconsin Press, 2006). Scholars of South African and other black elites have long struggled to categorise this class more precisely within the schemas of Max Weber (for whom elites were defined by their social status) or Karl Marx (for whom elites were defined by their relation to the means of production): see Kristin Mann, *Marrying Well: Marriage, Status, and Social Change among the Educated Elite in Colonial Lagos* (New York: Cambridge University Press, 1985), 1–7 and 133–134, for a discussion of these camps. In the South African context, the most influential Weberian analysis remains Leo Kuper, *An African Bourgeoisie*. For Marxist analyses, see Brian Willan, 'An African in Kimberley: Sol T. Plaatje, 1894–1898', in *Industrialisation and Social Change in South Africa: African Class Formation, Culture, and Consciousness, 1870–1930*, eds. Shula Marks and Richard Rathbone (New York: Longman, 1982), 238–258; Shula Marks, *The Ambiguities of Dependence in South Africa: Class, Nationalism, and the State in Twentieth-Century Natal* (Baltimore: Johns Hopkins, 1986); and Helen Bradford, *A Taste of Freedom: The ICU in Rural South Africa* (New Haven: Yale University Press, 1987). The Marxist term 'petty bourgeoisie' seems to

have been naturalised to describe black elites in recent southern Africanist historiography: see Natasha Erlank, 'Gender and Masculinity in South African Nationalist Discourse, 1912–1950', *Feminist Studies* 29, no. 3 (Autumn 2003): 653–671; and Michael O. West, *The Rise of an African Middle Class: Colonial Zimbabwe, 1898–1965* (Bloomington: Indiana University Press, 2002).

17. See Paul La Hausse, *Restless Identities: Signatures of Nationalism, Zulu Ethnicity and History in the Lives of Petros Lamula and Lymon Maling* (Pietermaritzburg: University of Natal Press, 2000), 14; and La Hausse, 'So Who Was Elias Kuzwayo? Nationalism, Collaboration and the Picaresque in Natal', *Cahiers d'études africaines* 32, no. 127 (1992): 469–507, p. 470.

18. See La Hausse, *Restless Identities*, 259; and Thomas, 'The Modern Girl', 97.

19. See Thomas, 'The Modern Girl'; David Goodhew, *Respectability and Resistance: A History of Sophiatown* (Westport, CT: Praeger, 2004); and John Nauright, ' "Black Island in a White Sea": Black and White in the Making of Alexandra Township, South Africa, 1912–1948' (PhD diss., Queen's University, 1992).

20. Evelyn Brooks Higginbotham, 'The Politics of Respectability', in *Righteous Discontent: The Women's Movement in the Black Baptist Church, 1880–1920* (Cambridge, MA: Harvard University Press, 1993), 185–229; and Thomas, 'The Modern Girl'. See also Glenda Gilmore, *Gender and Jim Crow: Women and the Politics of White Supremacy in North Carolina, 1896–1920* (Chapel Hill: University of North Carolina, 1996); Kevin Gaines, *Uplifting the Race: Black Leadership, Politics, and Culture in the Twentieth Century* (Chapel Hill: University of North Carolina, 1996).

21. See Sol T. Plaatje, *Native Life in South Africa, Before and Since the European War and the Boer Rebellion* (London: P.S. King and Son, 1915), 89.

22. See George Fredrickson, *Black Liberation: A Comparative History of Black Ideologies in the United States and South Africa* (New York: Oxford University Press, 1995), 117–121; and R.V. Selope Thema, 'How Congress Began', originally published in *Drum* (July 1953). Reprinted in *Seme: The Founder of the ANC*, eds. Richard Rive and Tim Couzens (Braamfontein, South Africa: Skotaville, 1991), 85–87.

23. 'Constitution of the South African Native National Congress', 1919, accessed 19 February 2011, http://www.anc.org.za/main.php?include=docs/const/1919/constitution_sanncx.html. See also Marks, *The Ambiguities of Dependence*, 60–67.

24. See Peter Limb, *The ANC's Early Years: Nation, Class, and Place in South Africa before 1940* (Pretoria: Unisa Press, 2010); Saul Dubow, *The African*

National Congress (Johannesburg: Jonathan Ball, 2000); Peter Walshe, *The Rise of African Nationalism in South Africa: The African National Congress, 1912–1952* (Berkeley: University of California Press, 1970; 1982); and Cherryl Walker, *Women and Resistance in South Africa* (London: Onyx Press, 1982; Cape Town: David Philip, 1991), 87.

25. See Marks, *The Ambiguities of Dependence*, 60–67. See also Nicholas Cope, *To Bind the Nation: Solomon kaDinuzulu and Zulu Nationalism, 1913–1933* (Pietermaritzburg: University of Natal Press, 1993), 103.

26. Farming and mining interests summoned Solomon to address Zulu employees when unrest loomed; as Natal planter and politician George Heaton Nicholls put it in 1929, 'If we do not get back to communalism we will most certainly arrive very soon at communism.' Cited in Shula Marks, 'Patriotism, Patriarchy and Purity: Natal and the Politics of Zulu Ethnic Consciousness', in *The Creation of Tribalism in Southern Africa*, ed. Leroy Vail (Berkeley: University of California Press, 1991), 215–240, p. 217.

27. See Marks, *The Ambiguities of Dependence*, 74–109; and Bradford, *A Taste of Freedom*.

28. 'The Charter of the Zulu Society', 1937, in the Zulu Society Papers (ZSP), Series A1381, Volume I/1/1, National Archives of South Africa, Pietermaritzburg, KwaZulu-Natal. See also Marks, 'Patriotism, Patriarchy and Purity'.

29. Sibusisiwe Makhanya, 'Primitive Zulu Women', address at the Zulu Cultural Society Second Annual Conference, 30 January 1937, ZSP, Series A1381, Volume I/3/1.

30. Personal communication with Ntongela Masilela, Pitzer College, 8 December 2009; Tim Couzens, 'Pseudonyms in Black South African Writing, 1920–1950', *Research in African Literatures* 6, no. 2 (1975): 226–231; Thomas, 'The Modern Girl'.

31. X.Y.Z., 'Women and Their Responsibility', *The Bantu World* (30 September 1939): 9.

32. X.Y.Z., 'Failure of Responsibility', *The Bantu World* (14 October 1939): 9.

33. H.I.E. Dhlomo, 'Bantu Womanhood', *Umteteli wa Bantu* (10 May 1930), accessed 19 February 2011, http://pzacad.pitzer.edu/NAM/newafrre/writers/hdhlomo/umteteli/10_5_30.gif. Dhlomo anticipates Michel Foucault's understanding of modern governmentality: see Foucault, *Discipline and Punish: The Birth of the Prison* (New York: Vintage, 1995).

34. See 'Discipline of Bantu Trained Nurses', *Ilanga Lase Natal* (27 June 1936): 9; Editress' note, P.E. Ngozwana, BA, 'Emancipation of Women', *The Bantu World* (18 May 1935): 13.

35. S.H.D. Lee Mnyandu, 'An Appeal for Educated Girls', *Ilanga Lase Natal* (16 May 1936): 9. See also Spectator, 'Women Must Also Be Educated',

The Bantu World (14 December 1935): 5; and Spectator, 'The Influence of Educated Women', *The Bantu World* (28 December 1935): 16.

36. James R. Korombi, 'Women, the Leaders of Races', *The Bantu World* (27 February 1937): 12.

37. Erlank, 668. See also Carole Pateman, *The Sexual Contract* (Cambridge: Polity Press, 1988), 77–78.

38. Frene Ginwala, 'Women and the African National Congress, 1912–1943', *Agenda* 8 (1990): 77–93.

39. 1940 Constitution of the Daughters of Africa, cited in John Nauright, ' "I Am with You as Never Before": Women in Urban Protest Movements, Alexandra Township, South Africa, 1912–1945', in *Courtyards, Markets, City Streets: Urban Women in Africa*, ed. Kathleen Sheldon (Boulder, CO: Westview Press, 1996), 259–283, pp. 276–277. See also Cecilia Lillian Tshabalala, 'What is the Club Woman?' *The Bantu World* (4 April 1936): 12; and Angeline Dube, interviewed at Ohlange Institute by A. Manson, D. Collins and A. Mngomezulu, 8 March 1979, Killie Campbell Audio Visual Collection (KCAV), 116, Killie Campbell Oral History Programme (KCOHP), Campbell Collections, University of KwaZulu-Natal, Durban.

40. H.I.E. Dhlomo, 'African Attitudes to the European', *The Democrat* (1 December 1945): 21 and 24.

41. X. (H.I.E. Dhlomo), 'Woman', *Ilanga Lase Natal* (26 August 1944).

42. P.E. Ngozwana, BA, 'Emancipation of Women', *The Bantu World* (18 May 1935): 13. Transcript of speech continued in *The Bantu World* (25 May 1935): 13; and *The Bantu World* (1 June 1935): 12. See also 'The Emancipation of Women and What Has Resulted From It: An Address Delivered by Miss E. Ngozwana, B.A., at Inanda Seminary – 4th May 1935', *Ilanga Lase Natal* (17 May 1935): 3. Ngozwana married a Ugandan man in 1939 and spent the rest of her career working in Ugandan politics: see 'Kisosonkole, Pumla Ellen Ngozwana', in Kathleen E. Sheldon, *Historical Dictionary of Women in Sub-Saharan Africa* (Lanham, MD: Scarecrow Press, 2005), 120.

43. On the wide appeal of 'Invictus' for African nationalists, see Elleke Boehmer, *Nelson Mandela: A Very Short Introduction* (New York: Sterling, 2008), 92.

44. Mitta Mbili, 'Men and Women of To-morrow', *The Torchbearer* (November 1933): 48.

45. Janet Mtshali, 'The Aims of Standard IX of 1935', *The Torchbearer* (December 1935).

46. Sophia Mafukuzela, 'Completers', *The Torchbearer* (December 1940): 85.

47. See 'Editorial: "Shine Where You Are!" ' *The Torchbearer* (December 1940): 55. This motto has endured down to the present. Popular memory holds that it was inspired by Philippians 2:15: 'That ye may be blameless

and harmless, the sons of God, without rebuke, in the midst of a crooked and perverse nation, among whom ye shine as lights in the world' (King James). Although I have not found information on the precise timing of the motto's introduction, it seems a quintessential *amarespectable* mantra. It is both reminiscent of and transcends Booker T. Washington's 1895 injunction for African Americans to 'cast down your bucket where you are'. The motto aptly combines an appeal to state officials – suggesting that alumnae will be 'blameless and harmless' – with an exhortation to students to uplift the 'crooked and perverse nation' beyond campus. This was a multivalent call, which could justify evangelical or political engagements.

48. Catherine Burns, ' "A Man Is a Clumsy Thing Who Does Not Know How to Handle a Sick Person": Aspects of the History of Masculinity and Race in the Shaping of Male Nursing in South Africa, 1900–1950', *Journal of Southern African Studies* 24, no. 4 (December 1998): 695–717.

49. Marks, *Divided Sisterhood*, 100.

50. Dorothy Kambule, 'From Our Old Girls: My First Experience as a Nurse', *The Torchbearer* (December 1940): 90–91.

51. Cited in Marks, *Divided Sisterhood*, 101.

52. See Deborah Gaitskell, ' "Doing a Missionary Hard Work . . . in the Black Hole of Calcutta": African Women Teachers Pioneering a Profession in the Cape and Natal, 1880–1950', *Women's History Review* 13, no. 3 (September 2004): 407–425, p. 421.

53. See Walbridge, Wood and Anne Brookings, Inanda, to 'The Members of the Mission', 7 April 1933, ABC, Series 15.4, Volume 46; and Walbridge, Inanda, to Emerson, Boston, 19 March 1935, ABC, Series 15.4, Volume 47. Single missionary women received less than half the salary of ministers until 1933, accentuating their subordination: see Walbridge, Inanda, to Emerson, Boston, 9 May 1932, ABC, Series 15.4, Volume 45; and Walbridge, Inanda, to Emerson, Boston, 1 December 1932, ABC, Series 15.4, Volume 45.

54. See Walbridge, Inanda, to Riggs, Boston, 10 November 1926, ABC, Series 15.4, Volume 41: 'With the growing national feeling among our Native people here, it would be better to have no white people on the staff than poor ones of whom we are ashamed, and who cannot perform their duties as well as a Native teacher.'

55. Walbridge, Boston, to Riggs, Boston, 4 April 1929, ABC, Series 15.4, Volume 41.

56. See 'Résumé of Sibusisiwe Makhanya (Fifi) – Her Life and Activities', Sibusisiwe Makhanya Papers (SMP), File 4, Campbell Collections, University of KwaZulu-Natal, Durban; Umehani Khan, 'A Critical Study of the Life of Sibusisiwe Makanya and Her Work as Educator and Social

Worker in the Umbumbulu District of Natal, 1894–1971' (master's thesis, University of Natal, 1995); Shula Marks, *Not Either an Experimental Doll: The Separate Worlds of Three South African Women* (Bloomington: Indiana University Press, 1987), 30–42; and R. Hunt Davis, Jr, 'Producing the "Good African": South Carolina's Penn School as a Guide for African Education in South Africa', in *Independence without Freedom: The Political Economy of Colonial Education in Southern Africa*, eds. Agrippah T. Mugomba and Mougo Nyaggah (Santa Barbara, CA: ABC-Clio, 1980), 83–103.

57. Wood, Inanda, to Emerson, Boston, 13 September 1938, ABC, Series 15.4, Volume 41. See also Khan, 'A Critical Study of the Life of Sibusisiwe Makanya', 79–111; Walbridge, Inanda, to Emerson, Boston, 1 September 1927, ABC, Series 15.4, Volume 41; and 'Conference Regarding the Training of Young Women as Home Demonstrators at Inanda Seminary', 17 February 1927, ABC, Series 15.4, Volume 41. Makhanya maintained cordial relations with American missionaries until the early 1950s, when she opened a beer hall at Umbumbulu to much controversy and left the church for the universalist Baha'i faith. See Sibusisiwe Makhanya, Umbumbulu, to Dr Philip C. Jones, New York, 8 March 1954, SMP, File 5; and Khan, 'A Critical Study of the Life of Sibusisiwe Makanya', 134–138.

58. Carter, Bethel, Connecticut, to Emerson, Boston, 4 November 1929, ABC, Series 15.4, Volume 40; Walbridge, Inanda, to Emerson, Boston, 30 December 1929, ABC, Series 15.4, Volume 41; and Minnie Carter, 'Inanda Seminary Report, July 1, 1927 to July 1, 1928', ABC, Series 15.4, Volume 39. Skota called Ntlabati Inanda's 'vice-principal', but I have not found substantiating evidence for this: see T.D. Mweli Skota, *The African Yearly Register: Being an Illustrated National Biography Dictionary (Who's Who) of Black Folks in Africa* (Johannesburg: Esson, 1930), 228.

59. See Scott, Inanda, to Emerson, Boston, 19 April 1940, ABC, Series 15.4, Volume 54. Ellen Kuzwayo, an Adams- and Lovedale-trained teacher who came to Inanda in 1937, also left on account of a nervous breakdown, but she attributed it to overwork in her final year at Lovedale rather than to Inanda. Kuzwayo went on to be a social worker, political activist, writer and post-apartheid parliamentarian. See Kuzwayo, *Call Me Woman* (London: The Women's Press, 1985), 97.

60. Carter, Inanda, to Emerson, Boston, 9 November 1940, ABC, Series 15.4, Volume 53.

61. Carter, Inanda, to Emerson, Boston, 13 May 1941, ABC, Series 15.4, Volume 53.

62. Phyllis Ntantala, *A Life's Mosaic: The Autobiography of Phyllis Ntantala* (Berkeley: University of California Press, 1992), 71.

63. See 'New Scales of Teachers' Salaries', *Native Teachers' Journal* 7, no. 3 (April 1928): A 'European' man with a degree and professional training received a standard salary of 285 pounds; a 'European' woman with these qualifications received 200 pounds; a 'Native man' with these qualifications received 175 pounds; and an equally qualified 'Native woman', only 120 pounds.

64. See Scott, Inanda, to Emerson, Boston, 12 July 1937, ABC, Series 15.4, Volume 47.

65. Walbridge, 12–15 August 1923, in *Thokozile*, ed. Walbridge (Topeka, KS: Mainline Printing, 1978), 39.

66. Walbridge, 23 October 1927, in *Thokozile*, 98.

67. See Enoch Mnguni, 'Inanda', *The Torchbearer* (December 1936): 23.

68. See 'The "Zoo" Invades the "Zebras"', *Ilanga Lase Natal* (3 April 1937): 6; and G. Stou Shezi, 'Zoo', *The Torchbearer* (December 1937): 5.

69. 'Inanda Seminary Report for 1920–1921', ABC, Series 15.4, Volume 39; 'Inanda Seminary Report for 1926', ABC, Series 15.4, Volume 39; 'Inanda Seminary Report for 1927', ABC, Series 15.4, Volume 39; 'Inanda Seminary Report for 1929', ABC, Series 15.4, Volume 39; and Sibusisiwe Makhanya, 'The Bantu Youth League in South Africa: A Statement of Purpose and Program, April, 1930', SMP, File 34.

70. 'Prospectus: St. Francis Training College, Mariannhill', 1925, Inanda Seminary Papers (ISP), File 3b, Campbell Collections, University of KwaZulu-Natal, Durban.

71. See Susan Michelle du Rand, 'From Mission School to Bantu Education: A History of Adams College' (master's thesis, University of Natal, 1990), 91–93.

72. See Sibusisiwe Makhanya, 'The Problem of the Zulu Girl', *Native Teachers' Journal* 10, no. 3 (April 1931): 116–120; Lynn Thomas, 'Gendered Reproduction: Placing Schoolgirl Pregnancies in African History', in *Africa after Gender?* eds. Catherine M. Cole, Takyiwaa Manuh and Steven F. Miescher (Bloomington: Indiana University Press, 2007), 48–62; and Peter Delius and Clive Glaser, 'Sexual Socialisation in South Africa: A Historical Perspective', *African Studies* 61, no. 1 (2002): 27–54.

73. Albertina Mzimela/Mnguni, interviewed at her home in Umlazi by Simeon Zulu, 23 September 1980, KCAV, 329, KCOHP. Revealing the recent importation of Christian ideas of public and private space, Mzimela used the English words 'engagement' and 'public' in an otherwise isiZulu interview: 'Nayesikhathi se Daughters of Africa o-Miss Makhanya, lo owayefundisa inhlanzeko ephindela futhi lapho ukuthi makuhlanzekwe intombazane nje ingahlanzani nomfana. [During the time of the Daughters of Africa, Miss Makhanya, who taught sex purity, also repeated that a girl

should not unite with a boy just like that.] Kwenziwe konke lokhu o-engagement, public. [These things should be done after an engagement, made public.]'

74. Beatrice Mdolo, 'Visit of Mrs. Ray E. Phillips', *The Torchbearer* (December 1937): 23. See also Irene Thelejane, Amy Gumede and Eleanor Njapha, 'Visit of Mrs. Ray E. Phillips', *The Torchbearer* (December 1937): 24, for comparisons between Phillips and mothers.

75. Scott, Inanda, to Emerson, Boston, 25 September 1940, ABC, Series 15.4, Volume 54; see also Scott, Inanda, to Emerson, Boston, 26 September 1939, ABC, Series 15.4, Volume 47a; and Scott, Inanda, to John Reuling, Boston, 5 November 1957, ISP, File 7.

76. Local leaders of the Daughters of Africa included Bertha Mkhize; John Dube's wife, Angeline Khumalo Dube; Albert Luthuli's wife, Nokukhanya Bhengu Luthuli; Inanda teacher Margaret Nduna; and Durban Bantu Child Welfare Society secretary Isabel Sililo.

77. Scott, Inanda, 'Dearest Family', 13 October 1940, LSP, Box 3, File 12; and Scott, Inanda, 'Dearest Family', 5 November 1941, LSP, Box 3, File 12.

78. Constance Miriam (Dlomo) Koza, Inanda student (1941–1945) and principal (1980–1986), interviewed by the author, 2 June 2009, Centurion, Gauteng, ISOHP. Her former students recall such lessons: Pamela Dube, Inanda student (1980–1984); Siphokazi Koyana, Inanda student (1981–1985); Nomsa Makhoba, Inanda student (1981–1985); Nozizwe Maneli, Inanda student (1981–1985); and Vuyo Ncwaiba, Inanda student (1984–1985), all interviewed by the author, 1 June 2009, Johannesburg, ISOHP. See Chapter 5.

79. On 'sodomy' in Johannesburg, see, for instance, Herbert Goodenough, 'The Johannesburg Field', July 1909, ABC, Series 15.4, Volume 23.

80. Caroline Sililo, Inanda student (1934–1936) and teacher (1943–1950); and Faith (Nomvete) Nyongo, Inanda student (1943–1945), interviewed by the author, 17 March 2009, Groutville, KwaZulu-Natal, ISOHP.

81. 'Prize-Winning Essays about Old Inanda Girls', *EzakwamahEdwards* (November 1948): 33–38.

82. On Hawes, see Chapter 1.

83. On Cele, see Chapter 2.

84. Jordan K. Ngubane, 'The Woman Who Saved Her Tribe: Florence Nightingale of the Bantu, Story of Sacrifice and Devotion', *The Forum* (12 October 1946): 31–33. See also Constance Makhanya, 'Need for Native Nurses and Midwives in Rural Areas', *Native Teachers' Journal* 12, no. 3 (April 1933): 149–150.

85. See Kenneth King, *Pan-Africanism and Education: A Study of Race Philanthropy and Education in the Southern States of America and East Africa* (Oxford: Clarendon Press, 1971).

86. At Teachers College, Loram came to believe in the wide applicability of black American industrial models: see Charles T. Loram, *The Education of the South African Native* (New York: Longmans, Green, and Co., 1917; Negro Universities Press, 1969); and Brahm Fleisch, 'The Teachers College Club: American Educational Discourse and the Origins of Bantu Education in South Africa (1914-1951)', (PhD diss., Columbia University, 1995), 130-163. Loram then shaped new 'industrial' curricula in the Cape and in Natal, where he was Chief Inspector of Native Education from 1917 to 1920: see R. Hunt Davis, Jr, 'Charles T. Loram and an American Model for African Education in South Africa', *African Studies Review* 19, no. 2 (1976): 87-99; and James T. Campbell, 'Models and Metaphors: Industrial Education in the United States and South Africa', in *Comparative Perspectives on South Africa*, ed. Ran Greenstein (New York: St Martin's, 1998), 90-134. Over the next decade, as a state 'expert' on 'race relations' with the newly created South African Native Affairs Commission (1920-1929) and then as the leading Natal educational official (1930-1931), Loram espoused a programme of 'adapted' schooling that he termed 'education for life' – education that emphasised students' development as rural labourers and docile political subjects as interdependent processes: see Sue Krige, 'Segregation, Science and Commissions of Enquiry: The Contestation over Native Education Policy in South Africa, 1930-36', *Journal of Southern African Studies* 23, no. 3 (September 1997): 491-506. Loram headed to Yale in 1933, where he presided over the graduate programme in Culture Contacts and Race Relations: see R. Glotzer, 'The Career of Mabel Carney: The Study of Race and Rural Development in the United States and South Africa', *International Journal of African Historical Studies* 29, no. 2 (1996): 309-336.

87. See 'Dr. and Mrs. Anson Phelps Stokes at Inanda', September 1932, ABC, Series 15.4, Volume 45; and 'An Address of Welcome to Dr. and Mrs. Stokes, on the Occasion of Their Visit to Inanda', September 1932, ABC, Series 15.4, Volume 45.

88. Thomas Jesse Jones, *Education in East Africa: A Study of East, Central and South Africa by the Second African Education Commission under the Auspices of the Phelps-Stokes Fund, in Cooperation with the International Education Board* (New York: Phelps-Stokes Fund, 1925), 340-343.

89. Anson Phelps Stokes, 'Introduction', in Jones, *Education in East Africa*, xv-xvii.

90. List of desirable character traits, Frederick Gordon Guggisberg, Governor of the Gold Coast, quoted in Stokes, 'Introduction', xvii; latter quote is from Stokes, 'Introduction', xvii.

91. Stokes, 'Introduction', xviii.

92. See Carnegie Corporation of New York, *Village Education in Africa: Report of the Inter-territorial 'Jeanes' Conference, Salisbury, S. Rhodesia* (Alice, South Africa: Lovedale Press, 1935); and Timothy Burke, *Lifebuoy Men, Lux Women: Commodification, Consumption, and Cleanliness in Modern Zimbabwe* (Durham, NC: Duke University Press, 1996), 44–52.

93. 'Girls School Committee Minutes', 6 July 1918, ISP, File 1b.

94. American Zulu Mission, 'General Letter, July 1920 – July 1921', ABC, Series 15.4, Volume 39.

95. Walbridge, in Clarke, 'Inanda Seminary Report, June 1922–1923', ABC, Series 15.4, Volume 39.

96. 'Inanda Seminary Report for 1924', ABC, Series 15.4, Volume 39.

97. 'Prospectus of Inanda Seminary', 1929, ISP, File 3b.

98. Agnes Wood, 'My Thirty-six Years in Africa' (unpublished memoirs, 1984), 48. Thanks to Cherif Keita of Carleton College for sharing these memoirs with me.

99. Wood, 'My Thirty-six Years in Africa', 5.

100. See Lucy Twala, 'Inanda Seminary Beats Adams', *The Bantu World*, 12 October 1935: 12; Twala, 'Inanda Seminary News', *The Bantu World* (13 June 1936): 12; and W.M.B. Ntlapo, 'Mrs. Lucy Mvulelo (nee) Twala', *The Bantu World* (19 August 1939): 12.

101. Iris Berger, *Threads of Solidarity: Women in South African Industry, 1900–1980* (Bloomington: Indiana University Press, 1992), 120; and Berger, 'Generations of Struggle: Trade Unions and the Roots of Feminism, 1930–1960', in *Women in South African History: Basus'iimbokodo, bawel'imilambo/They Remove Boulders and Cross Rivers*, ed. Nomboniso Gasa (Cape Town: HSRC Press, 2007), 185–205, pp. 194–195. Twala's defence of domestic workers' gendered propriety served as a path to more strident activism, as she built on her skills to become an activist in the garment industry and later, with Inanda alumna Bertha Mkhize, in the Federation of South African Women, an anti-apartheid women's group formed in 1954. Twala's married name was Lucy Mvubelo.

102. The 1936 census counted 241 230 African female domestic workers. See Deborah Gaitskell, Judy Kimble, Moira Maconachie and Elaine Unterhalter, 'Class, Race and Gender: Domestic Workers in South Africa', *Review of African Political Economy* 27/28 (1983): 86–108, p. 102.

103. Africans in Natal resisted the feminisation of domestic labour longer than their peers in the other three provinces, drawing upon the relatively greater structural integrity of African family units in Natal to avoid women's waged domestic service: up to the Second World War, domestic service remained a male-dominated profession in Natal. See Gaitskell, Kimble, Maconachie and Unterhalter, 'Class, Race and Gender', 99–100.

104. Clarke, 'Inanda Seminary Report, 1919–1920', ABC, Series 15.4, Volume 39; and American Zulu Mission, 'Annual Letter for Year 1921–1922', ABC, Series 15.4, Volume 39.

105. 'Inanda Seminary: New Dormitory Opened, by Chief Commissioner', *Natal Mercury* (22 April 1922). Clipping in ISP, File 2a.

106. Wheelwright, 1926, cited in Fleisch, 'The Teachers College Club', 153.

107. Scott, Inanda, 'Dearest Family', 3 March 1946, LSP, Box 3, File 12. See also E.G. Wyatt, 'Adams College Annual Report, Year Ending June, 1946', ABC, Series 15.4, Volume 52.

108. See Jonathan Hyslop, *The Classroom Struggle: Policy and Resistance in South Africa, 1940–1990* (Pietermaritzburg: University of Natal Press, 1999), 10–21; Hyslop, 'Food, Authority, and Politics: Student Riots in South African Schools, 1945–1976', *Africa Perspective* 1, no. 3–4 (June 1987): 3–42; and T. White, 'Master of the Night: The Context and Evolution of the Lovedale Riot of 1946', *Historia* 42, no. 1 (May 1997): 81–97. See also 'Mission Stations and Missionaries', *Ilanga Lase Natal* (24 November 1946): 15.

109. Anne Mager, *Gender and the Making of a South African Bantustan: A Social History of the Ciskei, 1945–1959* (Portsmouth, NH: Heinemann, 1999), 198.

110. Mager, *Gender and the Making of a South African Bantustan*, 202–204.

111. Quoted in Marks, *Divided Sisterhood*, 110.

112. On the foregoing, see 'Commission of Enquiry into Disturbances at Native Educational Institutions, 1947 – Evidence and Report', Ken Hartshorne Papers (KHP), Series A2857, File C1, Historical Papers Collection, William Cullen Library, University of the Witwatersrand, Johannesburg.

113. See, for instance, Walbridge, 29 May 1926, *Thokozile*, 77; Walbridge, 8 September 1929, *Thokozile*, 110; Scott, Inanda, 'Dearest Family', 23 September 1937, LSP, Box 3, File 11; Scott, Inanda, 'Dearest Family', 7 May 1940, LSP, Box 3, File 12; Scott, Inanda, 'Dearest Family', 8 November 1942, LSP, Box 3, File 12; and Scott, Inanda, 'Dearest Family', 9 September 1945, LSP, Box 3, File 12. For broader perspectives on *ufufunyana*, see Julie Parle, *States of Mind: Searching for Mental Health in Natal and Zululand, 1868–1918* (Pietermaritzburg: University of KwaZulu-Natal Press, 2007); and Leslie Swartz, *Culture and Mental Health: A Southern African View* (Cape Town: Oxford University Press, 1998).

114. On the politics of spirit possession, hysteria and gendered pressures elsewhere, see Aihwa Ong, *Spirits of Resistance and Capitalist Discipline: Factory Women in Malaysia* (Albany: State University of New York, 1987); and C.C. Adomakoh, 'The Pattern of Epidemic Hysteria in a Girls' School in Ghana', *African Journal of Psychiatry* 1 (1976): 177–182.

115. Scott, Inanda, 'Dearest Family', 3 March 1946, LSP, Box 3, File 12.

116. Decima Ntshingila, 'The Library at Inanda Seminary', *The Torchbearer* (November 1933): 49. On the significance of Inanda's library, see also Alan Cobley, *The Rules of the Game: Struggles in Black Recreation and Social Welfare Policy in South Africa* (Westport, CT: Greenwood, 1997), 46; and Mazo Sybil T. MaDlamini Buthelezi, *African Nurse Pioneers in KwaZulu-Natal, 1920–2000* (Victoria, British Columbia: Trafford Publishing, 2004), 192.

117. See Mary Rabotapi, 'Current Events', *The Torchbearer* (December 1937): 36.

118. Beauty Nkuku, 'Intercollege Debate', *The Torchbearer* (December 1937): 29.

119. Orah Khanyile, 'The Debate: Inanda and Ohlange', *The Torchbearer* (December 1937): 33.

120. 'Debate', *The Torchbearer* (December 1940): 74.

121. Jane H. Kubheka, 'My Study of Mercantile Law', *The Torchbearer* (December 1940): 41–42.

122. Eunice Makhaye, 'School Government', *EzakwamahEdwards* (November 1948): 7.

123. Walbridge, Inanda, to C. Walbridge, Topeka, Kansas, 14 February 1926, in *Thokozile*, 73; Scott, Adams, 'Dearest Family', 27 May 1935, LSP, Box 3, File 11; and Lauretta (Gwina) Ngcobo, Inanda student (1945–1949), interviewed by the author, 19 March 2009, Durban, ISOHP.

124. Ngcobo, ISOHP.

125. Sililo and Nyongo, ISOHP. Goba's husband, Reggie, would lose a scholarship for advocating 'non-white nationalism' to teachers: see Scott to Reuling, 30 December 1951, ISP, File 5b.

126. Nomangcobo Sibusisiwe Zamakhosi Bhengu, Inanda student (1949–1951); Melodious (Blose) Gumede, Inanda student (1944–1946); and Dorcas Sibusisiwe (Gumbi) Meyiwa, Inanda student (1944–1948), interviewed by the author, 20 January 2009, Inanda, ISOHP.

127. Bhengu, Gumede and Meyiwa, ISOHP.

128. See Joanna Lewis, *Empire State-Building: War and Welfare in Kenya, 1925–1952* (Athens: Ohio University Press, 2000), 52–81; and Carol Summers, *Colonial Lessons: Africans' Education in Southern Rhodesia, 1918–1940* (Portsmouth, NH: Heinemann, 2002).

129. See Catherine Burns, 'Reproductive Labors: The Politics of Women's Health in South Africa, 1900 to 1960' (PhD diss., Northwestern University, 1995), 314–316 and 450–451.

130. Scott, Inanda, 'Dearest Family', 6 June 1948, LSP, File 3, Folder 12.

Chapter Four

1. 'Adams Holds Its Last Service before Hand-Over to Government', *Natal Daily News* (3 December 1956), Edgar Brookes Papers (EBP), File 30, Campbell Collections, University of KwaZulu-Natal, Durban.

2. 'Century-Old Adams College Era Ending', *Natal Mercury* (3 December 1956), in EBP, File 30.

3. See John Reuling, Boston, to David Rubenstein, Adams Mission, 27 February 1957, Adams College Papers (ACP), File 1D, Campbell Collections, University of KwaZulu-Natal, Durban.

4. See Lavinia Scott, Inanda Seminary, to Reuling, Boston, 4 November 1958, Inanda Seminary Papers (ISP), File 8, Campbell Collections, University of KwaZulu-Natal, Durban.

5. See, e.g., Mangosuthu Gatsha Buthelezi, 'Adams College Reunion Address', 7 January 1978, ACP, File 15; Norman Etherington, *Preachers, Peasants, and Politics in Southeast Africa, 1835–1880: African Christian Communities in Natal, Pondoland, and Zululand* (London: Royal Historical Society, 1978), 176.

6. English- and Afrikaans-speaking pupils received free, compulsory schooling. See Peter Kallaway, ed., *The History of Education under Apartheid, 1948–1994: The Doors of Learning and Culture Shall Be Opened* (New York: P. Lang, 2002); Jonathan Hyslop, *The Classroom Struggle: Policy and Resistance in South Africa, 1940–1990* (Pietermaritzburg: University of Natal Press, 1999).

7. Muriel Horrell, *A Decade of Bantu Education* (Johannesburg: South African Institute of Race Relations, 1964), 30. Officials also seemed to assume that high school students would be more manageable in single-sex institutions: the state prohibited male high school attendance at St Matthew's, where girls had rioted in the 1940s, while Lovedale, which had been marked by male student unrest in the 1940s, became an all-male, industrially oriented school after it was taken over by the state. See Phyllis Ntantala, 'The Abyss of Bantu Education', *Africa South* 4, no. 2 (January–March 1960): 42–47; and Anne Mager, *Gender and the Making of a South African Bantustan: A Social History of the Ciskei, 1945–1959* (Portsmouth, NH: Heinemann, 1999), 212.

8. See Harold Wolpe, 'Capitalism and Cheap Labour Power in South Africa: From Segregation to Apartheid', *Economy and Society* 1, no. 4 (1972): 425–456; and Philip Bonner, Peter Delius and Deborah Posel, eds, *Apartheid's Genesis: 1935–1962* (Johannesburg: Ravan, 1993).

9. See Frederick Cooper, *Africa since 1940: The Past of the Present* (New York: Cambridge University Press, 2002); Cooper, *Decolonization and African Society: The Labor Question in French and British Africa* (New York: Cambridge University Press, 1996); and Myles Osborne, 'The

Kamba and Mau Mau: Ethnicity, Development, and Chiefship, 1952–1960', *International Journal of African Historical Studies* 43, no. 1 (2010): 63–87.

10. On the limits of development in settler colonies, see Caroline Elkins and Susan Pedersen, eds, *Settler Colonialism in the Twentieth Century: Projects, Practices, Legacies* (New York: Routledge, 2005).

11. Ten homelands would eventually form: Transkei and Ciskei (Xhosa), Bophuthatswana (Tswana), KwaZulu (Zulu), Venda (Venda), Gazankulu (Tsonga), KaNgwane (Swazi), KwaNdebele (Ndebele), Lebowa (Pedi) and QwaQwa (Southern Sotho).

12. See William Beinart and Saul Dubow, 'Introduction: The Historiography of Segregation and Apartheid', in *Segregation and Apartheid in Twentieth-Century South Africa*, eds. Beinart and Dubow (New York: Routledge, 1995), 1–24, pp. 16–17.

13. Wolpe, 'Capitalismn and Cheap Labour Power'; Belinda Bozzoli, 'Marxism, Feminism, and South African Studies', *Journal of Southern African Studies* 9, no. 2 (1983): 139–171; Cherryl Walker, *Women and Resistance in South Africa* (London: Onyx Press, 1982; Cape Town: David Philip, 1991), 123–133; Julia Wells, *We Now Demand! The History of Women's Resistance to Pass Laws in South Africa* (Johannesburg: Wits University Press, 1993); and Mark Hunter, *Love in the Time of AIDS: Inequality, Gender, and Rights in South Africa* (Bloomington: University of Indiana Press, 2010), 84–102.

14. Hyslop, *The Classroom Struggle*, 1.

15. The son of German missionaries, Eiselen was a trained anthropologist and former Chief Inspector of Native Education in the Transvaal. With six other white, male 'experts' – trained in education, history, social work and 'mission science' – Eiselen toured schools around the country, soliciting views from nearly 500 white 'experts' and missionaries as well as a small number of African teachers and parents. See Cynthia Kros' intellectual biography of Eiselen, *The Seeds of Separate Development: Origins of Bantu Education* (Pretoria: Unisa Press, 2010). See also 'Questionnaire on Native Education', in Native Education Commission Papers (NECP), BC 282, A 1.2, University of Cape Town Manuscripts and Archives.

16. Union of South Africa, *Report of the Commission on Native Education, 1949–1951 - U.G. No. 53/1951* (Pretoria: Government Printer, 1951), 103–105. See also Kenneth Hartshorne, *Native Education in the Union of South Africa: A Summary of the Report of the Commission on Native Education in South Africa - U.G. 53-1951* (Johannesburg: South African Institute of Race Relations, 1953), 3–5.

17. *Report of the Commission on Native Education*, 115. See also Hartshorne, *Native Education in the Union of South Africa*, 12.
18. *Report of the Commission on Native Education*, 52.
19. *Report of the Commission on Native Education*, 116; see also Hartshorne, *Native Education in the Union of South Africa*, 12–13.
20. *Report of the Commission on Native Education*, 120; see also Hartshorne, *Native Education in the Union of South Africa*, 14-16.
21. *Report of the Commission on Native Education*, 128; see also Hartshorne, *Native Education in the Union of South Africa*, 25.
22. *Report of the Commission on Native Education*, 122; see also Hartshorne, *Native Education in the Union of South Africa*, 18.
23. See *Report of the Commission on Native Education*, 63: it cited a 1948 National Health Foundation report on the nursing shortage which indicated that 47 per cent of African female school-leavers wanted to be nurses, while 42 per cent hoped to teach.
24. See *Report of the Commission on Native Education*, 122.
25. Hartshorne, *Native Education in the Union of South Africa*, 21.
26. Hartshorne, *Native Education in the Union of South Africa*, 53.
27. *Report of the Commission on Native Education*, 117.
28. Hendrik Verwoerd, *Bantu Education: Policy for the Immediate Future* (Pretoria: Information Service of the Department of Native Affairs, 1954), 20. In Department of Information Series (INL), Volume 115/26, Reference 1/9/8(a), National Archives of South Africa, Pretoria, Gauteng. See also Shirley Mahlase, *The Careers of Women Teachers under Apartheid* (Harare: SAPES Trust, 1997), 59; and Owen Crankshaw, *Race, Class, and the Changing Division of Labour under Apartheid* (New York: Routledge, 1997), 88.
29. Verwoerd, *Bantu Education*, 20.
30. Mager, *Gender and the Making of a South African Bantustan*, 209–210.
31. Quoted in I.B. Tabata, *Education for Barbarism: Bantu Education in South Africa* (Durban: Prometheus, 1959), 14–15. See also Hilda Kuper, 'Nurses', in Leo Kuper, *An African Bourgeoisie: Race, Class, and Politics in South Africa* (New Haven: Yale University Press, 1965), 216–235. The Nursing Amendment Act of 1957 introduced segregated nursing advisory boards – placing the profession under white gatekeepers – and made it illegal for a black nurse to be employed in a position of authority over a white nurse. It also required racial registration of all nurses to account for the 'nursing resources in each racial group'.
32. *Bantu Education Act, Act No. 47 of 1953* (Pretoria: Government Printer, 1953), 265.
33. W.W.M. Eiselen, Secretary for Native Affairs, 'File No. 252/302 (Re: The transfer of control of teacher training schools to the State)', 2 August 1954, Roger Aylard Papers (RAP).

34. See Pam Christie, *The Right to Learn: The Struggle for Education in South Africa* (Johannesburg: Ravan, 1985), 79–81; Horrell, *A Decade of Bantu Education*, 20–23.

35. See Scott, Inanda, to Reuling, Boston, 28 July 1949, ISP, File 5b: Inanda then received $19 710 in state grants for teachers' salaries and $3 544 from the state for equipment. It also received $15 745 in student fees, $6 409 from the American Board, and $3 000 in gifts from South Africans and Americans.

36. The Group Areas Act, promulgated in 1950, established unprecedentedly thorough racialised restrictions on where South Africans could live and conduct business. See David Welsh, *The Rise and Fall of Apartheid* (Johannesburg: Jonathan Ball, 2009), 55–56.

37. Practically nothing has been written about Seventh-Day Adventist schools, perhaps because they never educated significant numbers of black students or produced prominent leaders. From the late nineteenth century, the church attracted growing numbers of black members, but the church was rigidly segregated. See Gary Land, *Historical Dictionary of Seventh-Day Adventists* (Lanham, MD: Scarecrow Press, 2005), 280–281. The only comment on the Adventists' experience under Bantu Education is in Alven Makapela, *The Problem with Africanity in the Seventh-Day Adventist Church* (Lewiston, NY: The Edwin Mellen Press, 1996), 277: 'Because of the government's attitude to legislate against equal education, most private and mission schools either voluntarily closed their doors or were nationalized by the state. [Some of] the exceptions were Seventh-Day Adventist schools. These schools were exempt from seizure by the government because they had never accepted government subsidies and also were never involved in opposition to its policies.' Nelson Mandela sent his own children to Adventist schools briefly.

38. In 1948, the Catholics ran over 740 schools, serving some 85 000 students. Nearly half of these schools were in Natal. In 1960, the Catholics controlled 640 schools, serving nearly 100 000 students. These included nine high schools that extended to matriculation, and three teacher training colleges that could only train teachers for Catholic schools. Under Bantu Education, the Catholic Church went from being a minority player in African schooling to being almost the only provider of private schooling to Africans, and Natal replaced the Cape as the centre of elite education for black South Africans. From 1962, the state more rigorously required that students at Catholic institutions be confirmed Catholics. See Garth Abraham, *The Catholic Church and Apartheid: The Response of the Catholic Church of South Africa to the First Decade of National Party Rule, 1948-1957* (Johannesburg: Ravan, 1989); and 'Catholics Join the

Church Fight against Racialism: "Going It Alone" over Schools', *Contact* (March 1958): 4.

39. See Albert Luthuli, *Let My People Go* (Johannesburg: Collins, 1962), 118. Other participants in the Congress Alliance were the South African Indian Congress, the South African Coloured People's Organisation, the South African Congress of Democrats and the South African Congress of Trade Unions. See African National Congress, 'The Freedom Charter', 1955, accessed 19 February 2011, http://www.anc.org.za/show.php?include = docs/misc/1955/charter.html.

40. 'Editorial: Fighting against Bantu Education', *Liberation: A Journal of Democratic Discussion*, no. 14 (November 1955): 1–7, p. 4.

41. Luthuli, *Let My People Go*, 135.

42. Hyslop, *The Classroom Struggle*, 73.

43. See Scott, 'Dear Friends', 20 November 1957, Lavinia Scott Papers (LSP), Box 4, File 1, Melville J. Herskovits Library of African Studies, Northwestern University, Evanston, Illinois.

44. Grant had previously taught in Trinidad, Grenada, Southern Rhodesia and Zanzibar. See Jack Grant, Maphumulo, to Reka and Sam Kaetzel, 8 February 1954, American Board Mission Collection (ABMC), Box A/2/32, National Archives of South Africa, Pietermaritzburg, KwaZulu-Natal.

45. Grant, 'To Be Read with Discretion', 30 January 1954, ABMC, Box A/2/32.

46. Ironically, De Villiers was himself a former Adams College teacher. Scott, Inanda, to Reuling, Boston, 25 March 1954, ISP, File 6.

47. He applied thrice, as officials reported that two applications had been lost in the mail. On the foregoing, see George C. [Jack] Grant, *The Liquidation of Adams College* (Durban: George Grant, 1957), 17–26.

48. 'Repeal of Bantu Education Act Demanded', *Ilanga Lase Natal* (28 November 1953): 15.

49. On the foregoing, see Grant, *The Liquidation of Adams College*, 27–41.

50. See Mark Gevisser, *A Legacy of Liberation: Thabo Mbeki and the Future of the South African Dream* (New York: Palgrave Macmillan, 2009), 19–24.

51. M.T. Moerane, 'Presidential Address', *Ilanga Lase Natal* (11 July 1953): 14.

52. On the foregoing, see Grant, *The Liquidation of Adams College*, 38–41.

53. F.J. de Villiers, Department of Native Affairs, Pretoria, to the Secretary, Adams College, Inc., Adams Mission Station, 12 July 1956, ACP, File 1C.

54. 'Conversation at Inanda, August 2, 1956', Inanda Seminary Campus Archive (ISCA), Inanda, KwaZulu-Natal. On this meeting, see also Scott

Couper, 'Fearing for Its Future: Bantu Education's Threat of Closure to Inanda Seminary', *Journal of Gender and Religion in Africa* 17, no. 1 (July 2011): 74–95.

55. Ida Grant, 'Remember Adams?' in *Contact* (August 1956): 3–4. See also Ida Grant, 'A Tragic Happening: Adams Sacrificed to Apartheid', *Ilanga Lase Natal* (15 September 1956).

56. Scott to Reuling, 13 October 1956, ISP, File 7. See also Scott's handwritten notes about this meeting: 'Mr. Dent – Sept. 21, '56', ISCA.

57. Lynette S'phiwe Hlongwane, 'The Role of Inanda Seminary in the Education of African Girls in South Africa: A Report of Graduates' Views' (PhD diss., Teachers College, Columbia University, 1998), 166.

58. See, for instance, Scott, Mary Beals, Virginia Nichols, Phyllis Spafford, Beatrice Cowey and Minnie Carter, Inanda Seminary, to the 'Members of the Mission', 23 September 1954, ABMC, Box A/2/32; Jack Grant, Adams, to 'The Inanda Ladies', 29 September 1954, ISP, File 6; and Grant, Adams, to Lavinia Scott, Inanda, 4 October 1954, ISP, File 6.

59. Natal Native Education Advisory Board, 'Minutes of a Meeting of the Natal Native Education Advisory Board, 23 September 1953', *Native Teachers' Journal* (January 1954): 190–192, p. 190. Scott chaired the Advisory Board between 1952 and 1954 – at which point the state dissolved the group. The Board had been similarly critical of the Eiselen Commission: see 'Minutes of an Extraordinary Meeting of the Natal Native Education Advisory Board', Pietermaritzburg, 28 May 1952, Natal Native Education Advisory Board Minutes (NNEAB), Campbell Collections, University of KwaZulu-Natal, Durban. See also Inanda Seminary High School Staff, 'Replies to Questionnaire, Native Education Enquiry Commission', response to question #8, NECP, BC 282, A 1.11; 'The New Bantu Education Act – Report by Lavinia Scott to the American Board and the Mission', 22 March 1954, ISP, File 7; John W. de Gruchy, 'Grappling with a Colonial Heritage: The English-Speaking Churches under Imperialism and Apartheid', in *Christianity in South Africa: A Political, Social, and Cultural History*, eds. Richard Elphick and Rodney Davenport (Berkeley: University of California Press, 1997), 155–172, p. 161.

60. See Scott Couper, *Albert Luthuli: Bound by Faith* (Pietermaritzburg: University of KwaZulu-Natal Press, 2010), 34–35.

61. Secretary, American Zulu Mission, Maphumulo Mission Station, to the Minister of Native Affairs, Pretoria, 13 July 1954, ISP, File 6.

62. Scott, Inanda, to Reuling, Boston, 15 July 1954, ISP, File 6.

63. Regional Director of Bantu Education, Pietermaritzburg, to Secretary, American Board Mission Council, Mapumulo, 'Registration: Inanda Seminary', 23 November 1957, RAP.

64. Regional Director of Bantu Education, Pietermaritzburg, to Secretary, American Board Mission Council, Mapumulo, 23 November 1957, RAP.

65. See S.R. Dent, Regional Director of Bantu Education, to Sam Kaetzel, Secretary, American Zulu Mission, Pietermaritzburg, n.d. (circa November 1957), ABMC, Box A/2/26; F.J. de Villiers, Director of Bantu Education, Pretoria, to Kaetzel, Mapumulo, 6 May 1958, ABMC, Box A/2/26; Scott to Reuling, 4 December 1957, ISP, File 7; and Scott to Reuling, 20 November 1958, ISP, File 8.

66. Notes of 20 November 1958 on copy of Regional Director of Bantu Education, Pietermaritzburg, to Secretary, American Board Mission Council, Mapumulo, 'Registration: Inanda Seminary', 23 November 1957, RAP.

67. See Scott to Reuling, 29 July 1959, ISP, File 8; Scott to David Rubenstein, 11 February 1961, ISP, File 10; and Scott to Reuling, 28 February 1961, ISP, File 10.

68. Tellingly, homecraft would actually be replaced with an accounting course in 1976. See 'Minutes of the 44th Meeting of the Governing Council', 22 February 1975, EBP, File 43.

69. South African Association of University Women, Pietermaritzburg Branch, 'Visit to Inanda Seminary', 1965, Mabel Palmer Papers (MPP), File 2, Campbell Collections, University of KwaZulu-Natal, Durban. See also Mazo Sybil T. MaDlamini Buthelezi, *African Nurse Pioneers in KwaZulu-Natal, 1920–2000* (Victoria, British Columbia: Trafford Publishing, 2004), 281–284: Buthelezi, who attended Inanda between 1955 and 1957, found Inanda's mathematics training poor and felt that she was therefore unable to pursue a career as a doctor.

70. See Roger Aylard, 'Principal's Annual Report for the 1971 School Year', 26 February 1972, RAP.

71. The Central African Federation comprised present-day Malawi, Zambia and Zimbabwe. See 'Inanda Seminary', 1971, ISP, File 2a.

72. Shula Marks, *Divided Sisterhood: Race, Class, and Gender in the South African Nursing Profession* (Johannesburg: Wits University Press, 1994), 169.

73. Lavinia Scott, '33 Years at Inanda Seminary', *Race Relations News* (December 1969): 6; and Marks, *Divided Sisterhood*, 170.

74. See 'Inanda Seminary', 1971, ISP, File 2a; and Roger Aylard, 'Principal's Letter', *EzakwamahEdwards* (1971): 1. That year, the school reportedly received 1 500 applications for ninety openings – a 6 per cent admission rate.

75. Mabel Christofersen, interviewed by A. Manson and D. Collins, 20 February 1979, Inanda Seminary, Killie Campbell Audio Visual

Collection (KCAV), 112, Killie Campbell Oral History Programme (KCOHP), Campbell Collections, University of KwaZulu-Natal, Durban.

76. Mabel Christofersen, Inanda teacher (1946–1980), interviewed by the author, 9 December 2008, Durban, Inanda Seminary Oral History Project (ISOHP).

77. Roger Aylard, Inanda teacher and principal (1968–1973), interviewed by the author, via Skype from California, 30 June 2009, ISOHP.

78. Scott, Inanda, 'Dearest Family', 11 November 1951, LSP, File 4.1. Scott was right: officials lauded the school as a 'showpiece of positive apartheid'. See Vanessa Noble, 'Doctors Divided: Gender, Race, and Class Anomalies in the Production of Black Medical Doctors in Apartheid South Africa, 1948 to 1994' (PhD diss., University of Michigan, 2005), 50–51 and 67–68.

79. McCord was another necessary evil for the state: it continued as a private institution through apartheid, despite repeated threats of closure for contravening the Group Areas Act, because the state did not offer sufficient health services to sustain black communities around Durban. Catherine Burns, Vanessa Noble and Julie Parle have a manuscript on McCord's history in progress.

80. Noble, 'Doctors Divided', 2. See also H.L. Watts, *Black Doctors: An Investigation into Aspects of the Training and Career of Students and Graduates from the Medical School of the University of Natal* (Durban: University of Natal Institute for Social Research, 1975), 37–38.

81. See B.T. Naidoo, 'A History of the Durban Medical School', *South African Medical Journal* 50, no. 9 (1976): 1625–1628.

82. See Roger Aylard, 'Principal's Annual Report for the 1971 School Year', 26 February 1972, RAP; and 'South African Black Women Medical Doctors Qualified 1947–1981', in Ellen Kuzwayo, *Call Me Woman* (London: The Women's Press, 1985), 264–265.

83. Under the 1959 Extension of University Education Act, students classified as Zulu or Swazi were to attend Zululand, while students classified as Sotho, Tswana, Venda and Tsonga were to attend the University College of the North in the Transvaal, which also opened in 1960. Fort Hare was reserved for Xhosa students. 'Coloured' and Indian students were to attend, respectively, the new University of the Western Cape, opened in 1960 as a constituent college of Unisa, and the University College for Indians in Durban, also established in 1960 as a Unisa affiliate. The English-medium universities of Cape Town, the Witwatersrand and Natal were closed to blacks, unless they received approval from the Minister of Bantu Education because their courses of study were not available elsewhere; the correspondence school Unisa remained open to all. Most faculty at 'bush colleges' were white, and many had been trained at

rabidly pro-apartheid Afrikaans universities. See Freda Troup, *Forbidden Pastures: Education under Apartheid* (London: International Defence and Aid Fund, 1976), 55–65; Horrell, *A Decade of Bantu Education*, 121–152; and Seán Morrow, 'Race, Redress and Historically Black Universities', in *Racial Redress and Citizenship in South Africa*, eds. Kristina Bentley and Adam Habib (Cape Town: HSRC Press, 2008), 263–288.

84. South African Association of University Women, Pietermaritzburg Branch, 'The University College of Zululand', 1965, MPP, File 2.

85. Horrell, *A Decade of Bantu Education*, 86.

86. Horrell, *A Decade of Bantu Education*, 33.

87. 'A List of Inanda Seminary Former Students (Compiled by Daphne Nene) Who Have Attended the University College of Zululand at Ongoye', RAP; and Muriel Horrell, *Bantu Education to 1968* (Johannesburg: South African Institute of Race Relations, 1968), 125.

88. 'Inanda Seminary', 1971, ISP, File 2a.

89. Deborah Gaitskell, '"Doing a Missionary Hard Work . . . in the Black Hole of Calcutta": African Women Teachers Pioneering a Profession in the Cape and Natal, 1880–1950', *Women's History Review* 13, no. 3 (September 2004): 407–425, p. 421; Mahlase, *The Careers of Women Teachers under Apartheid*, 59; Amelia Mariotti, 'The Incorporation of African Women into Wage Employment in South Africa, 1920–1970' (PhD diss., University of Connecticut, 1980), 197; and *South African Statistics 1990* (Pretoria: Central Statistical Service, 1990), 5:2–5:5.

90. Leo Kuper, *An African Bourgeoisie*, 173.

91. Charlotte Searle, *The History of the Development of Nursing in South Africa, 1652–1960: A Socio-Historical Survey* (Cape Town: Struik, 1965), 276.

92. Marks, *Divided Sisterhood*, 170.

93. The 1970 census recorded 641 180 African female domestic servants, out of 1 985 947 'economically active' African women. See Deborah Gaitskell, Judy Kimble, Moira Maconachie and Elaine Unterhalter, 'Class, Race and Gender: Domestic Workers in South Africa', *Review of African Political Economy* 27/28 (1983): 86–108, p. 102.

94. 'Inanda Seminary: One Hundred Years, 1869–1969', ISCA.

95. Inanda's transformation followed the state's construction of a massive new township in neighboring KwaMashu. This development extended transport services to make the area a commuter suburb of Durban – but KwaMashu also propelled growing numbers of people who did not qualify for or refused to occupy government houses to build shacks in Inanda. See Heather Hughes, 'The City Closes In: The Incorporation of Inanda into Metropolitan Durban', in *The People's City: African Life in Twentieth-Century Durban*, eds. Paul Maylam and Iain Edwards (Pietermaritzburg: University of KwaZulu-Natal Press, 1996), 299–309.

96. See Gerhard Maré and Georgina Hamilton, *An Appetite for Power: Buthelezi's Inkatha and South Africa* (Johannesburg: Ravan, 1987); and Shula Marks, *The Ambiguities of Dependence in South Africa: Class, Nationalism, and the State in Twentieth-Century Natal* (Baltimore: Johns Hopkins, 1986).

97. P. Allen Myrick, 'Report of the Acting Field Secretary, South Africa Mission, for the Year 1965, to the United Church Board for World Ministries', 22 January 1966, United Congregational Church of Southern Africa Archives (UCCSA), Brixton, Gauteng.

98. See Dee Shirley Deane, *Black South Africans: A Who's Who of Natal's Leading Blacks* (Cape Town: Oxford University Press, 1978), 24–32.

99. See David Rubenstein, 'The Significance of Inanda Seminary', 12 August 1966, RAP.

100. See, for example, 'Mission with a Water Problem', *Daily News* (26 August 1971): 50; and 'Inanda's Perennial Problem: Water – and Sewage Disposal', n.d. (circa 1973), ISP, Book 72.

101. 'Student Centre an Enlightened Gift – Buthelezi', *Natal Mercury* (27 September 1972), in ISCA.

102. Shirley Deane, Inanda Seminary Public Relations Office, Durban, to Thorne, Braamfontein, 17 September 1973, EBP, File 42.

103. See Brigid Flanagan, 'Education: Policy and Practice', in *Catholics in Apartheid Society*, ed. Andrew Prior (Cape Town: David Philip, 1982), 83–96.

104. Aylard, Inanda, to Buthelezi, Mahlabathini, 8 June 1972, RAP; and Buthelezi, Mahlabathini, 'To Whom It May Concern', 12 January 1973, RAP.

105. Roger Aylard, 'Principal's Annual Report for the 1971 School Year', 26 February 1972, RAP.

106. See Aylard, Inanda, 'To Whom It May Concern', November 1972, RAP; Buthelezi, Mahlabathini, 12 January 1973, RAP; and P.G. Henwood, Secretary, Group Chairman's Fund, Anglo American Corporation of South Africa, Johannesburg, to Aylard, 1 May 1973, EBP.

107. J.F. Thorne and G. Owen Lloyd, UCCSA, 'Report on Survey of Inanda Seminary as a Church-Related Institution', February 1973, EBP, File 42.

108. See Aylard, 'Principal's Annual Report for the 1972 School Year', 10 February 1973, EBP; and 'To Staff, Re: Survey of Inanda Seminary', n.d. (circa 1972), EBP, File 42.

109. Thorne and Lloyd, 'Report on Survey of Inanda Seminary as a Church-Related Institution', February 1973, EBP, File 42. The UCCSA was not unanimous in finding Inanda 'commendable'. The report also indicated that 'a section' of UCCSA members questioned the role of Catholic and 'coloured' staff and the presence of non-Zulu students. On tensions in

the UCCSA, see Desmond van der Water and Steve de Gruchy, 'Submission to the Truth and Reconciliation Commission of South Africa, October 1997', in *Changing Frontiers: The Mission Story of the United Congregational Church of Southern Africa*, ed. Steve de Gruchy (Gaborone, Botswana: Pula Press, 1999), 231–253.

110. Inanda Seminary would not finalise a deal for aid from KwaZulu until 1984. See Roger Aylard, Dumi Zondi, Faith Gcabashe and B.P. Simelane, 'Analysis and Study of UCCSA Financial Survey Report', 8 June 1973, ISCA; J.W. Nxumalo, Councillor for Education and Culture, KwaZulu Department of Education and Culture, Eshowe, to Aylard, Inanda, 19 June 1973, EBP, File 42; F.M. Hallows, KwaZulu Department of Education and Culture, Pietermaritzburg, to the Principal, Inanda Seminary, 3 June 1975, RAP; and 'Minutes of the 87th Meeting of the Governing Council of Inanda Seminary', 27 May 1983, ISCA.

111. By 1980 there were just twenty-three private schools in KwaZulu, out of 2 164 institutions: see 'Report of the KwaZulu Department of Education and Culture, 1980', 21, in *Official Publications of South African States* (Pretoria: State Library, 1986).

112. For Inkatha's invocation of 'woman-power', see Roger Southall, 'Buthelezi, Inkatha, and the Politics of Compromise', *African Affairs* 80, no. 321 (October 1981): 453–481, p. 457.

113. Ad Hoc Consultative Education Committee, KwaZulu Government, 'The Education Manifesto of KwaZulu', February 1973, EBP, File 42.

114. See 'Short Address: At the Opening of the Inanda Seminary Secretarial School – by the Honorable M.G. Buthelezi: Chief Executive Councillor of KwaZulu', 6 April 1974, Speech 22, Mangosuthu Gatsha Buthelezi Speeches (MGBS), Campbell Collections, University of KwaZulu-Natal, Durban; and Erica Rudden, 'Black Breakthrough: Inanda's New Secretarial School', *Daily News* (26 September 1974): 25. KwaZulu officials had long emphasised to Inanda's administrators that 'highly trained secretaries are an immediate need in the Government of KwaZulu'; IBM and Anglo American both expressed interest in hiring the school's graduates, and Anglo American followed up its interest with a grant to the high school. See summary of meeting with Nxumalo, in Aylard, Inanda, to Buthelezi, Mahlabathini, 8 June 1972, RAP; and 'Minutes of Governing Council Meeting of Inanda Seminary', 23 February 1974, EBP, File 43.

115. See Ruth Ann Nomathemba Sidzumo-Sanders, 'The Bantu Education System: Impact on Black Women in South Africa' (PhD diss., Wayne State University, 1989), 138; see also Table 1 in the Introduction to this volume.

116. See Hyslop, *The Classroom Struggle*, 134–149; and Elaine Unterhalter, 'Changing Aspects of Reformism in Bantu Education, 1953–1989', in *Apartheid Education and Popular Struggles*, eds. Unterhalter et al. (London: Zed, 1991), 35–72.

117. Mamphela Ramphele, *Across Boundaries: The Journey of a South African Woman Leader* (New York: The Feminist Press at the City University of New York, 1996; 1999), 35.

118. Daniel Massey, *Under Protest: The Rise of Student Resistance at the University of Fort Hare* (Pretoria: Unisa Press, 2010).

119. Lauretta (Gwina) Ngcobo, Inanda student (1945–1949), interviewed by the author, 19 March 2009, Durban, ISOHP.

120. See Edmie Mali, Fort Hare, to Scott, Inanda, 25 October 1960, ISCA.

121. For Tshabalala-Msimang, this was despite her father's refusal to pay for her university education, because 'he won't sharpen a knife that will cut somebody else'; she earned a scholarship from the American Board, with Lavinia Scott's support. See Ethel Mali, Durban, to Scott, Inanda, 26 February 1958, ISCA.

122. See Massey, *Under Protest*, 272.

123. Ethel Mali, Durban, to Scott, Inanda, 10 April 1962, ISCA.

124. Bongekile (Makhoba) Dlomo, Inanda student (1951–1952), interviewed by the author, 11 March 2009, Durban, ISOHP.

125. 'Obituary: Dudu Mate Mfusi', *EzakwamahEdwards* (2001): 37.

126. See Simonne Horwitz, ' "Black Nurses in White": Exploring Young Women's Entry into the Nursing Profession at Baragwanath Hospital, Soweto, 1948–1980', *Social History of Medicine* 20, no. 1 (2007): 131–146; and Horwitz, 'A Phoenix Rising: A History of Baragwanath Hospital, Soweto, South Africa, 1942–1990' (PhD diss., Oxford University, 2006), for an incisive examination of the personal factors impelling young women to take up nursing in the country's largest hospital during this period, and the political transformations that some underwent.

127. 'Joyce Sikhakhane-Rankin', in *The Road to Democracy: South Africans Telling Their Stories*, Volume 1, *1950–1970*, ed. South African Democracy Trust (Pretoria: Unisa Press, 2008), 441–449, p. 441. Interview conducted by Gregory Houston, 16 May 2001; edited by Mbulelo Vizikhungo Mzamane.

128. 'Joyce Sikhakhane-Rankin', 441.

129. Joyce Sikhakhane, Orlando West, to Scott, Inanda, 30 December 1963, ISCA.

130. Lindiwe (Gumede) Baloyi, Inanda student (1960–1964), interviewed by the author, 12 June 2010, Westville, KwaZulu-Natal, ISOHP. See also Mwelela Cele, member of Gumede family and *kholwa* historian, interviewed by the author, 24 May 2009, Durban, ISOHP.

131. Gloria (Mbalula) Malindi, Inanda student (1962–1964), interviewed by the author, 2 June 2009, Johannesburg, ISOHP.

132. Steve Biko, 'We Blacks', in Biko, *I Write What I Like* (London: Bowerdean Press, 1978; Johannesburg: Picador, 2004), 29–35, p. 29.

133. Daniel R. Magaziner, *The Law and the Prophets: Black Consciousness in South Africa, 1968–1977* (Athens: Ohio University Press, 2010), 57.

134. Biko, 'We Blacks', 31.

135. See Kopano Ratele, 'We Black Men', *International Journal of Intercultural Relations* 27, no. 2 (March 2003): 237–249; Daniel R. Magaziner, 'Pieces of a (Wo)man: Feminism, Gender, and Adulthood in Black Consciousness, 1968–1977', *Journal of Southern African Studies* 37, no. 1 (March 2011): 45–61; Ian MacQueen, 'Categories of Struggle: Reassessing Black Consciousness in South Africa through Gender, 1967–1976', in *Paths to Gender: European Historical Perspectives on Men and Women*, eds. Carla Salvaterra and Berteke Waaldijk (Pisa: Pisa University Press, 2009), 259–267.

136. See Leslie Hadfield, 'Restoring Human Dignity and Building Self-Reliance: Youth, Women, and Churches and Black Consciousness Community Development, South Africa, 1969–1977' (PhD diss., Michigan State University, 2010).

137. Clive Glaser, *Bo-Tsotsi: The Youth Gangs of Soweto, 1935–1976* (Portsmouth, NH: Heinemann, 2000), 172.

138. 2006 interview with Magaziner; see Magaziner, *The Law and the Prophets*, 39 and 134.

139. Nozizwe Madlala-Routledge, 'University of KwaZulu-Natal Award Speech', 30 October 2006, accessed 19 February 2011, http://www.polity.org.za/article/madlalaroutledge-university-of-kwazulunatal-award-30102006-2006-10-30.

40. Darlene Woodburn, Inanda teacher and choir director (1968–1973), interviewed by the author, via telephone from California, 30 June 2009, ISOHP.

141. 'South African Students' Organisation: Executive Council Meeting, Edendale Ecumenical Centre, 1–8 December 1971', accessed 19 February 2011, http://www.aluka.org/action/showMetadata?doi=10.5555/AL.SFF.DOCUMENT.min19711200.032.009.748. See also Bennie Khoapa, 'Youth and Student Organizations', *The Black Review* (1972): 181–189, pp. 183–184; and Alan Brooks and Jeremy Brickhill, *Whirlwind before the Storm: The Origins and Development of the Uprising in Soweto and the Rest of South Africa from June to December 1976* (London: International Defence and Aid Fund for Southern Africa, 1980), 80.

142. Aylard, ISOHP. I have not been able to verify whether this anecdote is apocryphal or not – in any event, it is indicative of Inanda administrators' attitudes towards student engagement in overt political organisation at the time.

143. Dumi Zondi, Inanda teacher and principal (1966–1976), interviewed by the author, 14 October 2008, Inanda, ISOHP.

144. Dumi Zondi, 'Profile of a Black Boarding School', *Institute for Black Research Quarterly Comment* (January 1976): 25. In 1972, for the first time in its history, Inanda's salary scales were not based on race. The scale remained gendered – an arrangement that remained typical for women of all hues in apartheid South Africa. See 'Inanda Seminary Salary Schedule (Effective from 1st April 1972 through 31st March 1974)', RAP.

145. Zondi, ISOHP.

146. On connections between interracial and predominantly white Christian groups and Black Consciousness, see Ian MacQueen, 'Re-imagining South Africa: Black Consciousness, Radical Christianity, and the New Left, 1967–1977' (PhD diss., University of Sussex, 2011); and Mabel Raisibe Maimela, 'Black Consciousness and White Liberals in South Africa: Paradoxical Anti-apartheid Politics' (PhD diss., University of South Africa, 1999).

147. Carohn Cornell, Inanda teacher (1968–1970), interviewed by the author, Kalk Bay, Western Cape, 6 May 2009, ISOHP.

148. Madlala-Routledge, 'University of KwaZulu-Natal Award Speech'.

149. Zamakhosi Mpanza, Inanda student (1964–1969) and librarian (1974–1978), interviewed by the author, 21 March 2009, Durban, ISOHP. The significance of librarians and reading in creating the requisite imaginative space to develop alternatives to apartheid has been preliminarily explored in Archie L. Dick, *The Hidden History of South Africa's Book and Reading Cultures* (Toronto: University of Toronto Press, 2012). The rich history of student debating societies under segregation and apartheid, as discussed in this chapter and in the previous chapter, await further investigation.

150. Baleka Mbete, 'Application for Admission', 1966, ISCA.

151. Faith Duma, 'How I, as a Woman, Can Contribute to Society', *Who's Who in the Zoo* (5 March 1971), ISCA.

152. Khathija Phili, 'What Am I Fit For?????' *Who's Who in the Zoo* (August 1971), ISCA.

153. Nomvuyo Qubeka, 'The Place of Women's Liberation in Society', *Who's Who in the Zoo* (3 September 1975), ISCA.

154. Esther Sbongile (Cele) Sangweni, Inanda student (1965–1969) and teacher (1974–1979), interviewed by the author, 12 March 2009, Durban, ISOHP.

155. Khonzaphi (Nduli) Zimu, Inanda student (1965–1969) and principal and teacher (1999–2009), interviewed by the author, 14 December 2008, KwaMashu, KwaZulu-Natal, ISOHP.

156. Cecilia (Mvelase) Khuzwayo, Inanda student (1966–1970), interviewed by the author, 7 December 2008, via telephone from Johannesburg, ISOHP.

157. See also Sindiwe Magona, *Forced to Grow* (London: The Women's Press, 1992), 52–115, on her experiences as a student and teacher near Cape Town in the 1960s and early 1970s.

158. Ramphele, *Across Boundaries*, 43.

159. Ramphele, *Across Boundaries*, 44.

160. Ramphele, *Across Boundaries*, 184–185.

161. Robert Morrell, Debbie Epstein, Elaine Unterhalter, Deevia Bhana and Relebohile Moletsane, *Towards Gender Equality: South African Schools During the HIV and AIDS Epidemic* (Pietermaritzburg: University of KwaZulu-Natal Press, 2009), 29; and Morrell and Moletsane, 'Inequality and Fear: Living and Working inside Bantu Education Schools', in *The History of Education under Apartheid, 1948–1994*, 238.

Chapter Five

1. Sikose Mji, 'Application for Admission', 7 January 1976, Inanda Seminary Campus Archive (ISCA), Inanda, KwaZulu-Natal.

2. Mji, 'The World of Inanda Seminary', in *Who's Who in the Zoo* (June 1976), ISCA.

3. See Sikose Mji, 'Freedom is Choice', *The Warsaw Voice* (25 April 2003), accessed 19 February 2011, http://www.warsawvoice.pl/WVpage/pages/article.php/2152/article.

4. See Alan Brooks and Jeremy Brickhill, *Whirlwind before the Storm: The Origins and Development of the Uprising in Soweto and the Rest of South Africa from June to December 1976* (London: International Defence and Aid Fund for Southern Africa, 1980); Harry Mashabela, *A People on the Boil: Reflections on June 16, 1976 and Beyond* (Braamfontein, South Africa: Skotaville, 1987; Auckland Park, South Africa: Jacana, 2006); Sifiso Mxolisi Ndlovu, 'The Soweto Uprising', in *The Road to Democracy in South Africa*, Volume 2, *1970–1980*, ed. South African Democracy Education Trust (Pretoria: Unisa Press, 2006), 317–368; and Daniel R. Magaziner, *The Law and the Prophets: Black Consciousness in South Africa, 1968–1977* (Athens: Ohio University Press, 2010).

5. Clive Glaser, *Bo-Tsotsi: The Youth Gangs of Soweto, 1935–1976* (Portsmouth, NH: Heinemann, 2000), 172.

6. See Rachel Johnson, 'Making History, Gendering Youth: Young Women and South Africa's Liberation Struggles from 1976' (PhD diss., University of Sheffield, 2010). She draws on a nascent body of political memoirs, such as Sibongile Mkhabela, *Open Earth and Black Roses: Remembering 16 June 1976* (Braamfontein, South Africa: Skotaville, 2001). See also Monica Eileen Patterson, 'Constructions of Childhood in Apartheid's Last Decades' (PhD diss., University of Michigan, 2009), 22–54.

7. For rich inquiries into female students' educational visions elsewhere, see Heather Switzer, 'Disruptive Discourses: Kenyan Maasai Schoolgirls Make Themselves', *Girlhood Studies* 3, no. 1 (Summer 2010): 137–155; and Amy Stambach, *Lessons from Mount Kilimanjaro: Schooling, Community, and Gender in East Africa* (New York: Routledge, 2000).

8. For this term, see Colin Bundy, 'Street Sociology and Pavement Politics: Aspects of Youth and Student Resistance in Cape Town, 1985', *Journal of Southern African Studies* 13, no. 3 (April 1987): 303–330.

9. Elaine Unterhalter, 'The Impact of Apartheid on Women's Education in South Africa', *Review of African Political Economy* 48 (Autumn 1990): 66–75, p. 70. Seventy-five per cent of African girls between ages five and fourteen were in primary school that year.

10. Elaine Unterhalter, 'Can Education Overcome Women's Subordinate Position in the Occupation Structure?' in *Education in a Future South Africa: Policy Issues for Transformation*, eds. Unterhalter, Harold Wolpe and Thozamile Botha (Portsmouth, NH: Heinemann, 1991), 65–84, pp. 79 and 82.

11. ANC Women's League, *Status of South African Women: A Sourcebook in Tables and Graphs* (Marshalltown, South Africa: ANC Women's League Policy Division, 1993), 57: 48.5 per cent of African men and 48.8 per cent of African women had attained their Standard Four certificates or above.

12. Bundy, 'Street Sociology and Pavement Politics', 311.

13. Many young women, however, were students at the correspondence-only University of South Africa (Unisa): more than two-fifths of African female university students attended Unisa in 1990, for example. See ANC Women's League, 47.

14. See Robert Morrell and Relebohile Moletsane, 'Inequality and Fear: Learning and Working inside Bantu Education Schools', in *The History of Education under Apartheid, 1948-1994: The Doors of Learning and Culture Shall Be Opened*, ed. Peter Kallaway (New York: P. Lang, 2002), 224–242, p. 228. Male teachers also preyed upon female students, stimulating student protests. See Isak Niehaus, 'Towards a Dubious Liberation: Masculinity, Sexuality and Power in South African Lowveld Schools, 1953-1999', *Journal of Southern African Studies* 26, no. 3 (September 2000): 387–407.

15. Mark Hunter, *Love in the Time of AIDS: Inequality, Gender, and Rights in South Africa* (Bloomington: University of Indiana Press, 2010), 85.

16. See Anne Mager, *Gender and the Making of a South African Bantustan: A Social History of the Ciskei, 1945–1959* (Portsmouth, NH: Heinemann, 1999); and Thembisa Waetjen, *Workers and Warriors: Masculinity and the Struggle for Nation in South Africa* (Urbana: University of Illinois Press, 2004).

17. Thokozani Xaba, 'Masculinity and Its Malcontents: The Confrontation between "Struggle Masculinity" and "Post-struggle Masculinity" (1990–1997)', in *Changing Men in Southern Africa*, ed. Robert Morrell (Pietermaritzburg: University of Natal Press, 2001), 105–124.

18. See Hunter, *Love in the Time of AIDS*, 84–102.

19. Jimmy Kruger, quoted in *Rand Daily Mail*, 4 July 1976; cited in Elaine Unterhalter, 'Changing Aspects of Reformism in Bantu Education, 1953–89', in *Apartheid Education and Popular Struggles*, eds. Unterhalter et al. (London: Zed, 1991), 64.

20. Brooks and Brickhill, *Whirlwind before the Storm*, 65.

21. Census figures, cited in Owen Crankshaw, *Race, Class, and the Changing Division of Labour under Apartheid* (New York: Routledge, 1997), 163.

22. See Shirley Mahlase, *The Careers of Women Teachers under Apartheid* (Harare: SAPES Trust, 1997), for an illustrative ethnography of the careers of female teachers in the Lebowa Bantustan in the early 1990s.

23. Shula Marks, *Divided Sisterhood: Race, Class, and Gender in the South African Nursing Profession* (Johannesburg: Wits University Press, 1994), 170; this was based on data from the South African Nursing Council.

24. Census data, in Crankshaw, *Race, Class, and the Changing Division of Labour*, 161.

25. United Party MP, quoted in Marks, *Divided Sisterhood*, 189.

26. Quoted in Marks, *Divided Sisterhood*, 191.

27. Crankshaw, *Race, Class, and the Changing Division of Labour*, 35.

28. Inanda's Secretarial School heralded the growing presence of African women in clerical jobs. In 1975, according to Manpower Surveys, there were some 27 000 African women and 131 000 African men in such jobs; by 1985, 96 000 women and 180 000 men; and by 1989, 217 000 women and 270 000 men. See Crankshaw, *Race, Class, and the Changing Division of Labour*, 159.

29. On Baragwanath, see Simonne Horwitz, 'A Phoenix Rising: A History of Baragwanath Hospital, Soweto, South Africa, 1942–1990' (PhD diss., Oxford University, 2006).

30. Marks, *Divided Sisterhood*, 203–206.

31. See Mahlase, *The Careers of Women Teachers under Apartheid*, 158–163; Shireen Motala and Salim Vally, 'People's Education: From People's Power

to Tirisano', in *The History of Education under Apartheid*, 174–194; Alan Wieder, 'Informed by Apartheid: Mini-Oral Histories of Two Cape Town Teachers', in *The History of Education under Apartheid*, 198–210; and Paul Kihn, 'Comrades and Professionals: Teacher Ideology and Practice in the Western Cape, 1985 to 1990', in *The History of Education under Apartheid*, 325–336.

32. See Vanessa Noble, 'Doctors Divided: Gender, Race, and Class Anomalies in the Production of Black Medical Doctors in Apartheid South Africa, 1948 to 1994' (PhD diss., University of Michigan, 2005), 149. MEDUNSA was originally intended to phase out African students from the politicised University of Natal Medical School – retaining only 'coloured' and Indian students in Durban – but the vociferousness of student protests ensured that the state accepted African medical students at both.

33. M. Saleem Badat, *Black Student Politics, Higher Education, and Apartheid: From SASO to SANSCO, 1968–1990* (Pretoria: HSRC Press, 1999), 198.

34. Badat, 190–192.

35. The state followed the lead of white Catholic schools that had admitted black students in 'instances that merit special consideration' since 1977. See Pam Christie, *Open Schools: Racially Mixed Catholic Schools in South Africa, 1976–1986* (Johannesburg: Ravan, 1990), 31.

36. Alex Callinicos, 'The Soweto Uprising: South Africa's Black Townships Have Finally Exploded', *International Socialism* 90 (July/August 1976): 4–7.

37. Brooks and Brickhill, *Whirlwind before the Storm*, 127.

38. See Doug Tilton, 'Creating an "Educated Workforce": Inkatha, Big Business, and Educational Reform in KwaZulu', *Journal of Southern African Studies* 18, no. 1 (March 1992): 166–189.

39. See Gerhard Maré and Georgina Hamilton, *An Appetite for Power: Buthelezi's Inkatha and South Africa* (Johannesburg: Ravan, 1987); and Sibusisiwe Nombuso Dlamini, *Youth and Identity Politics in South Africa, 1990–1994* (Toronto: University of Toronto Press, 2005).

40. Dee Shirley Deane, *Black South Africans: A Who's Who of Natal's Leading Blacks* (Cape Town: Oxford University Press, 1978), 8.

41. See Meghan Elisabeth Healy, 'Magogo kaDinuzulu, Constance', in *Dictionary of African Biography*, eds. Emmanuel K. Akyeampong and Henry Louis Gates, Jr (New York: Oxford University Press, 2011), 30–32.

42. Shireen Abdool Aziz Hassim, 'Black Women in Political Organisations: A Case Study of the Inkatha Women's Brigade, 1976 to the Present' (master's thesis, University of Natal, 1990), 58 and 127.

43. 'Inanda Seminary – IBM Executives Visit. A Short Address to the Students by Umtwana Mangosuthu G. Buthelezi, Chief Minister of KwaZulu and

President of Inkatha, Tuesday, 14 February 1978', Speech 136, Mangosuthu Gatsha Buthelezi Speeches (MGBS), Campbell Collections, University of KwaZulu-Natal, Durban.

44. Khanyisile Kweyama, Inanda student (1976–1980), interviewed by the author, 29 May 2010, Johannesburg, Inanda Seminary Oral History Project (ISOHP).

45. Mamsie Ntshangase, Inanda student (1977–1981), interviewed by the author, 12 June 2010, Durban, ISOHP.

46. Nozizwe Maneli, Inanda student (1981–1985), interviewed by the author, 1 June 2009, Johannesburg, ISOHP.

47. Magaziner, *The Law and the Prophets*, 23.

48. Thanks to Tim Gibbs of Trinity College, Cambridge University, for discussing the elite history of St John's that he uncovered in his research on ANC networks in the Transkei; and to Mwelela Cele of Campbell Collections, University of KwaZulu-Natal, Durban, for our many conversations about his schooling at Adams, Mariannhill and Ohlange during the late-apartheid years.

49. Rebekah Lee, *African Women and Apartheid: Migration and Settlement in Urban South Africa* (New York: I.B. Tauris, 2009), 57–58.

50. Kweyama, ISOHP.

51. Ndo Nyembezi, Inanda student (1975–1980), interviewed by the author, 16 April 2009, Durban, ISOHP.

52. Kweyama, ISOHP.

53. Faith Gcabashe, Acting Principal, 'Inanda Seminary Principal's Report', March 1977, ISCA.

54. Nonhlanhla Khumalo, Inanda student (1979–1982), interviewed by the author, 4 May 2009, Cape Town, ISOHP.

55. Khumalo, ISOHP.

56. Karen Roy-Guglielmi, Inanda teacher (1980–1985), interviewed by the author, 23 July 2009, Vernon, Connecticut, ISOHP.

57. Khumalo, ISOHP.

58. Vuyo Ncwaiba, Inanda student (1984–1985), interviewed by the author, June 2009, Johannesburg, ISOHP.

59. Thandeka (Zama) Dloti, Inanda student (1982–1986), interviewed by the author, 2 June 2009, Johannesburg, ISOHP.

60. Nomsa Makhoba, Inanda student (1981–1985), interviewed by the author, 1 June 2009, Johannesburg, ISOHP.

61. Pamela Dube, Inanda student (1980–1984), interviewed by the author, 1 June 2009, Johannesburg, ISOHP.

62. Carroll Jacobs, Inanda Secretarial School teacher (1972–1974) and school secretary (1981–1984), interviewed by the author, 5 May 2009, Plumstead, Western Cape, ISOHP.

63. Constance Miriam (Dlomo) Koza, Inanda student (1941–1945) and principal (1980–1986), interviewed by the author, 2 June 2009, Centurion, Gauteng, ISOHP.

64. Maneli, ISOHP.

65. Dube, ISOHP.

66. Siphokazi Koyana (Inanda student, 1981–1985), interviewed by the author, 1 June 2009, Johannesburg, ISOHP.

67. Dube, ISOHP; Koyana, ISOHP.

68. Ntshangase, ISOHP; see also Dloti, ISOHP.

69. Mandisa (Mesatywa) Zungu, Inanda Seminary student (1978–1982), interviewed by the author, 4 May 2009, Cape Town, ISOHP.

70. Kweyama, ISOHP.

71. Lungi (Mkhize) Kwitshana, Inanda student (1976–1980), interviewed by the author, 5 June 2010, Durban, ISOHP.

72. Ntshangase, ISOHP.

73. Thuthula Balfour-Kaipa, Inanda student (1976–1980), interviewed by the author, 29 May 2010, Johannesburg, ISOHP.

74. Thembi (Ndlela) Msane, Inanda student (1980–1984), interviewed by the author, 3 March 2009, Durban, ISOHP.

75. See 'Minutes of the 44th Meeting of the Governing Council', 22 February 1975, Edgar Brookes Papers (EBP), File 43, Campbell Collections, University of KwaZulu-Natal, Durban.

76. Kweyama, ISOHP.

77. Kwitshana, ISOHP.

78. Zungu, ISOHP.

79. Nyembezi, ISOHP.

80. Nyembezi, ISOHP.

81. Msane, ISOHP; Khumalo, ISOHP.

82. See also Khumalo, ISOHP.

83. Dube, ISOHP.

84. Koyana, ISOHP.

85. Balfour-Kaipa, ISOHP.

86. 'Principal's Report to the Governing Council Meeting', 22 February 1985, ISCA.

87. See Heather Hughes, 'Violence in Inanda, August 1985', *Journal of Southern African Studies* 13, no. 3 (April 1987): 331–354.

88. Koza apprehended that 'Fund-Raising is a game of politics', in which 'a project could be attractive as a salve to one's conscience': see 'Principal's Report to the Governing Council Meeting', 19 August 1983, ISCA. Koza tapped into funds from Anglo American and the Urban Foundation, which were investing heavily in education and social welfare projects to stave off

revolution and capital flight (see Constance Koza, 'Principal's Report, to Be Read at the 75th Meeting of the Governing Council of Inanda Seminary', 10 May 1980, ISCA). She mobilised support from IBM and Mobil (see 'Inanda Seminary Principal's Report to the Governing Council Meeting', 25 November 1983, ISCA). Both were signatories to the Sullivan Principles, which compelled American corporations to invest in black social welfare. See also Nicola Swanison, 'Corporate Intervention in Education and Training, 1960–1989', in *Apartheid Education and Popular Struggles*, 95–116.

89. 'Minutes of the 87th Meeting of the Governing Council of Inanda', 27 May 1983, ISCA.

90. Allen Myrick, Interim Africa Secretary, United Church Board for World Ministries, New York, to E.C. Gilfillan, Chairman, Inanda Seminary Governing Council, Maidstone, Natal, 30 October 1987, ISCA; Wing, Braamfontein, to Gilfillan, Maidstone, 29 December 1987, ISCA.

91. E.C. Gilfillan, Chairman, Inanda Governing Council, Maidstone, Natal, to Rev. Joseph Wing, Secretary, United Congregational Church of Southern Africa, Braamfontein, 7 December 1987, ISCA.

92. Dr Bonganjalo Goba to Rev. Sam Arends, General Secretary, UCCSA, 28 March 1989, ISCA.

93. F.G. Mhlambo, 'Principal's Report to the At Home Meeting Held on 10 October 1992', ISCA.

94. Siza Ntshakala, 'Fire Destroys Famous Girls' Boarding Establishment', *Natal Mercury* (5 October 1993), ISCA.

95. Mhlambo to Dr S. Bhengu, Department of National Education, Pretoria, 24 June 1994, ISCA.

96. R. Duma, Umlazi, 'Call to Former Inanda Pupils', *Daily News* (26 May 1997), clipping in ISCA; see also Chris Hlongwa, 'Illustrious Girls' School Threatened with Sad Closure', *City Press* (11 September 1997), clipping in ISCA.

Epilogue

1. Elaine Unterhalter, 'Gender Equality and Education in South Africa: Measurements, Scores, and Strategies', in *Gender Equity in South African Education, 1994–2004: Perspectives from Research, Government and Unions*, eds. Linda Chisholm and Jean September (Cape Town: HSRC Press, 2005), 77–91, p. 82; and Mignonne Breier and Angelique Wildschut, 'Changing Gender Profile of Medical Schools in South Africa', *South African Medical Journal* 98, no. 7 (July 2008): 557–560. African women remain under-represented: in 2005, African women were 23 per cent of medical students;

white women, 19 per cent; Indian women, 9 per cent; and mixed-race women, 5 per cent.

2. Thidziambi Phendla, 'Women on the Rise: Women Navigating across Social, Political, Economic and Cultural Arenas to Claim Their Stake in Educational Leadership Positions in South Africa', in *Women Leading Education across the Continents: Sharing the Spirit, Fanning the Flame*, ed. Helen C. Sobehart (Lanham, MD: Rowman and Littlefield, 2009), 57–64; Mark Hunter, *Love in the Time of AIDS: Inequality, Gender, and Rights in South Africa* (Bloomington: University of Indiana Press, 2010), 130–154; and Rowena Martineau, 'Women and Education in South Africa: Factors Influencing Women's Educational Progress and Their Entry into Traditionally Male-Dominated Fields', *The Journal of Negro Education* (Autumn 1997): 383–395.

3. Daniela Casale and Dorrit Posel, 'The Continued Feminization of the Labour Force in South Africa: An Analysis of Recent Data and Trends', *South African Journal of Economics* 701 (March 2002): 156–184; and Casale and Posel, 'Women and the Economy: How Far Have We Come?' *Agenda* 64 (2005): 21–29.

4. Naledi Pandor, 'The Hidden Face of Gender Inequality in South African Education', in *Gender Equity in South African Education*, 19–24, p. 23.

5. See Carole Leathwood and Barbara Read, *Gender and the Changing Face of Higher Education: A Feminized Future?* (New York: Open University Press, 2009), 26–47.

6. Robert Morrell, Debbie Epstein, Elaine Unterhalter, Deevia Bhana and Relebohile Moletsane, *Towards Gender Equality: South African Schools During the HIV and AIDS Epidemic* (Pietermaritzburg: University of KwaZulu-Natal Press, 2009), 23.

7. See Chisholm and September, 'Overview', in *Gender Equity in South African Education*, 1–18; on the historical context of gendered violence in schools, see Shula Marks, 'Changing History, Changing Histories: Separations and Connections in the Lives of South African Women', *Journal of African Cultural Studies* 13, no. 1 (June 2000): 94–106.

8. For discussion of these themes, see Hunter, *Love in the Time of Aids*; Morrell et al., *Towards Gender Equality*; and Didier Fassin, *When Bodies Remember: Experiences and Politics of AIDS in South Africa* (Berkeley: University of California Press, 2007). On nurses' aspirations to deal with South Africa's crisis of social reproduction by taking their skills overseas, see Elizabeth Hull, 'International Migration, "Domestic Struggles", and Status Aspiration among Nurses in South Africa', *Journal of Southern African Studies* 36, no. 4 (December 2010): 851–867.

9. Memorandum, 22 December 1997, Inanda Seminary Campus Archive (ISCA), Inanda, KwaZulu-Natal.

10. Chris Hlongwa, 'Inanda to Rise Like a Phoenix', *City Press* (4 January 1998): 16.

11. 'Inanda Seminary: 130 Years of Academic Excellence', *EzakwamahEdwards* (1999), ISCA.

12. Cynthia Mpati, 'From the Principal's Desk: Fighting Battles That Matter', *EzakwamahEdwards* (2001): 3–4, ISCA.

13. Mpati, 'From the Principal's Desk'.

14. Esther Sbongile (Cele) Sangweni, Inanda student (1965–1969) and teacher (1974–1979), interviewed by the author, 12 March 2009, Durban, Inanda Seminary Oral History Project (ISOHP).

15. Ntombi Mngomezulu, Inanda student (2002–2006), interviewed by the author, 4 May 2009, Cape Town, ISOHP.

16. 'How Did the Historic Schools Restoration Project Begin?' accessed 19 February 2011, http://www.historicschools.org.za/view.asp?/pg= Schools&subm=Pilot%20Schools.

17. Other pilot schools were taken over or closed by the apartheid state: Adams (the co-educational American Board institution in KwaZulu-Natal); Tiger Kloof (London Missionary Society, Northern Cape); Healdtown (Methodist, Eastern Cape); St Matthew's (Anglican, Eastern Cape); and Lemana (Swiss Mission, Limpopo).

18. 'Speech Given by President Thabo Mbeki at an HSRP Function at Healdtown Comprehensive School', Fort Beaufort, Eastern Cape, 24 May 2008, accessed 19 February 2011, http://www.historicschools.org.za/ view.asp?=4&tname=tblComponent4&oname=Speeches&pg=front& subm=Speeches.

19. On these experiences, see Mark Gevisser, *A Legacy of Liberation: Thabo Mbeki and the Future of the South African Dream* (New York: Palgrave Macmillan, 2009), 25–32 and 50–57.

20. Gevisser, *A Legacy of Liberation*, 276–345.

21. 'Identification of Historic Schools', accessed 19 February 2011, http:// www.historicschools.org.za/view.asp?pg=Schools&submIdentification %20of%20historic%20schools.

22. Italics in original. See 'The Z.K. Matthews Educational Trust', accessed 19 February 2011, http://www.historicschools.org.za/view.asp?pg=ZK %20Matthews&subm=The%20ZK%20Matthews%20Educational %20Trust.

23. See the sociological work of Nicoli Nattrass and Jeremy Seekings, ' "Two Nations"? Race and Economic Inequality in South Africa', *Daedalus* 130, no. 1 (Winter 2001): 45–70; and the satirical work of Zakes Mda, *Black Diamonds* (Cape Town: Penguin, 2009).

24. Nonhlanhla Khumalo (Inanda student, 1979–1982) and Mandisa Zungu (Inanda student, 1978–1982), interviewed by the author, 4 May 2009, Cape Town, ISOHP.

25. Lynette Hlongwane, 'The Role of Inanda Seminary in the Education of African Girls in South Africa: A Report of Graduates' Views' (PhD diss., Teachers College, Columbia University, 1998).

26. Mngomezulu, ISOHP.

27. See Frances R. Spielhagen, *Debating Single-Sex Education: Separate and Equal?* (Lanham, MD: Rowman and Littlefield, 2008); Ilana DeBare, *Where Girls Come First: The Rise, Fall and Surprising Revival of Girls' Schools* (New York: Penguin, 2004); and Rosemary C. Salomone, *Same, Different, Equal: Rethinking Single-Sex Schooling* (New Haven: Yale University Press, 2003).

28. Robert Morrell, 'Considering the Case for Single-Sex Schools in South Africa', *McGill Journal of Education* (Fall 2000): 221–244. For a critique of this 'protective' rationale for girls' schooling, see Deevia Bhana and Nalini Pillay, 'Beyond Passivity: Constructions of Femininities in a Single-Sex South African School', *Educational Review* 63, no. 1 (2011): 65–78.

29. Pusch Commey, 'South Africa: Oprah to the Rescue?' *New African* (February 2007): 10–15; and Oprah Winfrey Leadership Academy, *Building a Dream: The Oprah Winfrey Leadership Academy*, DVD (Chicago: Harpo Productions, 2007).

30. 'Academy Fact Sheet, October 2009', accessed 19 February 2011, http://www.oprahwinfreyleadershipacademy.o-philanthropy.org/site/Page Server?pagename=owla_about.

Bibliography

A. **Oral sources**

1. **Inanda Seminary Oral History Project (ISOHP)**

Between October 2008 and June 2010, the author interviewed the following Inanda affiliates (listed by type and dates of affiliation). Interviews were conducted in English and one-on-one, except where specified. Transcripts and recordings may be consulted at the Inanda Seminary Campus Archive; at the Campbell Collections, University of KwaZulu-Natal; and on the author's website.

Inanda Seminary Students

Caroline Sililo
  Inanda student, 1934–1936; teacher, 1943–1950.
  Interviewed with Nyongo in Groutville, KwaZulu-Natal, 17 March 2009.
Constance Miriam Koza (née Dlomo)
  Inanda student, 1941–1945; principal, 1980–1986.
  Interviewed in Centurion, Gauteng, 2 June 2009.
Faith Nyongo (née Nomvete)
  Inanda student, 1943–1945.
  Interviewed with Sililo in Groutville, KwaZulu-Natal, 17 March 2009.
Melodious Gumede (née Blose)
  Inanda student, 1944–1946.
  Interviewed with Bhengu and Meyiwa in Inanda, 20 January 2009.
Dorcas Sibusisiwe Meyiwa (née Gumbi)
  Inanda student, 1944–1948.
  Interviewed with Bhengu and Gumede in Inanda, 20 January 2009.
Lauretta Ngcobo (née Gwina)
  Inanda student, 1945–1949.
  Interviewed in Durban, 19 March 2009.
Nomangcobo Sibusisiwe Zamakhosi Bhengu
  Inanda student, 1949–1951.
  Interviewed with Gumede and Meyiwa in Inanda, 20 January 2009.

Bongekile Dlomo (née Makhoba)
    Inanda student, 1951–1952.
    Interviewed in Durban, 11 March 2009.
Lindiwe Baloyi (née Gumede)
    Inanda student, 1960–1964.
    Interviewed in Westville, KwaZulu-Natal, 12 June 2010.
Gloria Malindi (née Mbalula)
    Inanda student, 1962–1964.
    Interviewed in Johannesburg, 2 June 2009.
Zamakhosi Mpanza
    Inanda student, 1964–1969; librarian, 1974–1978.
    Interviewed in Durban, 21 March 2009.
Esther Sbongile Sangweni (née Cele)
    Inanda student, 1965–1969; teacher, 1974–1979.
    Interviewed in Durban, 12 March 2009.
Khonzaphi Zimu (née Nduli)
    Inanda student, 1965–1969; principal, 1999–2000; teacher, 2000–2009.
    Interviewed in KwaMashu, KwaZulu-Natal, 14 December 2008.
Cecilia Khuzwayo (née Mvelase)
    Inanda student, 1966–1970.
    Interviewed via telephone from Johannesburg, 7 December 2008.
Ndo Nyembezi
    Inanda student, 1975–1980.
    Interviewed in Durban, 16 April 2009.
Thuthula Balfour-Kaipa
    Inanda student, 1976–1980.
    Interviewed in Johannesburg, 29 May 2010.
Khanyisile Kweyama
    Inanda student, 1976–1980.
    Interviewed in Johannesburg, 29 May 2010.
Lungi Kwitshana (née Mkhize)
    Inanda student, 1976–1980.
    Interviewed in Durban, 5 June 2010.
Mamsie Ntshangase
    Inanda student, 1977–1981.
    Interviewed in Durban, 12 June 2010.
Mandisa Zungu (née Mesatywa)
    Inanda student, 1978–1982.
    Interviewed with Khumalo, Mngomezulu and Mphasane in Cape Town,
    4 May 2009.

Nonhlanhla Khumalo
Inanda student, 1979–1982.
Interviewed with Mngomezulu, Mphasane and Zungu in Cape Town,
4 May 2009.

Pamela Dube
Inanda student, 1980–1984.
Interviewed with Koyana, Makhoba, Maneli and Ncwaiba in Johannesburg,
1 June 2009.

Thembi Msane (née Ndlela)
Inanda student, 1980–1984.
Interviewed in Durban, 3 March 2009.

Siphokazi Koyana
Inanda student, 1981–1985.
Interviewed with Dube, Makhoba, Maneli and Ncwaiba in Johannesburg,
1 June 2009.

Nomsa Makhoba
Inanda student, 1981–1985.
Interviewed with Dube, Koyana, Maneli and Ncwaiba in Johannesburg,
1 June 2009.

Nozizwe Maneli
Inanda student, 1981–1985.
Interviewed with Dube, Koyana, Makhoba and Ncwaiba in Johannesburg,
1 June 2009.

Thandeka Dloti (née Zama)
Inanda student, 1982–1986.
Interviewed in Johannesburg, 2 June 2009.

Vuyo Ncwaiba
Inanda student, 1984–1985.
Interviewed with Dube, Koyana, Makhoba and Maneli in Johannesburg,
1 June 2009.

Ntombi Mngomezulu
Inanda student, 2002–2006.
Interviewed with Khumalo, Mphasane and Zungu in Cape Town,
4 May 2009.

Rudo Mphasane
Inanda student, 2006–2008.
Interviewed with Khumalo, Mngomezulu and Zungu in Cape Town,
4 May 2009.

Inanda Seminary Staff

Mabel Christofersen
    Inanda teacher, 1946–1980.
    Interviewed in Durban, 9 December 2008.
Thembekile Cybele Zondi
    Inanda teacher, 1954–1982.
    Interviewed in Inanda, 11 October 2008.
Reverend B.K. Dludla
    Inanda Seminary Governing Council Chair, 1965–1981.
    Interviewed in Durban, 20 March 2009.
Dumi Zondi
    Inanda teacher, 1966–1973; principal, 1974–1976.
    Interviewed in Inanda, 14 October 2008.
Carohn Cornell
    Inanda teacher, 1968–1970.
    Interviewed in Kalk Bay, Western Cape, 6 May 2009.
Roger Aylard
    Inanda teacher, 1968–1973; principal, 1970–1973.
    Interviewed via Skype from California, 30 June 2009.
Darlene Woodburn
    Inanda teacher and choir director, 1968–1973.
    Interviewed via telephone from California, 30 June 2009.
Carroll Jacobs
    Inanda teacher, 1972–1974; secretary, 1981–1984.
    Interviewed in Plumstead, Western Cape, 5 May 2009.
Karen Roy-Guglielmi
    Inanda teacher, 1980–1985.
    Interviewed in Vernon, Connecticut, 23 July 2009.

Relatives of Inanda Seminary students

Andile Hawes
    Descendant of Thomas Hawes and Hawes family historian.
    Interviewed in Inanda, 21 March 2009. Jeff Guy also participated.
Mwelela Cele
    Member of Gumede family and historian of *amakholwa* community.
    Interviewed in Durban, 24 May 2009. Jason Hickel also participated.

2. Killie Campbell Oral History Programme (KCOHP)

Collection archived at Campbell Collections, University of KwaZulu-Natal, Durban.

Killie Campbell Audio Visual Collection (KCAV), 112, Mabel Christofersen
  Inanda teacher, 1946–1980.
  Interviewed on 20 February 1979 in Inanda by A. Manson and D. Collins.
  Interview conducted in English; tape and transcript in archive.
KCAV, 115, Margaret Nduna
  Inanda student, 1924–1926; teacher, 1930–1932 and 1937–1977.
  Interviewed on 2 March 1979 in Inanda by A. Manson and D. Collins.
  Interview conducted in English; tape and transcript in archive.
KCAV, 116, Angeline Dube
  Member of Daughters of Africa and widow of John Dube.
  Interviewed on 8 March 1979 in Inanda by A. Manson, D. Collins and A.
  Mngomezulu. Interview conducted in English; transcript in archive.
KCAV, 147, 151 and 180, Bertha Mkhize
  Inanda student, circa 1901–1903; teacher, circa 1904–1910.
  Interviewed on 14 and 22 August 1979 in Inanda by A. Mason and D.
  Collins. Interview conducted in English; tapes and transcript in archive.
KCAV, 354, Bertha Mkhize
  Interviewed on 27 August 1980 in Inanda by Julia Wells and Heather
  Hughes. Interview conducted in English; tape and transcript in archive.
KCAV, 329, Albertina Mzimela/Mnguni
  Inanda student, circa early 1920s; teacher, circa 1930s; Daughters of Africa
  member.
  Interviewed on 23 September 1980 in Umlazi, KwaZulu, by Simeon Zulu.
  Interview conducted in isiZulu; isiZulu and English transcripts in archive.

B. Archival sources

In addition to the collections listed below, the author referenced the papers of
Carohn Cornell (CCP) and Roger Aylard (RAP), and the unpublished memoirs
of Inanda teacher Agnes Wood; all have been donated to the Inanda Seminary
Campus Archive.

1. Campbell Collections, University of KwaZulu-Natal, Durban
   Adams College Papers (ACP)
   Edgar Brookes Papers (EBP)
   Karl Robert Brueckner Papers (KRBP)
   Inanda Seminary Papers (ISP)
   Mabel Palmer Papers (MPP)
   Mangosuthu Gatsha Buthelezi Speeches (MGBS)
   Natal Native Education Advisory Board Minutes (NNEAB)
   Sibusisiwe Makhanya Papers (SMP)

2. William Cullen Library, Historical Papers Collection, University of the Witwatersrand, Johannesburg
   Ken Hartshorne Papers (KHP)

3. Melville J. Herskovits Library of African Studies, Northwestern University, Evanston, Illinois
   Lavinia Scott Papers (LSP)

4. Houghton Library, Harvard University, Cambridge, Massachusetts
   American Board of Commissioners for Foreign Missions: African Missions Records (ABC)

5. Inanda Seminary Campus Archive (ISCA), Inanda, KwaZulu-Natal

6. National Archives of South Africa, Pietermaritzburg, KwaZulu-Natal
   American Board Mission Collection (ABMC)
   Colonial Secretary's Office Series (CSO)
   Master of the Supreme Court, Estates Records (MSCE)
   Secretary for Native Affairs Series (SNA)
   Zulu Society Papers (ZSP)
   National Archives of South Africa, Pretoria, Gauteng
   Department of Information Series (INL)

8. United Congregational Church of Southern Africa Archives (UCCSA), Brixton, Gauteng

9. University of Cape Town Manuscripts and Archives
   Native Education Commission Papers (NECP)

C. Periodicals and newspapers

The Bantu World (Johannesburg)
City Press (Durban)
Contact (Cape Town)
EzakwamahEdwards (Inanda)
Ilanga Lase Natal (Durban)
Life and Light for Heathen Women (Boston)
The Missionary Herald (Boston)
Natal Daily News/Daily News (Durban)
Natal Mercury (Durban)

Native Teachers' Journal (Pretoria)
The Torchbearer (Inanda)
Umteteli wa Bantu (Johannesburg)
Who's Who in the Zoo (Inanda)

D. Theses and unpublished manuscripts

Burns, Catherine. 'Reproductive Labors: The Politics of Women's Health in South Africa, 1900 to 1960'. PhD diss., Northwestern University, 1995.

Carton, Benedict. ' "Get Thee to Church": Zulu Women and American Board Missionaries in the Early Twentieth Century'. Seminar paper, Southern African Research Program, Yale University, 1991.

Dinnerstein, Myra. 'The American Board Mission to the Zulu, 1835–1900'. PhD diss., Columbia University, 1971.

Du Rand, Susan Michelle. 'From Mission School to Bantu Education: A History of Adams College'. Master's thesis, University of Natal, 1990.

Duke, Debra L. 'From True Woman to New Woman: Mary Kelly Edwards, Single Woman Missionary to Natal, South Africa, 1868–1927'. PhD diss., Princeton Theological Seminary, 2004.

Fleisch, Brahm. 'The Teachers College Club: American Educational Discourse and the Origins of Bantu Education in South Africa (1914–1951)'. PhD diss., Columbia University, 1995.

Guy, Jeff. 'An Accommodation of Patriarchs: Theophilus Shepstone and the System of Native Administration in Natal'. Seminar paper, Colloquium on Masculinities in Southern Africa, University of Natal, Durban, 1997.

———. 'Tradition in Transition: The Gendered Origins of Our Time'. Seminar paper, History and African Studies Seminar, University of KwaZulu-Natal, Durban, 2010.

———. 'Women in Labour: The Birth of Colonial Natal'. Seminar paper, History and African Studies Seminar, University of KwaZulu-Natal, Durban, 2009.

Hadfield, Leslie. 'Restoring Human Dignity and Building Self-Reliance: Youth, Women, and Churches and Black Consciousness Community Development, South Africa, 1969–1977'. PhD diss., Michigan State University, 2010.

Hassim, Shireen Abdool Aziz. 'Black Women in Political Organisations: A Case Study of the Inkatha Women's Brigade, 1976 to the Present'. Master's thesis, University of Natal, 1990.

Hlongwane, Lynette. 'The Role of Inanda Seminary in the Education of African Girls in South Africa: A Report of Graduates' Views'. PhD diss., Teachers College, Columbia University, 1998.

Horwitz, Simonne. 'A Phoenix Rising: A History of Baragwanath Hospital, Soweto, South Africa, 1942–1990'. PhD diss., Oxford University, 2006.

Hughes, Heather. 'Politics and Society in Inanda, Natal: The Qadi under Chief Mqhawe, c. 1840–1906'. PhD diss., University of London, 1995.

Johnson, Rachel. 'Making History, Gendering Youth: Young Women and South Africa's Liberation Struggles from 1976'. PhD diss., University of Sheffield, 2010.

Khan, Umehani. 'A Critical Study of the Life of Sibusisiwe Makanya and Her Work as Educator and Social Worker in the Umbumbulu District of Natal, 1894–1971'. Master's thesis, University of Natal, 1995.

Khandlhela, Risimati Samuel. 'Mariannhill Mission and African Education, 1882–1915'. Master's thesis, University of Natal, 1993.

Kiernan, A.M.P. 'The Work for Education in Natal of Robert James Mann (1857–1865)'. Master's thesis, University of Manchester, 1982.

MacDougall, Lyndsay. 'Inanda Seminary, 1950–1980: Educating a Nation'. Honours thesis, University of Natal, 1990.

MacQueen, Ian. 'Re-imagining South Africa: Black Consciousness, Radical Christianity, and the New Left, 1967–1977'. PhD diss., University of Sussex, 2011.

Maimela, Mabel Raisibe. 'Black Consciousness and White Liberals in South Africa: Paradoxical Anti-apartheid Politics'. PhD diss., University of South Africa, 1999.

Mariotti, Amelia. 'The Incorporation of African Women into Wage Employment in South Africa, 1920–1970'. PhD diss., University of Connecticut, 1980.

Mindry, Deborah. ' "Good Women": Philanthropy, Power, and the Politics of Femininity in Contemporary South Africa'. PhD diss., University of California-Irvine, 1999.

Motapanyane, J. Maki. 'The Politics of Feminism in South Africa: Gender Consciousness and Political Agency in the Twentieth Century'. PhD diss., York University, 2009.

Nauright, John. ' "Black Island in a White Sea": Black and White in the Making of Alexandra Township, South Africa, 1912–1948'. PhD diss., Queen's University, 1992.

Noble, Vanessa. 'Doctors Divided: Gender, Race, and Class Anomalies in the Production of Black Medical Doctors in Apartheid South Africa, 1948 to 1994'. PhD diss., University of Michigan, 2005.

Patterson, Monica Eileen. 'Constructions of Childhood in Apartheid's Last Decades'. PhD diss., University of Michigan, 2009.

Sidzumo-Sanders, Ruth Ann Nomathemba. 'The Bantu Education System: Impact on Black Women in South Africa'. PhD diss., Wayne State University, 1989.

E. Published materials

Abraham, Garth. *The Catholic Church and Apartheid: The Response of the Catholic Church of South Africa to the First Decade of National Party Rule, 1948–1957.* Johannesburg: Ravan, 1989.

Adomakoh, C.C. 'The Pattern of Epidemic Hysteria in a Girls' School in Ghana'. *African Journal of Psychiatry* 1 (1976): 177–182.

African National Congress. 'Constitution of the South African Native National Congress', 1919. Accessed 19 February 2011. http://www. anc/org/zamain. Php?includ=docs/Const/1919/constitution_sanncx.html.

———. 'The Freedom Charter', 1955. Accessed 19 February 2011. http://www.anc.org.za/show.php?include=docs/misc/1955/charter. html.

African National Congress Women's League. *Status of South African Women: A Sourcebook in Tables and Graphs.* Marshalltown, South Africa: ANC Women's League Policy Division, 1993.

American Anti-Slavery Society. *The Legion of Liberty! and Force of Truth, Containing the Thoughts, Words, and Deeds, of Some Prominent Apostles, Champions, and Martyrs.* New York: American Anti-Slavery Society, 1847. First published 1837.

American Board of Commissioners for Foreign Missions. *Brief Sketch of the American Ceylon Mission.* Jaffna, Ceylon: American Mission Press, 1849.

Anderson, Rufus. *Memorial of the First Fifty Years of the American Board of Commissioners for Foreign Missions.* Boston: American Board, 1862.

Andrew, John. 'Educating the Heathen: The Foreign Mission School Controversy and American Ideals'. *Journal of American Studies* 12, no. 3 (December 1978): 331–342.

Badat, M. Saleem. *Black Student Politics, Higher Education, and Apartheid: From SASO to SANSCO, 1968–1990.* Pretoria: HSRC Press, 1999.

Bantu Education Act, Act No. 47 of 1953. Pretoria: Government Printer, 1953.

Bean, Lucy, and Elizabeth van Heyningen, eds. *The Letters of Elizabeth Jane Waterston, 1866–1905.* Cape Town: Van Riebeeck Society, 1983.

Behr, A.L., and R.G. Macmillan. *Education in South Africa.* Pretoria: J.L. van Schaik, 1966.

Beinart, William, and Saul Dubow. 'Introduction: The Historiography of Segregation and Apartheid'. In *Segregation and Apartheid in Twentieth-*

Century South Africa, eds. Beinart and Dubow, 1–24. New York: Routledge, 1995.

Bendroth, Margaret Lamberts. *A School of the Church: Andover Newton across Two Centuries.* Grand Rapids, MI: William B. Eerdmans, 2008.

Berger, Iris. 'Generations of Struggle: Trade Unions and the Roots of Feminism, 1930–1960'. In *Women in South African History: Basus'iimbokodo, bawel'imilambo/They Remove Boulders and Cross Rivers*, ed. Nomboniso Gasa, 185–205. Cape Town: HSRC Press, 2007.

———. *Threads of Solidarity: Women in South African Industry, 1900–1980.* Bloomington: Indiana University Press, 1992.

Bhana, Deevia, and Nalini Pillay. 'Beyond Passivity: Constructions of Femininities in a Single-Sex South African School'. *Educational Review* 63, no. 1 (2011): 65–78.

Biko, Steve. *I Write What I Like.* Johannesburg: Picador, 2004. First published 1978.

Bloch, Marianne, Josephine A. Beoku-Betts and B. Robert Tabachnick, eds. *Women and Education in Sub-Saharan Africa: Power, Opportunities, and Constraints.* Boulder, CO: Lynne Rienner, 1998.

Boehmer, Elleke. *Nelson Mandela: A Very Short Introduction.* New York: Sterling, 2008.

Bonner, Philip, Peter Delius and Deborah Posel, eds. *Apartheid's Genesis: 1935–1962.* Johannesburg: Ravan, 1993.

Booth, Ian. 'Natal and Zululand: The Work of the American Board Mission'. In *Changing Frontiers: The Mission Story of the UCCSA*, ed. Steve de Gruchy, 80–92. Gaborone, Botswana: Pula Press, 1999.

Bozzoli, Belinda. 'Marxism, Feminism, and South African Studies'. *Journal of Southern African Studies* 9, no. 2 (1983): 139–171.

———. *Women of Phokeng: Consciousness, Life Strategy, and Migration in South Africa, 1900–1983.* Portsmouth, NH: Heinemann, 1991.

Bradford, Helen. *A Taste of Freedom: The ICU in Rural South Africa.* New Haven: Yale University Press, 1987.

Brain, Joy. *Christian Indians in Natal, 1860–1911: An Historical and Statistical Study.* Cape Town: Oxford University Press, 1983.

Breier, Mignonne, and Angelique Wildschut. 'Changing Gender Profile of Medical Schools in South Africa'. *South African Medical Journal* 98, no. 7 (July 2008): 557–560.

Brooks, Alan, and Jeremy Brickhill. *Whirlwind before the Storm: The Origins and Development of the Uprising in Soweto and the Rest of South Africa from June to December 1976.* London: International Defence and Aid Fund for Southern Africa, 1980.

Brumberg, Joan Jacobs. 'Zenanas and Girlless Villages: The Ethnology of American Evangelical Women, 1870–1900'. *Journal of American History* 69, no. 2 (September 1982): 347–371.

Bundy, Colin. *The Rise and Fall of the South African Peasantry*. Berkeley: University of California Press, 1979.

———. 'Street Sociology and Pavement Politics: Aspects of Youth and Student Resistance in Cape Town, 1985'. *Journal of Southern African Studies* 13, no. 3 (April 1987): 303–330.

Burke, Timothy. *Lifebuoy Men, Lux Women: Commodification, Con-sumption, and Cleanliness in Modern Zimbabwe*. Durham, NC: Duke University Press, 1996.

Burns, Catherine. ' "A Man Is a Clumsy Thing Who Does Not Know How to Handle a Sick Person": Aspects of the History of Masculinity and Race in the Shaping of Male Nursing in South Africa, 1900–1950'. *Journal of Southern African Studies* 24, no. 4 (December 1998): 695–717.

Buthelezi, Mazo Sybil T. MaDlamini. *African Nurse Pioneers in KwaZulu-Natal, 1920–2000*. Victoria, British Columbia: Trafford Publishing, 2004.

Callinicos, Alex. 'The Soweto Uprising: South Africa's Black Townships Have Finally Exploded'. *International Socialism* 90 (July/August 1976): 4–7.

Campbell, James T. 'Models and Metaphors: Industrial Education in the United States and South Africa'. In *Comparative Perspectives on South Africa*, ed. Ran Greenstein, 90–134. New York: St Martin's, 1998.

———. *Songs of Zion: The African Methodist Episcopal Church in the United States and South Africa*. New York: Oxford University Press, 1995.

Carnegie Corporation of New York. *Village Education in Africa: Report of the Inter-territorial Jeanes' Conference, Salisbury, S. Rhodesia*. Alice, South Africa: Lovedale Press, 1935.

Carton, Benedict. *Blood from Your Children: The Colonial Origins of Generational Conflict in South Africa*. Charlottesville: University of Virginia Press, 2000.

Casale, Daniela, and Dorrit Posel. 'The Continued Feminisation of the Labour Force in South Africa: An Analysis of Recent Data and Trends'. *South African Journal of Economics* 701 (March 2002): 156–184.

———. 'Women and the Economy: How Far Have We Come?' *Agenda* (2005) 64: 21–29.

Chisholm, Linda, and Jean September. 'Overview'. In *Gender Equity in South African Education, 1994–2004: Perspectives from Research, Government and Unions*, eds. Chisholm and September, 1–18. Cape Town: HSRC, 2005.

Christie, Pam. *Open Schools: Racially Mixed Catholic Schools in South Africa, 1976–1986*. Johannesburg: Ravan, 1990.

————. *The Right to Learn: The Struggle for Education in South Africa.* Johannesburg: Ravan, 1985.

Cobley, Alan. *Class and Consciousness: The Black Petty Bourgeoisie in South Africa, 1924–1950.* New York: Greenwood Press, 1990.

————. *The Rules of the Game: Struggles in Black Recreation and Social Welfare Policy in South Africa.* Westport, CT: Greenwood, 1997.

Cock, Jacklyn. 'Domestic Service and Education for Domesticity: The Incorporation of Xhosa Women into Colonial Society'. In *Women and Gender in Southern Africa to 1945*, ed. Cherryl Walker, 76–96. Cape Town: David Philip, 1990.

————. *Maids and Madams: A Study in the Politics of Exploitation.* Johannesburg: Ravan, 1980.

Colenso, Frances E. *History of the Zulu War and Its Origin.* London: Chapman and Hall, 1880.

Comaroff, Jean. 'Reading, Rioting, and Arithmetic: The Impact of Mission Education on Black Consciousness in South Africa'. *Bulletin of the Institute of Ethnology, Academia Sinica* 82 (Autumn 1996): 19–63.

Comaroff, Jean, and John Comaroff. 'Mansions of the Lord: Architecture, Interiority, Domesticity'. In *The Dialectics of Modernity on a South African Frontier.* Volume 2, *Of Revelation and Revolution*, eds. Comaroff and Comaroff, 274–322. Chicago: University of Chicago Press, 1991.

Commey, Pusch. 'South Africa: Oprah to the Rescue?' *New African* (February 2007): 10–15.

Cooper, Frederick. *Africa since 1940: The Past of the Present.* New York: Cambridge University Press, 2002.

————. *Decolonization and African Society: The Labor Question in French and British Africa.* New York: Cambridge University Press, 1996.

Cope, Nicholas. *To Bind the Nation: Solomon kaDinuzulu and Zulu Nationalism, 1913–1933.* Pietermaritzburg: University of Natal Press, 1993.

Couper, Scott. *Albert Luthuli: Bound by Faith.* Pietermaritzburg: University of KwaZulu-Natal Press, 2010.

————. 'Fearing for Its Future: Bantu Education's Threat of Closure to Inanda Seminary'. *Journal of Gender and Religion in Africa* 17, no. 1 (July 2011): 74–95.

Couzens, Tim. *The New African: A Study of the Life and Work of H.I.E. Dhlomo.* Johannesburg: Ravan, 1985.

————. 'Pseudonyms in Black South African Writing, 1920–1950'. *Research in African Literatures* 6, no. 2 (1975): 226–231.

Cott, Nancy. *The Bonds of Womanhood: 'Woman's Sphere' in New England, 1780–1835.* New Haven: Yale University Press, 1977.

Crankshaw, Owen. *Race, Class, and the Changing Division of Labour under Apartheid.* New York: Routledge, 1997.

Davis, R. Hunt, Jr. 'Charles T. Loram and an American Model for African Education in South Africa'. *African Studies Review* 19, no. 2 (1976): 87–99.

———. 'Producing the "Good African": South Carolina's Penn School as a Guide for African Education in South Africa'. In *Independence without Freedom: The Political Economy of Colonial Education in Southern Africa*, eds. Agrippah T. Mugomba and Mougo Nyaggah, 83–103. Santa Barbara, CA: ABC-Clio, 1980.

De Gruchy, John W. 'Grappling with a Colonial Heritage: The English-Speaking Churches under Imperialism and Apartheid'. In *Christianity in South Africa: A Political, Social, and Cultural History*, eds. Richard Elphick and Rodney Davenport, 155–172. Berkeley: University of California Press, 1997.

Deane, Dee Shirley. *Black South Africans: A Who's Who of Natal's Leading Blacks.* Cape Town: Oxford University Press, 1978.

DeBare, Ilana. *Where Girls Come First: The Rise, Fall and Surprising Revival of Girls' Schools.* New York: Penguin, 2004.

Delius, Peter, and Clive Glaser. 'Sexual Socialisation in South Africa: A Historical Perspective'. *African Studies* 61, no. 1 (2002): 27–54.

Dhlomo, H.I.E. 'African Attitudes to the European'. *The Democrat* (1 December 1945): 21 and 24.

———. 'Bantu Womanhood'. *Umteteli wa Bantu* (10 May 1930). Accessed 19 February 2011. http://pzacad.pitzer.edu/NAM/newafrre/writers/hdhlomo/umteteli/10_5_30.gif.

Dick, Archie L. *The Hidden History of South Africa's Book and Reading Cultures.* Toronto: University of Toronto Press, 2012.

Dinnerstein, Myra. 'The American Zulu Mission in the Nineteenth Century: Clash over Customs'. *Church History* 45, no. 2 (June 1976): 235–246.

Dlamini, Sibusisiwe Nombuso. *Youth and Identity Politics in South Africa, 1990–1994.* Toronto: University of Toronto Press, 2005.

Dube, Adelaide Charles. 'Africa: My Native Land'. In *Women Writing Africa: The Southern Region*, eds. M.J. Daymond, Dorothy Driver, Sheila Meintjes, Leloba Molema, Chiedza Musengezi, Margie Orford and Nobantu Rasebotsa, 161–162. New York: Feminist Press at the City University of New York, 2003.

Dube, John L. 'A Native View of Christianity in South Africa'. *Missionary Review of the World* 24 (1901): 421–426.

Dubow, Saul. *The African National Congress.* Johannesburg: Jonathan Ball, 2000.

Duff, S.E. ' "The Right Kind of Ambition": Discourses of Femininity at the Huguenot Seminary and College, 1895-1910'. In *Girlhood: A Global History*, eds. Jennifer Helgren and Colleen A. Vasconcellos, 234-249. New Brunswick, NJ: Rutgers University Press, 2010.

Duncan, Graham A. *Lovedale: Coercive Agency*. Pietermaritzburg: Cluster, 2003.

'Editorial: Fighting Against Bantu Education'. *Liberation: A Journal of Democratic Discussion*, no. 14 (November 1955): 1-7.

Elkins, Caroline, and Susan Pedersen, eds. *Settler Colonialism in the Twentieth Century: Projects, Practices, Legacies*. New York: Routledge, 2005.

Elphick, Richard. 'The Benevolent Empire and the Social Gospel: Missionaries and South African Christians in the Age of Segregation'. In *Christianity in South Africa: A Political, Social, and Cultural History*, eds. Elphick and Rodney Davenport, 347-369. Cape Town: David Philip, 1997.

Erlank, Natasha. 'Gender and Masculinity in South African Nationalist Discourse, 1912-1950'. *Feminist Studies* 29, no. 3 (Autumn 2003): 653-671.

Etherington, Norman. 'An American Errand into the South African Wilderness'. *Church History* 39 (1970): 62-71.

———. 'Gender Issues in Southeast African Missions, 1835-1885'. In *Missions and Christianity in South African History*, eds. Henry Bredekamp and Robert Ross, 135-152. Johannesburg: Wits University Press, 1995.

———. *The Great Treks: The Transformation of Southern Africa, 1815-1854*. New York: Longman, 2001.

———. *Preachers, Peasants, and Politics in Southeast Africa, 1835-1880: African Christian Communities in Natal, Pondoland, and Zululand*. London: Royal Historical Society, 1978.

Evans, Julie, and David Philips. ' "When There's No Safety in Numbers": Fear and the Franchise in South Africa: The Case of Natal'. In *Law, History, and Colonialism: The Reach of Empire*, eds. Diane Kirkby and Catharine Coleborne, 91-105. Manchester: Manchester University Press, 2001.

Fakier, Khayaat, and Jacklyn Cock. 'A Gendered Analysis of the Crisis of Social Reproduction in Contemporary South Africa'. *International Feminist Journal of Politics* 11, no. 3 (September 2009): 353-371.

Fassin, Didier. *When Bodies Remember: Experiences and Politics of AIDS in South Africa*. Berkeley: University of California Press, 2007.

Flanagan, Brigid. 'Education: Policy and Practice'. In *Catholics in Apartheid Society*, ed. Andrew Prior, 83-96. Cape Town: David Philip, 1982.

Foucault, Michel. *Discipline and Punish: The Birth of the Prison*. New York: Vintage, 1995. First published in French, 1975; first published in English, 1977.

Fredrickson, George. *Black Liberation: A Comparative History of Black Ideologies in the United States and South Africa*. New York: Oxford University Press, 1995.

Gaines, Kevin. *Uplifting the Race: Black Leadership, Politics, and Culture in the Twentieth Century*. Chapel Hill: University of North Carolina, 1996.

Gaitskell, Deborah. 'At Home with Hegemony? Coercion and Consent in African Girls' Education for Domesticity in South Africa before 1910'. In *Contesting Colonial Hegemony: State and Society in Africa and India*, eds. Dagmar Engels and Shula Marks, 110–128. London: British Academic Press, 1994.

———. ' "Doing a Missionary Hard Work . . . in the Black Hole of Calcutta": African Women Teachers Pioneering a Profession in the Cape and Natal, 1880–1950'. *Women's History Review* 13, no. 3 (September 2004): 407–425.

———. 'Race, Gender and Imperialism: A Century of Black Girls' Education in South Africa'. In *'Benefits Bestowed'? Education and British Imperialism*, ed. J.A. Mangan, 151–173. New York: Manchester University Press, 1988.

Gaitskell, Deborah, Judy Kimble, Moira Maconachie and Elaine Unterhalter. 'Class, Race and Gender: Domestic Workers in South Africa'. *Review of African Political Economy* 27/28 (1983): 86–108.

Geiger, Susan. *TANU Women: Gender and Culture in the Making of Tanganyikan Nationalism, 1955–1965*. Portsmouth, NH: Heinemann, 1998.

Gengenbach, Heidi. 'Truth-Telling and the Politics of Women's Life History Research in Africa: A Reply to Kirk Hoppe'. *The International Journal of African Historical Studies* 27, no. 3 (1994): 619–627.

Gevisser, Mark. *A Legacy of Liberation: Thabo Mbeki and the Future of the South African Dream*. New York: Palgrave Macmillan, 2009.

Gilley, Lawrence. 'Mozambique: The Work of the American Board Mission in Inhambane'. In *Changing Frontiers: The Mission Story of the UCCSA*, ed. Steve de Gruchy, 93–106. Gaborone, Botswana: Pula Press, 1999.

Gilmore, Glenda. *Gender and Jim Crow: Women and the Politics of White Supremacy in North Carolina, 1896–1920*. Chapel Hill: University of North Carolina, 1996.

Ginwala, Frene. 'Women and the African National Congress, 1912–1943'. *Agenda* 8 (1990): 77–93.

Ginzberg, Lori D. 'Global Goals, Local Acts: Grass-Roots Activism in Imperial Narratives'. *The Journal of American History* 88, no. 3 (December 2001): 870–873.

Girls Collegiate School. *Girls Collegiate School, 1878–1989*. Pietermaritz-burg: Girls Collegiate School, 1989.

Glaser, Clive. *Bo-Tsotsi: The Youth Gangs of Soweto, 1935–1976.* Portsmouth, NH: Heinemann, 2000.

Glotzer, R. 'The Career of Mabel Carney: The Study of Race and Rural Development in the United States and South Africa'. *International Journal of African Historical Studies* 29, no. 2 (1996): 309–336.

Gollock, G.A. *Daughters of Africa.* New York: Longmans, Green, and Co., 1932.

Goodhew, David. *Respectability and Resistance: A History of Sophiatown.* Westport, CT: Praeger, 2004.

Grant, George C. *The Liquidation of Adams College.* Durban: George Grant, 1957.

Green, Elizabeth Alden. *Mary Lyon and Mount Holyoke: Opening the Gates.* Hanover, NH: University Press of New England, 1979.

Grimshaw, Patricia. *Paths of Duty: American Missionary Wives in Nineteenth-Century Hawaii.* Honolulu: University of Hawaii Press, 1989.

Grimshaw, Patricia, and Peter Sherlock. 'Women and Cultural Exchanges'. In *Missions and Empire*, ed. Norman Etherington, 173–193. New York: Oxford University Press, 2005.

Guy, Jeff. 'Analysing Pre-capitalist Societies in Southern Africa'. *Journal of Southern African Studies* 14, no. 1 (October 1987): 18–37.

———. 'Gender Oppression in Southern Africa's Precapitalist Societies'. In *Women and Gender in Southern Africa to 1945*, ed. Cherryl Walker, 33–47. Cape Town: David Philip, 1990.

Hance, Gertrude R. *The Zulu Yesterday and To-day: Twenty-nine Years in South Africa.* New York: Negro Universities Press, 1969. First published 1916.

Hanretta, Sean. 'Women, Marginality, and the Zulu State: Women's Institutions and Power in the Early Nineteenth Century'. *The Journal of African History* 39, no. 3 (1998): 389–415.

Hansen, Karen Tranberg, ed. *African Encounters with Domesticity.* New Brunswick, NJ: Rutgers University Press, 1992.

Harries, Patrick. *Butterflies and Barbarians: Swiss Missionaries and Systems of Knowledge in South-East Africa.* Athens: Ohio University Press, 2007.

Harris, Paul William. *Nothing but Christ: Rufus Anderson and the Ideology of Protestant Foreign Missions.* New York: Oxford University Press, 1999.

Hartshorne, Kenneth. *Native Education in the Union of South Africa: A Summary of the Report of the Commission on Native Education in South Africa – U.G. 53-1951.* Johannesburg: South African Institute of Race Relations, 1953.

Healy, Meghan Elisabeth. ' "Like a Family": Global Models, Familial Bonds, and the Making of an American School for Zulu Girls'. *Safundi: The Journal of South African and American Studies* 11, no. 3 (July 2010): 279–300.

———. 'Magogo kaDinuzulu, Constance'. In *Dictionary of African Biography*, eds. Emmanuel K. Akyeampong and Henry Louis Gates, Jr, 30–32. New York: Oxford University Press, 2011.

———. '"To Control Their Destiny": The Politics of Home and the Feminisation of Schooling in Colonial Natal'. *Journal of Southern African Studies* 37, no. 2 (June 2011): 247–264.

Higginbotham, Evelyn Brooks. 'The Politics of Respectability'. In *Righteous Discontent: The Women's Movement in the Black Baptist Church, 1880–1920*, 185–229. Cambridge, MA: Harvard University Press, 1993.

Hill, Patricia R. *The World Their Household: The American Women's Foreign Mission Movement and Cultural Transformation, 1870–1920*. Ann Arbor: University of Michigan Press, 1985.

Historic Schools Restoration Project. 'How Did the Historic Schools Restoration Project Begin?' Accessed 19 February 2011. http://www.historicschools.org.za/view.asp?/pg=Schools&subm=Pilot%20 Schools.

———. 'Identification of Historic Schools'. Accessed 19 February 2011. http://www.historicschools.org.za/view.asp?pg=Schools&submIdentification 20of%20historic%20schools.

———. 'Speech Given by President Thabo Mbeki at an HSRP Function at Healdtown Comprehensive School', Fort Beaufort, Eastern Cape, 24 May 2008. Accessed 19 February 2011. http://www.historic schools.org.za/view.asp?=4&tname=tblComponent4&oname=Speeches&pg=front& subm=Speeches.

———. 'Z.K. Matthews Educational Trust'. Accessed 19 February 2011. http://www.historicschools.org.za/view.asp?pg=ZK%20Matthews&subm= The%20ZK%20 Matthews%20Educational%20Trust.

Horrell, Muriel. *African Education: Some Origins, and Development until 1953*. Johannesburg: South African Institute of Race Relations, 1963.

———. *Bantu Education to 1968*. Johannesburg: South African Institute of Race Relations, 1968.

———. *A Decade of Bantu Education*. Johannesburg: South African Institute of Race Relations, 1968.

Horwitz, Simonne. '"Black Nurses in White": Exploring Young Women's Entry into the Nursing Profession at Baragwanath Hospital, Soweto, 1948–1980'. *Social History of Medicine* 20, no. 1 (2007): 131–146.

Houle, Robert. 'Mbiya Kuzwayo's Christianity: Revival, Reformation and the Surprising Viability of Mainline Churches in South Africa'. *Journal of Religion in Africa* 38 (2008): 141–170.

Hughes, Heather. 'The City Closes In: The Incorporation of Inanda into Metropolitan Durban'. In *The People's City: African Life in Twentieth-*

Century Durban, eds. Paul Maylam and Iain Edwards, 299–309. Pietermaritzburg: University of KwaZulu-Natal Press, 1996.

———. 'Doubly Elite: Exploring the Life of John Langalibalele Dube', *Journal of Southern African Studies* 27, no. 3 (September 2001): 445–458.

———. *First President: A Life of John L. Dube, Founding President of the ANC*. Auckland Park, South Africa: Jacana, 2011.

———. ' "A Lighthouse for African Womanhood": Inanda Seminary, 1869–1945'. In *Women and Gender in Southern Africa to 1945*, ed. Cherryl Walker, 197–220. Cape Town: David Philip, 1990.

———. 'Violence in Inanda, August 1985'. *Journal of Southern African Studies* 13, no. 3 (April 1987): 331–354.

Hull, Elizabeth. 'International Migration, "Domestic Struggles", and Status Aspiration among Nurses in South Africa'. *Journal of Southern African Studies* 36, no. 4 (December 2010): 851–867.

Hunt, Nancy Rose. *A Colonial Lexicon of Birth Ritual, Medicalization, and Mobility in the Congo*. Durham, NC: Duke University Press, 1999.

Hunter, Jane H. 'Women's Mission in Historical Perspective: American Identity and Christian Internationalism'. In *Competing Kingdoms: Women, Mission, Nation, and the American Protestant Empire, 1812–1960*, eds. Barbara Reeves-Ellington, Kathryn Kish Sklar and Connie A. Shemo, 19–42. Durham, NC: Duke University Press, 2010.

Hunter, Mark. 'Beneath the "Zunami": Jacob Zuma and the Gendered Politics of Social Reproduction in South Africa'. *Antipode* (February 2011): 1–25.

———. *Love in the Time of AIDS: Inequality, Gender, and Rights in South Africa*. Bloomington: University of Indiana Press, 2010.

Hutchinson, William R. *Errand to the World: American Protestant Thought and Foreign Missions*. Chicago: University of Chicago Press, 1987.

Hyslop, Jonathan. *The Classroom Struggle: Policy and Resistance in South Africa, 1940–1990*. Pietermaritzburg: University of Natal Press, 1999.

———. 'Food, Authority, and Politics: Student Riots in South African Schools, 1945–1976'. *Africa Perspective* 1, no. 3–4 (June 1987): 3–42.

Ireland, William. *Historical Sketch of the Zulu Mission in South Africa, as Also of the Gaboon Mission, in Western Africa*. Boston: American Board, n.d., circa 1865.

Jacobs, Sylvia M. 'Give a Thought to Africa: Black Women Missionaries in Southern Africa'. In *Western Women and Imperialism: Complicity and Resistance*, eds. Nupur Chaudhuri and Margaret Strobel, 207–230. Bloomington: Indiana University Press, 1992.

Jones, Thomas Jesse. *Education in East Africa: A Study of East, Central and South Africa by the Second African Education Commission under the Auspices of the Phelps-Stokes Fund, in Cooperation with the International Education Board*. New York: Phelps-Stokes Fund, 1925.

'Joyce Sikhakhane-Rankin'. In *The Road to Democracy: South Africans Telling Their Stories*. Volume 1, *1950–1970*, ed. South African Democracy Education Trust, 441–449. Pretoria: Unisa Press, 2008.

Kadiz, Charles Fitzwilliam, ed. *Natal Ordinances, Laws, and Proclamations*. Pietermaritzburg: Government Printers, 1890.

Kallaway, Peter. 'An Introduction to the Study of Education for Blacks in South Africa'. In *Apartheid and Education: Education of Black South Africans*, ed. Kallaway, 1–44. Johannesburg: Ravan, 1984.

Kallaway, Peter, ed. *The History of Education under Apartheid, 1948–1994: The Doors of Learning and Culture Shall Be Opened*. New York: P. Lang, 2002.

Kaplan, Amy. 'Manifest Domesticity'. In *No More Separate Spheres!* eds. Cathy N. Davidson and Jessamyn Hatcher, 183–207. Durham, NC: Duke University Press, 2002.

Khoapa, Bennie. 'Youth and Student Organizations'. *The Black Review* (1972): 181–189.

Kihn, Paul. 'Comrades and Professionals: Teacher Ideology and Practice in the Western Cape, 1985 to 1990'. In *The History of Education under Apartheid, 1948–1994: The Doors of Learning and Culture Shall Be Opened*, ed. Peter Kallaway, 325–336. New York: P. Lang, 2002.

King, Kenneth. *Pan-Africanism and Education: A Study of Race Philanthropy and Education in the Southern States of America and East Africa*. Oxford: Clarendon Press, 1971.

Kotze, D.J., ed. *Letters of the American Missionaries, 1835–1838*. Cape Town: Van Riebeeck Society, 1950.

Krige, Sue. 'Segregation, Science and Commissions of Enquiry: The Contestation over Native Education Policy in South Africa, 1930–36'. *Journal of Southern African Studies* 23, no. 3 (September 1997): 491–506.

Kros, Cynthia. *The Seeds of Separate Development: Origins of Bantu Education*. Pretoria: Unisa Press, 2010.

Kuper, Adam. 'The "House" and Zulu Political Structure in the Nineteenth Century'. *The Journal of African History* 34, no. 3 (1993): 469–487.

Kuper, Hilda. 'Nurses'. In Leo Kuper, *An African Bourgeoisie: Race, Class, and Politics in South Africa*, 216–235. New Haven: Yale University Press, 1965.

Kuper, Leo. *An African Bourgeoisie: Race, Class, and Politics in South Africa*. New Haven: Yale University Press, 1965.

Kuzwayo, Ellen. *Call Me Woman*. London: The Women's Press, 1985.

Labode, Modupe. 'From Heathen Kraal to Christian Home: Anglican Mission Education and African Christian Girls, 1850–1900'. In *Women and Missions: Past and Present, Anthropological and Historical Perceptions*, eds. Fiona Bowie, Deborah Kirkwood and Shirley Ardener, 126–144. Providence, RI: Berg, 1993.

La Hausse, Paul. *Restless Identities: Signatures of Nationalism, Zulu Ethnicity and History in the Lives of Petros Lamula and Lymon Maling*. Pietermaritzburg: University of Natal Press, 2000.

———. 'So Who Was Elias Kuzwayo? Nationalism, Collaboration and the Picaresque in Natal'. *Cahiers d'études africaines* 32, no. 127 (1992): 469–507.

Lambert, John. *Betrayed Trust: Africans and the State in Colonial Natal*. Pietermaritzburg: University of Natal Press, 1995.

Land, Gary. *Historical Dictionary of Seventh-Day Adventists*. Lanham, MD: Scarecrow Press, 2005.

Laslett, Barbara, and Joanna Brenner. 'Gender and Social Reproduction'. *Annual Review of Sociology* 15 (1989): 381–404.

Lawrance, Benjamin N., Emily Lynn Osborn and Richard L. Roberts, eds. *Intermediaries, Interpreters, and Clerks: African Employees in the Making of Colonial Africa*. Madison: University of Wisconsin Press, 2006.

Leathwood, Carole, and Barbara Read. *Gender and the Changing Face of Higher Education: A Feminized Future?* New York: Open University Press, 2009.

Lee, Rebekah. *African Women and Apartheid: Migration and Settlement in Urban South Africa*. New York: I.B. Tauris, 2009.

LeRoy, A.E. *The Educated Native: Fact vs. Theory*. Dundee, Natal: Church of Sweden, 1906.

Lewis, Joanna. *Empire State-Building: War and Welfare in Kenya, 1925–1952*. Athens: Ohio University Press, 2000.

Limb, Peter. *The ANC's Early Years: Nation, Class, and Place in South Africa before 1940*. Pretoria: Unisa Press, 2010.

Loram, Charles T. *The Education of the South African Native*. New York: Negro Universities Press, 1969. First published 1917.

Luthuli, Albert. *Let My People Go*. Johannesburg: Collins, 1962.

Luxton, Meg, and Kate Bezanson. *Social Reproduction: Feminist Political Economy Challenges Neo-liberalism*. Montreal: McGill-Queen's University Press, 2006.

MacQueen, Ian. 'Categories of Struggle: Reassessing Black Consciousness in South Africa through Gender, 1967–1976'. In *Paths to Gender: European Historical Perspectives on Men and Women*, eds. Carla Salvaterra and Berteke Waaldijk, 259–267. Pisa: Pisa University Press, 2009.

Madlala-Routledge, Nozizwe. 'University of KwaZulu-Natal Award Speech', 30 October 2006. Accessed 19 February 2011. http://www.polity.org/za/article/Madlalaroutledge-university-of-kwazulunatal-award-30102006-2006-10-30.

Magaziner, Daniel R. *The Law and the Prophets: Black Consciousness in South Africa, 1968–1977.* Athens: Ohio University Press, 2010.

———. 'Pieces of a (Wo)man: Feminism, Gender, and Adulthood in Black Consciousness, 1968–1977'. *Journal of Southern African Studies* 37, no. 1 (March 2011): 45–61.

Mager, Anne. *Gender and the Making of a South African Bantustan: A Social History of the Ciskei, 1945–1959.* Portsmouth, NH: Heinemann, 1999.

Magona, Sindiwe. *Forced to Grow.* London: The Women's Press, 1992.

Mahlase, Shirley. *The Careers of Women Teachers under Apartheid.* Harare: SAPES Trust, 1997.

Mahoney, Michael R. 'Racial Formation and Ethnogenesis from Below: The Zulu Case, 1879–1906'. *The International Journal of African Historical Studies* 36, no. 3 (2003): 559–583.

Mahoney, Michael R., and Julie Parle. 'An Ambiguous Sexual Revolution: Intragenerational Conflict in Late Colonial Natal, 1879–1906'. *South African Historical Journal* 50 (2004): 134–151.

Makapela, Alven. *The Problem with Africanity in the Seventh-Day Adventist Church.* Lewiston, NY: The Edwin Mellen Press, 1996.

Makdisi, Ussama. *Artillery of Heaven: American Missionaries and the Failed Conversion of the Middle East.* Ithaca: Cornell University Press, 2008.

Mamdani, Mahmood. *Citizen and Subject: Contemporary Africa and the Legacy of Late Colonialism.* Princeton, NJ: Princeton University Press, 1996.

Manicom, Linzi. 'Ruling Relations: Rethinking State and Gender in South African History'. *The Journal of African History* 33, no. 3 (1992): 441–465.

Mann, Kristin. *Marrying Well: Marriage, Status, and Social Change among the Educated Elite in Colonial Lagos.* New York: Cambridge University Press, 1985.

Marable, Manning. 'John L. Dube and the Politics of Segregated Education in South Africa'. In *Independence without Freedom: The Political Economy of Colonial Education in Southern Africa*, eds. Agrippah T. Mugomba and Mougo Nyaggah. Santa Barbara, CA: ABC-Clio, 1977.

Maré, Gerhard, and Georgina Hamilton. *An Appetite for Power: Buthelezi's Inkatha and South Africa.* Johannesburg: Ravan, 1987.

Marks, Shula. *The Ambiguities of Dependence in South Africa: Class, Nationalism, and the State in Twentieth-Century Natal.* Baltimore: Johns Hopkins, 1986.

————. 'Changing History, Changing Histories: Separations and Con-nections in the Lives of South African Women'. *Journal of African Cultural Studies* 13, no. 1 (June 2000): 94–106.

————. *Divided Sisterhood: Race, Class, and Gender in the South African Nursing Profession*. Johannesburg: Wits University Press, 1994.

————. *Not Either an Experimental Doll: The Separate Worlds of Three South African Women*. Bloomington: Indiana University Press, 1987.

————. 'Patriotism, Patriarchy and Purity: Natal and the Politics of Zulu Ethnic Consciousness'. In *The Creation of Tribalism in Southern Africa*, ed. Leroy Vail, 215–240. Berkeley: University of California Press, 1991.

————. *Reluctant Rebellion: The 1906–8 Disturbances in Natal*. Oxford: Clarendon Press, 1970.

Martineau, Rowena. 'Women and Education in South Africa: Factors Influencing Women's Educational Progress and Their Entry into Traditionally Male-Dominated Fields'. *The Journal of Negro Education* (Autumn 1997): 383–395.

Marx, Karl. *Capital: A Critique of Political Economy*. New York: Vintage, 1977. First published in German, 1867; first published in English, 1887.

Masemann, Vandra. 'The "Hidden Curriculum" of a West African Girls' Boarding School'. *Canadian Journal of African Studies* 6, no. 3 (1974): 479–494.

Mashabela, Harry. *A People on the Boil: Reflections on June 16, 1976 and Beyond*. Auckland Park, South Africa: Jacana, 2006. First published 1987.

Massey, Daniel. *Under Protest: The Rise of Student Resistance at the University of Fort Hare*. Pretoria: Unisa Press, 2010.

McCord, James B., with John Scott Douglas. *My Patients Were Zulus*. London: Frederick Muller, 1951. First published 1946.

McCord, Margaret. *The Calling of Katie Makhanya*. Cape Town: David Philip, 1997.

McCormick, Kathleen K. 'Code-Switching, Code-Mixing, and Con-vergence in Cape Town'. In *Language and Social History: Studies in South African Sociolinguistics*, ed. Rajend Mesthrie. Cape Town: David Philip, 1995.

Mda, Zakes. *Black Diamonds*. Cape Town: Penguin, 2009.

Meintjes, Sheila. 'Family and Gender in the Christian Community at Edendale, Natal, in Colonial Times'. In *Women and Gender in Southern Africa to 1945*, ed. Cherryl Walker, 125–145. Cape Town: David Philip, 1990.

Mji, Sikose. 'Freedom is Choice'. *The Warsaw Voice* (25 April 2003). Accessed 19 February 2011. http://www.warsawvoice.pl/WVpage/pagesarticle.php/2152/article.

Mkhabela, Sibongile. *Open Earth and Black Roses: Remembering 16 June 1976.* Braamfontein, South Africa: Skotaville, 2001.

Moran, S.M. *The First 100 Years, 1882–1982: Durban Girls' Model School and Durban Girls' High School.* Durban: S.M. Moran, 1982.

Morrell, Robert. 'Considering the Case for Single-Sex Schools in South Africa'. *McGill Journal of Education* (Fall 2000): 221–244.

Morrell, Robert, Debbie Epstein, Elaine Unterhalter, Deevia Bhana and Relebohile Moletsane. *Towards Gender Equality: South African Schools During the HIV and AIDS Epidemic.* Pietermaritzburg: University of KwaZulu-Natal Press, 2009.

Morrell, Robert, and Relebohile Moletsane. 'Inequality and Fear: Living and Working inside Bantu Education Schools'. In *The History of Education under Apartheid, 1948–1994: The Doors of Learning and Culture Shall Be Opened*, ed. Peter Kallaway, 224–242. New York: P. Lang, 2002.

Morrow, Seán. 'Race, Redress and Historically Black Universities'. In *Racial Redress and Citizenship in South Africa*, eds. Kristina Bentley and Adam Habib, 263–288. Cape Town: HSRC Press, 2008.

Motala, Shireen, and Salim Vally. 'People's Education: From People's Power to Tirisano'. In *The History of Education under Apartheid, 1948–1994: The Doors of Learning and Culture Shall Be Opened*, ed. Peter Kallaway, 174–194. New York: P. Lang, 2002.

Mpanza, Khosi. 'Schooled for Success'. *Agenda* 21 (1994): 43–46.

Naidoo, B.T. 'A History of the Durban Medical School'. *South African Medical Journal* 50, no. 9 (1976): 1625–1628.

Nattrass, Nicoli, and Jeremy Seekings. ' "Two Nations"? Race and Economic Inequality in South Africa'. *Daedalus* 130, no. 1 (Winter 2001): 45–70.

Nauright, John. ' "I Am with You as Never Before": Women in Urban Protest Movements, Alexandra Township, South Africa, 1912–1945'. In *Courtyards, Markets, City Streets: Urban Women in Africa*, ed. Kathleen Sheldon, 259–283. Boulder, CO: Westview Press, 1996.

Ndlovu, Sifiso Mxolisi. 'The Soweto Uprising'. In *The Road to Democracy in South Africa*. Volume 2, *1970–1980*, ed. South African Democracy Trust, 317–368. Pretoria: Unisa Press, 2006.

Ngubane, Harriet. 'Marriage, Affinity and the Ancestral Realm: Zulu Marriage in Female Perspective'. In *Essays on African Marriage in Southern Africa*, eds. Eileen Krige and John Comaroff, 84–95. Cape Town: Juta, 1981.

Ngubane, Jordan K. 'The Woman Who Saved Her Tribe: Florence Nightingale of the Bantu, Story of Sacrifice and Devotion'. *The Forum* (12 October 1946): 31–33.

Niehaus, Isak. 'Towards a Dubious Liberation: Masculinity, Sexuality and Power in South African Lowveld Schools, 1953–1999'. *Journal of Southern African Studies* 26, no. 3 (September 2000): 387–407.

Ntantala, Phyllis. 'The Abyss of Bantu Education'. *Africa South* 4, no. 2 (January–March 1960): 42–47.

———. *A Life's Mosaic: The Autobiography of Phyllis Ntantala.* Berkeley: University of California Press, 1992.

Official Publications of South African States. Pretoria: State Library, 1986.

Ong, Aihwa. *Spirits of Resistance and Capitalist Discipline: Factory Women in Malaysia.* Albany: State University of New York, 1987.

Oprah Winfrey Leadership Academy. 'Academy Fact Sheet, October 2009'. Accessed 19 February 2011. http://oprahwinfreyleadershipacademy. ophilanthropy.org/site/PageServer? pagename=owla_about.

———. *Building a Dream: The Oprah Winfrey Leadership Academy.* DVD. Chicago: Harpo Productions, 2007.

Osborne, Myles. 'The Kamba and Mau Mau: Ethnicity, Development, and Chiefship, 1952–1960'. *International Journal of African Historical Studies* 43, no. 1 (2010): 63–87.

Pandor, Naledi. 'The Hidden Face of Gender Inequality in South African Education'. *Gender Equity in South African Education, 1994–2004: Perspectives from Research, Government and Unions,* eds. Linda Chisholm and Jean September, 19–24. Cape Town: HSRC Press, 2005.

Parle, Julie. *States of Mind: Searching for Mental Health in Natal and Zululand, 1868–1918.* Pietermaritzburg: University of KwaZulu-Natal Press, 2007.

Pateman, Carole. *The Sexual Contract.* Cambridge: Polity Press, 1988.

Phendla, Thidziambi. 'Women on the Rise: Women Navigating across Social, Political, Economic and Cultural Arenas to Claim Their Stake in Educational Leadership Positions in South Africa'. In *Women Leading Education across the Continents: Sharing the Spirit, Fanning the Flame,* ed. Helen C. Sobehart, 57–64. Lanham, MD: Rowman and Littlefield, 2009.

Pillay, Gerald J. 'Community Service and Conversion: Christianity among Indian South Africans'. In *Christianity in South Africa: A Political, Social, and Cultural History,* eds. Richard Elphick and Rodney Davenport, 286–296. Cape Town: David Philip, 1997.

Plaatje, Sol T. *Native Life in South Africa, Before and Since the European War and the Boer Rebellion.* London: P.S. King and Son, 1915.

Plant, Robert. *The Zulu in Three Tenses: Being a Forecast of the Zulu's Future in the Light of His Past and His Present.* Pietermaritzburg: P. Davis and Sons, 1905.

Porterfield, Amanda. *Mary Lyon and the Mount Holyoke Missionaries*. New York: Oxford University Press, 1997.

Prevost, Elizabeth E. *The Communion of Women: Missions and Gender in Colonial Africa and the British Metropole*. New York: Oxford University Press, 2010.

Pruitt, Lisa Joy. *A Looking-Glass for Ladies: American Protestant Women and the Orient in the Nineteenth Century*. Macon, GA: Mercer University Press, 2005.

Ramphele, Mamphela. *Across Boundaries: The Journey of a South African Woman Leader*. New York: The Feminist Press at the City University of New York, 1999. First published 1996.

Ratele, Kopano. 'We Black Men'. *International Journal of Intercultural Relations* 27, no. 2 (March 2003): 237–249.

Reeves-Ellington, Barbara. 'A Vision of Mount Holyoke in the Ottoman Balkans: American Cultural Transfer, Bulgarian Nation-Building and Women's Educational Reform, 1858–1870'. *Gender and History* 16, no. 1 (April 2004): 146–171.

Rive, Richard. 'The Early Years'. In *Seme: The Founder of the ANC*, eds. Richard Rive and Tim Couzens, 9–35. Braamfontein, South Africa: Skotaville, 1991.

Robert, Dana L. *American Women in Mission: A Social History of Their Thought and Practice*. Macon, GA: Mercer University Press, 1996.

———. 'The "Christian Home" as a Cornerstone of Anglo-American Missionary Thought and Practice'. In *Converting Colonialism: Visions and Realities in Mission History, 1706–1914*, ed. Robert, 134–165. Grand Rapids, MI: William B. Eerdmans, 2008.

Robertson, Claire. 'Women's Education and Class Formation in Africa, 1950–1980'. In *Women and Class in Africa*, eds. Iris Berger and Robertson, 92–116. New York: Africana Publishing, 1986.

Salomone, Rosemary C. *Same, Different, Equal: Rethinking Single-Sex Schooling*. New Haven: Yale University Press, 2003.

Scott, Lavinia. '33 Years at Inanda Seminary'. *Race Relations News* (December 1969): 6.

Searle, Charlotte. *The History of the Development of Nursing in South Africa, 1652–1960: A Socio-Historical Survey*. Cape Town: Struik, 1965.

Semple, Rhonda. 'Ruth, Miss Mackintosh, and Ada and Rose Marris: Biblewomen, *Zenana* Workers, and Missionaries in Nineteenth-Century British Missions to North India'. *Women's History Review* 17, no. 4 (September 2008): 561–574.

Sheldon, Kathleen E. *Historical Dictionary of Women in Sub-Saharan Africa*. Lanham, MD: Scarecrow Press, 2005.

Shepherd, R.H.W. *Lovedale, South Africa: 1824–1955*. Alice, South Africa: Lovedale Press, 1971.

Skota, T.D. Mweli. *The African Yearly Register: Being an Illustrated National Biography Dictionary (Who's Who) of Black Folks in Africa*. Johannesburg: Esson, 1930.

Smith, Edwin W. *The Life and Times of Daniel Lindley, 1801–1880*. London: The Epworth Press, 1949.

South African Statistics 1990. Pretoria: Central Statistical Service, 1990.

'South African Students' Organisation: Executive Council Meeting, Edendale Ecumenical Centre, 1–8 December 1971'. Accessed 19 February 2011. http://www.aluka.org/action/showMetadata? doi = 10.5555AL.SFF. DOCUMENT. min19711200.032.009.74.

Southall, Roger. 'Buthelezi, Inkatha, and the Politics of Compromise'. *African Affairs* 80, no. 321 (October 1981): 453–481.

Spielhagen, Frances R. *Debating Single-Sex Education: Separate and Equal?* Lanham, MD: Rowman and Littlefield, 2008.

Stambach, Amy. *Lessons from Mount Kilimanjaro: Schooling, Community, and Gender in East Africa*. New York: Routledge, 2000.

Stoler, Ann Laura. 'Tense and Tender Ties: The Politics of Comparison in North American History and (Post) Colonial Studies'. In *Haunted by Empire: Geographies of Intimacy in North American History*, ed. Stoler, 23–70. Durham, NC: Duke University Press, 2006.

Summers, Carol. *Colonial Lessons: Africans' Education in Southern Rhodesia, 1918–1940*. Portsmouth, NH: Heinemann, 2002.

Swanison, Nicola. 'Corporate Intervention in Education and Training, 1960–1989'. In *Apartheid Education and Popular Struggles*, eds. Elaine Unterhalter, Harold Wolpe, Thozamile Botha, Saleem Badat, Thulisile Dlamini and Benito Khotseng, 95–116. Johannesburg: Ravan, 1991.

Swartz, Leslie. *Culture and Mental Health: A Southern African View*. Cape Town: Oxford University Press, 1998.

Switzer, Heather. 'Disruptive Discourses: Kenyan Maasai Schoolgirls Make Themselves'. *Girlhood Studies* 3, no. 1 (Summer 2010): 137–155.

Tabata, I.B. *Education for Barbarism: Bantu Education in South Africa*. Durban: Prometheus, 1959.

Thema, R.V. Selope. 'How Congress Began'. In *Seme: The Founder of the ANC*, eds. Richard Rive and Tim Couzens, 85–87. Braamfontein, South Africa: Skotaville, 1991.

Thomas, Lynn. 'Gendered Reproduction: Placing Schoolgirl Pregnancies in African History'. In *Africa after Gender?* eds. Catherine M. Cole, Takyiwaa

Manuh and Steven F. Miescher, 48–62. Bloomington: Indiana University Press, 2007.

———. 'The Modern Girl and Racial Respectability in 1930s South Africa'. In *The Modern Girl Around the World: Consumption, Modernity, and Globalization*, eds. Alys Eve Weinbaum, Lynn M. Thomas, Priti Ramamurthy, Uta G. Poiger, Madeleine Yue Dong and Tani E. Barlow, 96–119. Durham, NC: Duke University Press, 2008.

Tilton, Doug. 'Creating an "Educated Workforce": Inkatha, Big Business, and Educational Reform in KwaZulu'. *Journal of Southern African Studies* 18, no. 1 (March 1992): 166–189.

Troup, Freda. *Forbidden Pastures: Education under Apartheid*. London: International Defence and Aid Fund, 1976.

Union of South Africa. *Report of the Commission on Native Education, 1949–1951 – U.G. No. 53/1951*. Pretoria: Government Printer, 1951.

Unterhalter, Elaine. 'Can Education Overcome Women's Subordinate Position in the Occupation Structure?' In *Education in a Future South Africa: Policy Issues for Transformation*, eds. Unterhalter, Harold Wolpe and Thozamile Botha, 65–84. Portsmouth, NH: Heinemann, 1991.

———. 'Changing Aspects of Reformism in Bantu Education, 1953–1989'. In *Apartheid Education and Popular Struggles*, eds. Unterhalter, Harold Wolpe, Thozamile Botha, Saleem Badat, Thulisile Dlamini and Benito Khotseng, 35–72. Johannesburg: Ravan, 1991.

———. 'Gender Equality and Education in South Africa: Measurements, Scores, and Strategies'. In *Gender Equity in South African Education, 1994–2004: Perspectives from Research, Government and Unions*, eds. Linda Chisholm and Jean September, 77–91. Cape Town: HSRC Press, 2005.

———. 'The Impact of Apartheid on Women's Education in South Africa'. *Review of African Political Economy* 48 (Autumn 1990): 66–75.

———. 'Remembering and Forgetting: Constructions of Education Gender Reform in Autobiography and Policy Texts of the South African Transition'. *History of Education* 29, no. 5 (2000): 457–472.

———. 'The Schooling of South African Girls'. In *Gender, Education, and Development: Beyond Access to Empowerment*, eds. Christine Heward and Sheila S. Bunwaree, 49–64. London: Zed, 1999.

Van der Water, Desmond, and Steve de Gruchy. 'Submission to the Truth and Reconciliation Commission of South Africa, October 1997'. In *Changing Frontiers: The Mission Story of the United Congregational Church of Southern Africa*, ed. Steve de Gruchy, 231–253. Gaborone, Botswana: Pula Press, 1999.

Verwey, C.T., P.D. Carstens and A. du Plessis, with E.B. Gumbi. *Statistical Review of Education in KwaZulu, 1979-1984*. Bloemfontein: Research Institute for Education Planning, University of the Orange Free State, 1985.

Verwoerd, Hendrik. *Bantu Education: Policy for the Immediate Future*. Pretoria: Information Service of the Department of Native Affairs, 1954.

Vietzen, Sylvia. *A History of Education for European Girls in Natal with Particular Reference to the Establishment of Some Leading Schools, 1837-1902*. Pietermaritzburg: University of Natal Press, 1973.

Vilakazi, Absolom. *Zulu Transformations: A Study of the Dynamics of Social Change*. Pietermaritzburg: University of Natal Press, 1962.

Vinson, Robert, and Robert Edgar. 'Zulus, African Americans and the African Diaspora'. In *Zulu Identities: Being Zulu, Past and Present*, eds. Benedict Carton, John Laband and Jabulani Sithole, 240-249. Pietermaritzburg: University of KwaZulu-Natal Press, 2008.

Waetjen, Thembisa. *Workers and Warriors: Masculinity and the Struggle for Nation in South Africa*. Urbana: University of Illinois Press, 2004.

Walbridge, Caroline, ed. *Thokozile*. Topeka, KS: Mainline Printing, 1978.

Walker, Cherryl. *Women and Resistance in South Africa*. Cape Town: David Philip, 1991. First published 1982.

Walshe, Peter. *The Rise of African Nationalism in South Africa: The African National Congress, 1912-1952*. Berkeley: University of California Press, 1982. First published 1970.

Watts, H.L. *Black Doctors: An Investigation into Aspects of the Training and Career of Students and Graduates from the Medical School of the University of Natal*. Durban: University of Natal Institute for Social Research, 1975.

Weiler, Kathleen, and Sue Middleton, eds. *Telling Women's Lives: Narrative Inquiries in the History of Women's Education*. Buckingham, UK: Open University Press, 1999.

Wells, Julia C. *We Now Demand! The History of Women's Resistance to Pass Laws in South Africa*. Johannesburg: Wits University Press, 1993.

Welsh, David. *The Rise and Fall of Apartheid*. Johannesburg: Jonathan Ball, 2009.

———. *The Roots of Segregation: Native Policy in Colonial Natal, 1845-1910*. New York: Oxford University Press, 1973. First published 1971.

West, Michael O. *The Rise of an African Middle Class: Colonial Zimbabwe, 1898-1965*. Bloomington: Indiana University Press, 2002.

White, Luise, Stephan F. Miescher and David William Cohen, eds. *African Words, African Voices: Critical Practices in Oral History*. Bloomington: Indiana University Press, 2001.

White, T. 'Master of the Night: The Context and Evolution of the Lovedale Riot of 1946'. *Historia* 42, no. 1 (May 1997): 81–97.

Wieder, Alan. 'Informed by Apartheid: Mini-Oral Histories of Two Cape Town Teachers'. In *The History of Education under Apartheid, 1948–1994: The Doors of Learning and Culture Shall Be Opened*, ed. Peter Kallaway, 198–210. New York: P. Lang, 2002.

Wilder, Royal Gould. *Mission Schools in India of the American Board of Commissioners for Foreign Missions*. New York: A.D.F. Randolph, 1861.

Willan, Brian. 'An African in Kimberley: Sol T. Plaatje, 1894–1898'. In *Industrialisation and Social Change in South Africa: African Class Formation, Culture, and Consciousness, 1870–1930*, eds. Shula Marks and Richard Rathbone, 238–258. New York: Longman, 1982.

Wilson, Monica Hunter. 'Co-operation and Conflict: The Eastern Cape Frontier'. In *The Oxford History of South Africa*, Volume 1, eds. Wilson and Leonard Thompson, 233–271. Oxford: Clarendon Press, 1969.

———. *Reaction to Conquest*. London: Oxford University Press, 1936.

Wolpe, Harold. 'Capitalism and Cheap Labour Power in South Africa: From Segregation to Apartheid'. *Economy and Society* 1, no. 4 (1972): 425–456.

Wood, Agnes. *Shine Where You Are: A History of Inanda Seminary, 1869–1969*. Alice, South Africa: Lovedale Press, 1972.

Woody, Thomas. *A History of Women's Education in the United States*. New York: Octagon Books, 1966.

Wright, John. 'Reflections on the Politics of Being "Zulu"'. In *Zulu Identities: Being Zulu, Past and Present*, eds. Benedict Carton, John Laband and Jabulani Sithole, 35–43. Pietermaritzburg: University of KwaZulu-Natal Press, 2008.

Xaba, Thokozani. 'Masculinity and Its Malcontents: The Confrontation between "Struggle Masculinity" and "Post-struggle Masculinity" (1990–1997)'. In *Changing Men in Southern Africa*, ed. Robert Morrell, 105–124. Pietermaritzburg: University of Natal Press, 2001.

Young, Robert. *African Wastes Reclaimed: Illustrated in the Story of the Lovedale Mission*. London: J.M. Dent and Company, 1902.

Zondi, Dumi. 'Profile of a Black Boarding School'. *Institute for Black Research Quarterly Comment* (January 1976): 25.

Index

Page numbers in *italics* refer to Tables and Figures.

Reconsiderations in Southern African History